"What has been lost will never return." This was one of the statements I set down when I first plotted this story.

Twenty-some years ago, my hale and hearty grandmother landed in the hospital. She soon couldn't remember her own name. After some time, she passed away, but the day I saw my grandmother after she had lost her heart was just as sad as the day she died.

"What has been lost will never return."

You must remember that and take care not to break things, I tell my three-year-old son.

But he always says to me, "You're wrong, Daddy."

—Hiroyuki Asada, 2015

Hiroyuki Asada made his debut in *Monthly Shonen Jump* in 1986. He's best known for his basketball manga *I'll*. He's a contributor to artist Range Murata's quarterly manga anthology *Robot*. *Tegami Bachi: Letter Bee* is his most recent series.

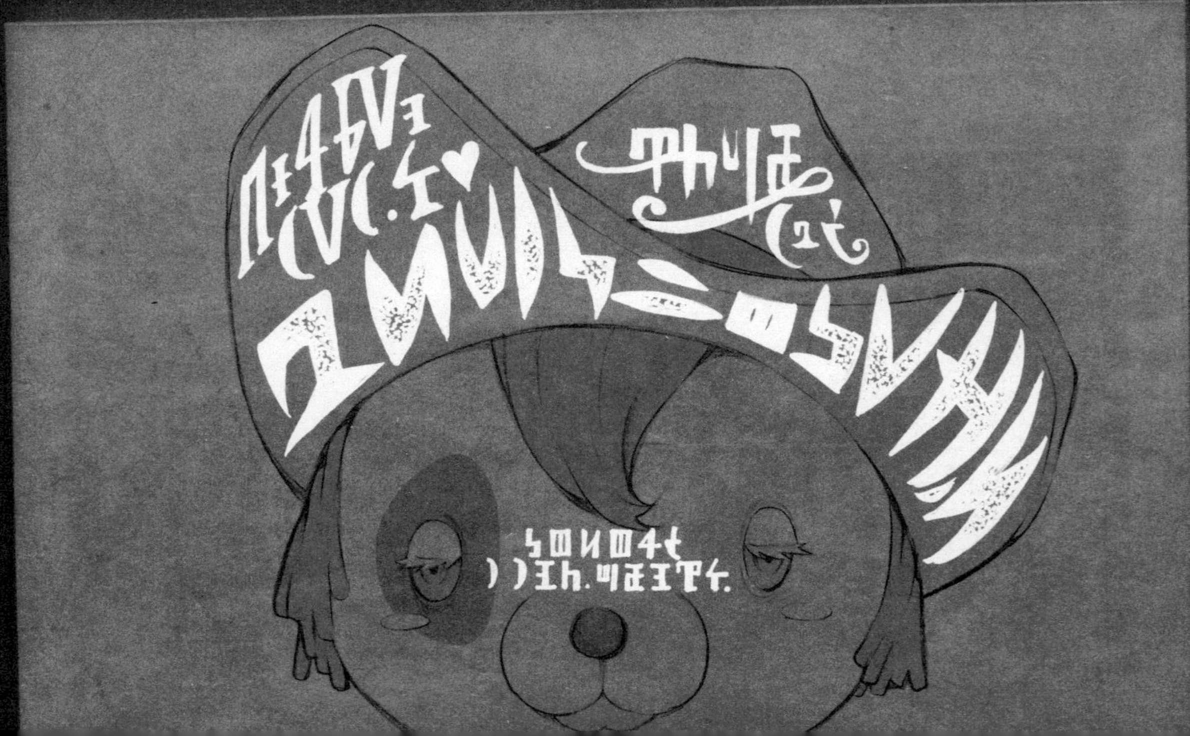

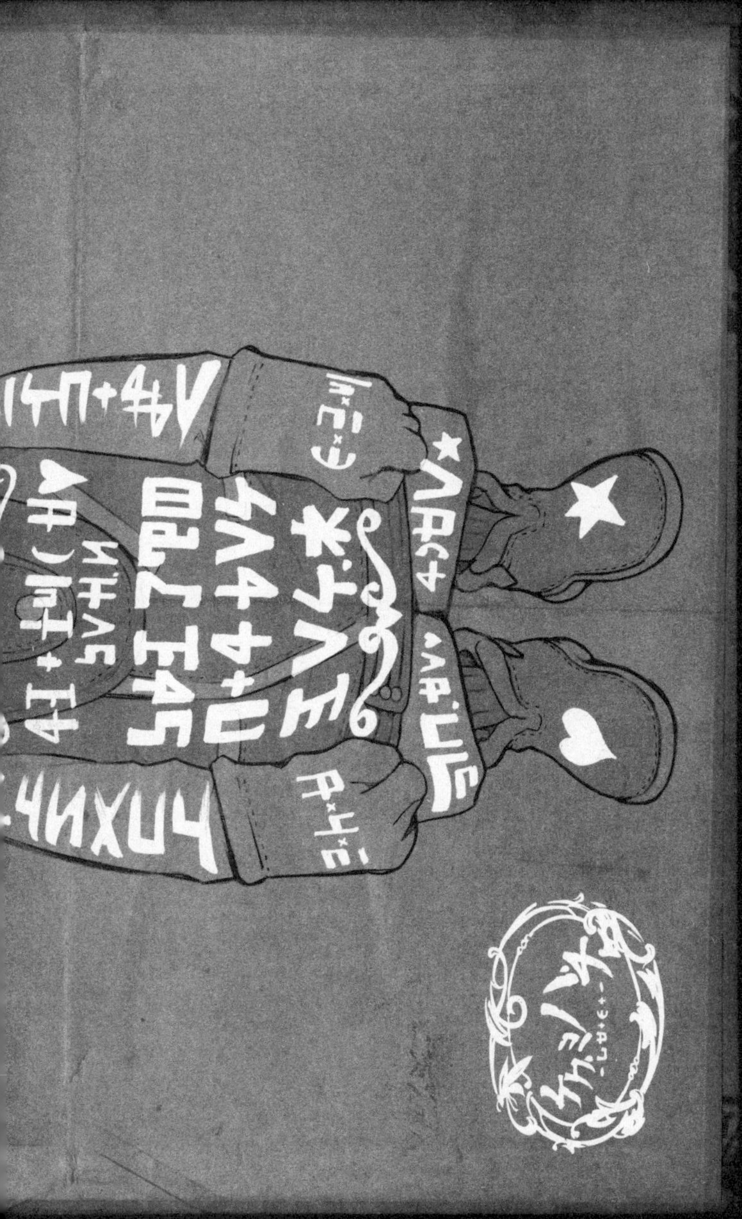

TegamiBachi
L E T T E R · B E E

Volume 19

SHONEN JUMP Manga Edition

Story and Art by Hiroyuki Asada

English Adaptation/Rich Amtower
Translation/JN Productions
Touch-up & Lettering/Annaliese Christman
Design/Amy Martin
Editor/Shaenon K. Garrity

Printed in the U.S.A.

Published by VIZ Media, LLC
P.O. Box 77010
San Francisco, CA 94107

10 9 8 7 6 5 4 3 2 1
First printing, June 2016

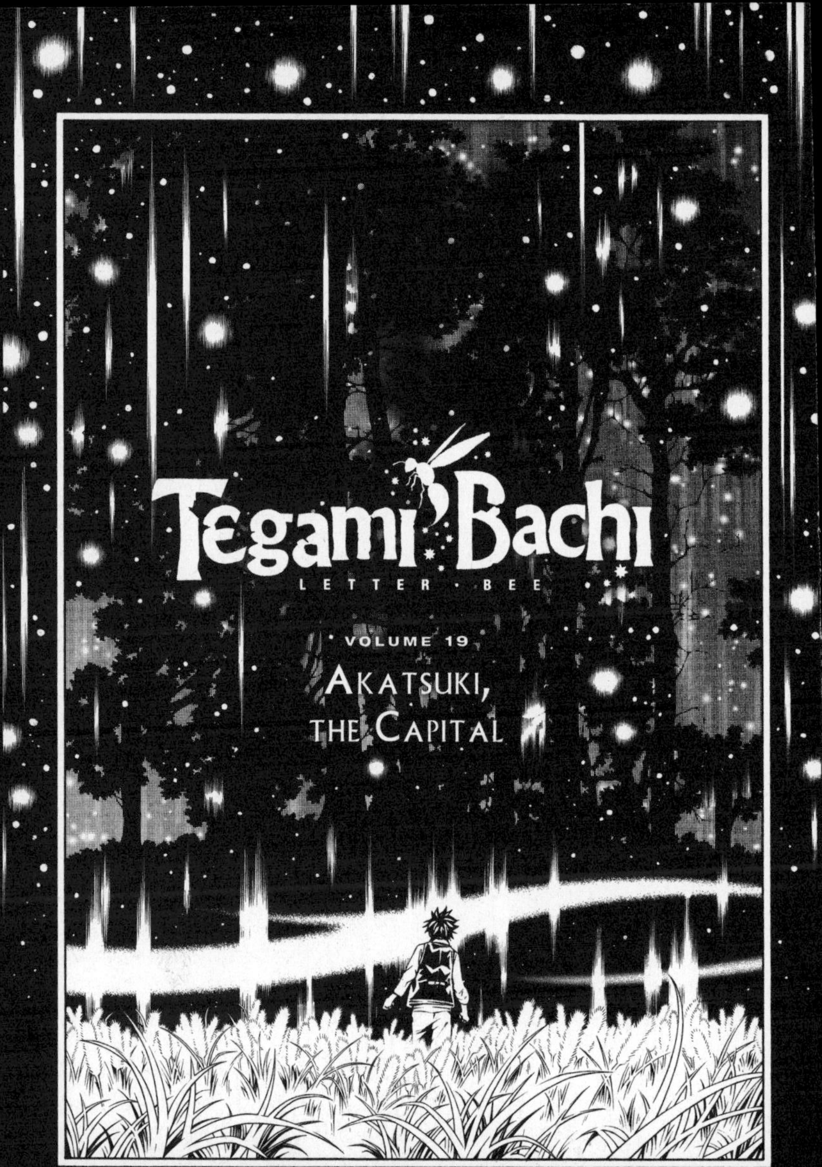
Tegami Bachi
LETTER · BEE
VOLUME 19
Akatsuki, the Capital

This is a country known as Amberground, where night never ends.

Its capital, Akatsuki, is illuminated by a man-made sun. The farther one strays from the capital, the weaker the light. The Yuusari region is cast in twilight; the Yodaka region survives only on pale moonlight.

Letter Bee Gauche Suede and young Lag Seeing meet in the Yodaka region— a postal worker and the "letter" he must deliver. In their short time together, they form a fast friendship, but when the journey ends, each departs down his own path. In time, Lag sets out for Yuusari to become a Letter Bee like Gauche. But Gauche is no longer there, having lost his *heart* and vanished.

Now a Bee, Lag continues delivering letters as he searches for Gauche. He discovers Gauche has taken on a new identity as Noir, a member of the rebel group Reverse. Reverse attempts to attack the capital with a massive Gaichuu, Cabernet, but the Bees foil their plan.

As Lag and his friends look for the five children born on the Day of the Flicker, cocky new hire Chico joins the Beehive. After Lag completes a delivery to one of the five children, an animal named Ponta, he receives an invitation from Largo Lloyd, head of Reverse. In the glacier town of Blue Notes Blues, Lloyd reveals to the Bees that within the artificial sun is a massive Gaichuu called Spiritus, which the government feeds with the *hearts of citizens.*

Lag tracks down the last living Spirit Insect and decides to remain with it until he learns how to defeat Spiritus. Now, after 358 days, Lag has finally returned...

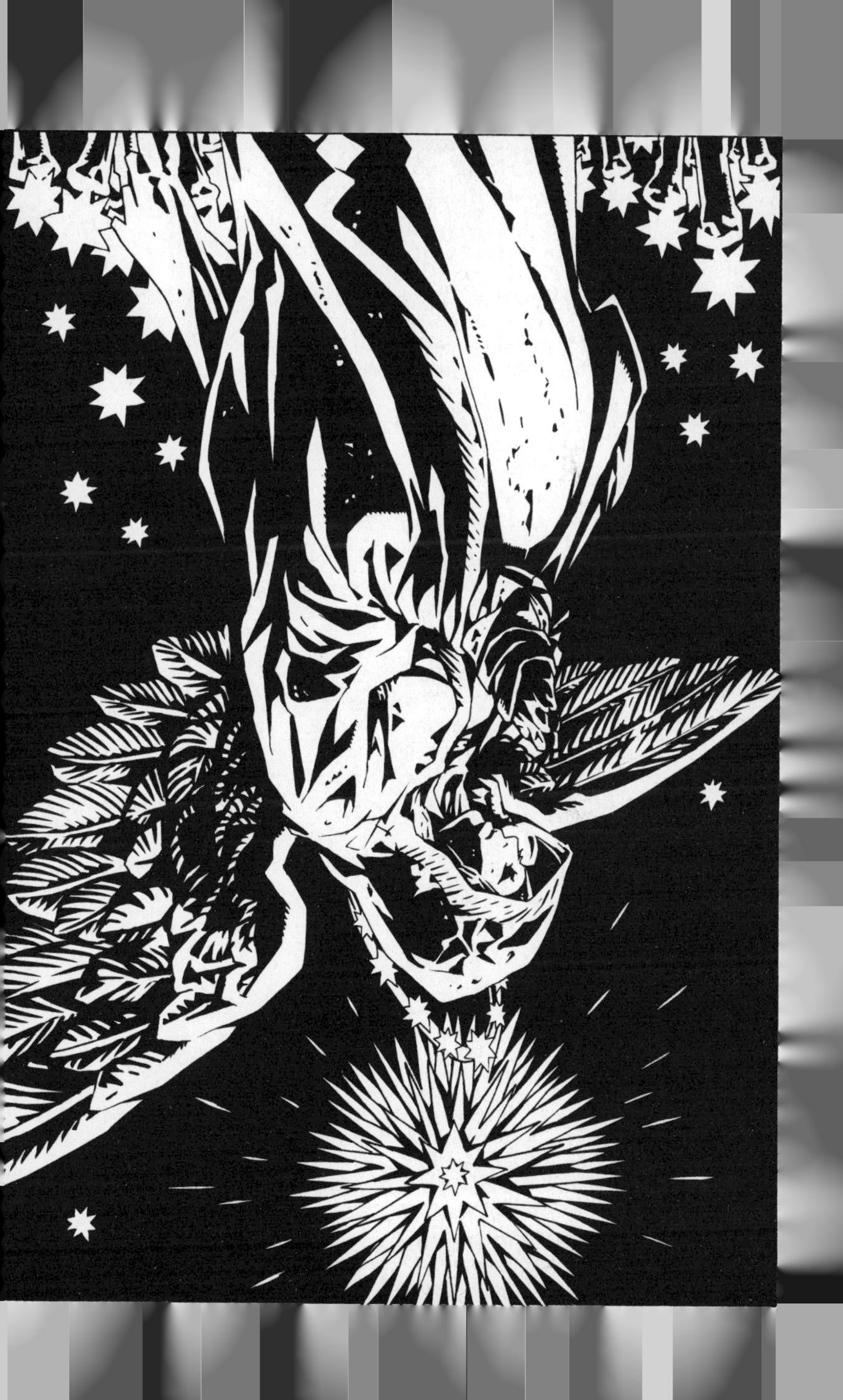

LIST OF CHARACTERS

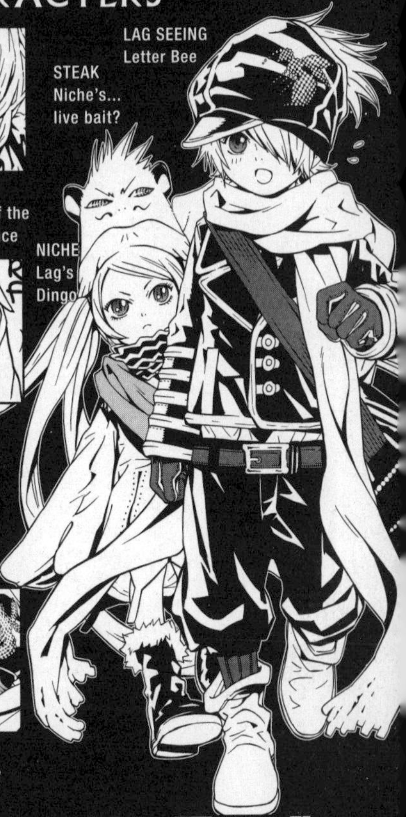

LAG SEEING
Letter Bee

STEAK
Niche's...
live bait?

NICHE
Lag's
Dingo

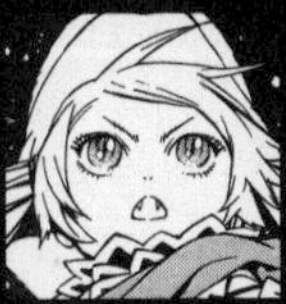

CHICO NEIGE
Letter Bee

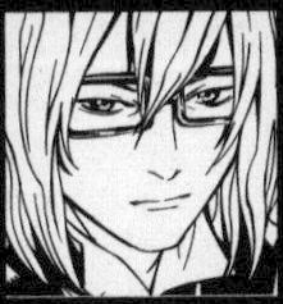

LARGO LLOYD
Ex-Beehive Director

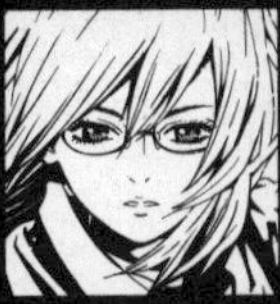

ARIA LINK
Section Chief of the
Dead Letter Office

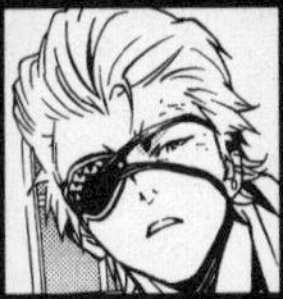

DR. THUNDERLAND, JR.
Member of the AG
Biological Science
Advisory Board,
Third Division and
head doctor at the
Beehive

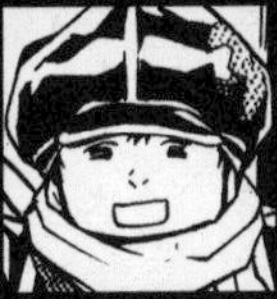

CONNOR KLUFF
Letter Bee

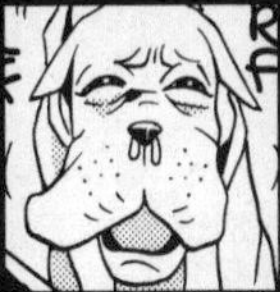

GUS
Connor's Dingo

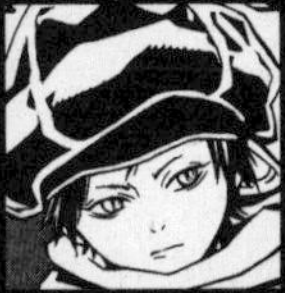

ZAZIE
Letter Bee

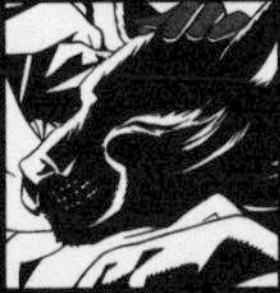

WASIOLKA
Zazie's Dingo

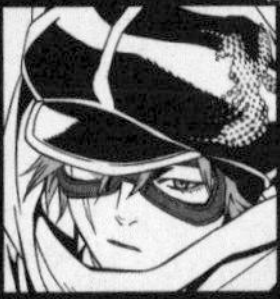

JIGGY PEPPER
Express Delivery
Letter Bee

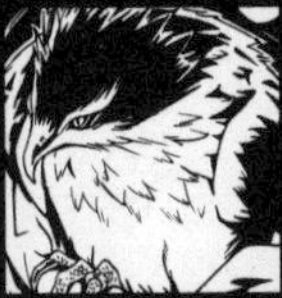

HARRY
Jiggy's Dingo

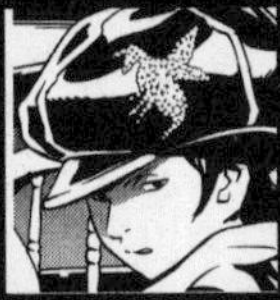

MOC SULLIVAN
Letter Bee

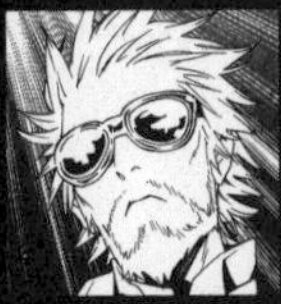

CHALYBS GARRARD
Inspector and
ex-Letter Bee

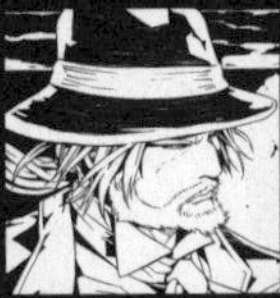

HAZEL VALENTINE
Inspector and
Garrard's ex-Dingo

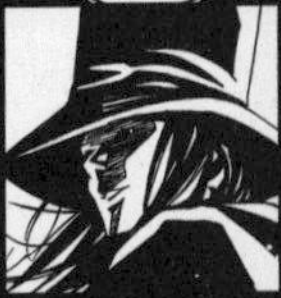

LAWRENCE
The ringleader of
Reverse

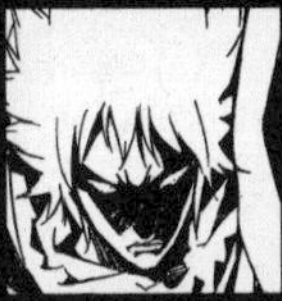

ZEAL
Marauder for
Reverse

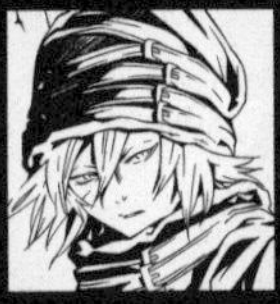

NOIR (FORMERLY
GAUCHE SUEDE)
Marauder for
Reverse and an
ex-Letter Bee

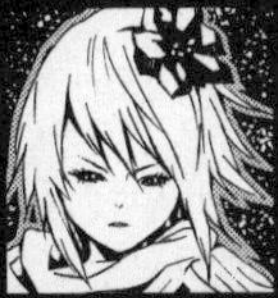

RODA
Noir's Dingo

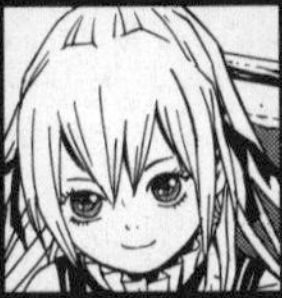

SYLVETTE SUEDE
Gauche's Sister

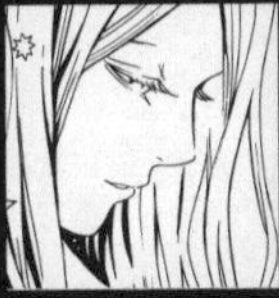

ANNE SEEING
Lag's Mother
(Missing)

Tegami Bachi
LETTER · BEE

VOLUME 19
AKATSUKI, THE CAPITAL

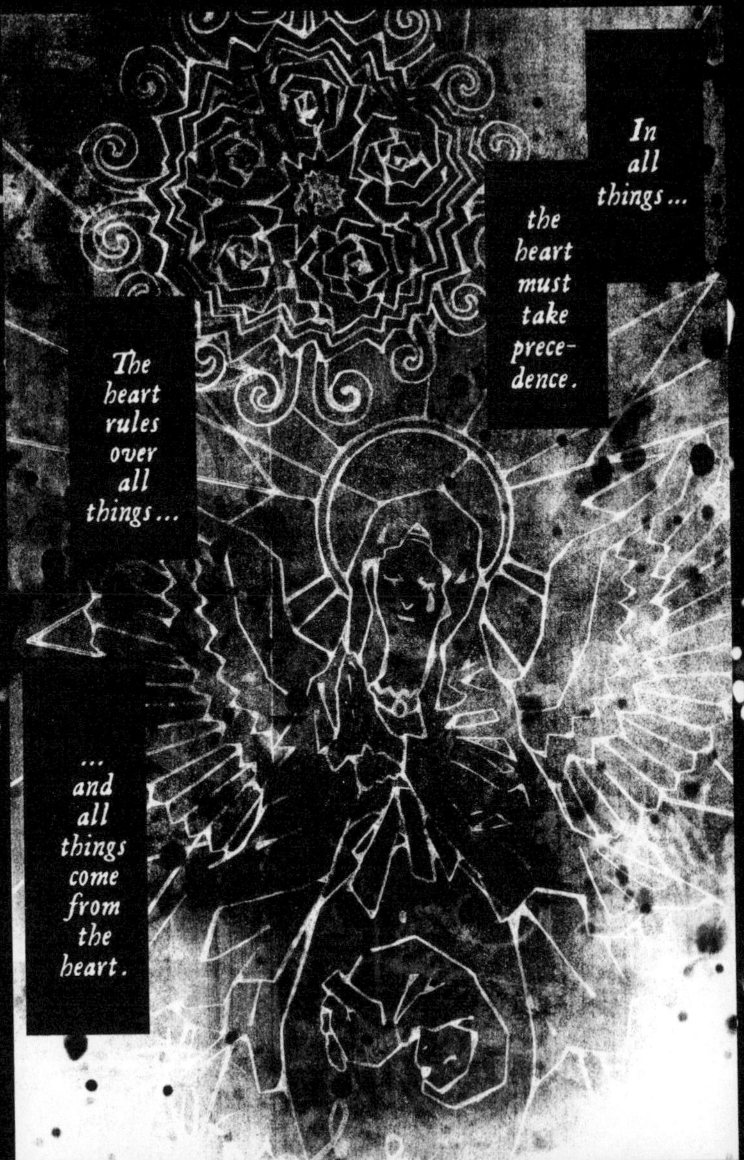
In all things...
the heart must take precedence.
The heart rules over all things...
... and all things come from the heart.

–THE SCRIPTURES OF AMBERGROUND, 1st verse

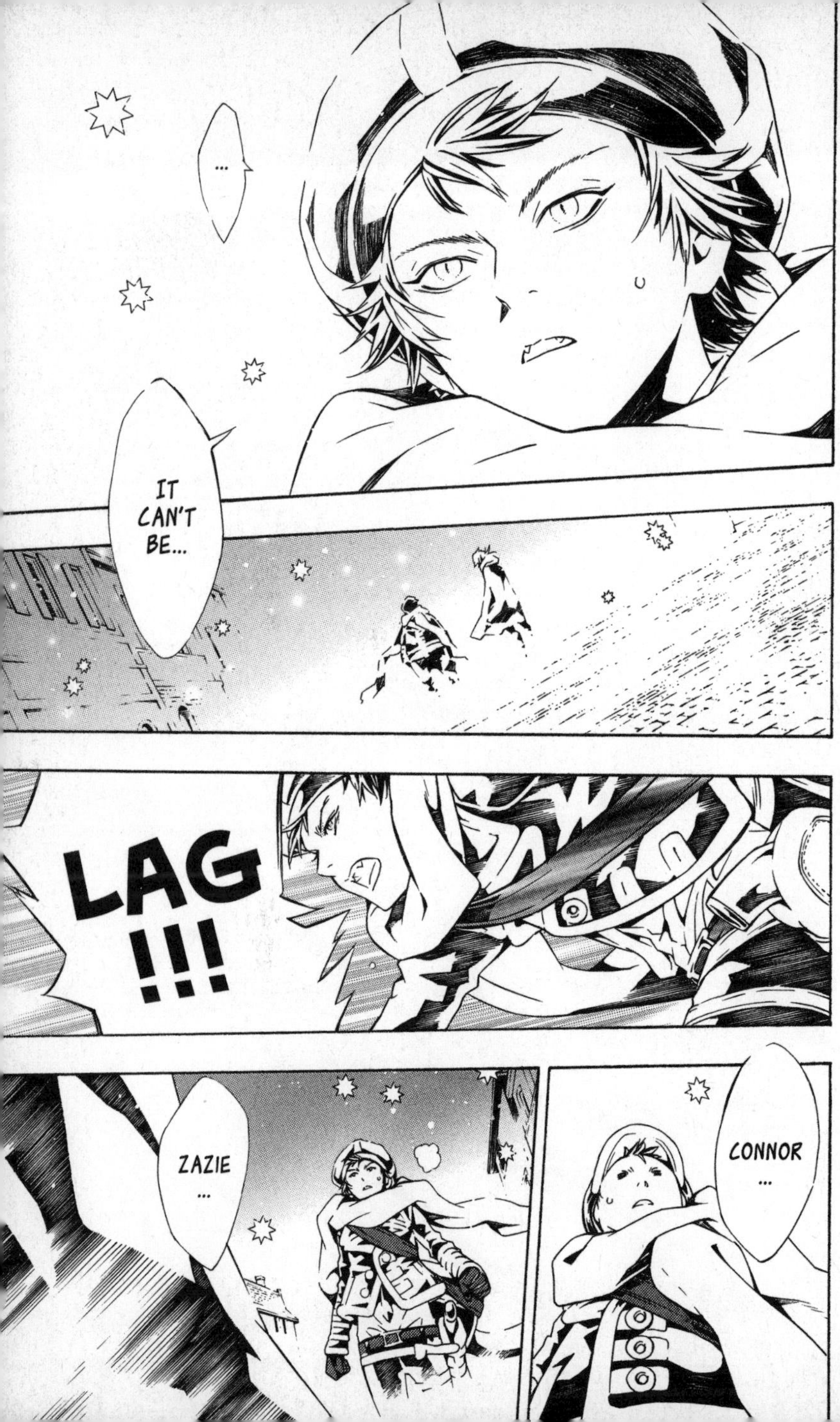
...
IT CAN'T BE...
LAG !!!
CONNOR ...
ZAZIE ...

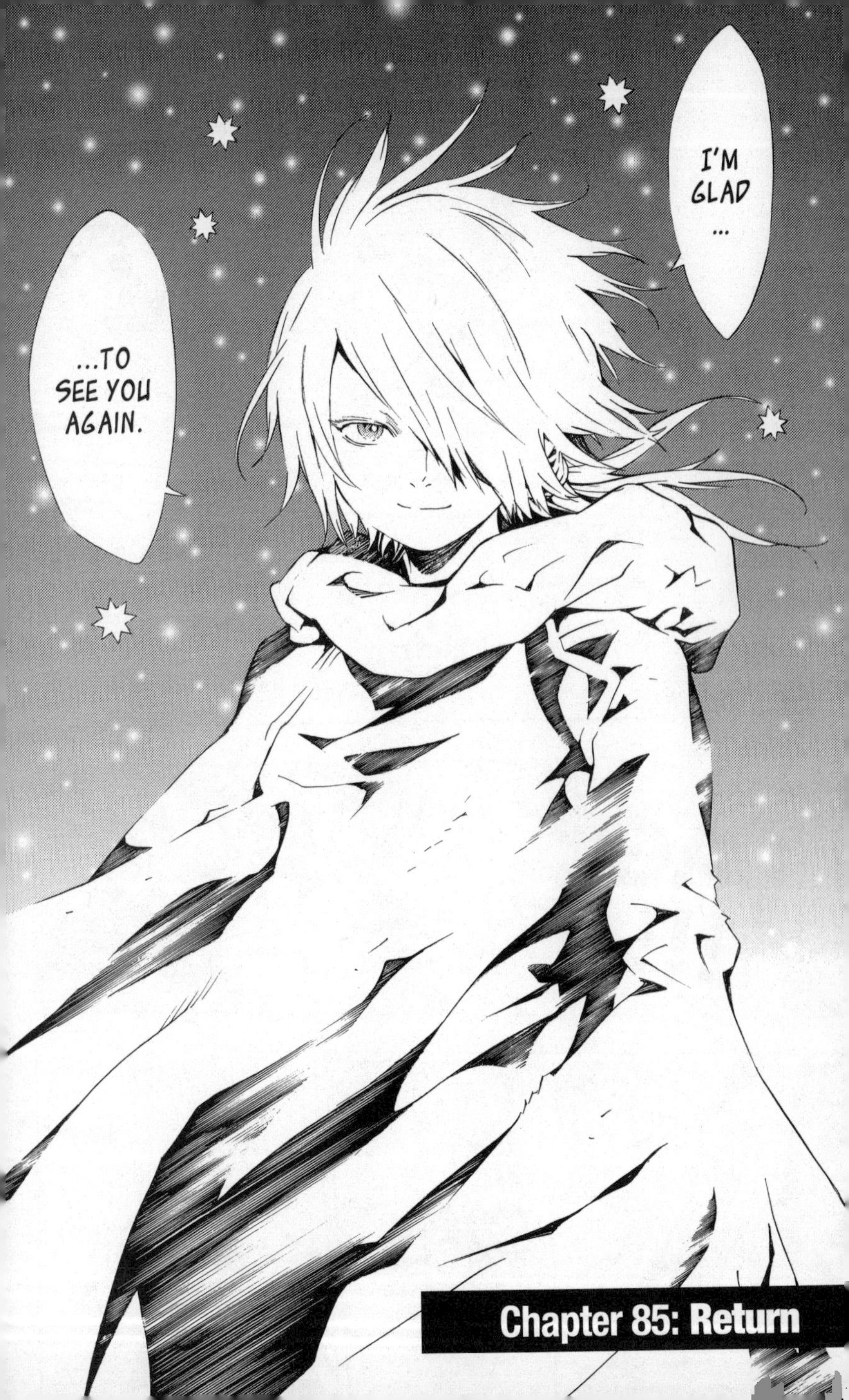
I'M GLAD ...
...TO SEE YOU AGAIN.

Chapter 85: Return

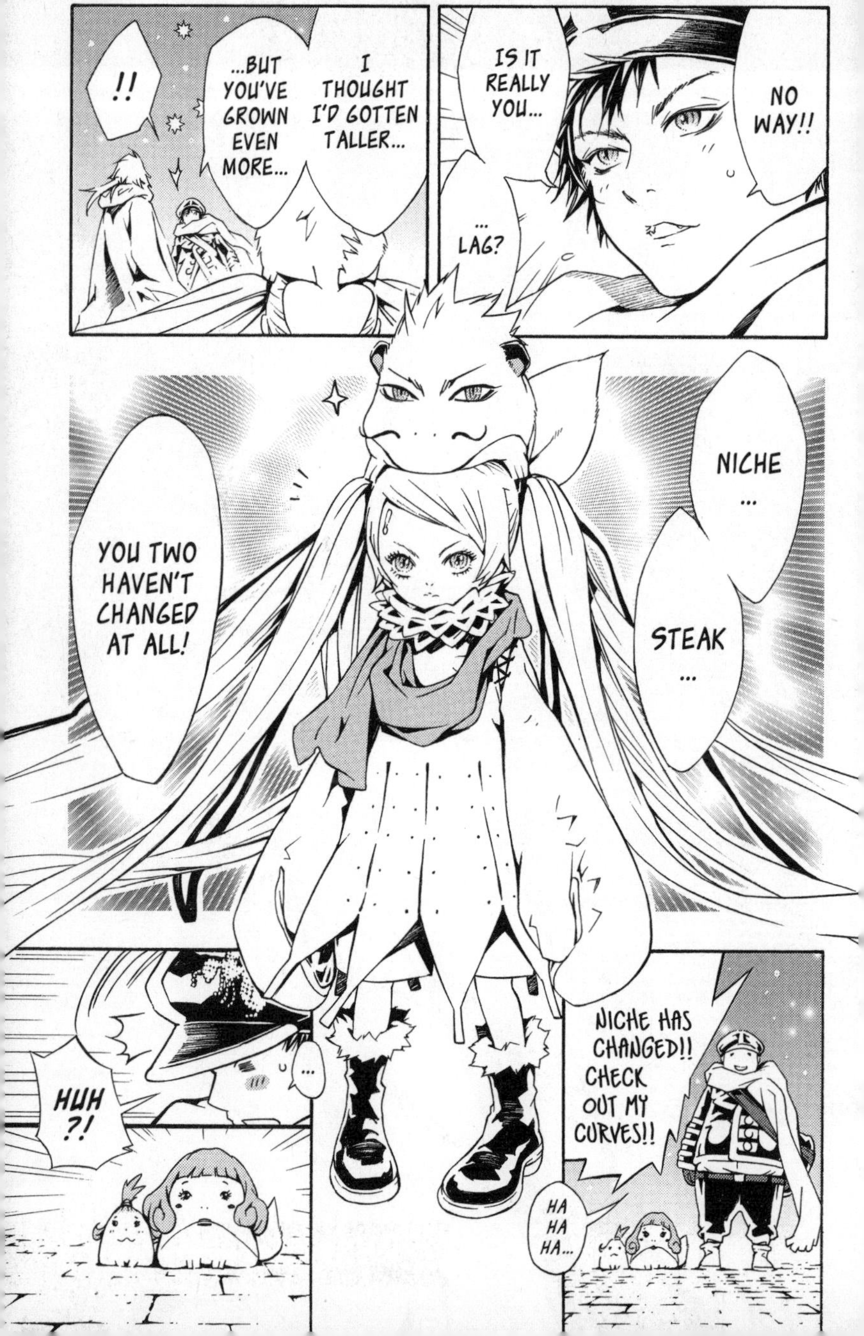
NO WAY!!
IS IT REALLY YOU...
... LAG?
I THOUGHT I'D GOTTEN TALLER...
...BUT YOU'VE GROWN EVEN MORE...
!!
NICHE ...
STEAK ...
YOU TWO HAVEN'T CHANGED AT ALL!
NICHE HAS CHANGED!! CHECK OUT MY CURVES!!
HA HA HA...
...
HUH ?!

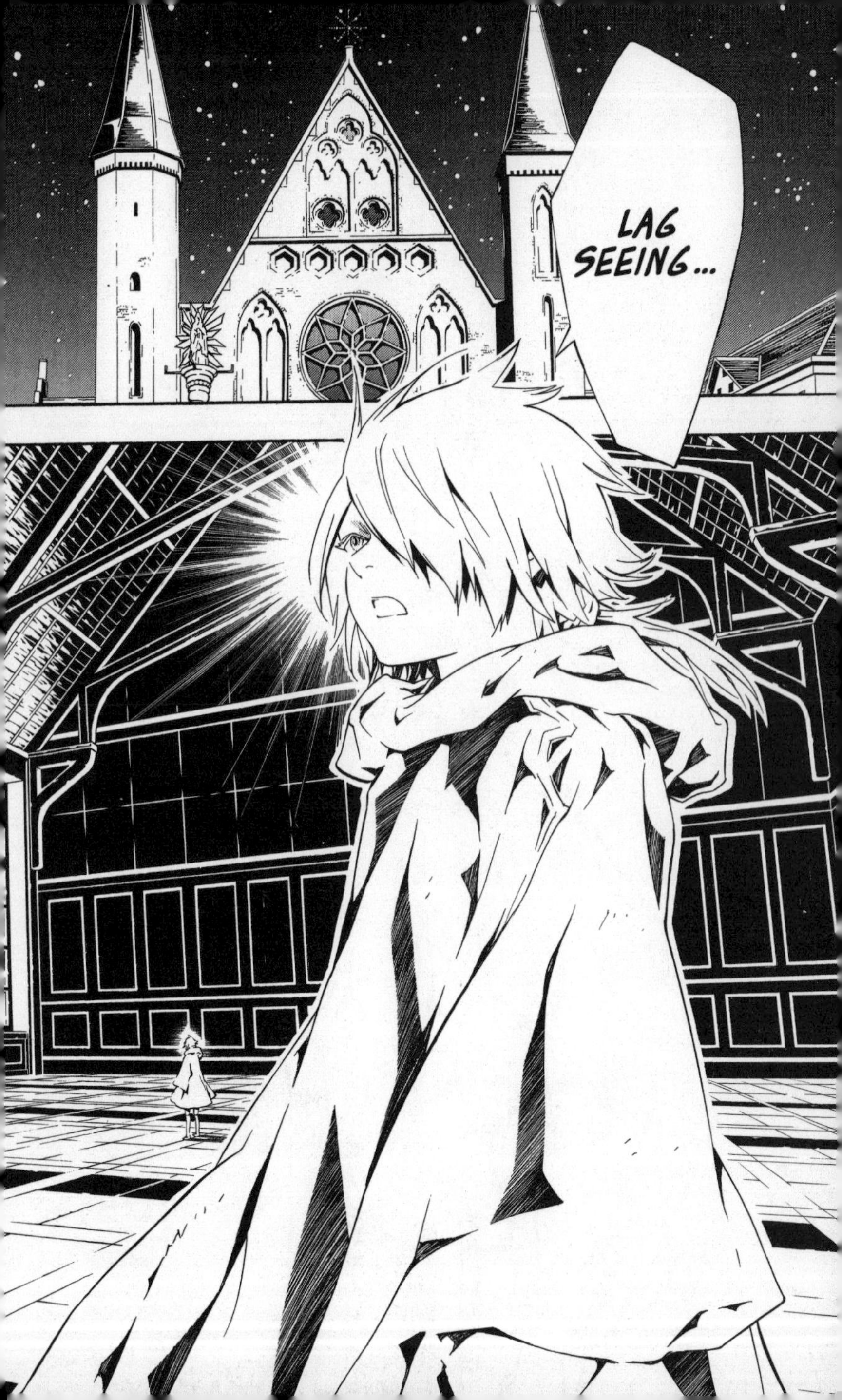
LAG SEEING...

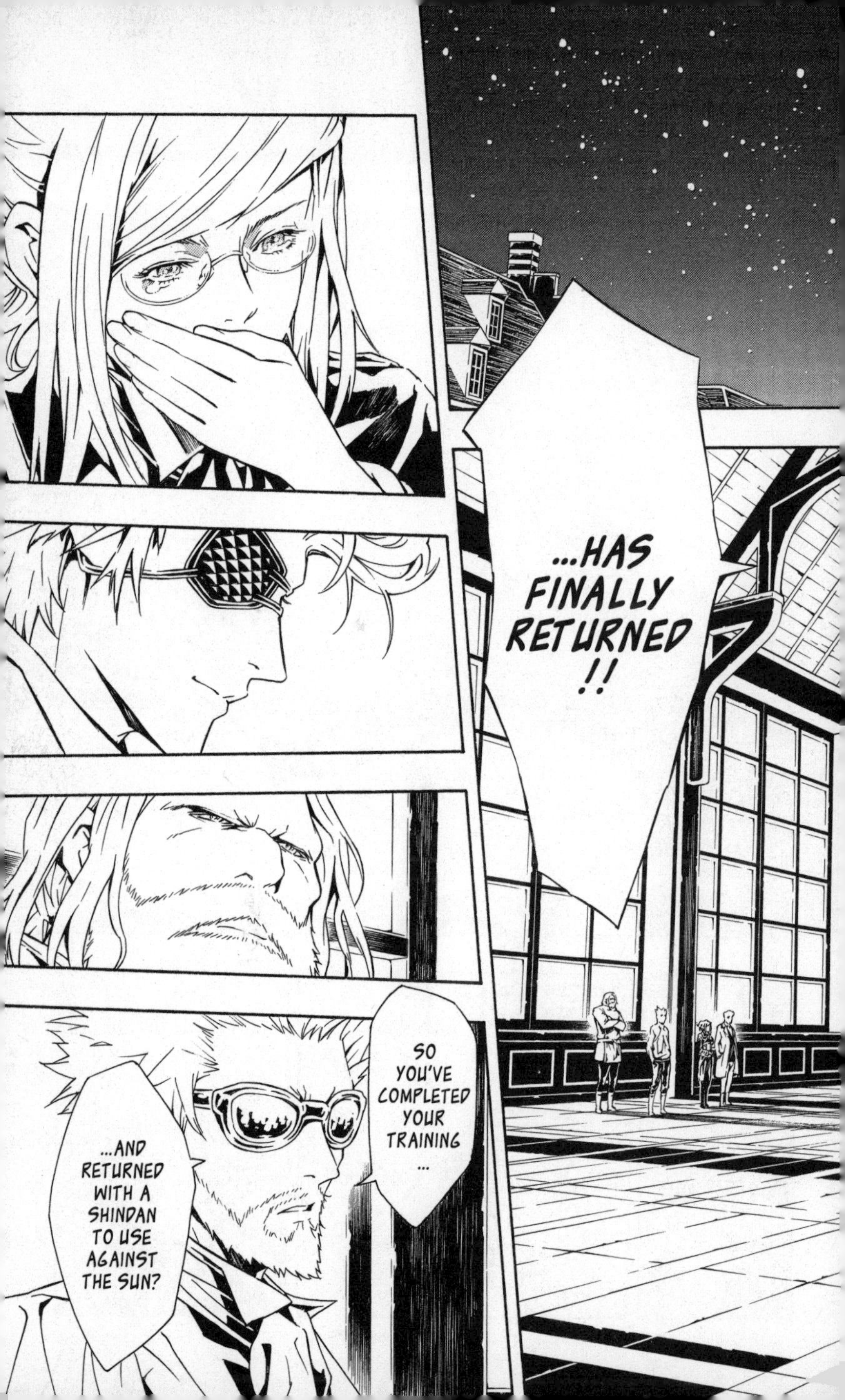
...HAS FINALLY RETURNED !!
SO YOU'VE COMPLETED YOUR TRAINING ...
...AND RETURNED WITH A SHINDAN TO USE AGAINST THE SUN?

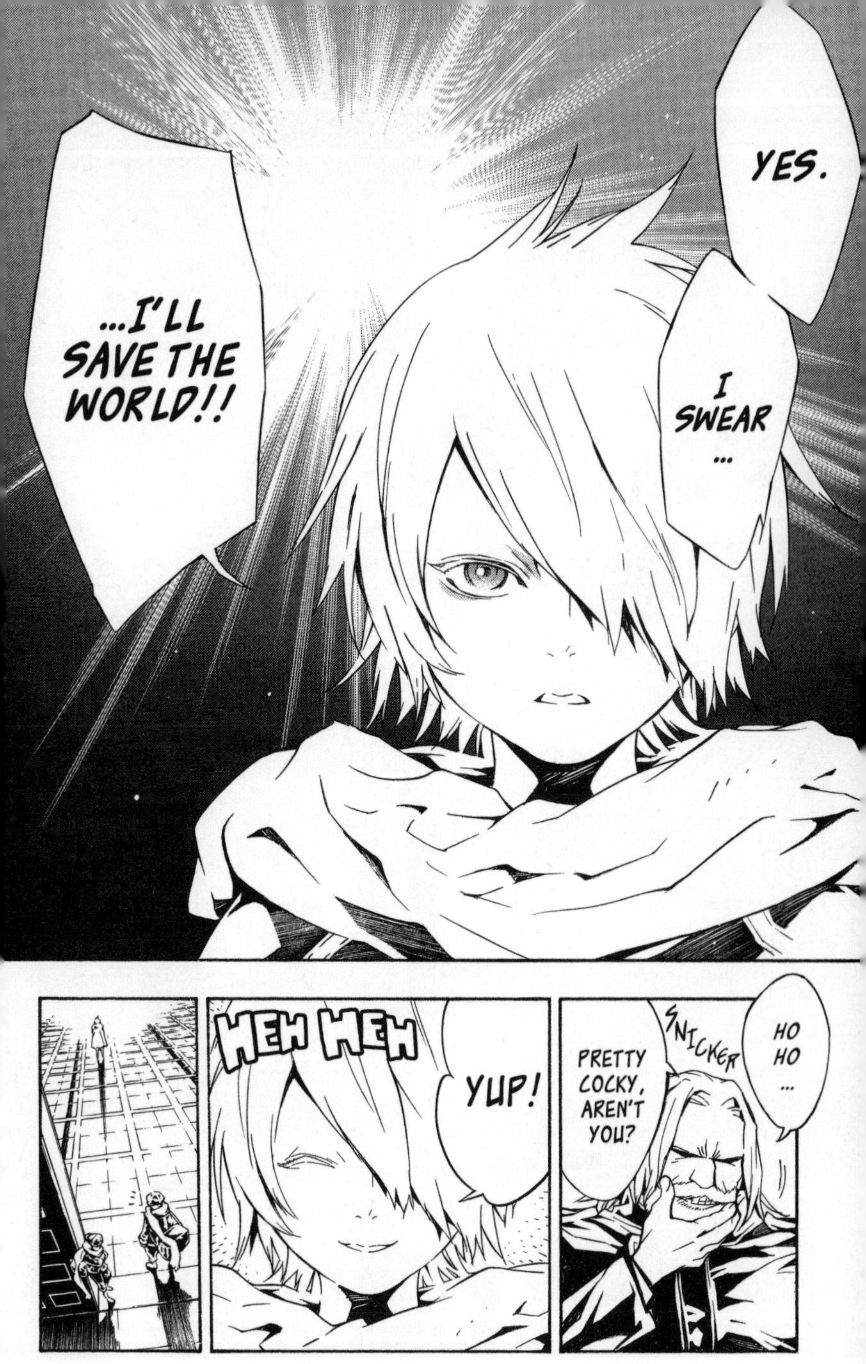
YES.
I SWEAR ...
...I'LL SAVE THE WORLD!!
HO HO ...
SNICKER
PRETTY COCKY, AREN'T YOU?
YUP!
HEH HEH

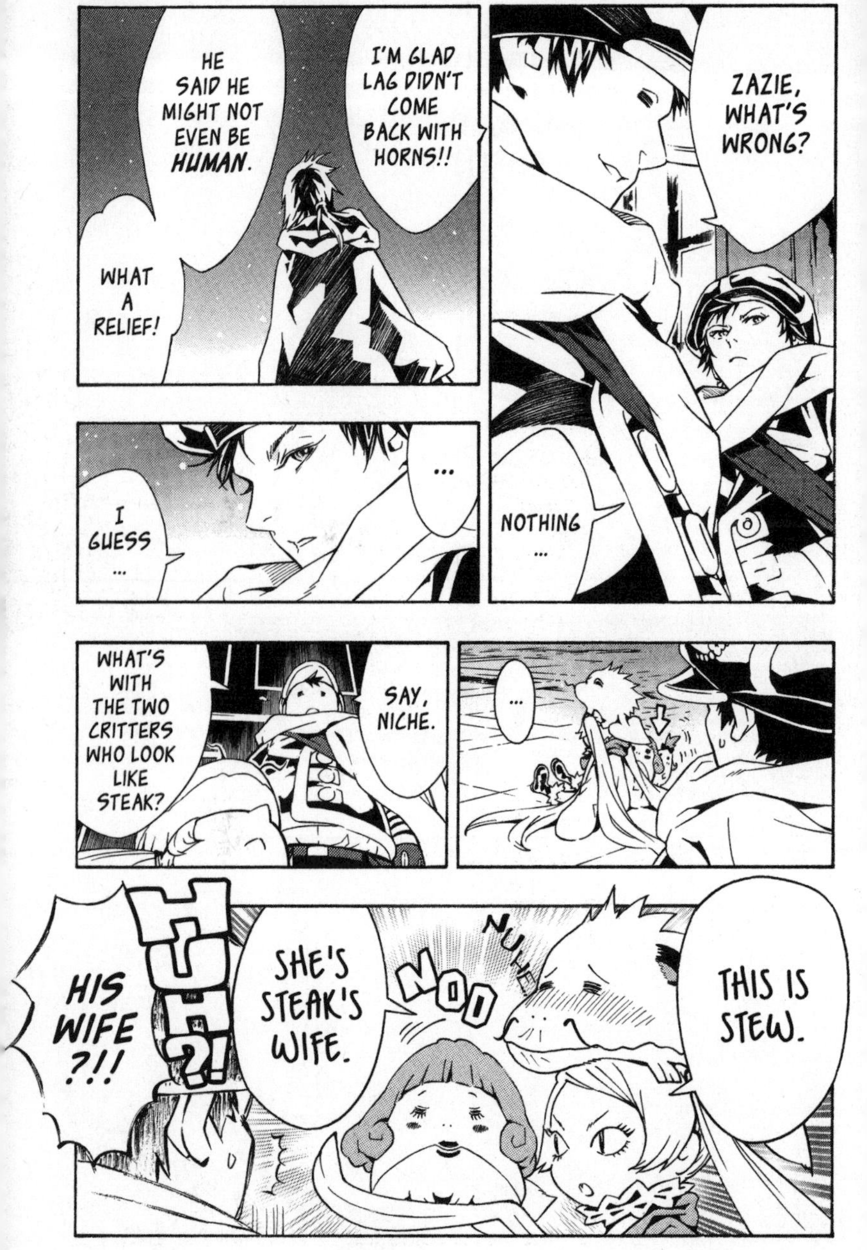
ZAZIE, WHAT'S WRONG?
NOTHING ...
I'M GLAD LAG DIDN'T COME BACK WITH HORNS!!
HE SAID HE MIGHT NOT EVEN BE **HUMAN**.
WHAT A RELIEF!
...
I GUESS ...
...
SAY, NICHE.
WHAT'S WITH THE TWO CRITTERS WHO LOOK LIKE STEAK?
THIS IS STEW.
NUHE
NOO
SHE'S STEAK'S WIFE.
HUH?!
HIS WIFE ?!!

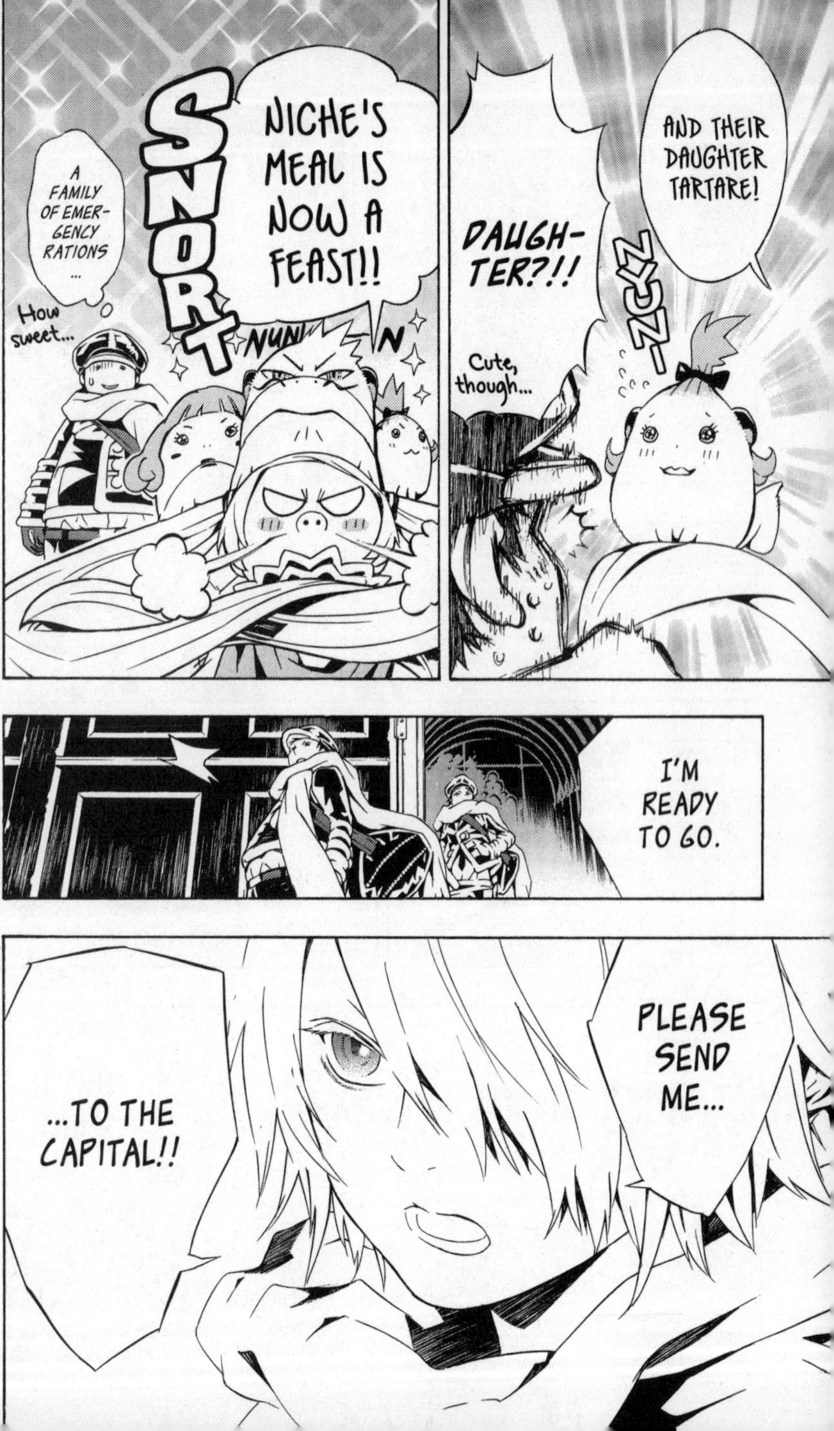
AND THEIR DAUGHTER TARTARE!
NYUN-
DAUGH-TER?!!
Cute, though...
NICHE'S MEAL IS NOW A FEAST!!
SNORT
NUN
N
A FAMILY OF EMER-GENCY RATIONS ...
How sweet...
I'M READY TO GO.
PLEASE SEND ME...
...TO THE CAPITAL!!

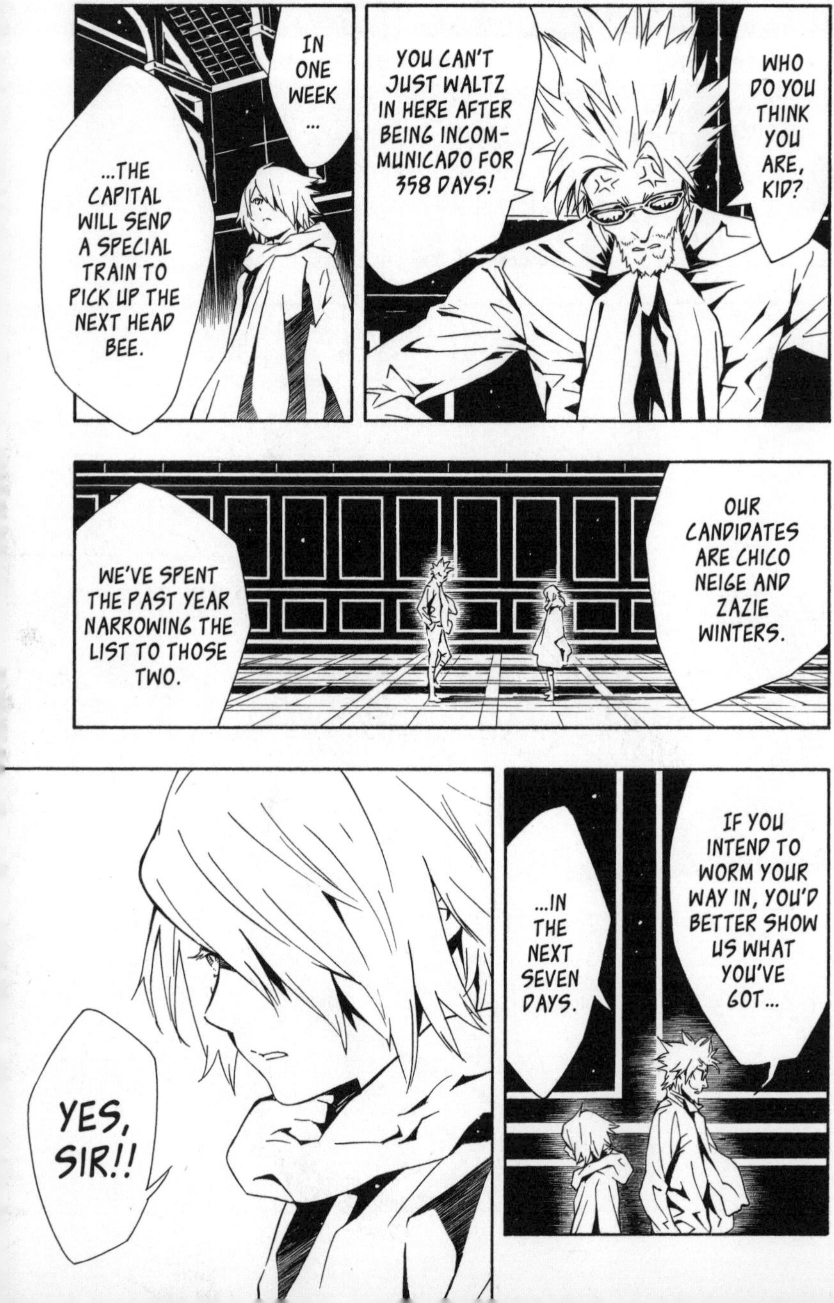
WHO DO YOU THINK YOU ARE, KID?
YOU CAN'T JUST WALTZ IN HERE AFTER BEING INCOM-MUNICADO FOR 358 DAYS!
IN ONE WEEK ...
...THE CAPITAL WILL SEND A SPECIAL TRAIN TO PICK UP THE NEXT HEAD BEE.
OUR CANDIDATES ARE CHICO NEIGE AND ZAZIE WINTERS.
WE'VE SPENT THE PAST YEAR NARROWING THE LIST TO THOSE TWO.
IF YOU INTEND TO WORM YOUR WAY IN, YOU'D BETTER SHOW US WHAT YOU'VE GOT...
...IN THE NEXT SEVEN DAYS.
YES, SIR!!

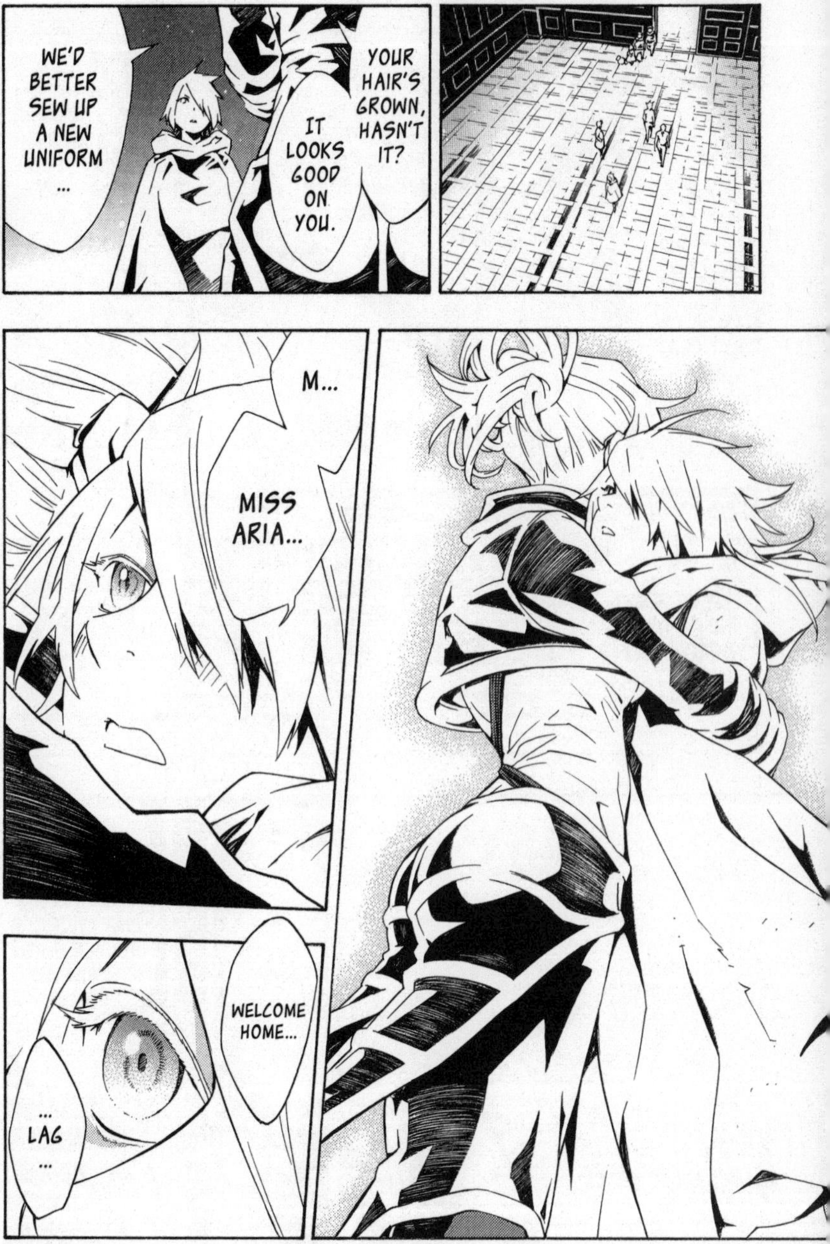
YOUR HAIR'S GROWN, HASN'T IT?
IT LOOKS GOOD ON YOU.
WE'D BETTER SEW UP A NEW UNIFORM ...
M...
MISS ARIA...
WELCOME HOME...
... LAG ...

WELCOME HOME...
I'M HOME...
SOB SOB
THUP THUP
...MISS ARIA...

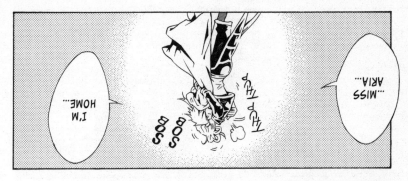

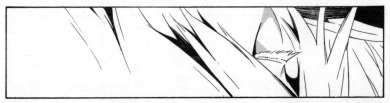

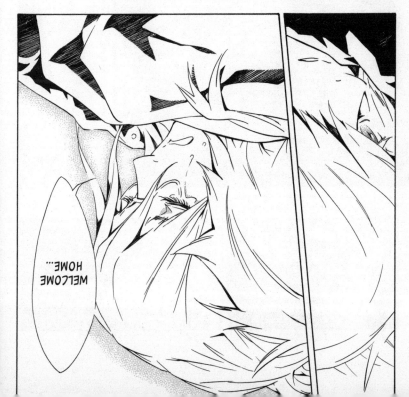

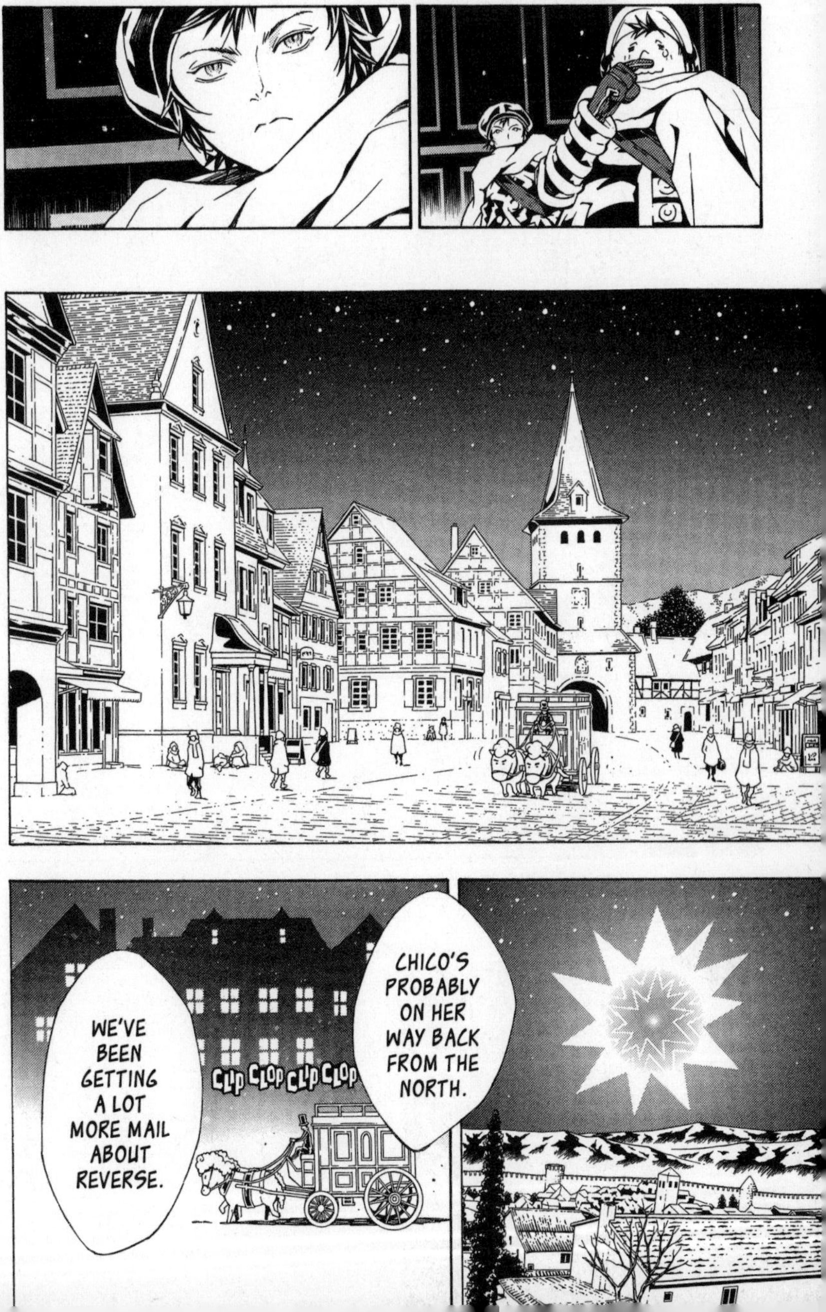
CHICO'S PROBABLY ON HER WAY BACK FROM THE NORTH.
CLIP CLOP CLIP CLOP
WE'VE BEEN GETTING A LOT MORE MAIL ABOUT REVERSE.

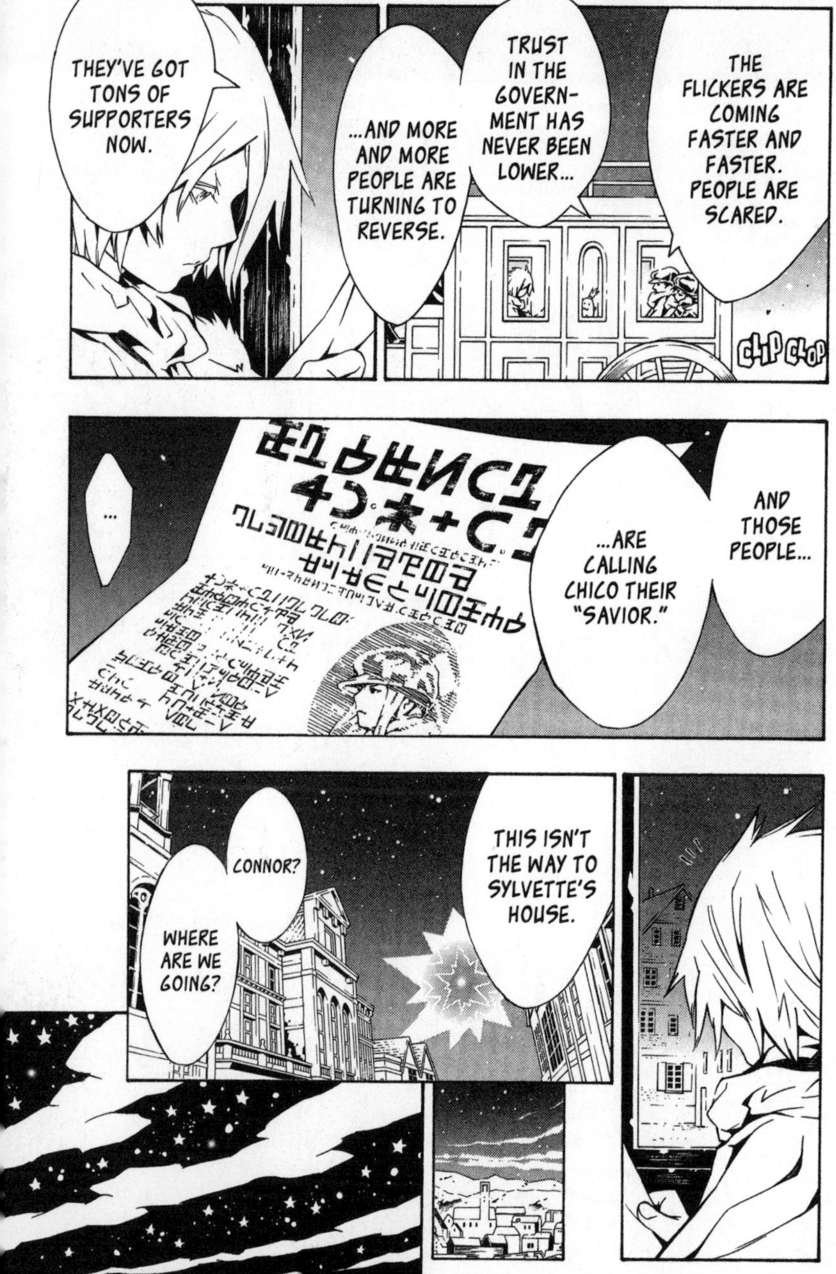
THE FLICKERS ARE COMING FASTER AND FASTER. PEOPLE ARE SCARED.
TRUST IN THE GOVERN-MENT HAS NEVER BEEN LOWER...
...AND MORE AND MORE PEOPLE ARE TURNING TO REVERSE.
CLIP CLOP
THEY'VE GOT TONS OF SUPPORTERS NOW.
AND THOSE PEOPLE...
...ARE CALLING CHICO THEIR "SAVIOR."
...
THIS ISN'T THE WAY TO SYLVETTE'S HOUSE.
CONNOR?
WHERE ARE WE GOING?

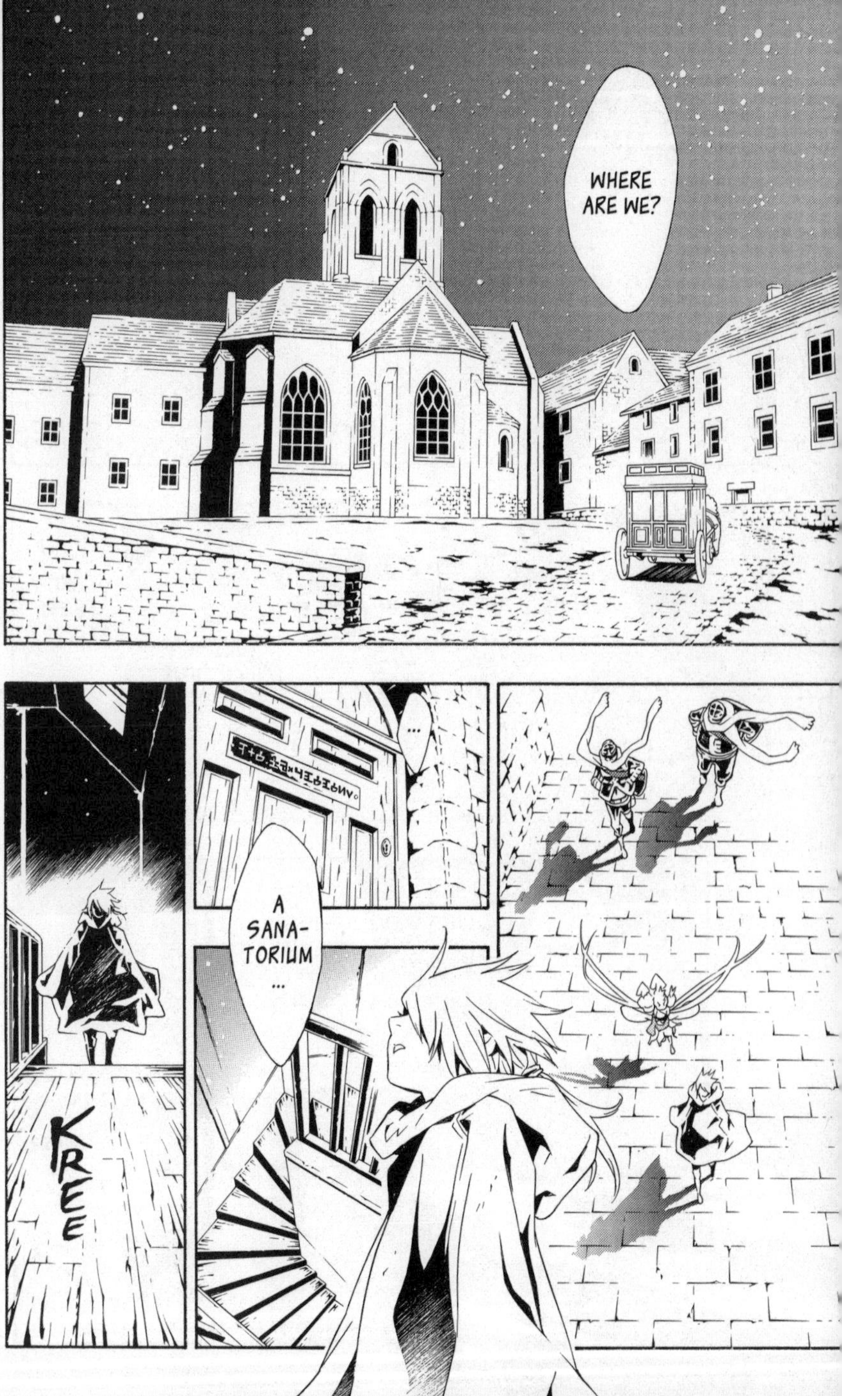
WHERE ARE WE?
...
A SANA-TORIUM...
KREE

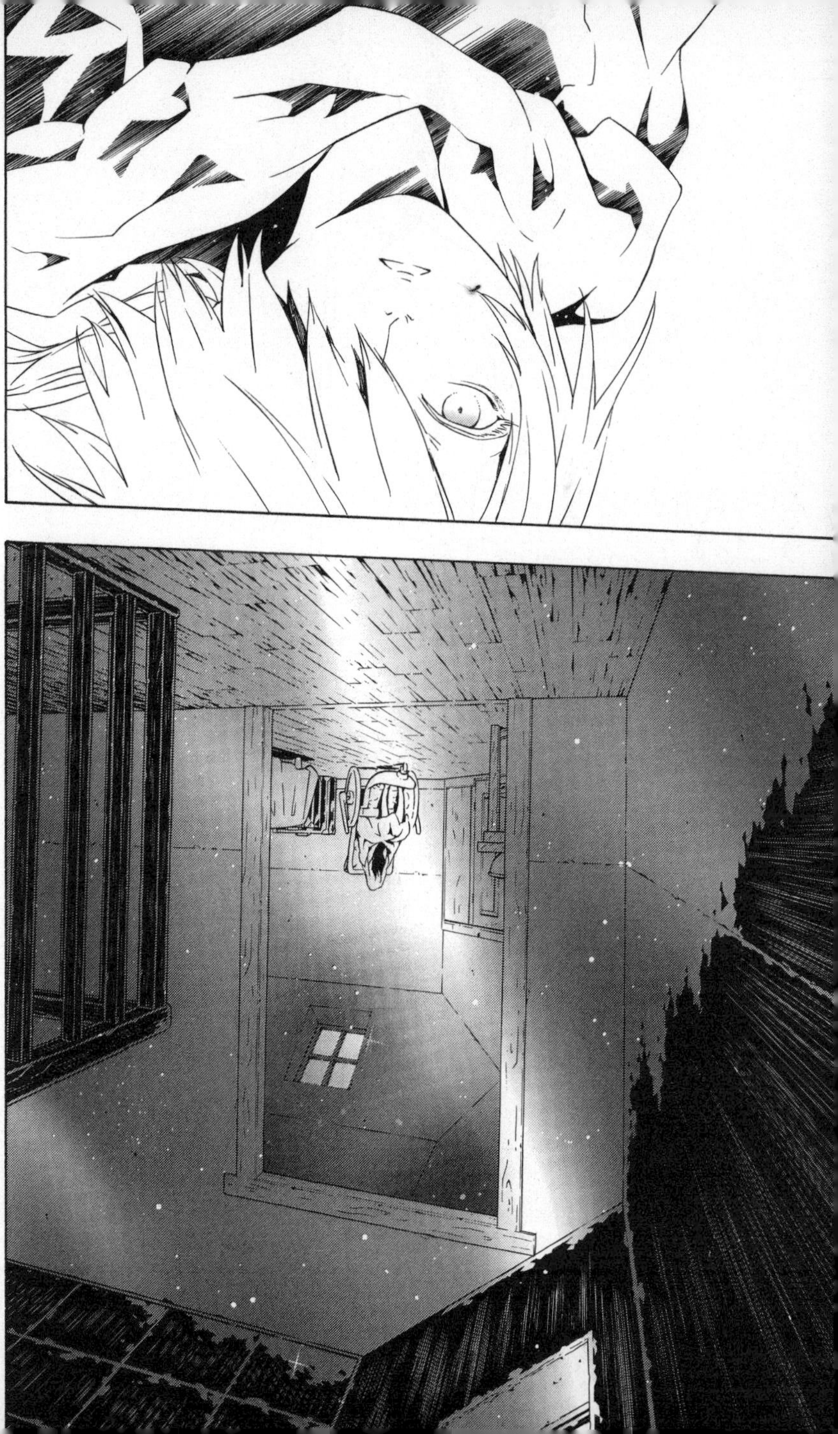

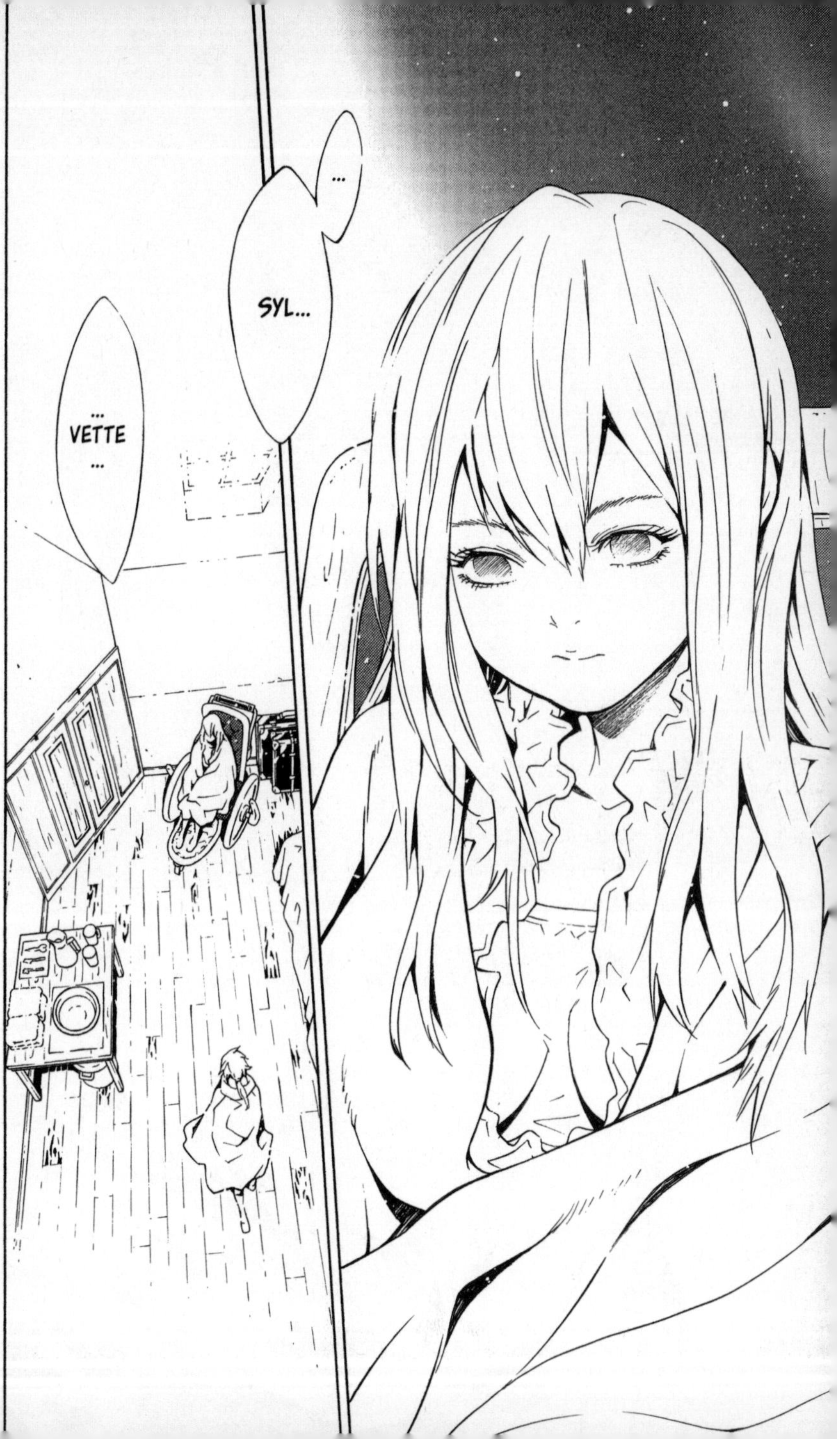
...
SYL...
... VETTE ...

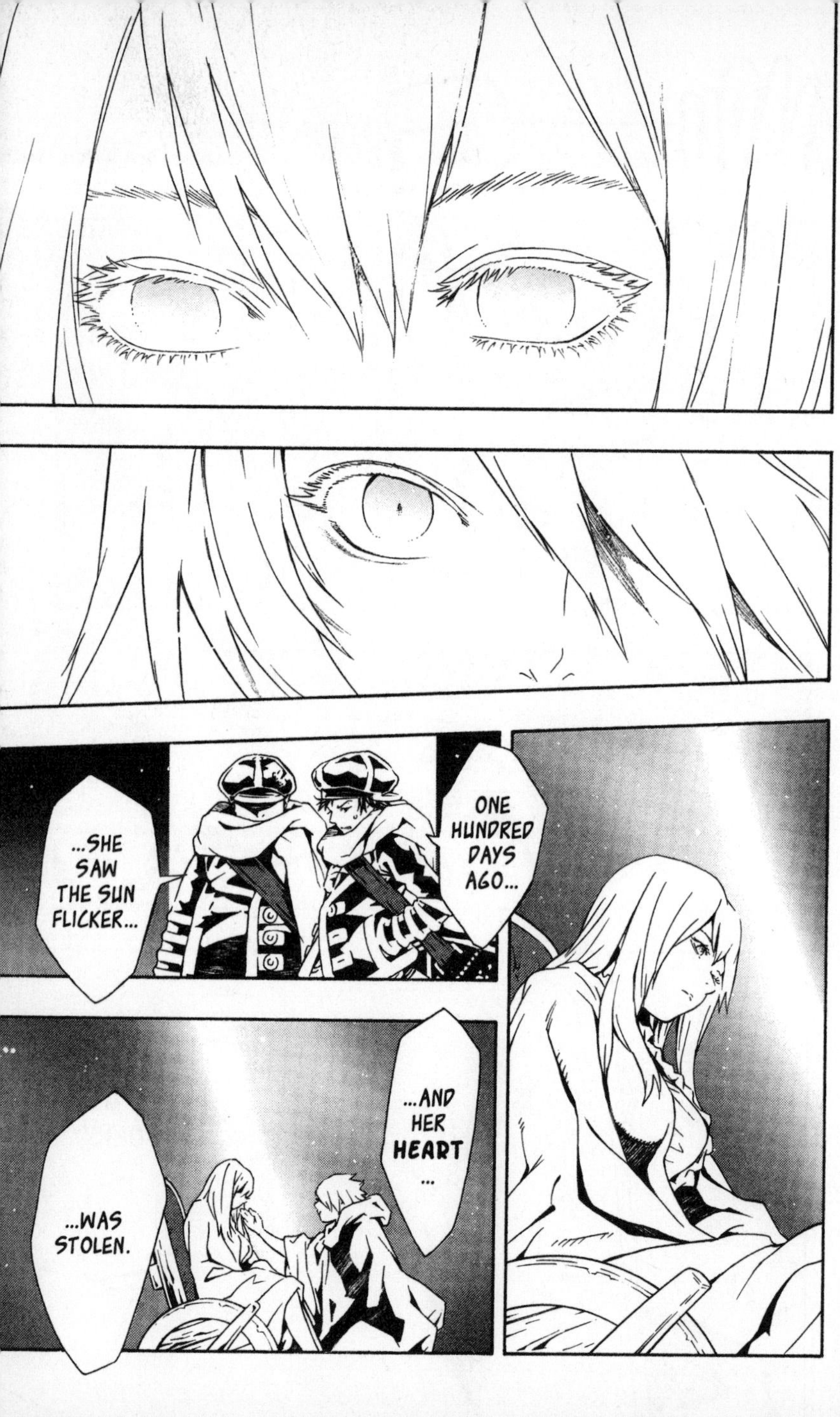
ONE HUNDRED DAYS AGO...
...SHE SAW THE SUN FLICKER...
...AND HER HEART ...
...WAS STOLEN.

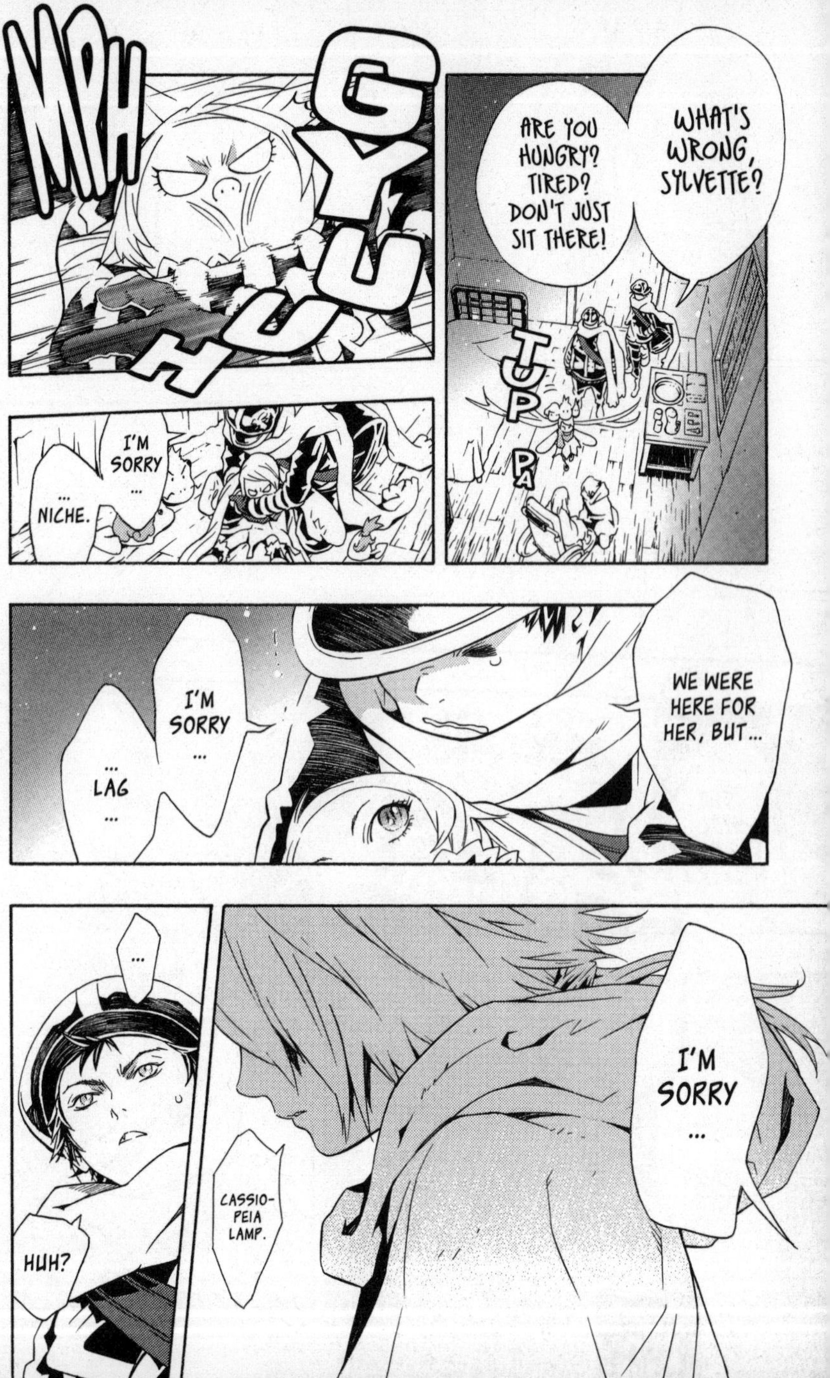
WHAT'S WRONG, SYLVETTE?
ARE YOU HUNGRY? TIRED? DON'T JUST SIT THERE!
TUP
PA
GYUU
HUH
MPH
I'M SORRY ...
... NICHE.
WE WERE HERE FOR HER, BUT...
I'M SORRY ...
... LAG ...
I'M SORRY ...
CASSIO-PEIA LAMP.
...
HUH?

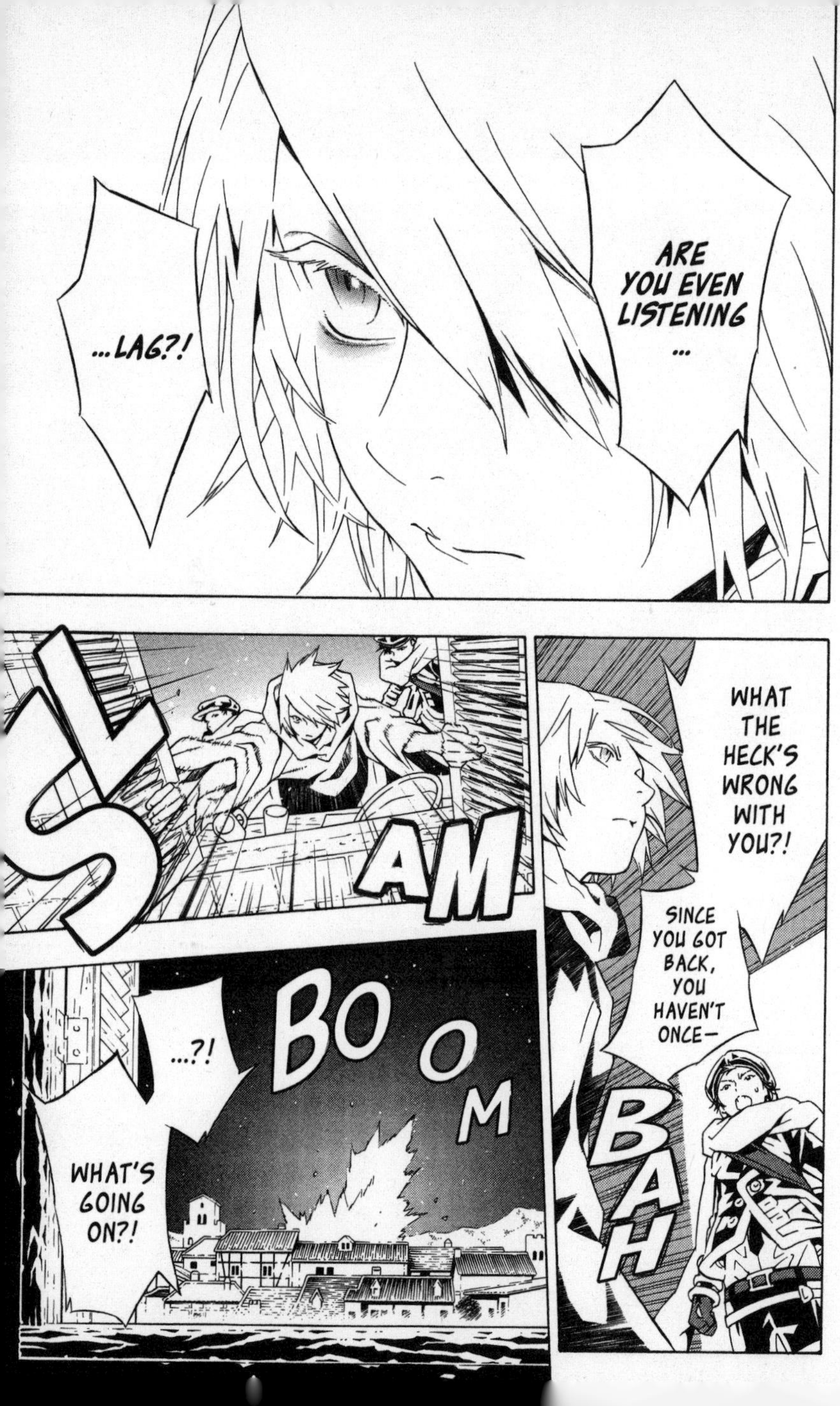
ARE YOU EVEN LISTENING...
...LAG?!
WHAT THE HECK'S WRONG WITH YOU?!
SINCE YOU GOT BACK, YOU HAVEN'T ONCE—
BAH
SLAM
BOOM
...?!
WHAT'S GOING ON?!

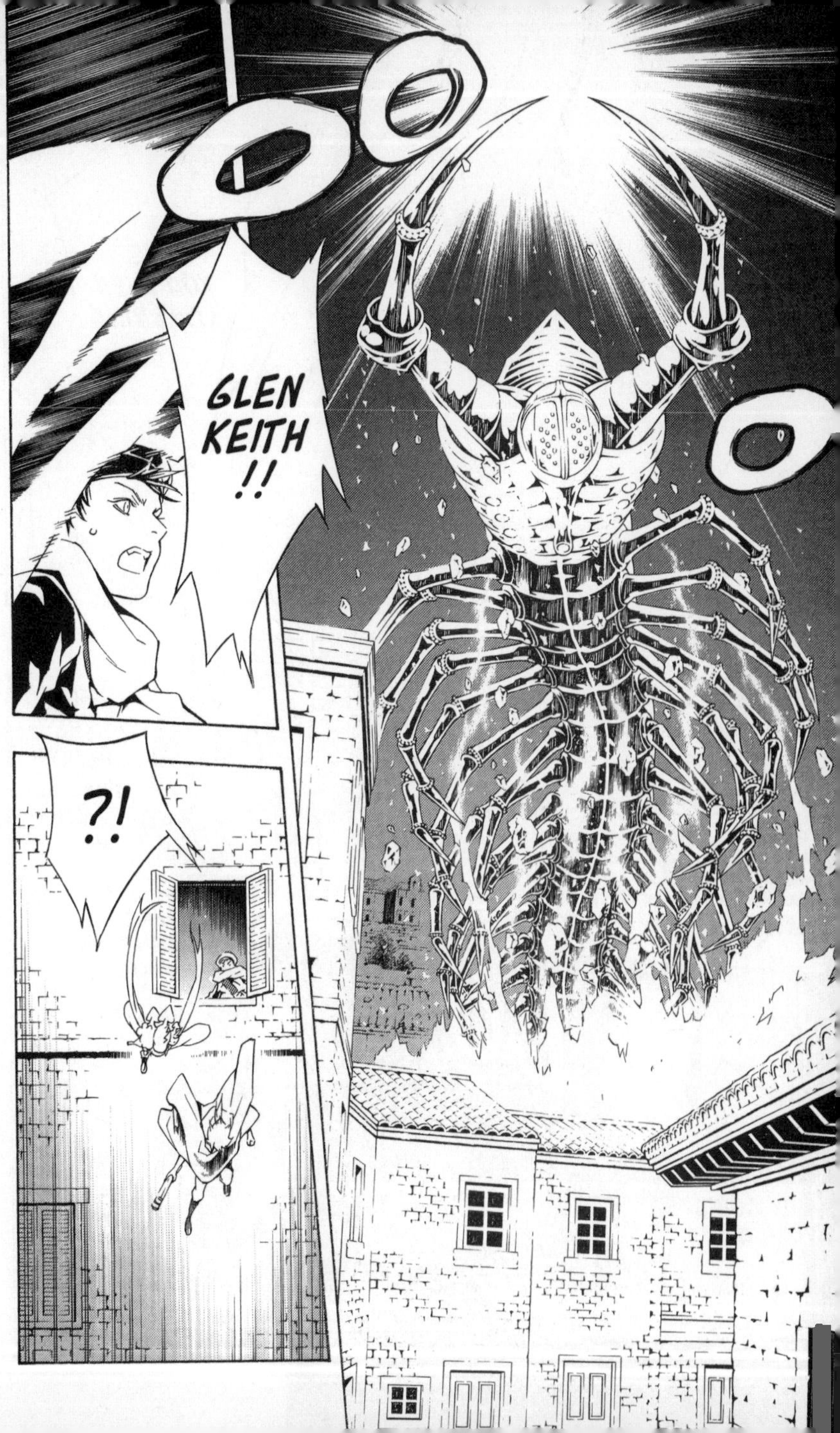
OOOO
GLEN KEITH !!
?!

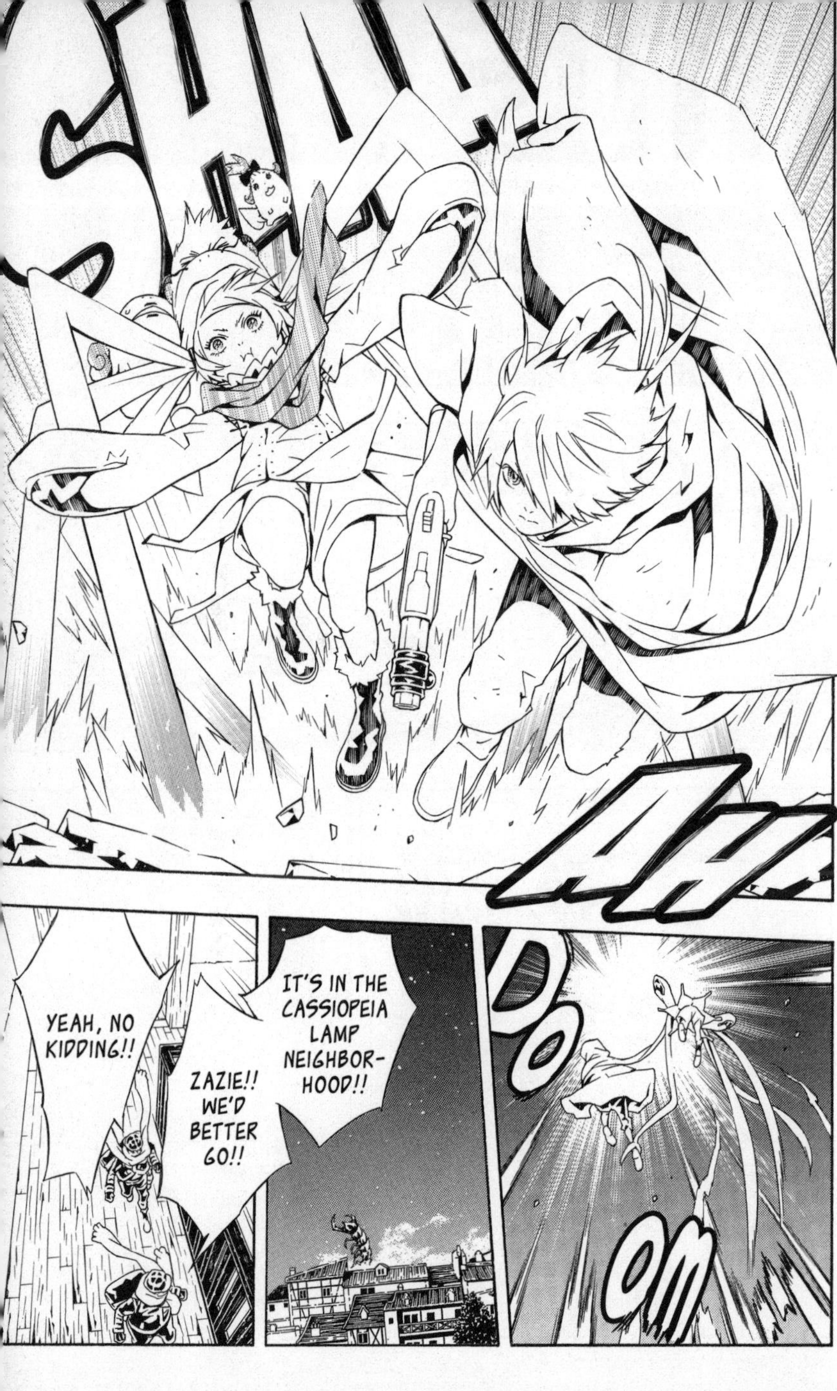
SHHA
AH
DOOOM
IT'S IN THE CASSIOPEIA LAMP NEIGHBOR-HOOD!!
ZAZIE!! WE'D BETTER GO!!
YEAH, NO KIDDING!!

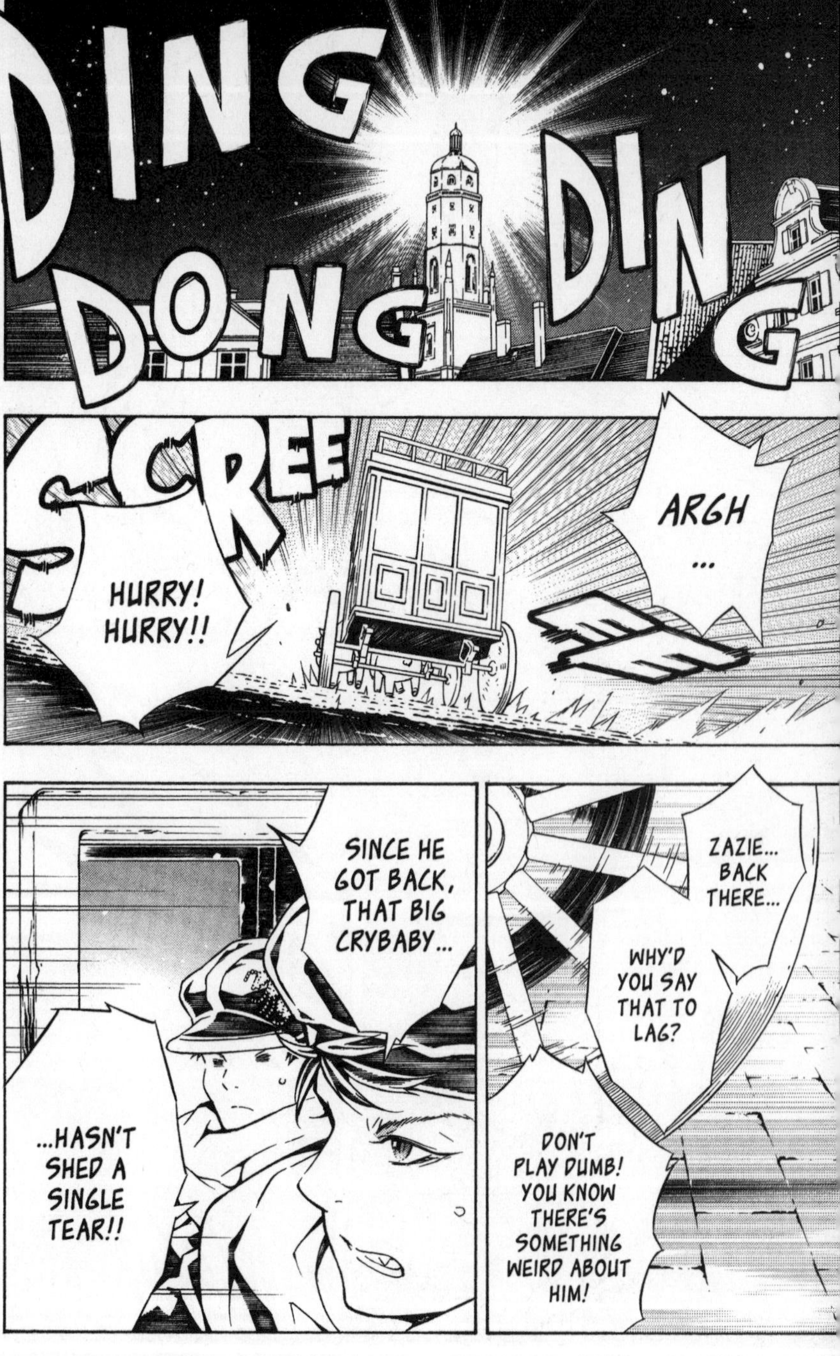
DING DONG DING
ARGH ...
CREE
HURRY! HURRY!!
ZAZIE... BACK THERE...
WHY'D YOU SAY THAT TO LAG?
DON'T PLAY DUMB! YOU KNOW THERE'S SOMETHING WEIRD ABOUT HIM!
SINCE HE GOT BACK, THAT BIG CRYBABY...
...HASN'T SHED A SINGLE TEAR!!

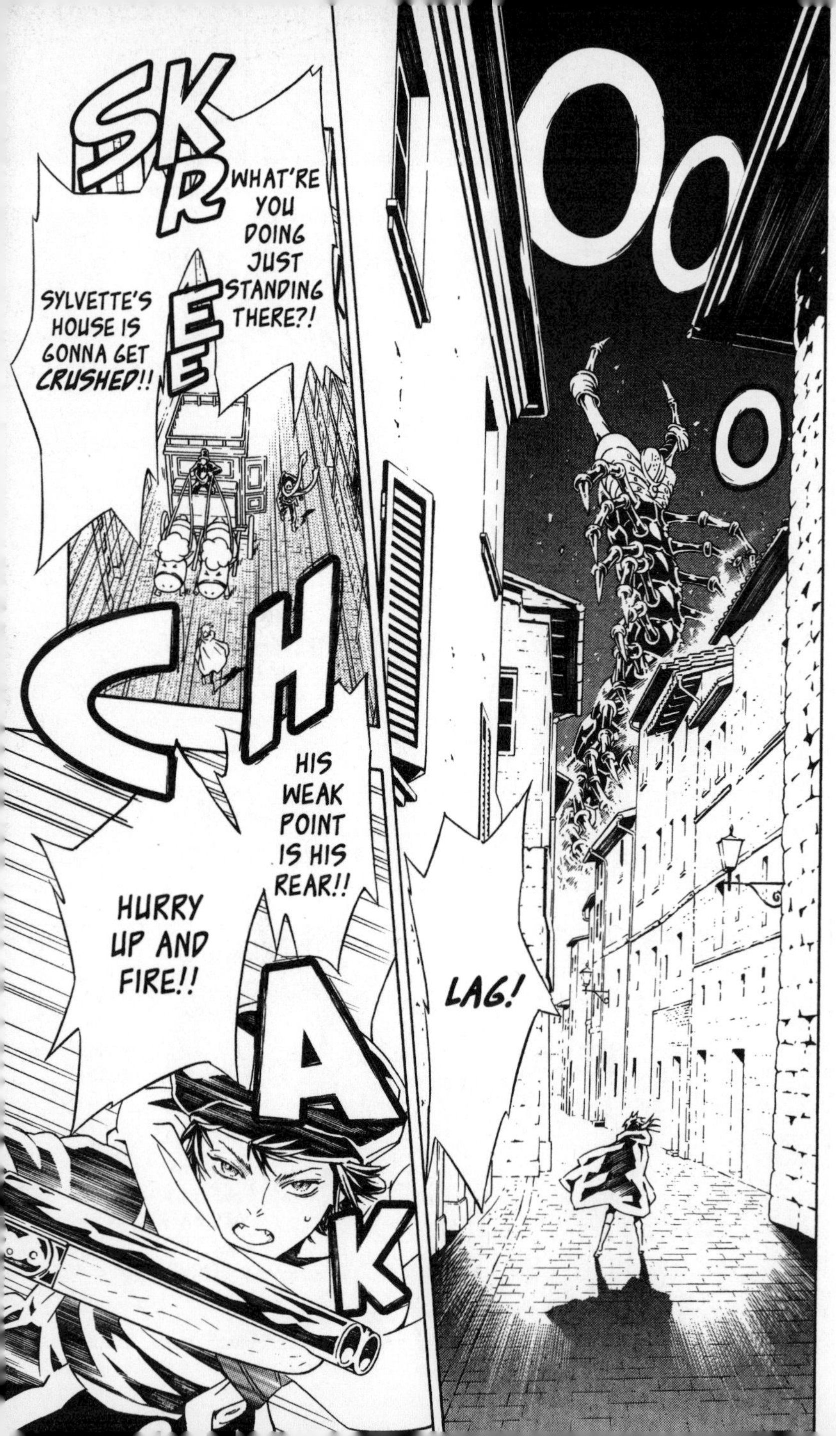
OOO
LAG!
SKREE
WHAT'RE YOU DOING JUST STANDING THERE?!
SYLVETTE'S HOUSE IS GONNA GET CRUSHED!!
CHAK
HIS WEAK POINT IS HIS REAR!!
HURRY UP AND FIRE!!

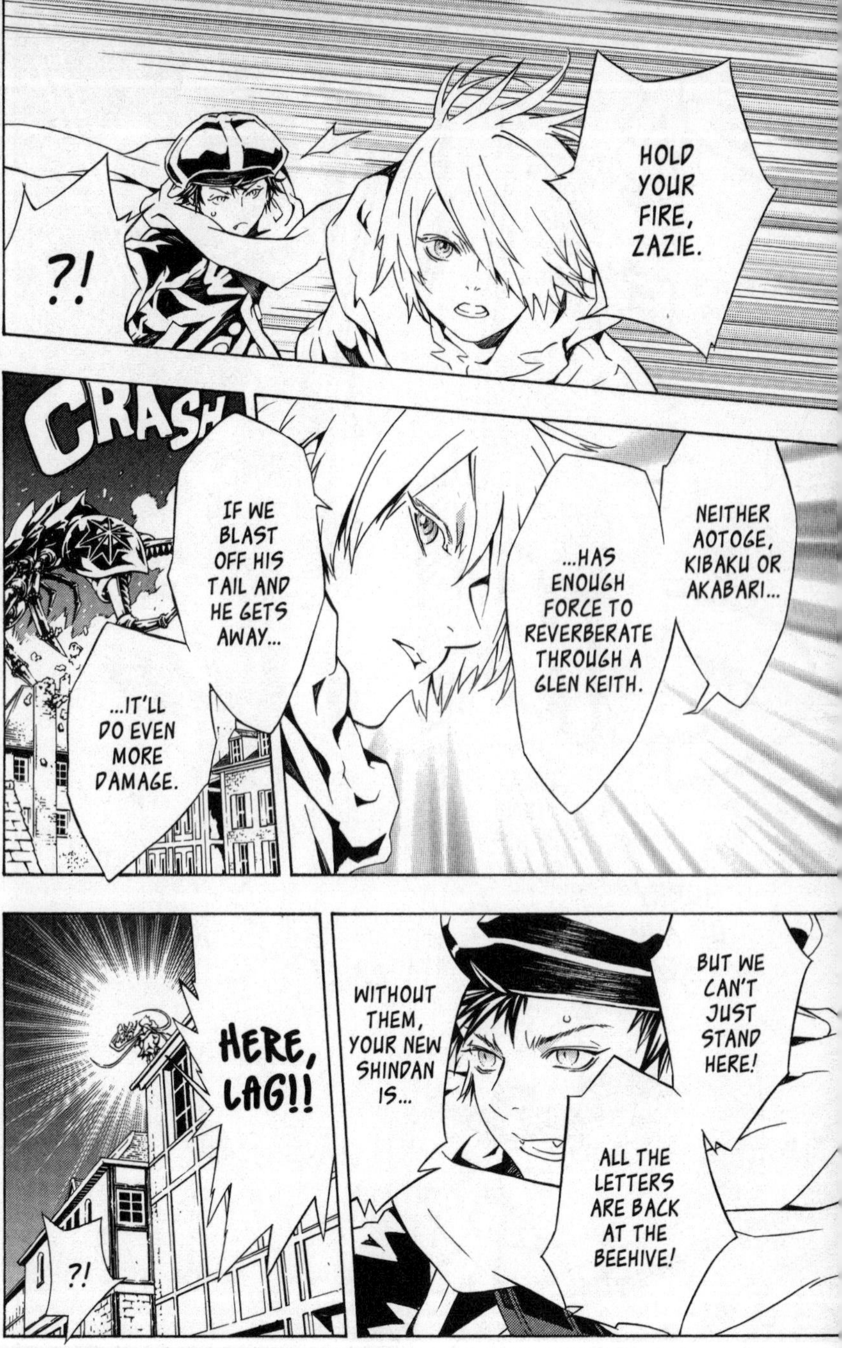
HOLD YOUR FIRE, ZAZIE.
?!
NEITHER AOTOGE, KIBAKU OR AKABARI...
...HAS ENOUGH FORCE TO REVERBERATE THROUGH A GLEN KEITH.
IF WE BLAST OFF HIS TAIL AND HE GETS AWAY...
...IT'LL DO EVEN MORE DAMAGE.
CRASH
BUT WE CAN'T JUST STAND HERE!
ALL THE LETTERS ARE BACK AT THE BEEHIVE!
WITHOUT THEM, YOUR NEW SHINDAN IS...
HERE, LAG!!
?!

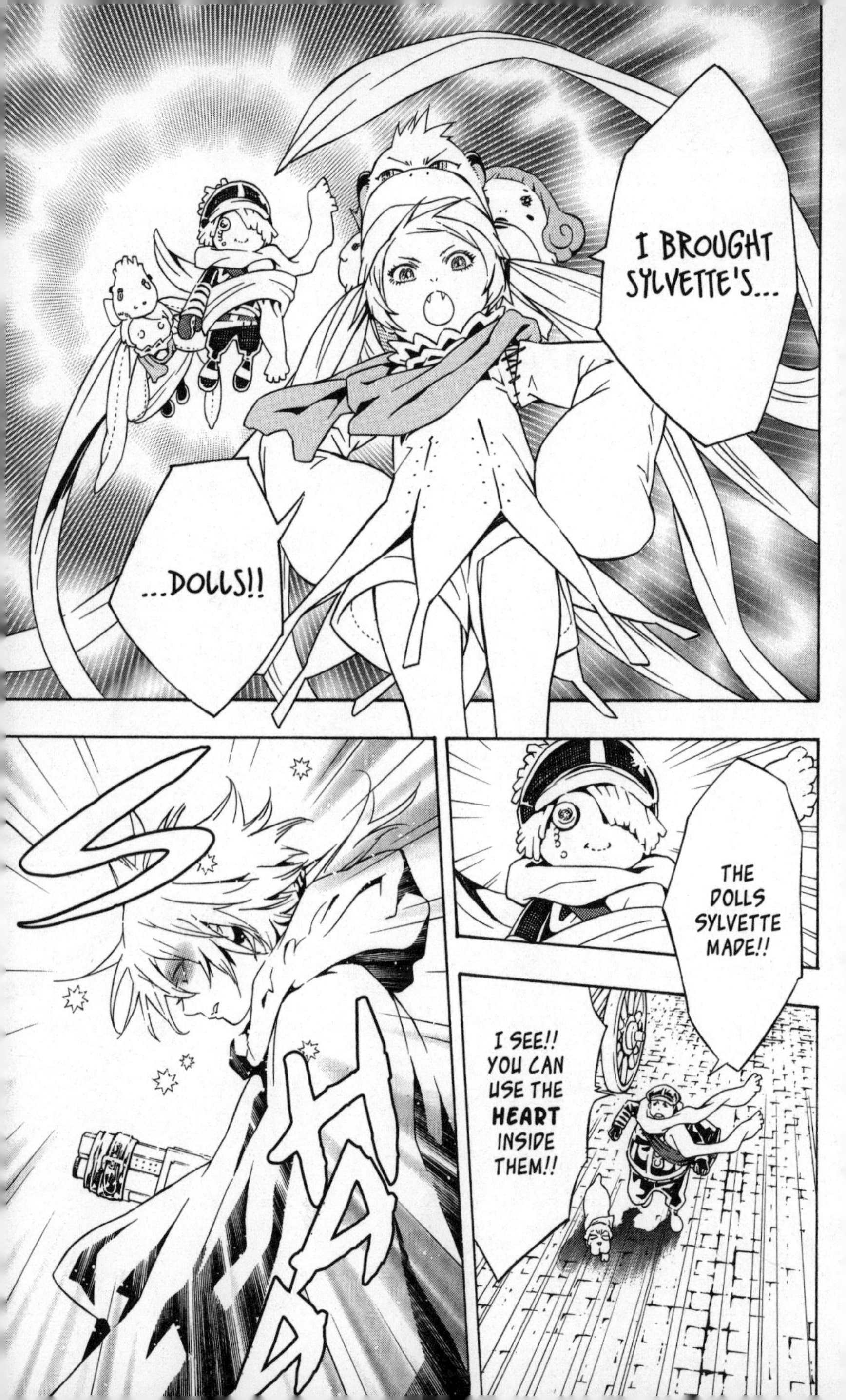
I BROUGHT SYLVETTE'S...
...DOLLS!!
THE DOLLS SYLVETTE MADE!!
I SEE!! YOU CAN USE THE **HEART** INSIDE THEM!!

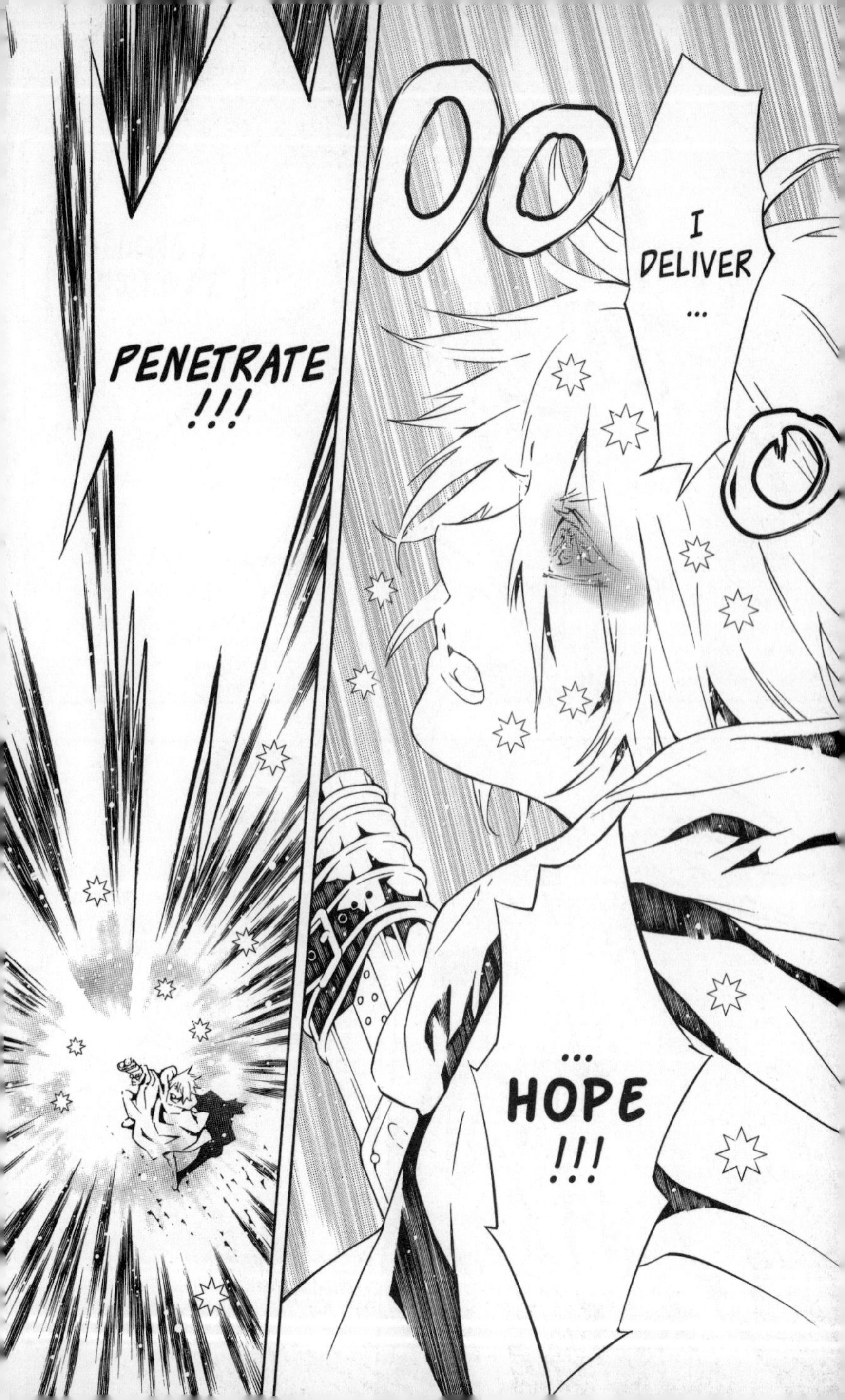
I DELIVER ...
... HOPE !!!
PENETRATE !!!

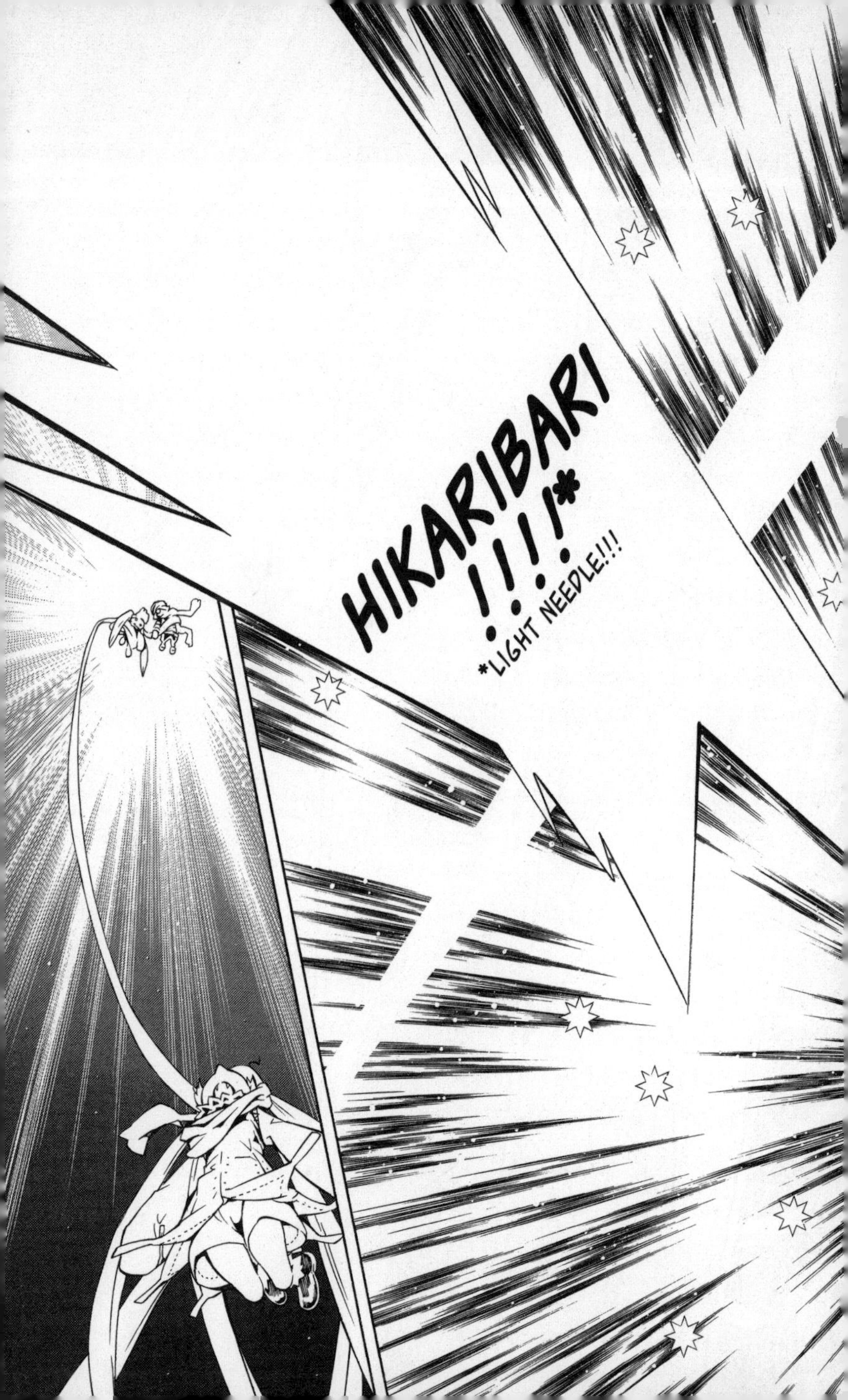
HIKARIBARI!!!!*
*LIGHT NEEDLE!!!

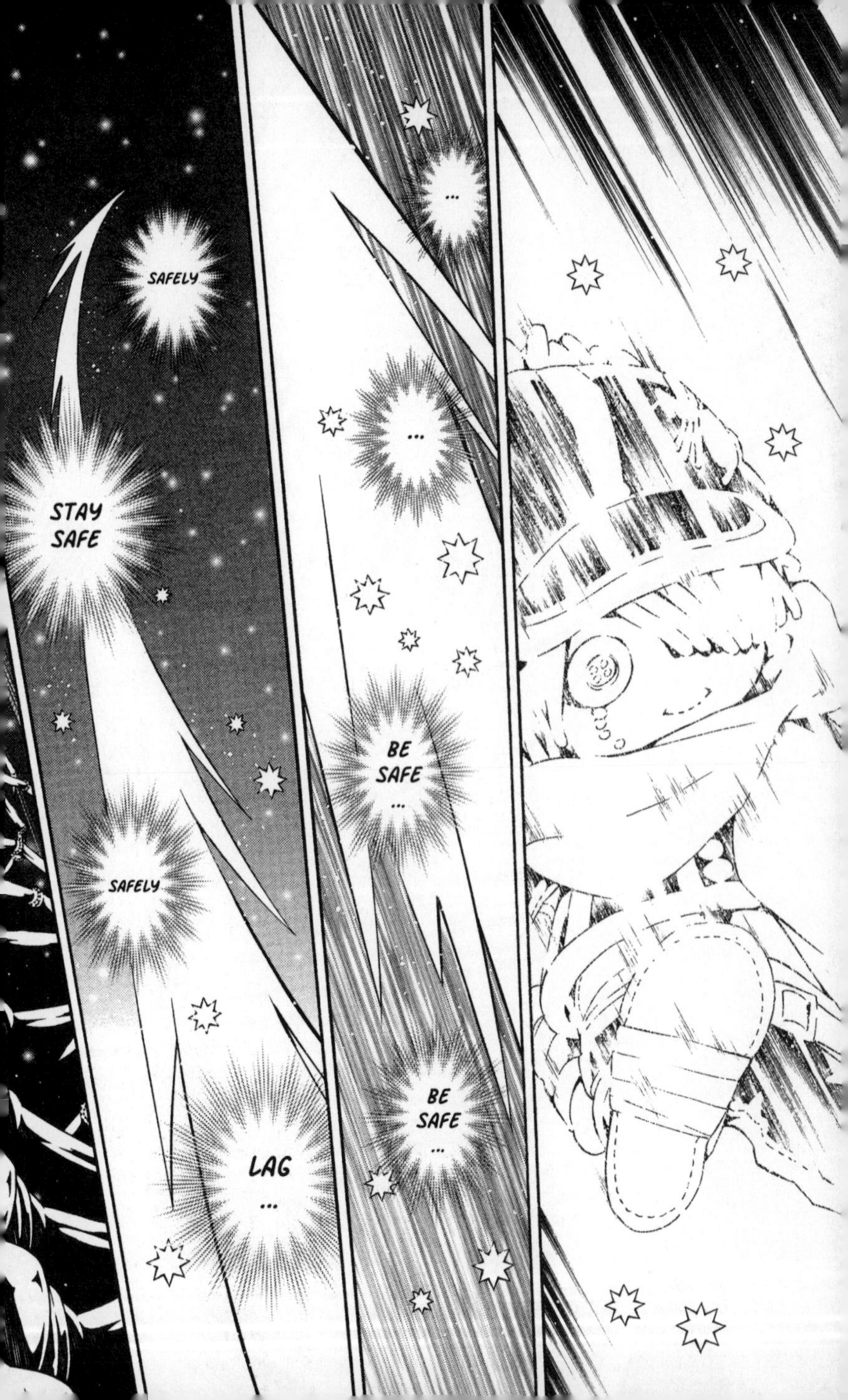
...
BE SAFE ...
...
BE SAFE ...
LAG ...
SAFELY
STAY SAFE
SAFELY

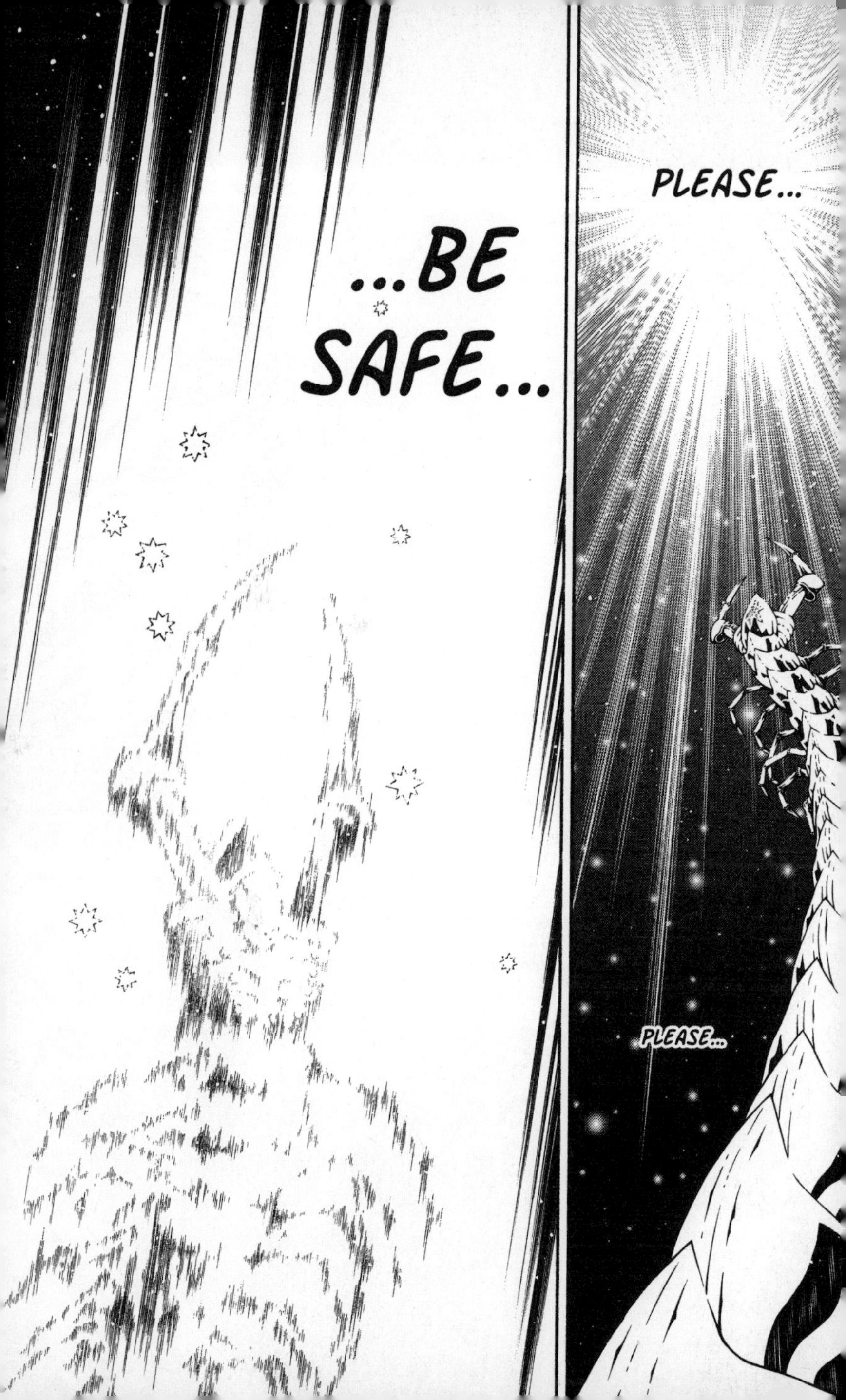
PLEASE...
PLEASE...
...BE SAFE...

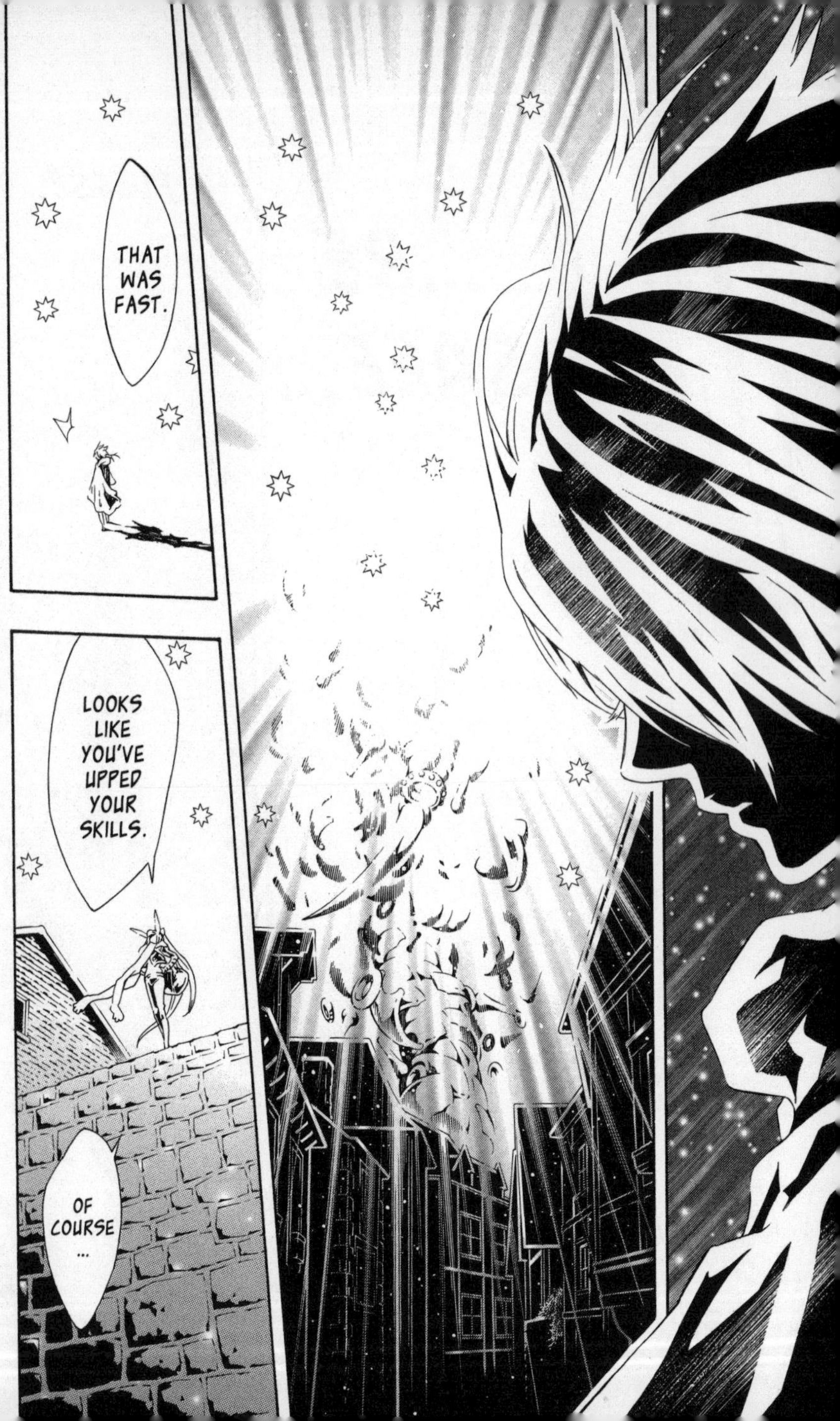
THAT WAS FAST.
LOOKS LIKE YOU'VE UPPED YOUR SKILLS.
OF COURSE ...

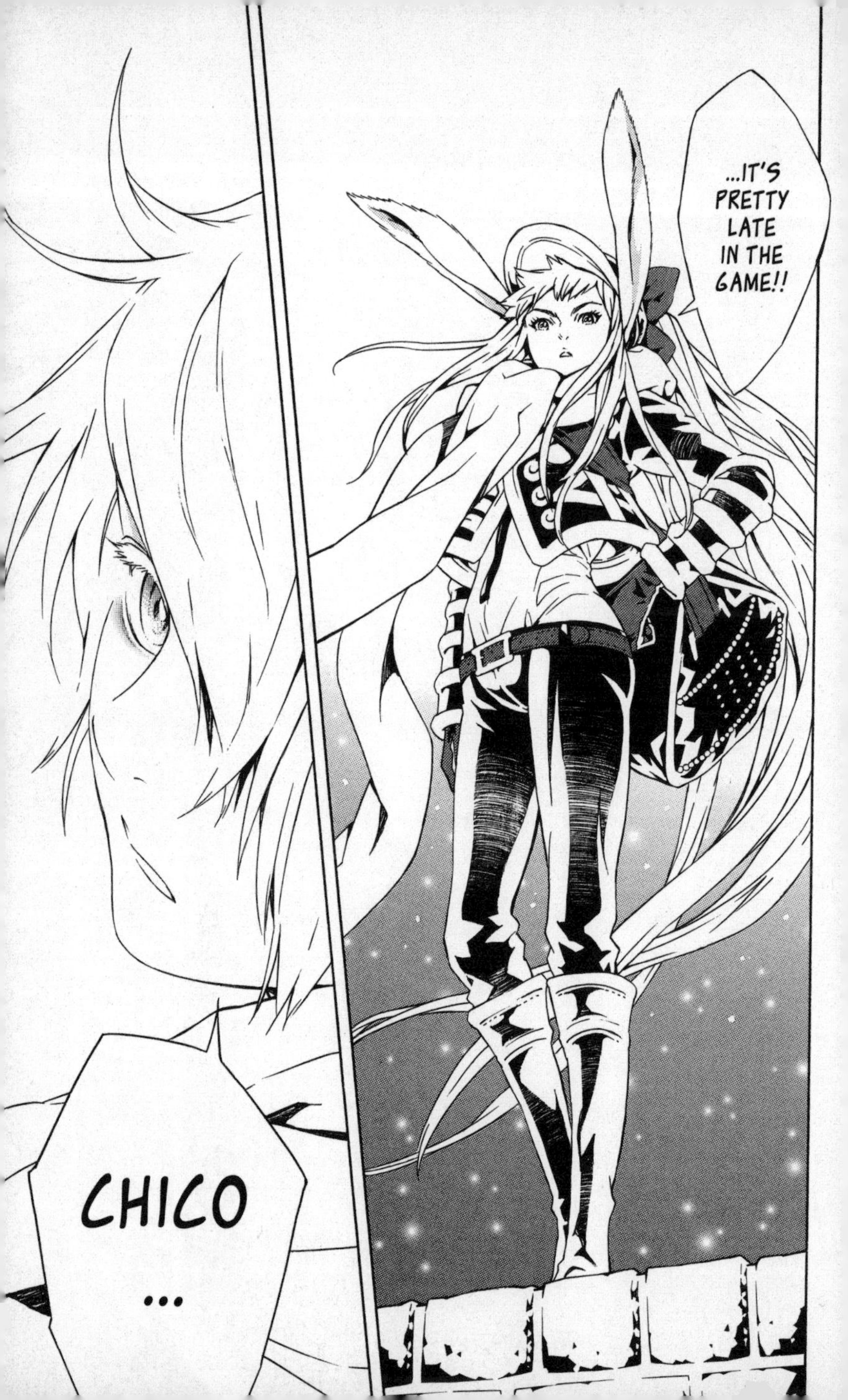
...IT'S PRETTY LATE IN THE GAME!!
CHICO
...

Dr. Thunderland's Reference Desk

Hey! What am I doing here? *Hmm…* Rumor has it there wasn't enough space for my section at the end of this volume. Honestly! How dare they treat me like this? It's an outrage!

But wait a minute. This may well be the chance I've been waiting for! If I jump to the page on the left, I'll finally be in the main story! This is so much better than being stuck at the end of the book!!

I work at the Yuusari Beehive, but I'm plotting to escape this barren page and break into the story. For the very first time, I can research developments in Amberground as they happen!

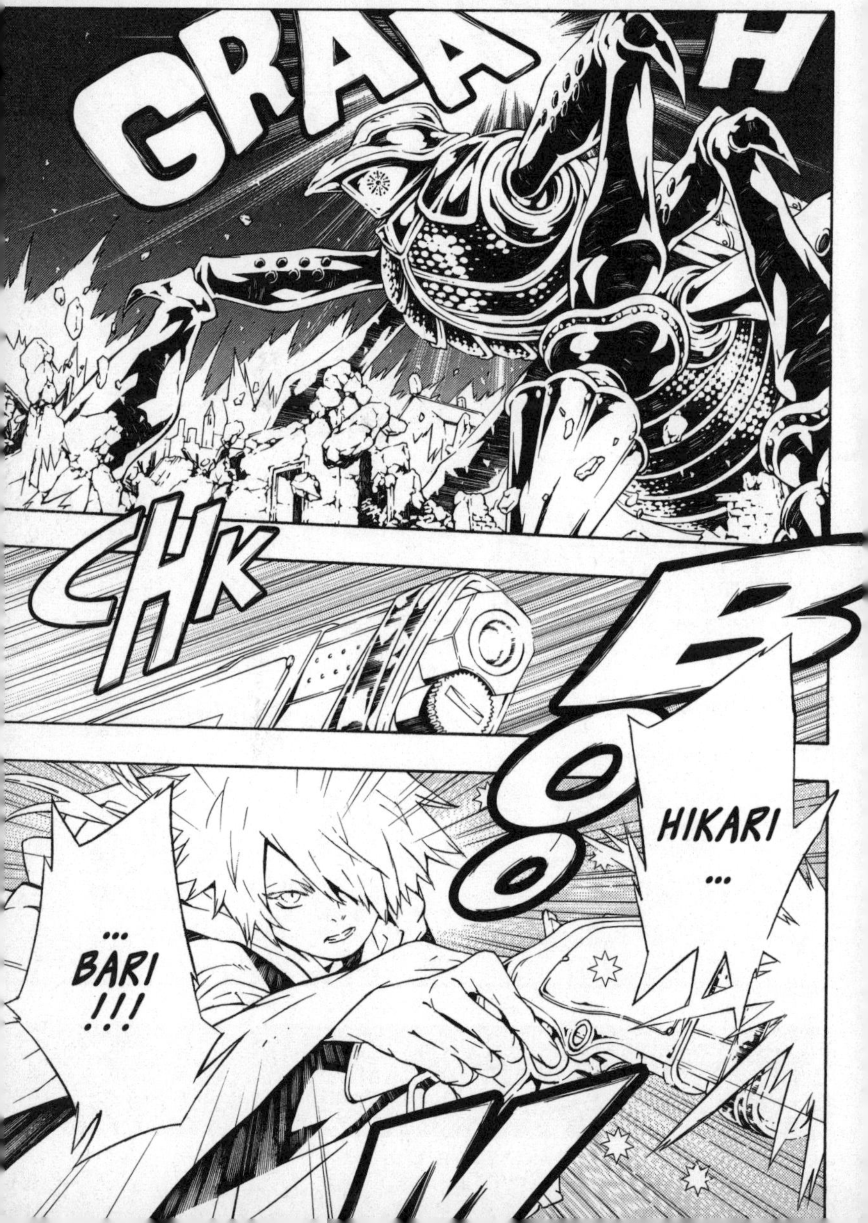
GRAAAH
CHK
HIKARI ...
... BARI !!!

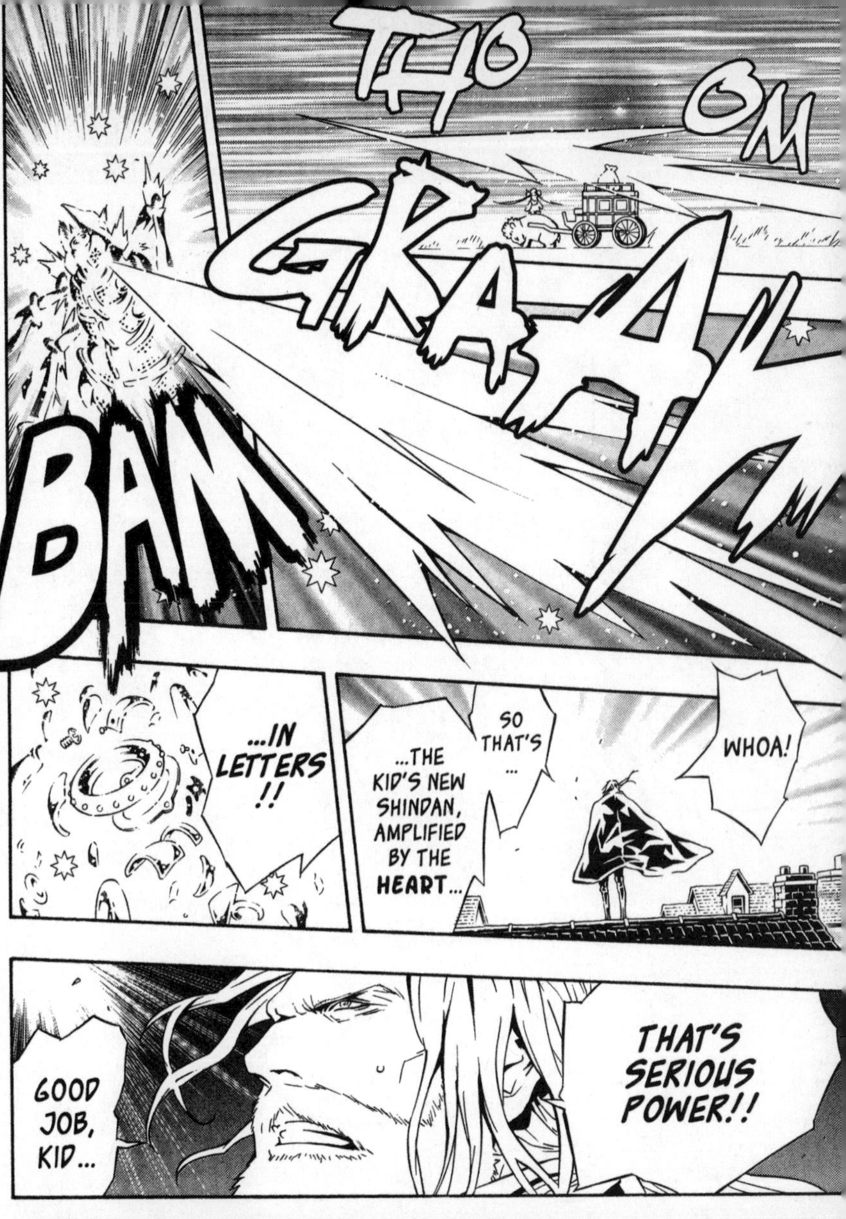
THOOM
GRAAA
BAM
WHOA!
SO THAT'S ...
...THE KID'S NEW SHINDAN, AMPLIFIED BY THE HEART...
...IN LETTERS!!
THAT'S SERIOUS POWER!!
GOOD JOB, KID...

third day

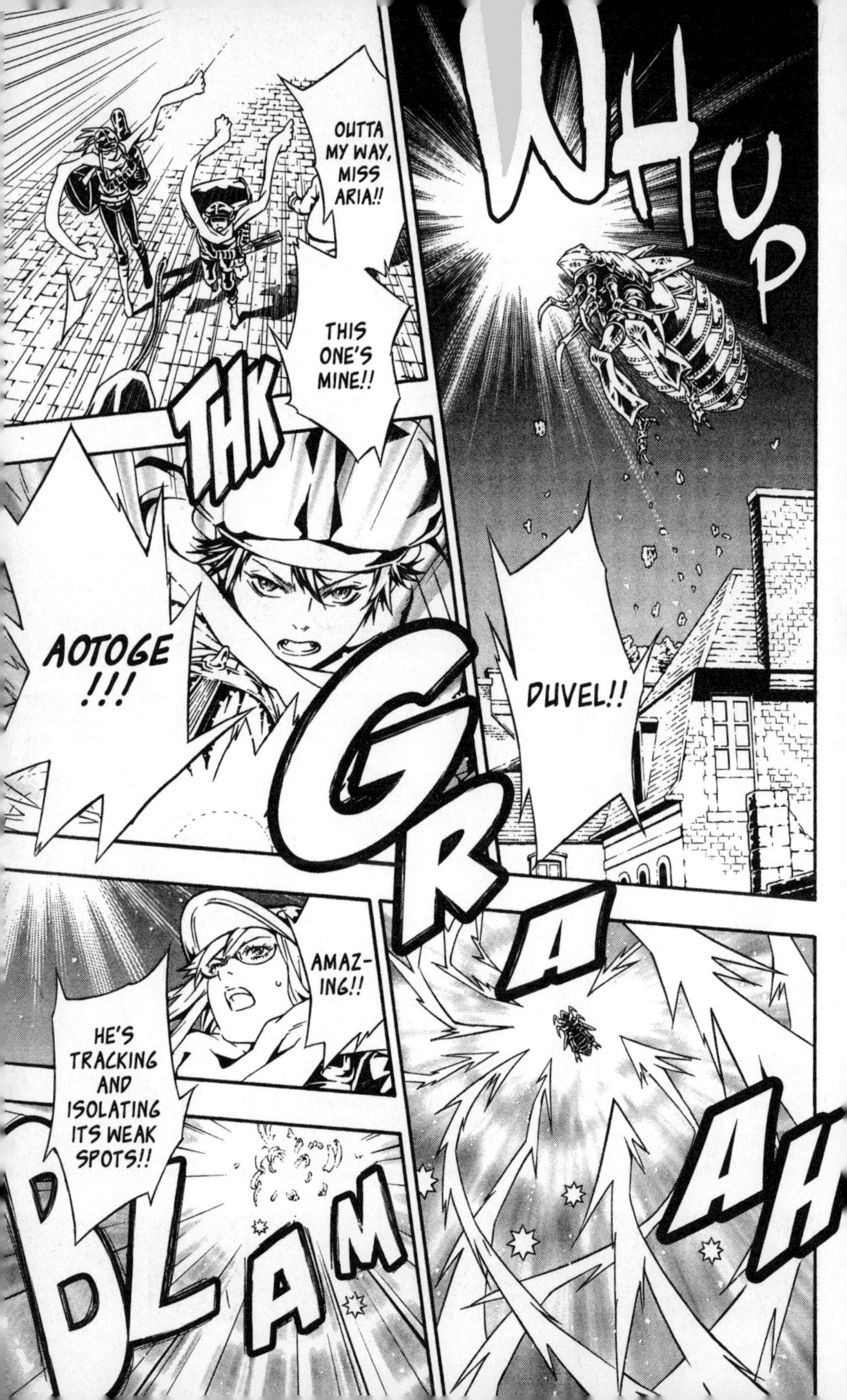
WHUP
DUVEL!!
OUTTA MY WAY, MISS ARIA!!
THIS ONE'S MINE!!
THK
AOTOGE!!!
GRA
AH
AMAZ-ING!!
HE'S TRACKING AND ISOLATING ITS WEAK SPOTS!!
BLAM

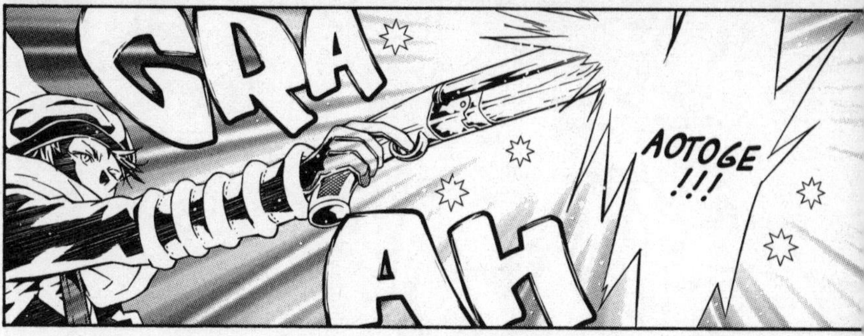
AOTOGE!!!
GRAAH

fifth day

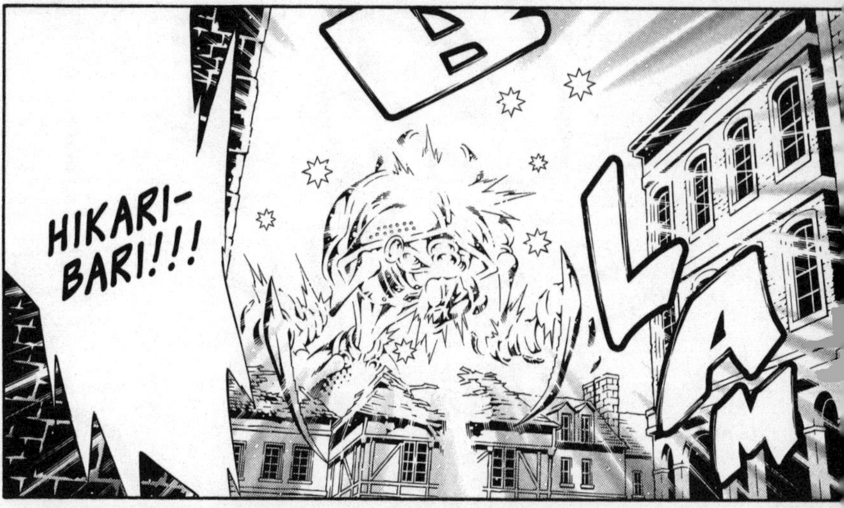
BLAM
HIKARI-BARI!!!

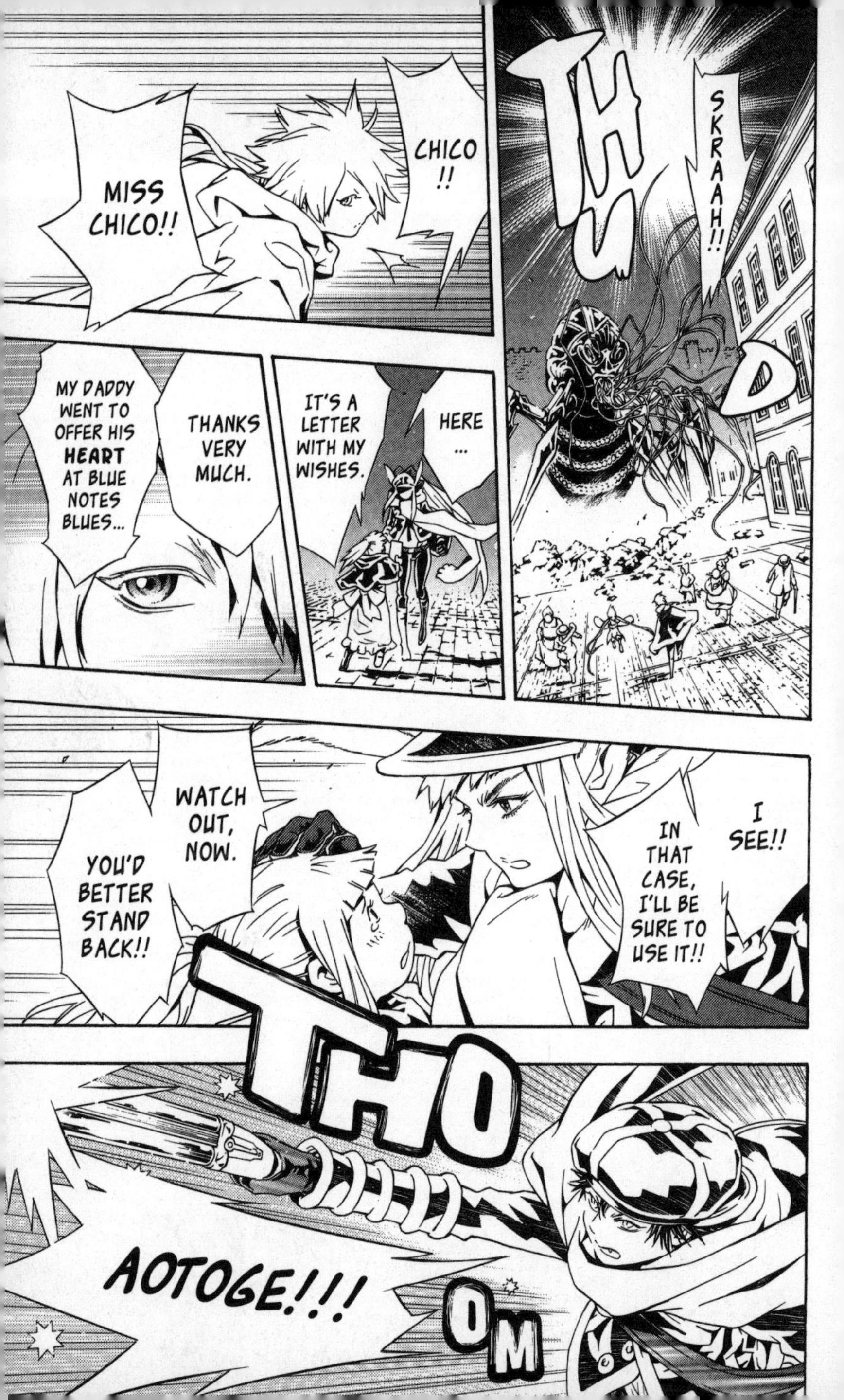
THUD
SKRAAAH!!
CHICO!!
MISS CHICO!!
HERE...
IT'S A LETTER WITH MY WISHES.
THANKS VERY MUCH.
MY DADDY WENT TO OFFER HIS **HEART** AT BLUE NOTES BLUES...
I SEE!!
IN THAT CASE, I'LL BE SURE TO USE IT!!
WATCH OUT, NOW.
YOU'D BETTER STAND BACK!!
THOOM
AOTOGE!!!

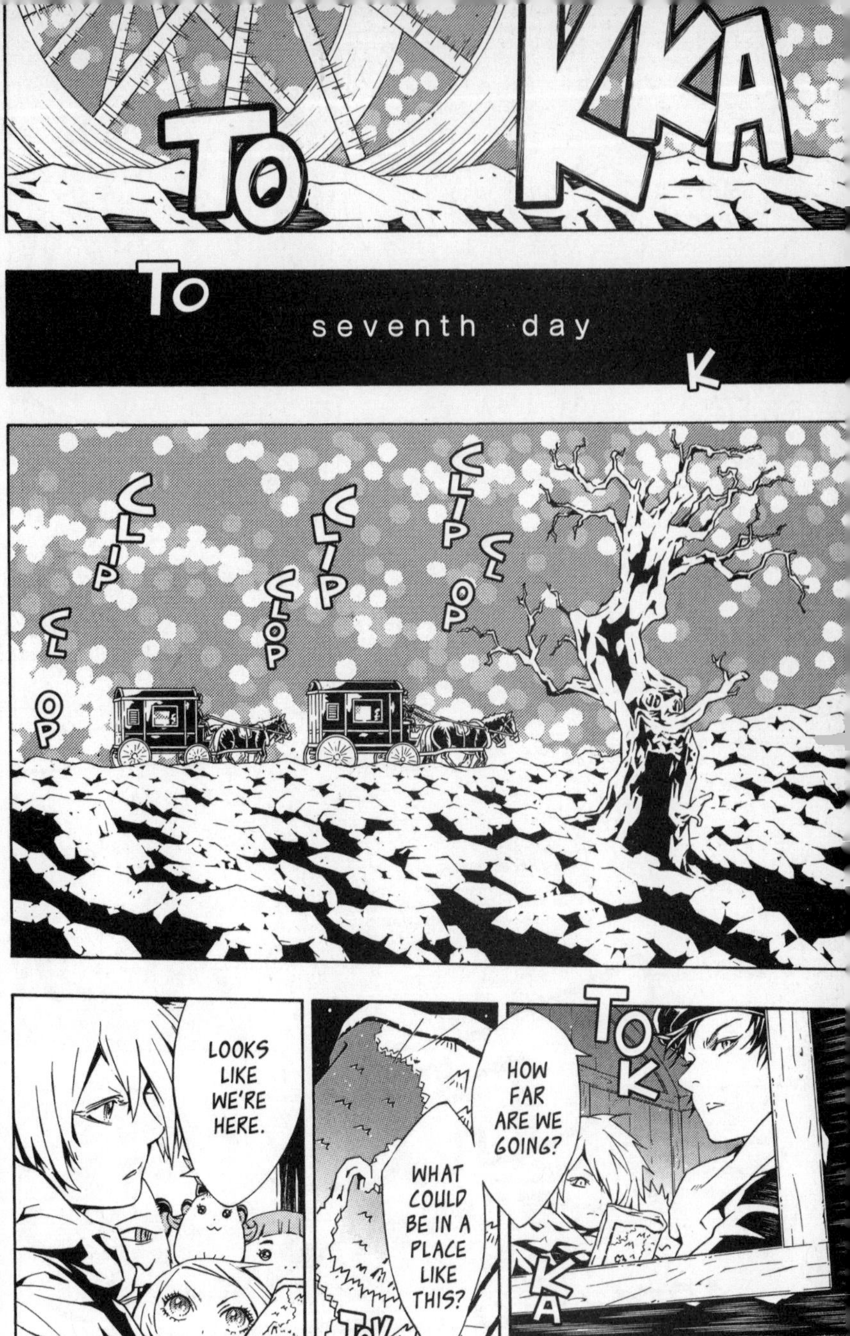
TO
KKA
TO
seventh day
K
CLIP
CLOP
CLIP
CLOP
CLIP
CLOP
HOW FAR ARE WE GOING?
TOK
KA
WHAT COULD BE IN A PLACE LIKE THIS?
TOK
LOOKS LIKE WE'RE HERE.

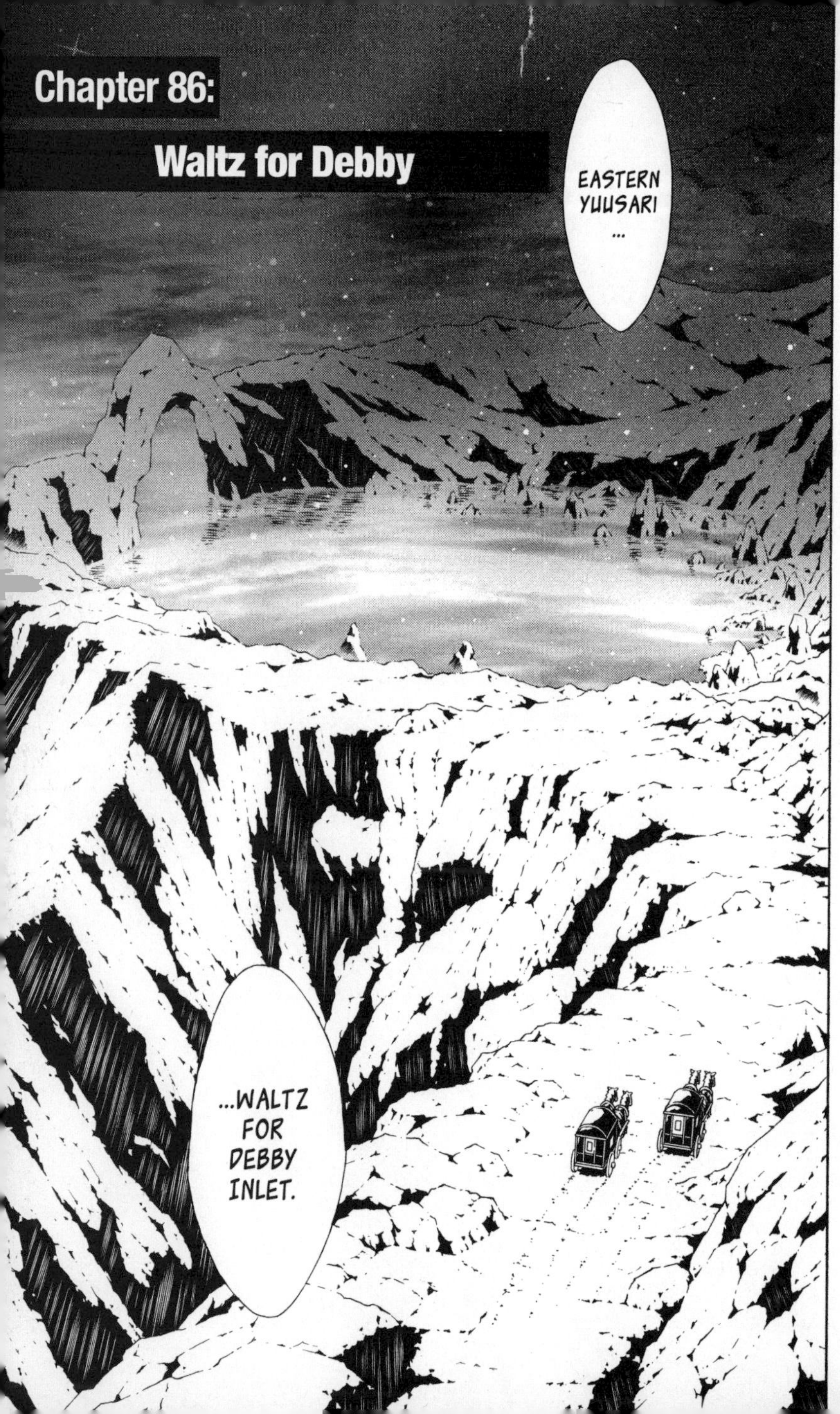
Chapter 86:
Waltz for Debby
EASTERN YUUSARI ...
...WALTZ FOR DEBBY INLET.

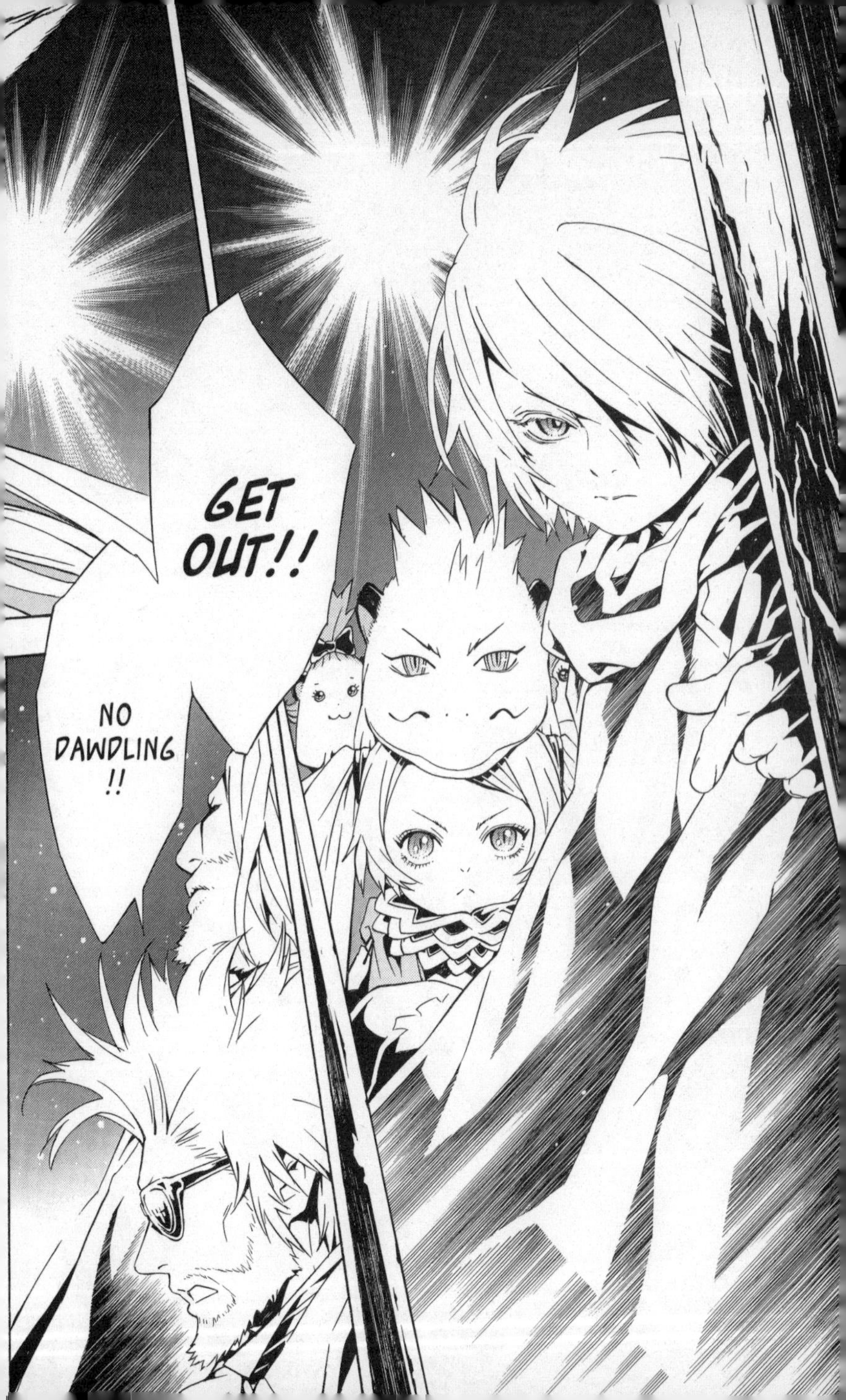
GET OUT!!
NO DAWDLING !!

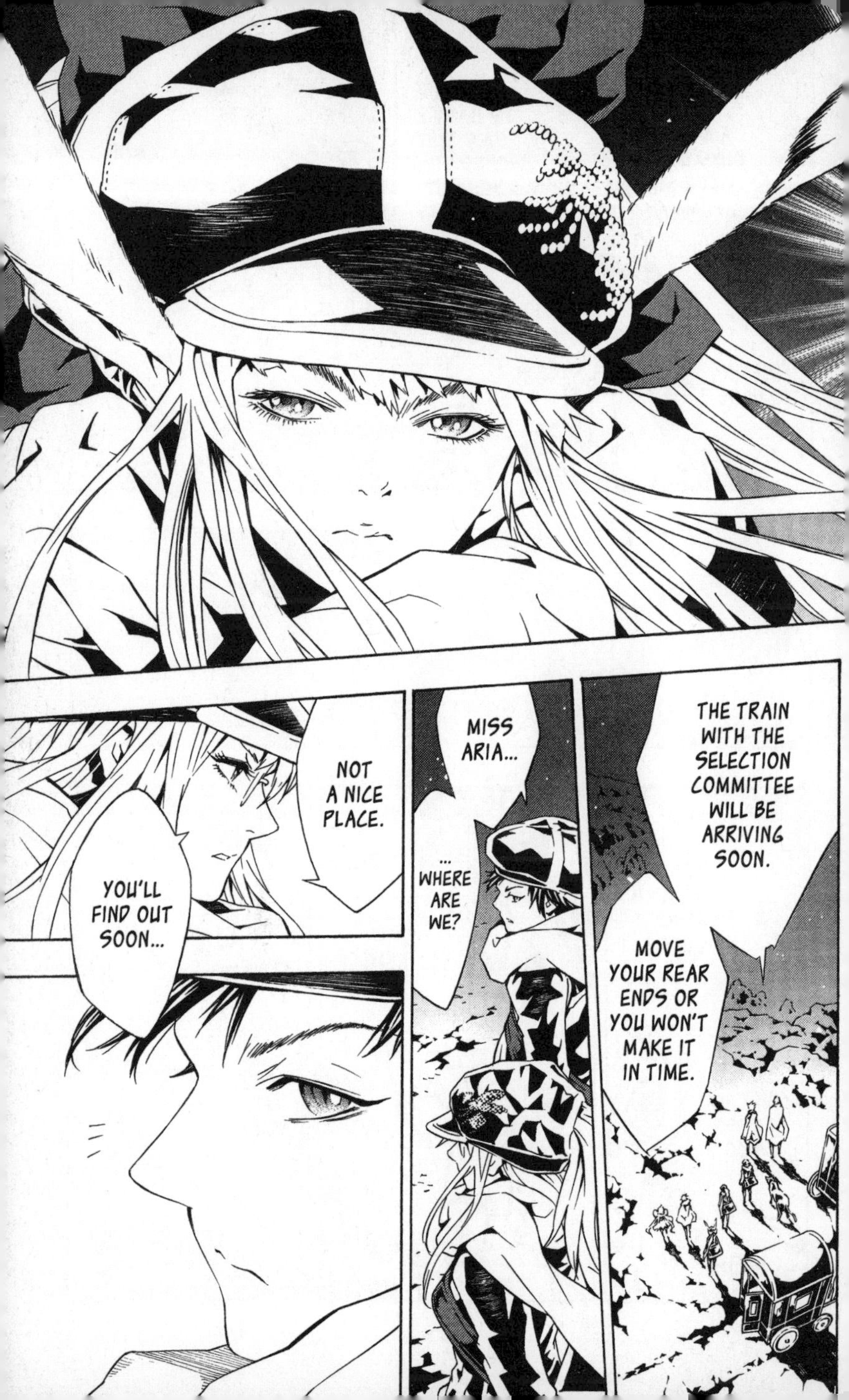
THE TRAIN WITH THE SELECTION COMMITTEE WILL BE ARRIVING SOON.
MOVE YOUR REAR ENDS OR YOU WON'T MAKE IT IN TIME.
MISS ARIA...
...WHERE ARE WE?
NOT A NICE PLACE.
YOU'LL FIND OUT SOON...

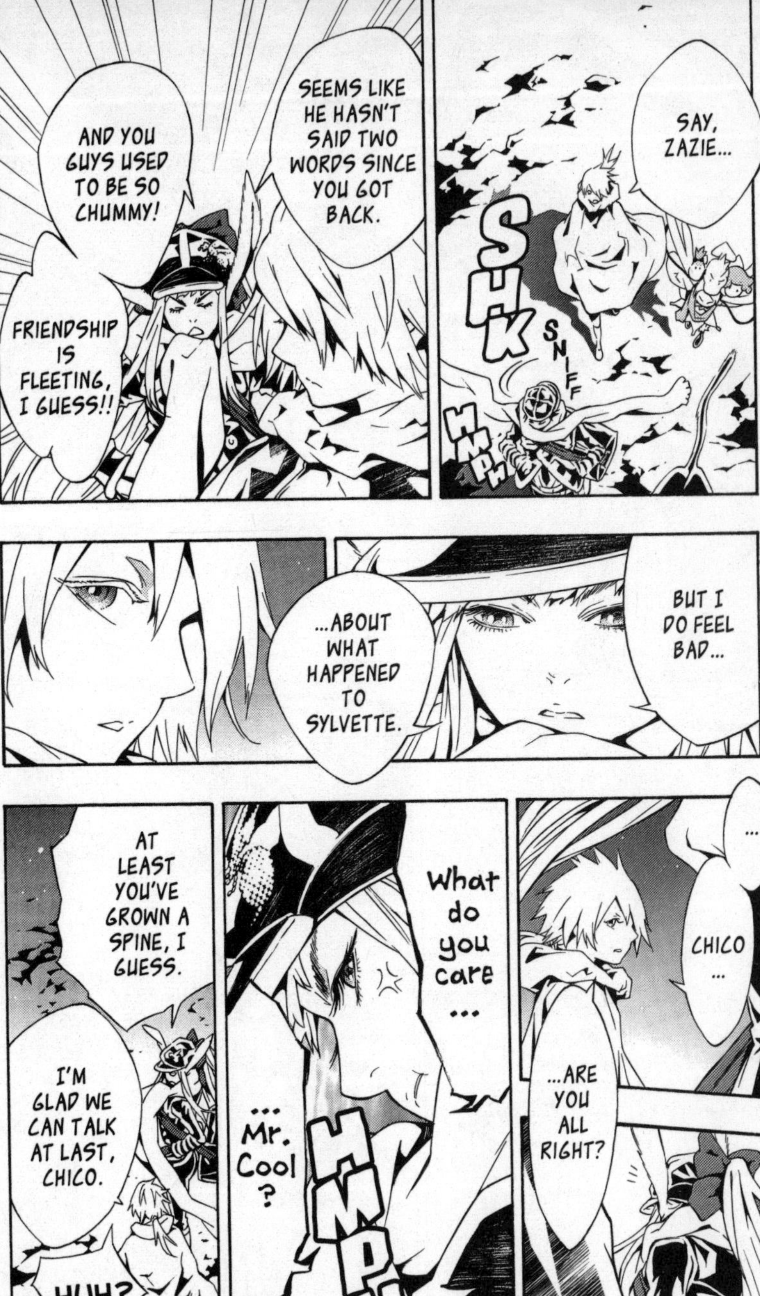
SAY, ZAZIE...
SHUK
SNIFF
HMPH
SEEMS LIKE HE HASN'T SAID TWO WORDS SINCE YOU GOT BACK.
AND YOU GUYS USED TO BE SO CHUMMY!
FRIENDSHIP IS FLEETING, I GUESS!!
BUT I DO FEEL BAD...
...ABOUT WHAT HAPPENED TO SYLVETTE.
...
CHICO ...
...ARE YOU ALL RIGHT?
What do you care ...
... Mr. Cool ?
HMPH
AT LEAST YOU'VE GROWN A SPINE, I GUESS.
I'M GLAD WE CAN TALK AT LAST, CHICO.
HUH?

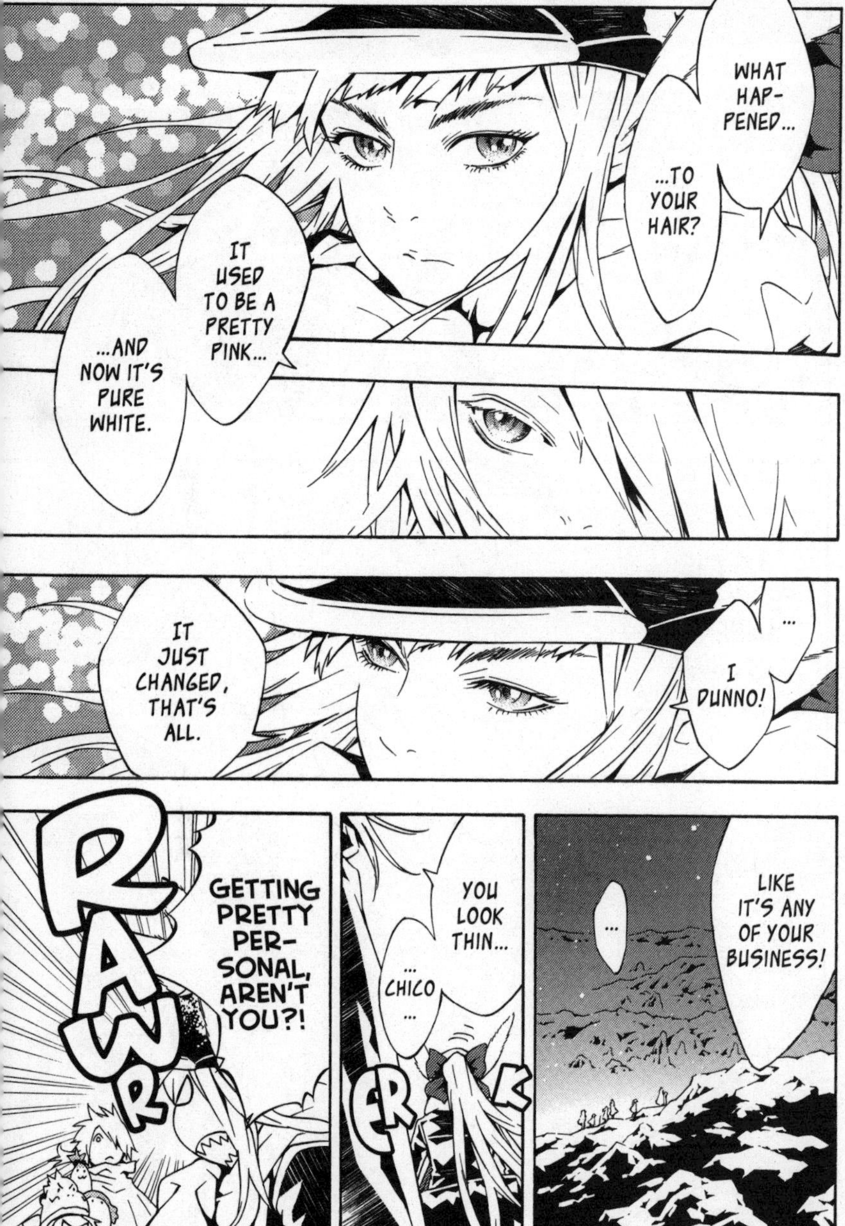
WHAT HAP-PENED...
...TO YOUR HAIR?
IT USED TO BE A PRETTY PINK...
...AND NOW IT'S PURE WHITE.
...
I DUNNO!
IT JUST CHANGED, THAT'S ALL.
LIKE IT'S ANY OF YOUR BUSINESS!
...
YOU LOOK THIN...
...CHICO...
GETTING PRETTY PER-SONAL, AREN'T YOU?!
RAWR

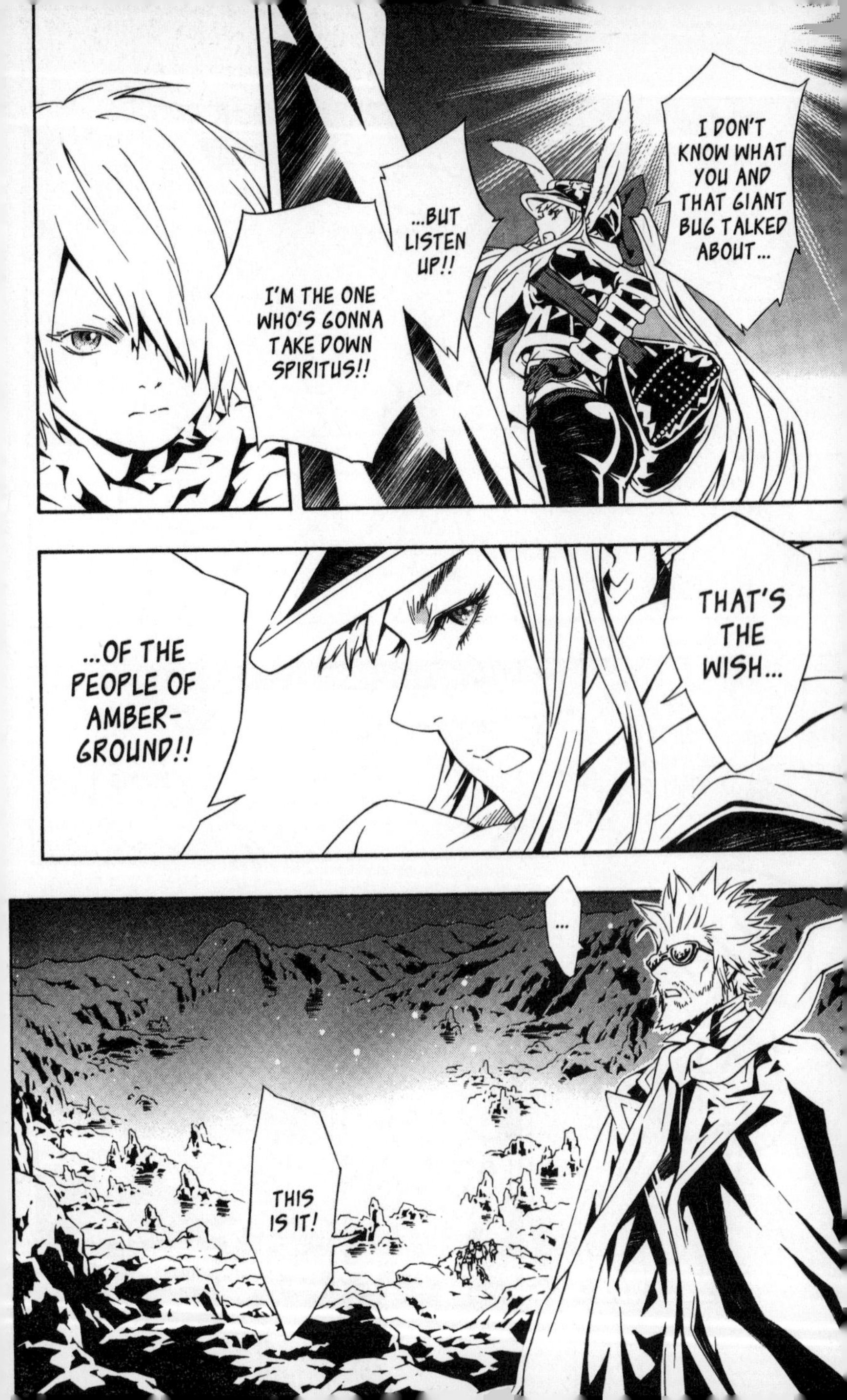
I DON'T KNOW WHAT YOU AND THAT GIANT BUG TALKED ABOUT...
...BUT LISTEN UP!!
I'M THE ONE WHO'S GONNA TAKE DOWN SPIRITUS!!
THAT'S THE WISH...
...OF THE PEOPLE OF AMBER-GROUND!!
...
THIS IS IT!

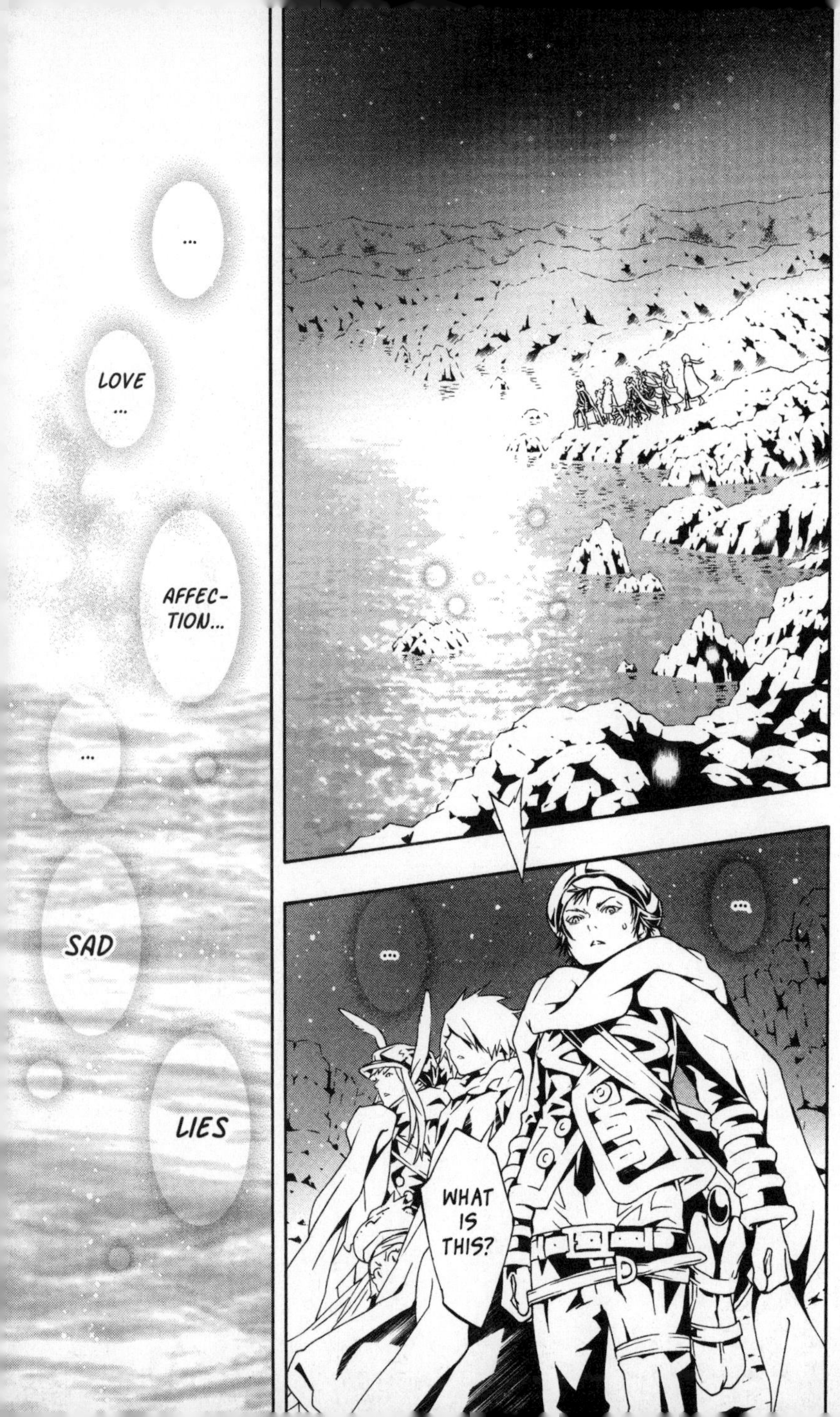
...
...
WHAT IS THIS?
...
LOVE ...
AFFEC-TION...
...
SAD
LIES

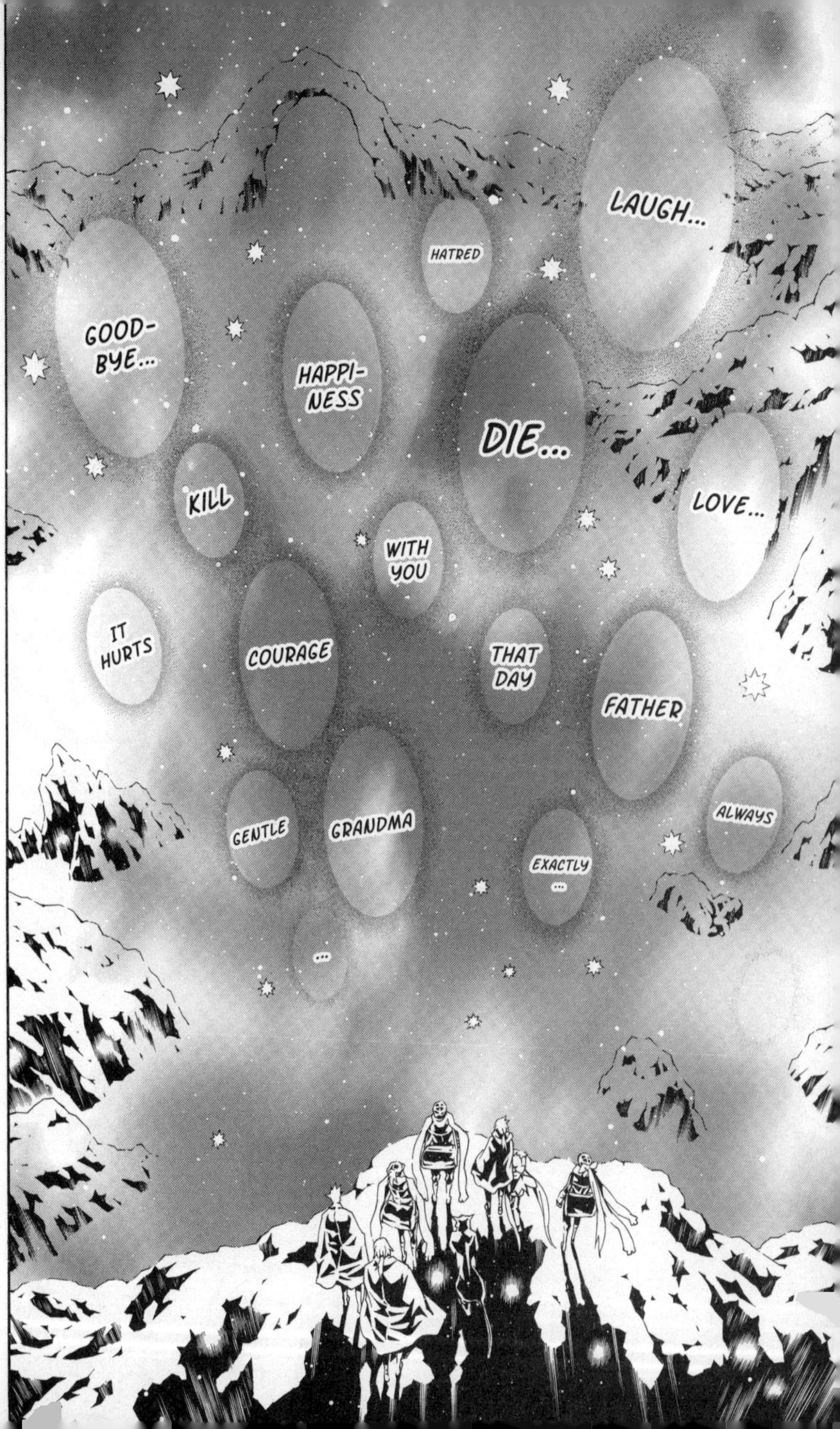
LAUGH...
HATRED
GOOD-BYE...
HAPPI-NESS
DIE...
LOVE...
KILL
WITH YOU
IT HURTS
COURAGE
THAT DAY
FATHER
ALWAYS
GRANDMA
GENTLE
EXACTLY...
...

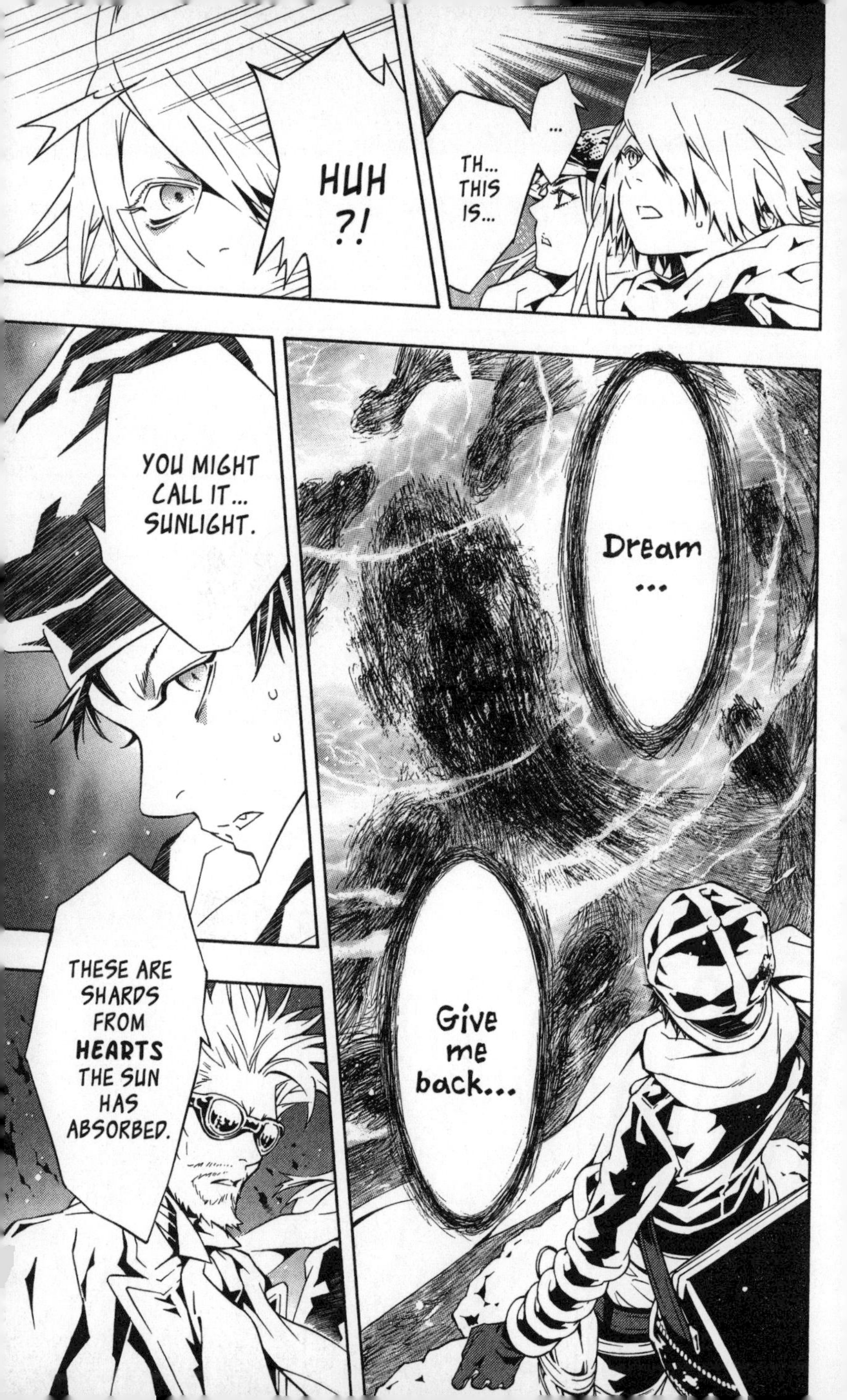
...
TH... THIS IS...
HUH ?!
Dream ...
Give me back...
YOU MIGHT CALL IT... SUNLIGHT.
THESE ARE SHARDS FROM **HEARTS** THE SUN HAS ABSORBED.

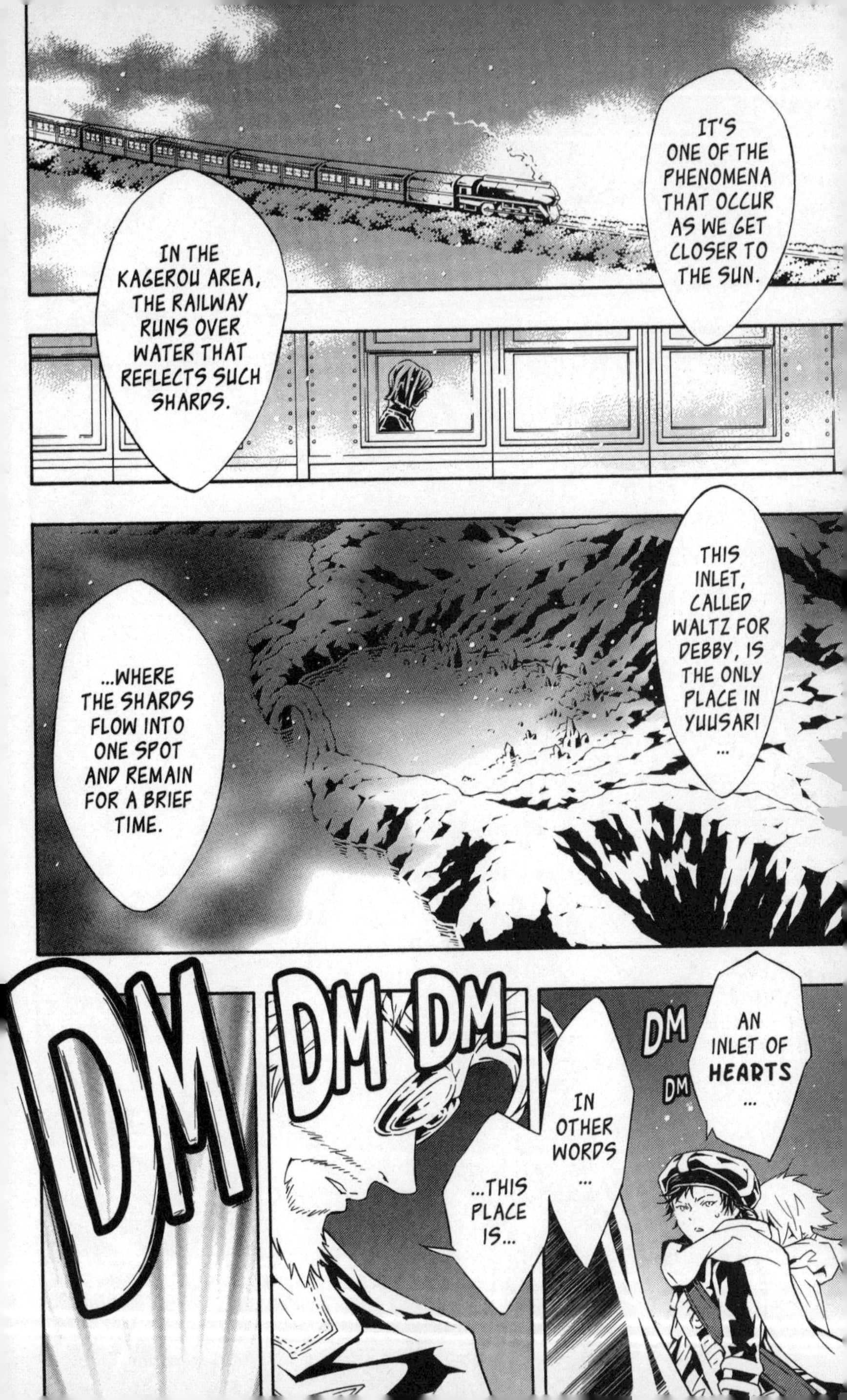
IT'S ONE OF THE PHENOMENA THAT OCCUR AS WE GET CLOSER TO THE SUN.
IN THE KAGEROU AREA, THE RAILWAY RUNS OVER WATER THAT REFLECTS SUCH SHARDS.
THIS INLET, CALLED WALTZ FOR DEBBY, IS THE ONLY PLACE IN YUUSARI ...
...WHERE THE SHARDS FLOW INTO ONE SPOT AND REMAIN FOR A BRIEF TIME.
AN INLET OF HEARTS ...
DM
DM
IN OTHER WORDS ...
...THIS PLACE IS...
DM DM
DM

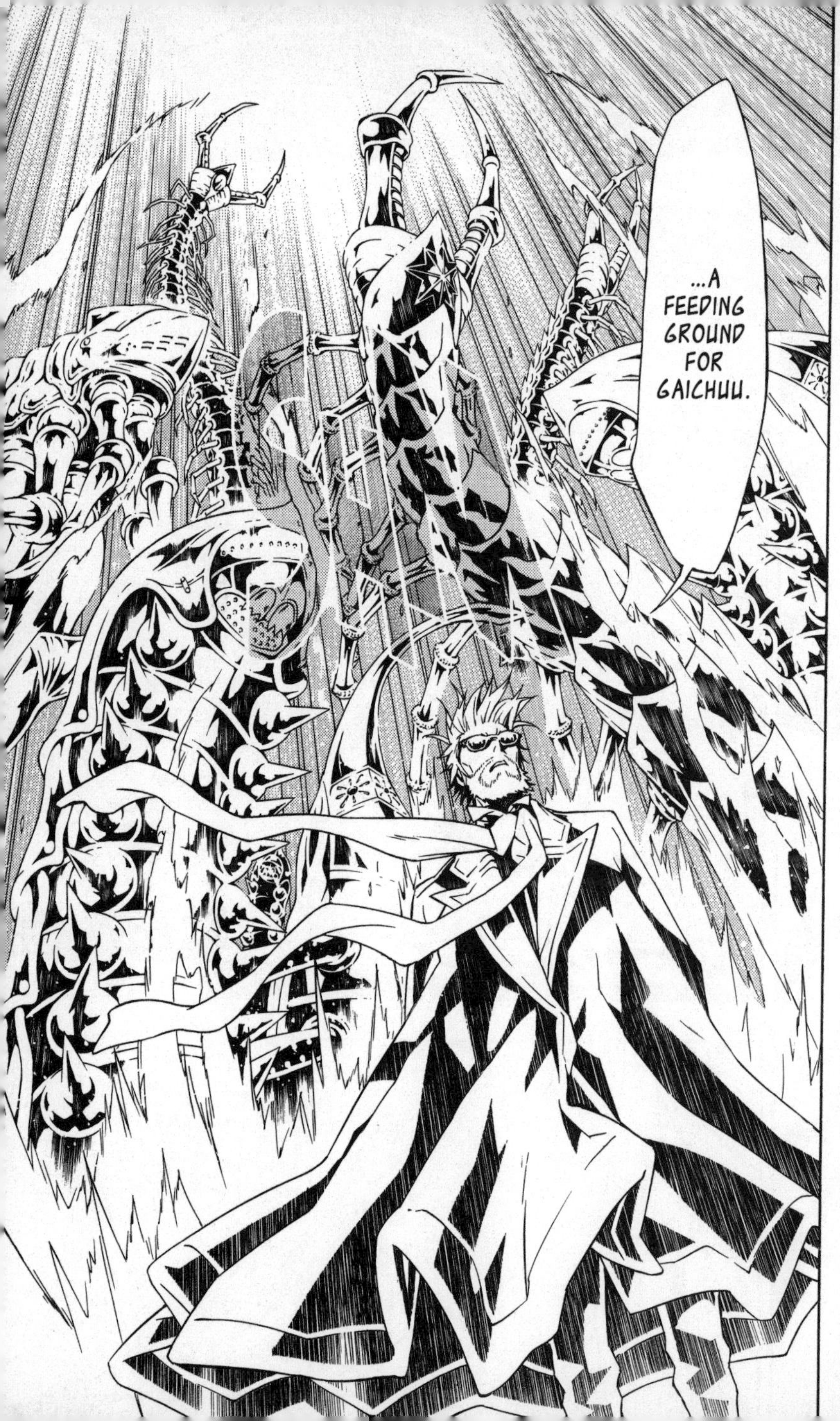
...A FEEDING GROUND FOR GAICHUU.

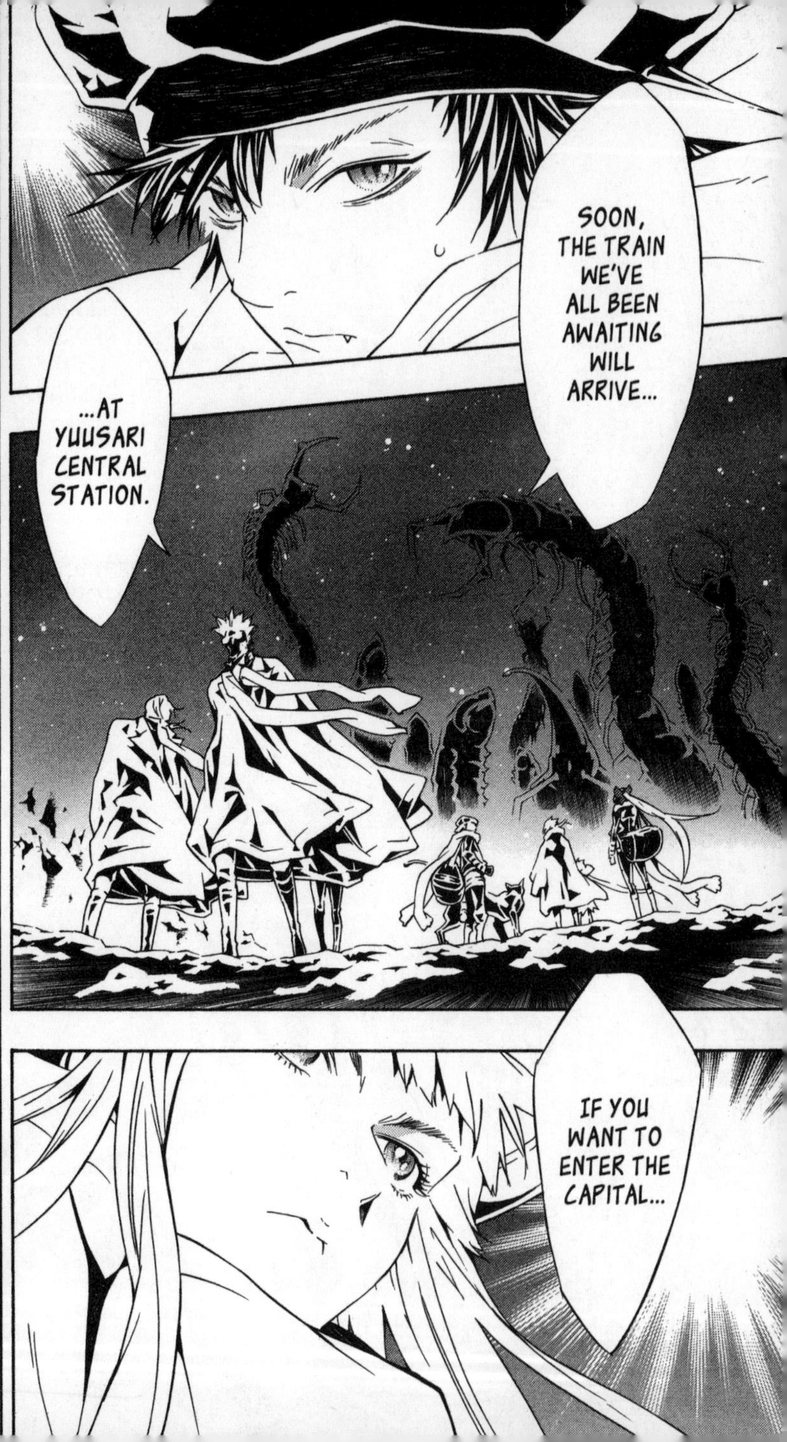
SOON, THE TRAIN WE'VE ALL BEEN AWAITING WILL ARRIVE...
...AT YUUSARI CENTRAL STATION.
IF YOU WANT TO ENTER THE CAPITAL...

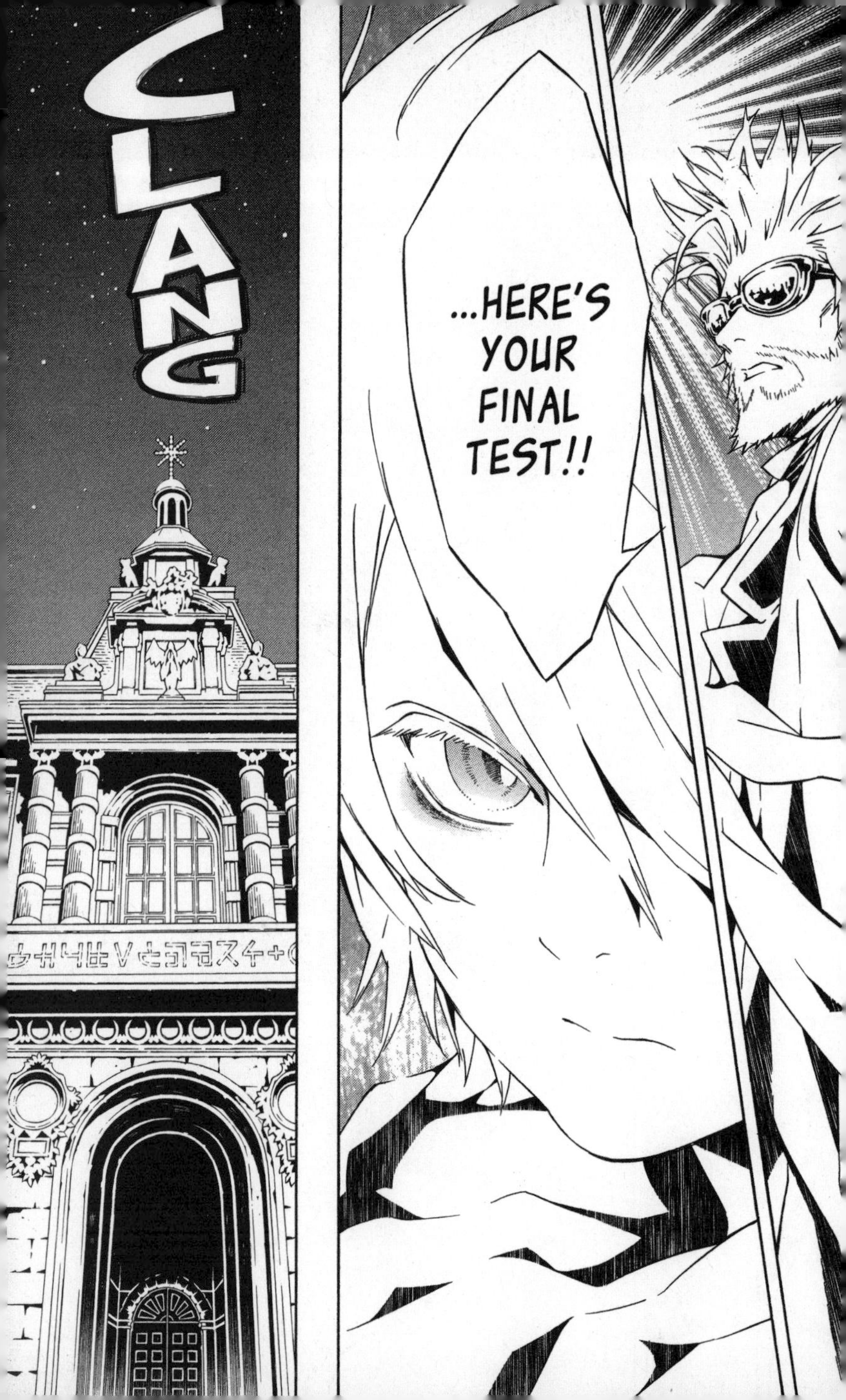
...HERE'S YOUR FINAL TEST!!
CLANG

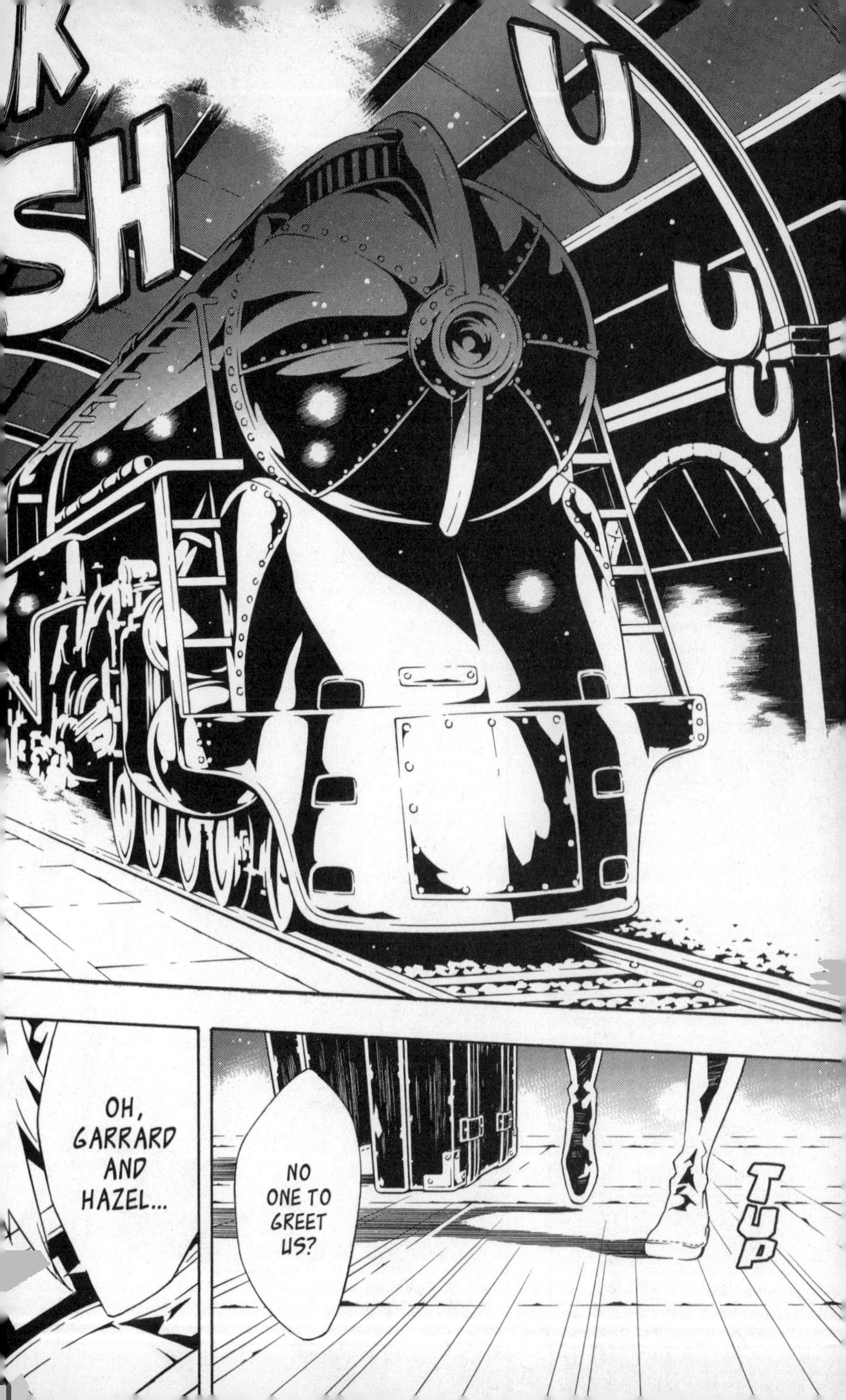
SHUUU
TUP
NO ONE TO GREET US?
OH, GARRARD AND HAZEL...

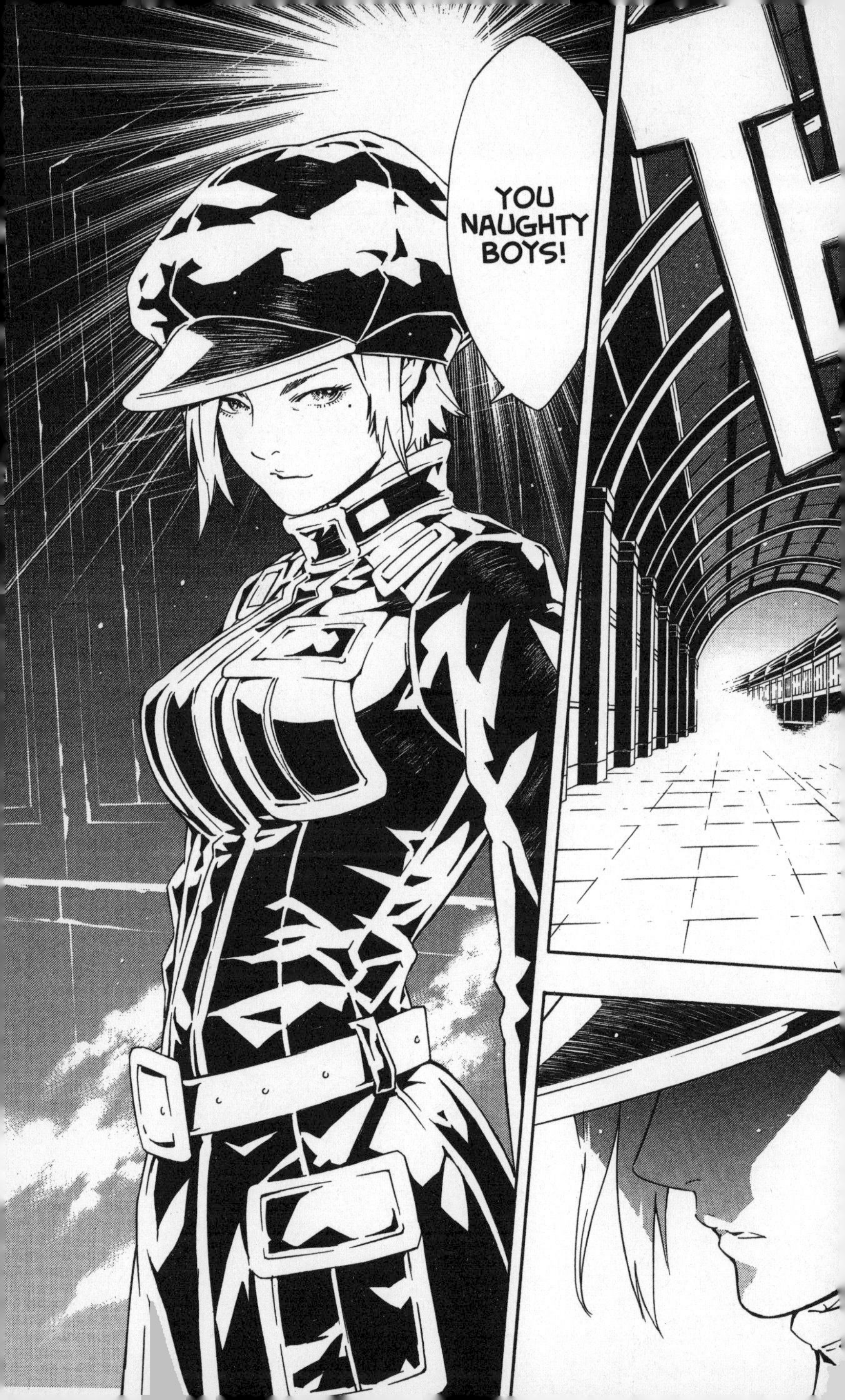
YOU NAUGHTY BOYS!

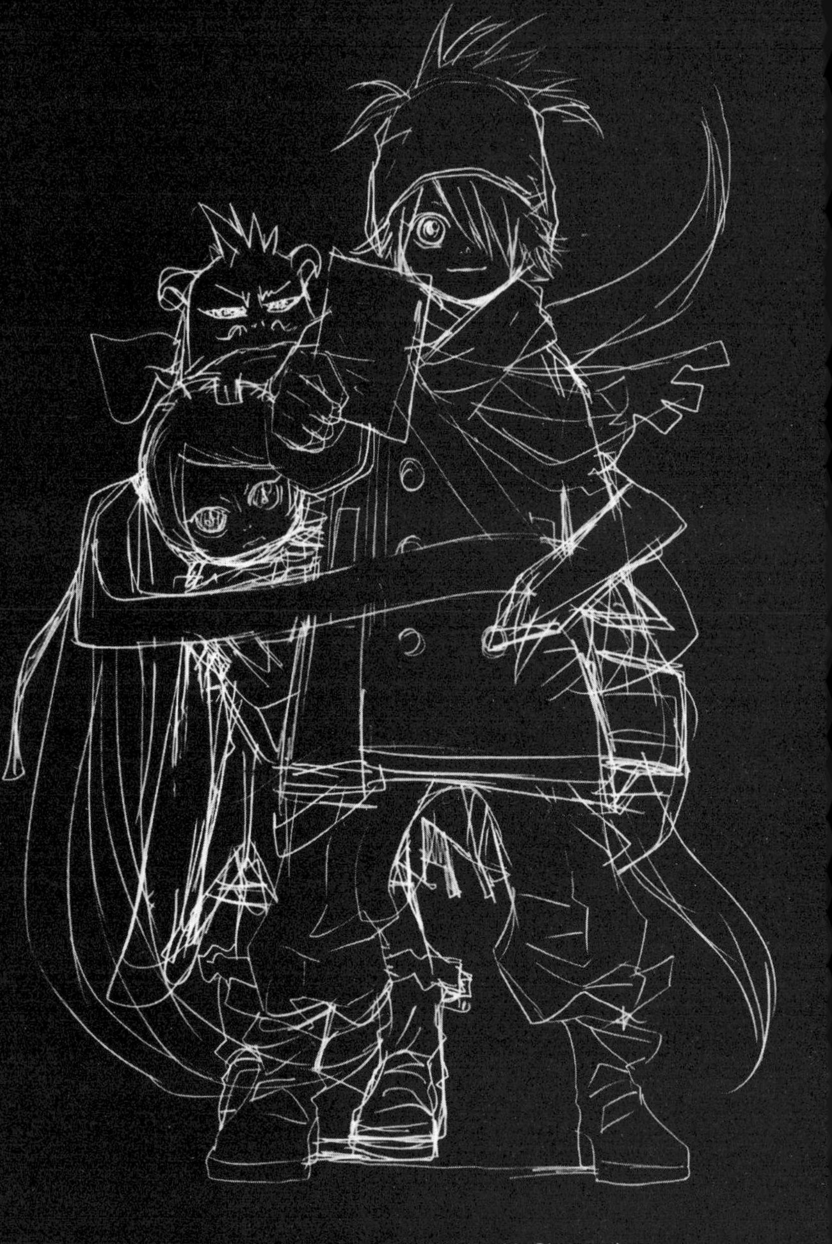

Rough sketch of the cover for the February 2007 *Monthly Shonen Jump*.

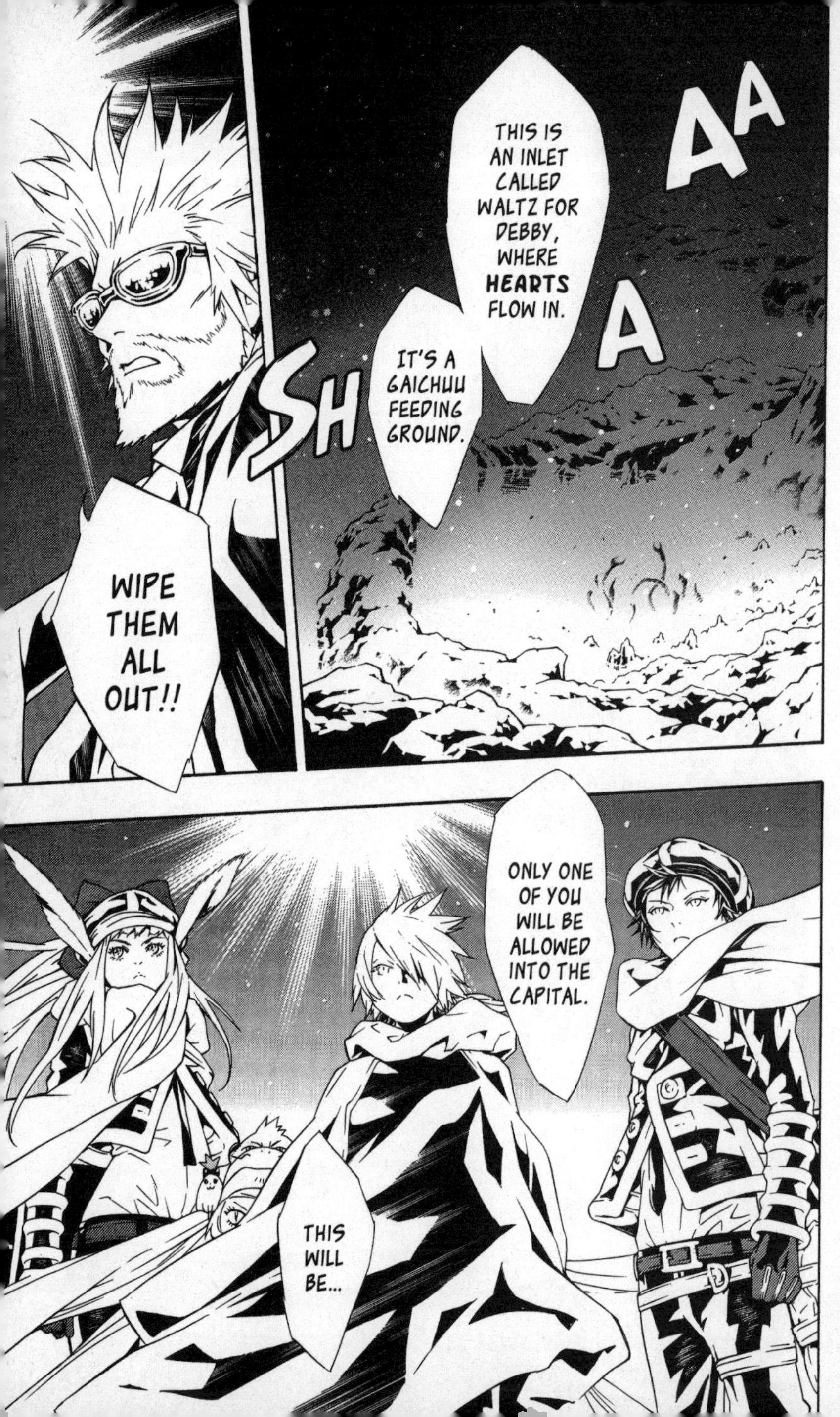

SHAAAA
THIS IS AN INLET CALLED WALTZ FOR DEBBY, WHERE **HEARTS** FLOW IN.
IT'S A GAICHUU FEEDING GROUND.
WIPE THEM ALL OUT!!
ONLY ONE OF YOU WILL BE ALLOWED INTO THE CAPITAL.
THIS WILL BE...

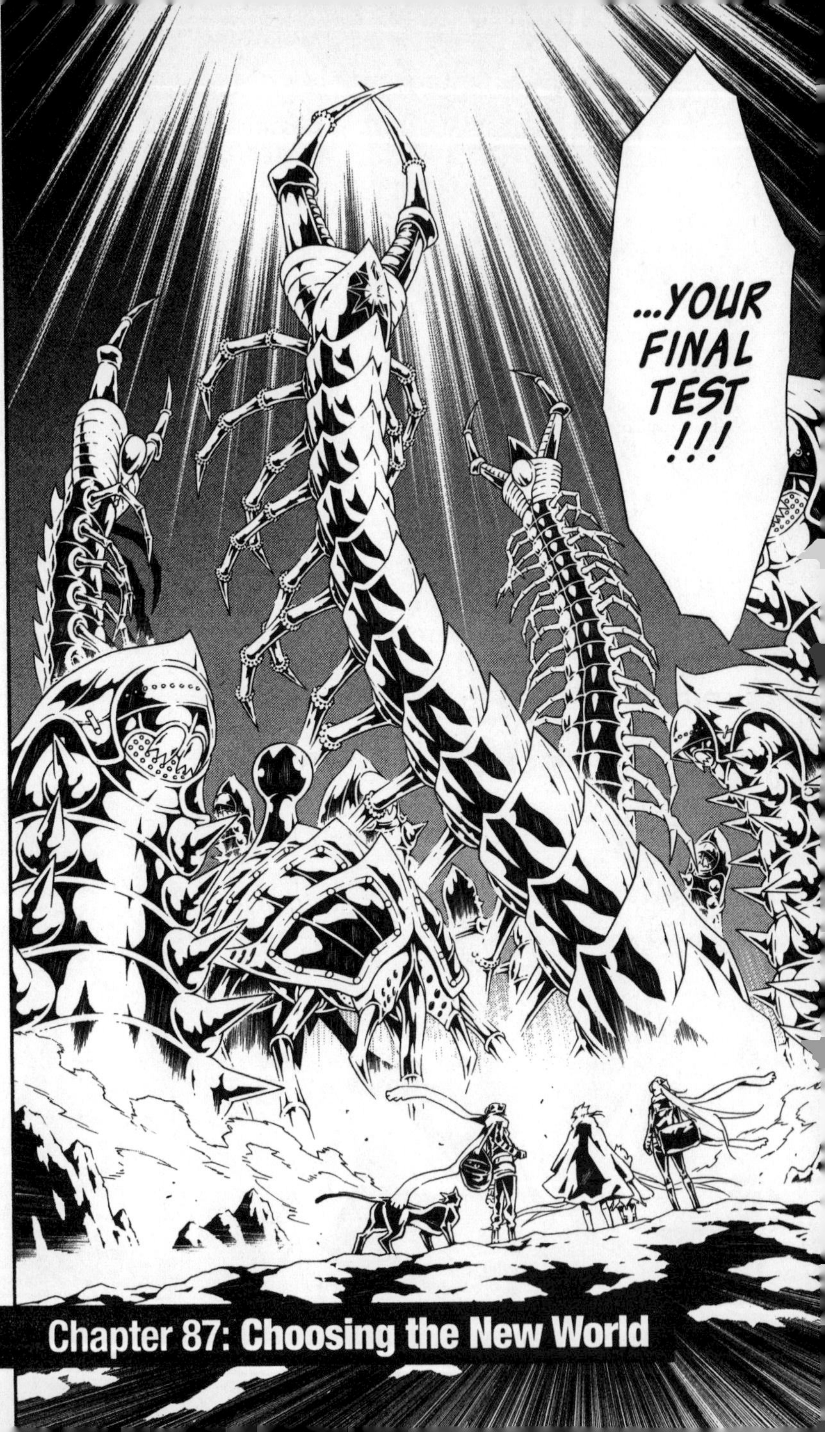
...YOUR FINAL TEST !!!

Chapter 87: Choosing the New World

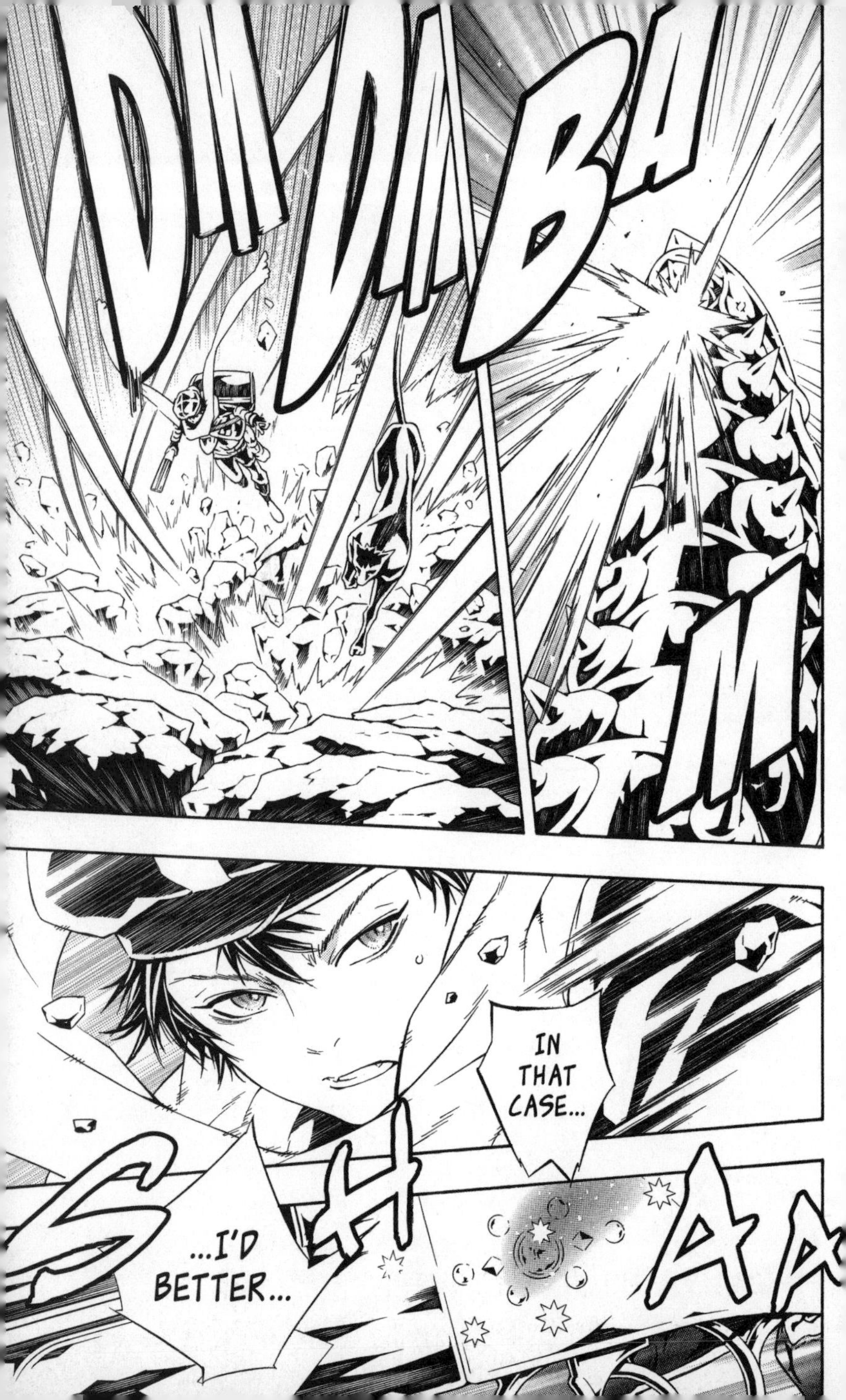
DADABAM
IN THAT CASE...
...I'D BETTER...
SHAA

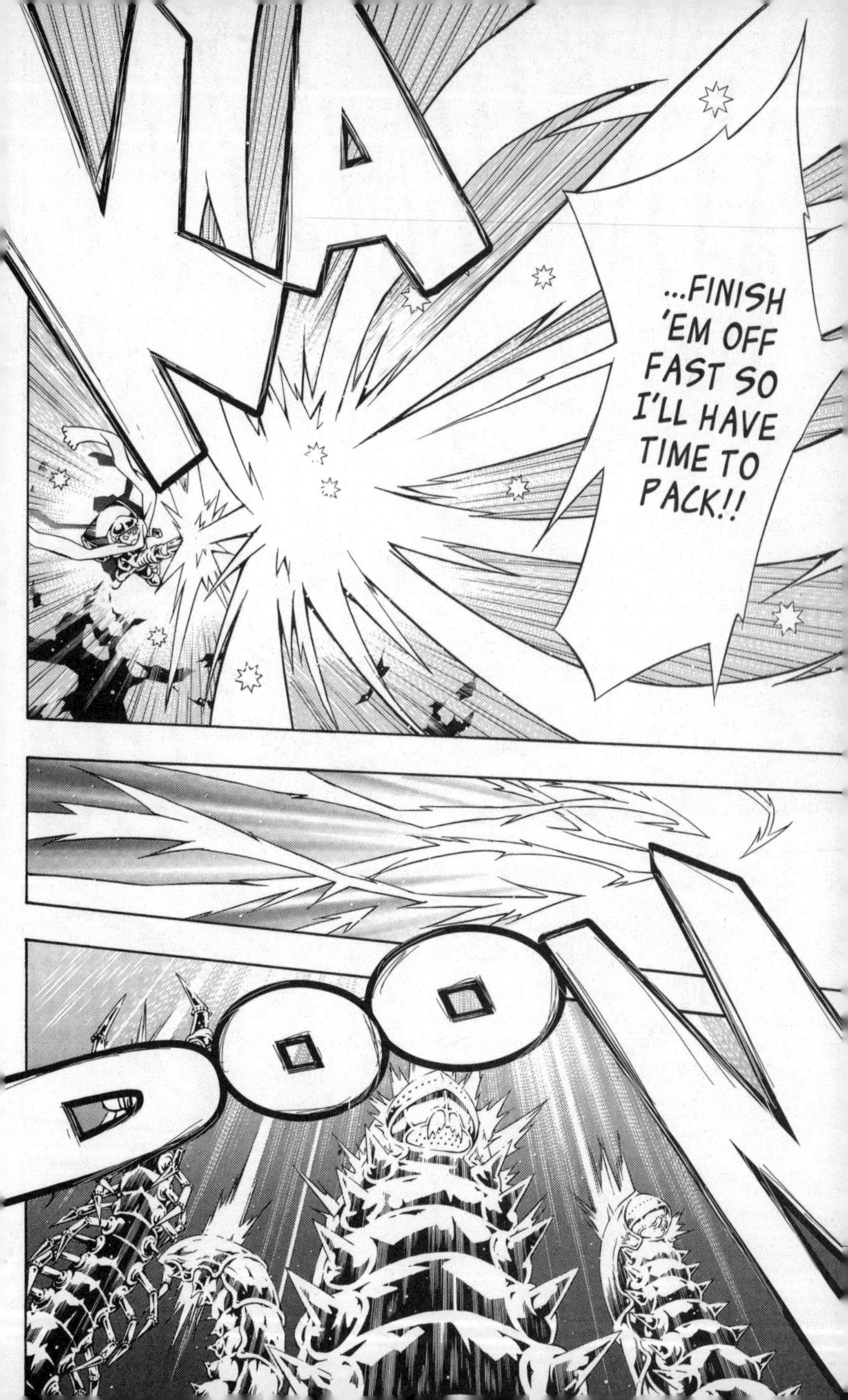
...FINISH 'EM OFF FAST SO I'LL HAVE TIME TO PACK!!

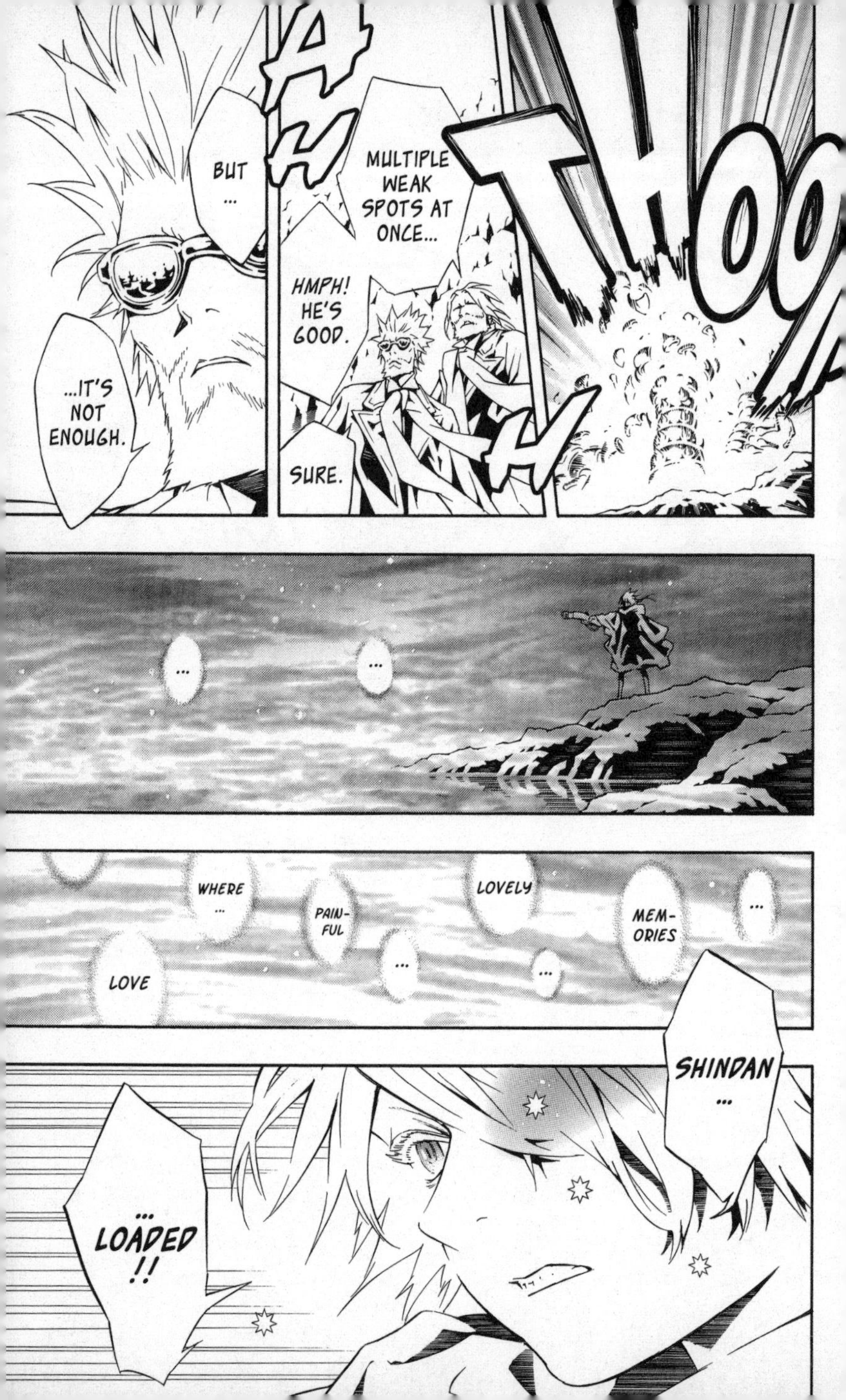
THOO
MULTIPLE WEAK SPOTS AT ONCE...
HMPH! HE'S GOOD.
SURE.
BUT ...
...IT'S NOT ENOUGH.
...
...
...
MEM-ORIES
LOVELY
...
...
PAIN-FUL
WHERE ...
LOVE
SHINDAN ...
...LOADED!!

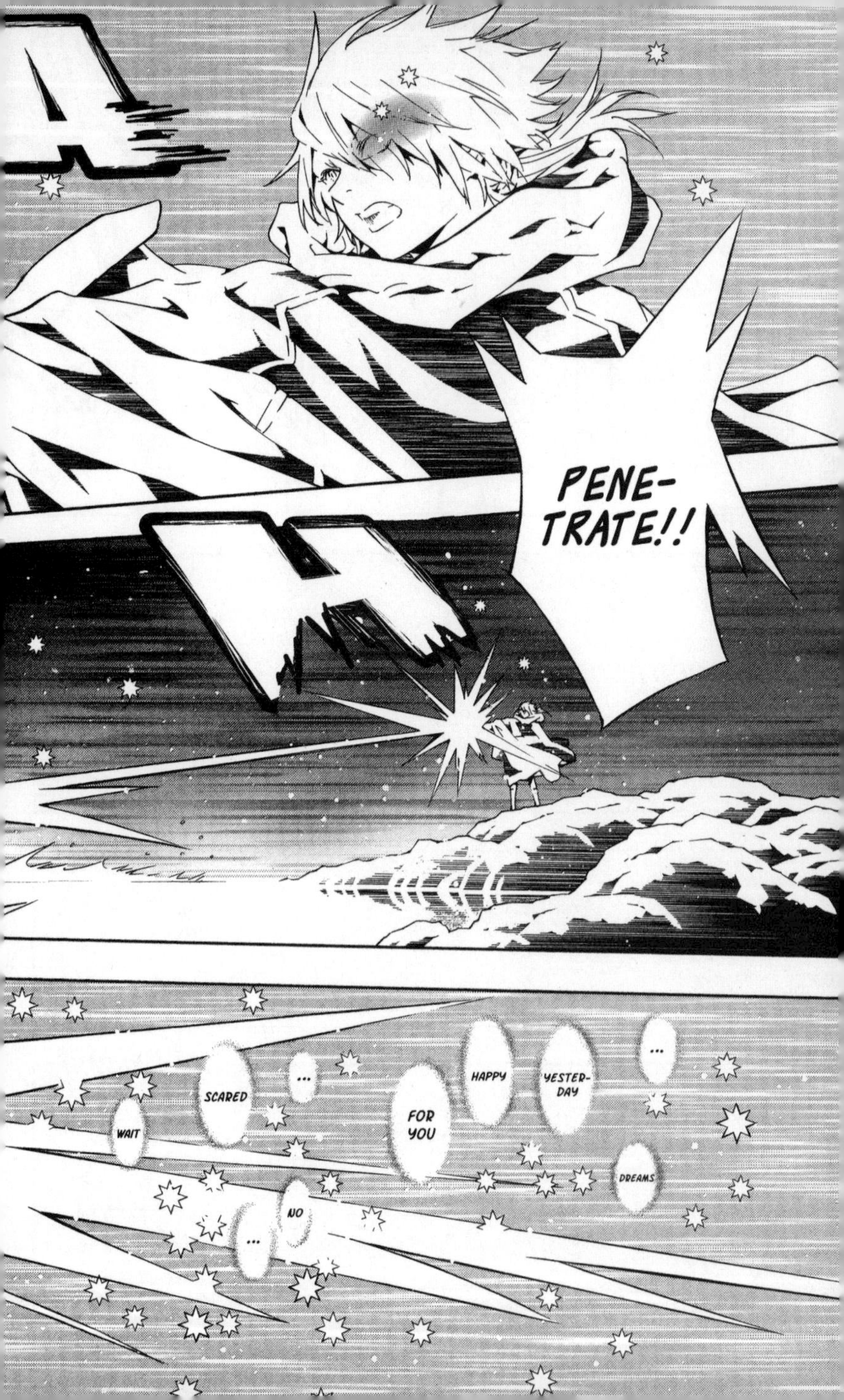
PENE-
TRATE!!
...
DREAMS
YESTER-
DAY
HAPPY
FOR
YOU
...
NO
SCARED
...
WAIT

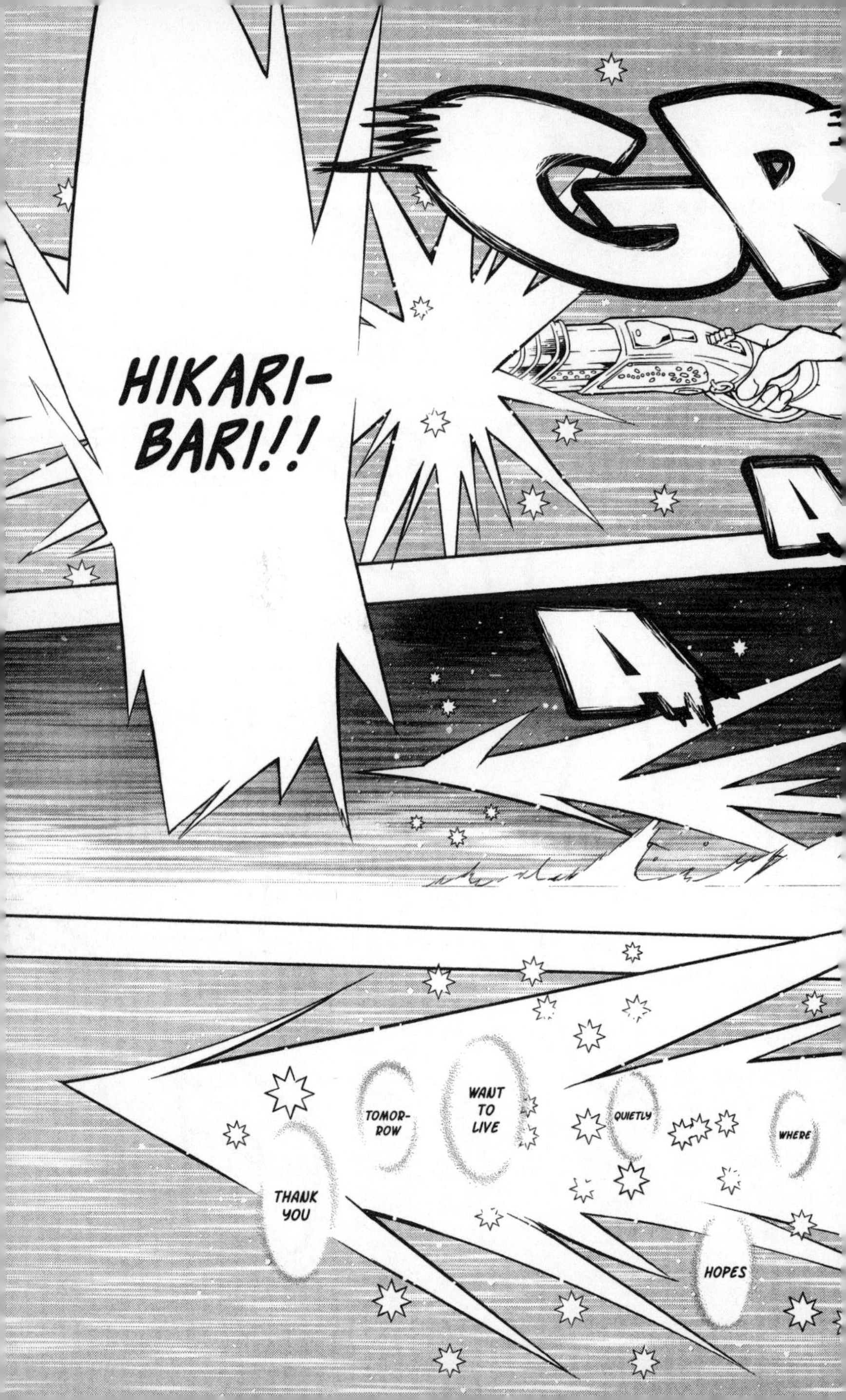
GRAA
HIKARI-BARI!!
WHERE
HOPES
QUIETLY
WANT TO LIVE
TOMOR-ROW
THANK YOU

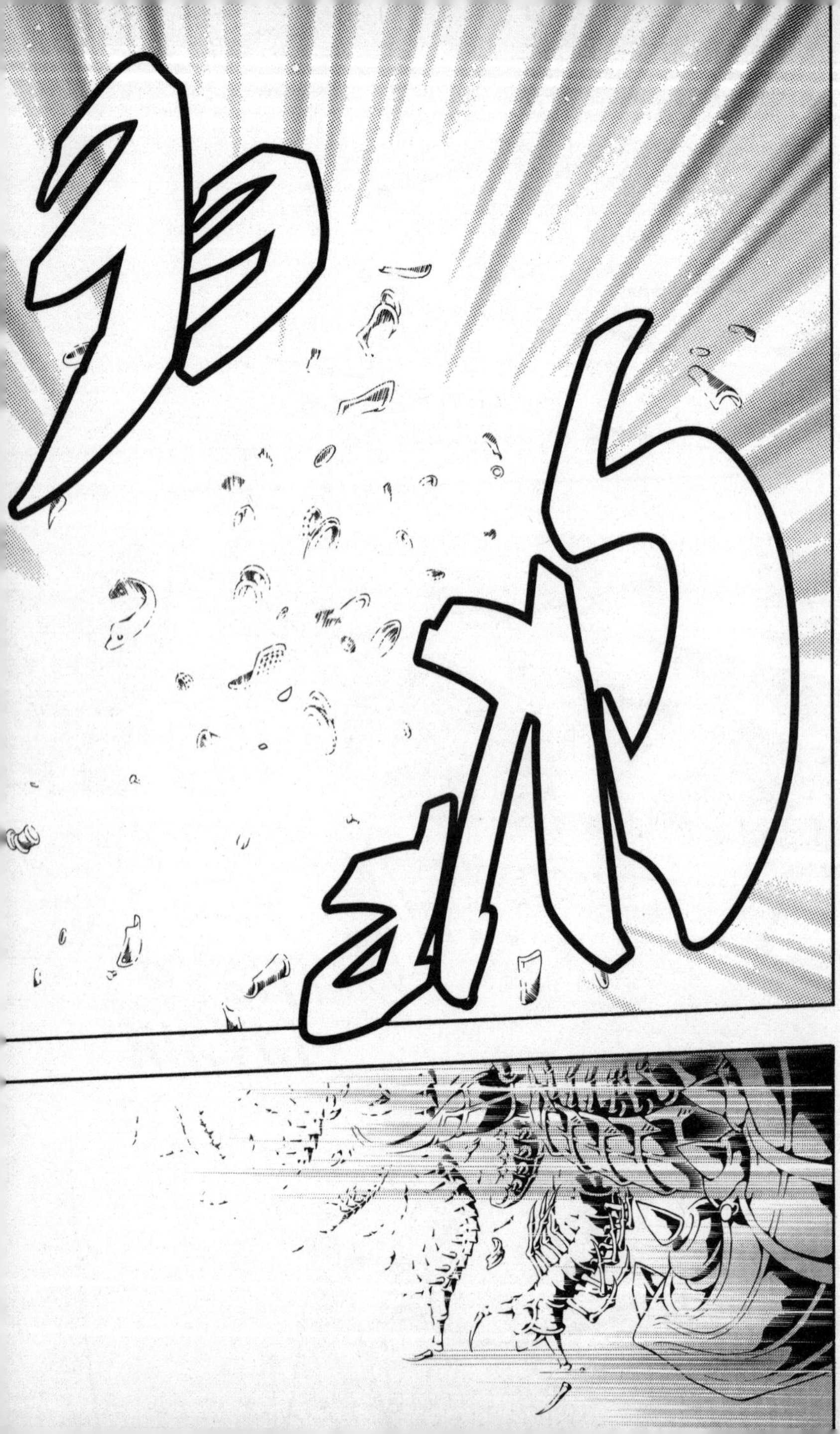

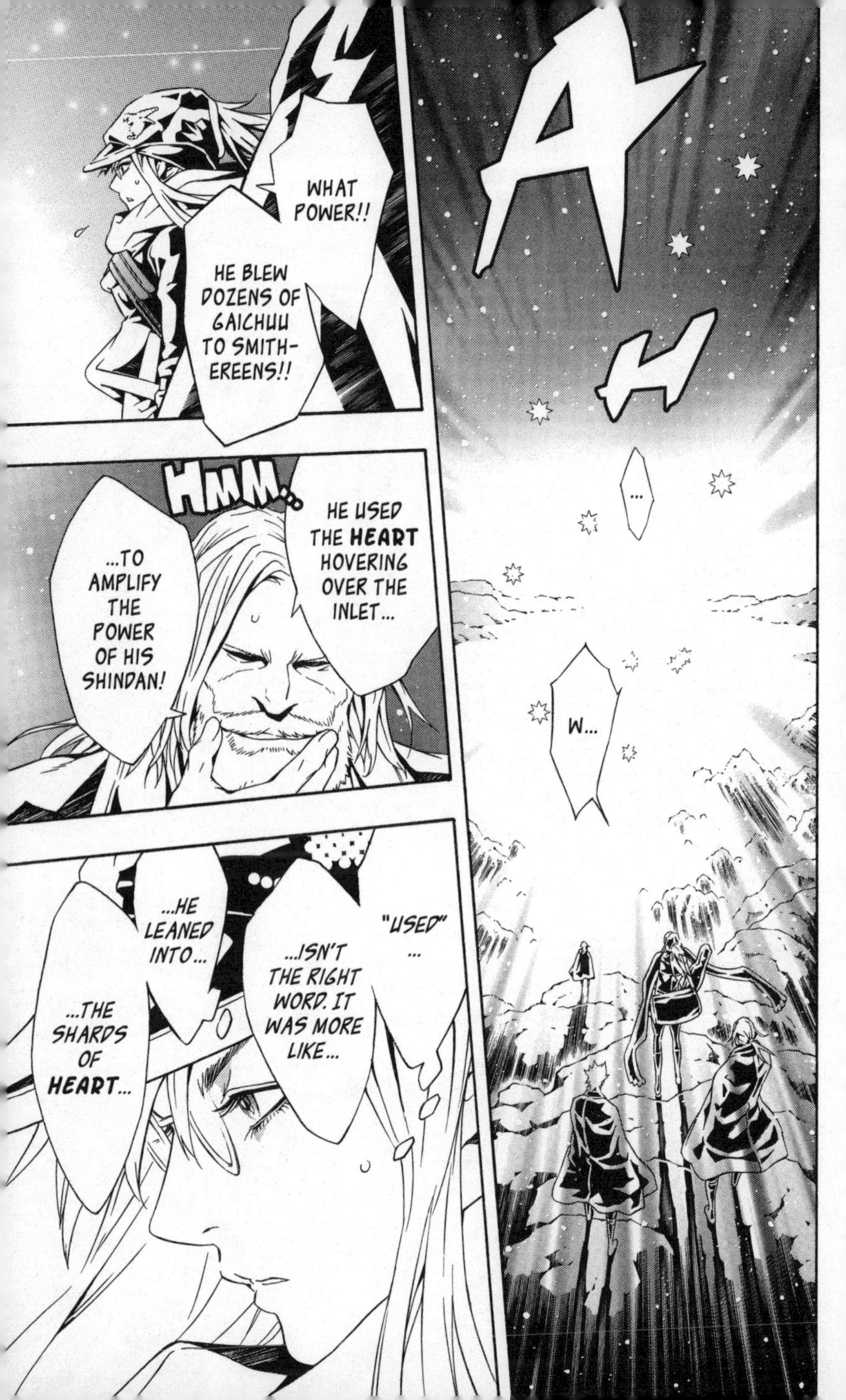
AH
...
W...
WHAT POWER!!
HE BLEW DOZENS OF GAICHUU TO SMITH-EREENS!!
HMM..
HE USED THE **HEART** HOVERING OVER THE INLET...
...TO AMPLIFY THE POWER OF HIS SHINDAN!
"USED" ...
...ISN'T THE RIGHT WORD. IT WAS MORE LIKE...
...HE LEANED INTO...
...THE SHARDS OF **HEART**...

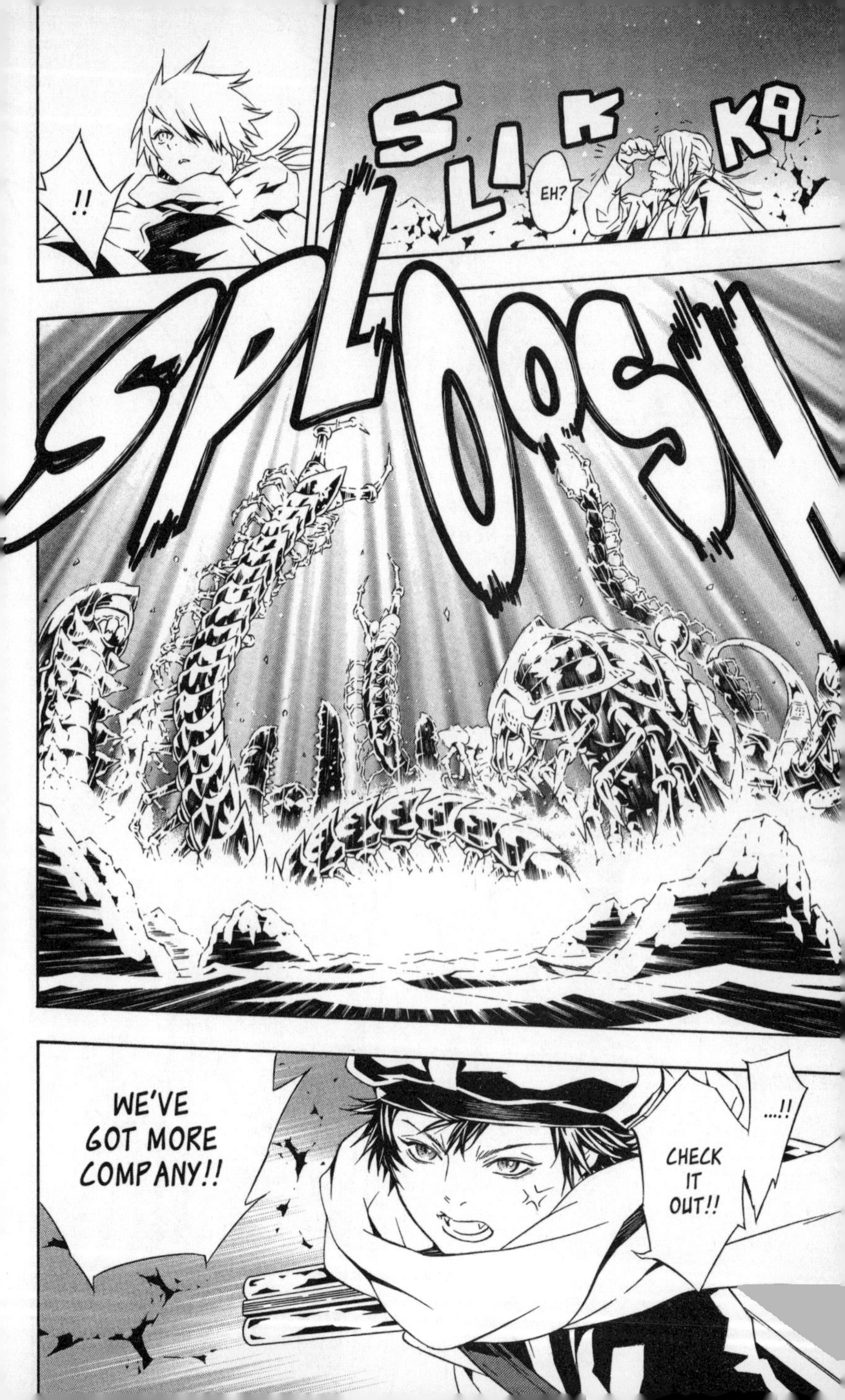
SLIK
KA
EH?
!!
SPLOOSH
...!!
CHECK IT OUT!!
WE'VE GOT MORE COMPANY!!

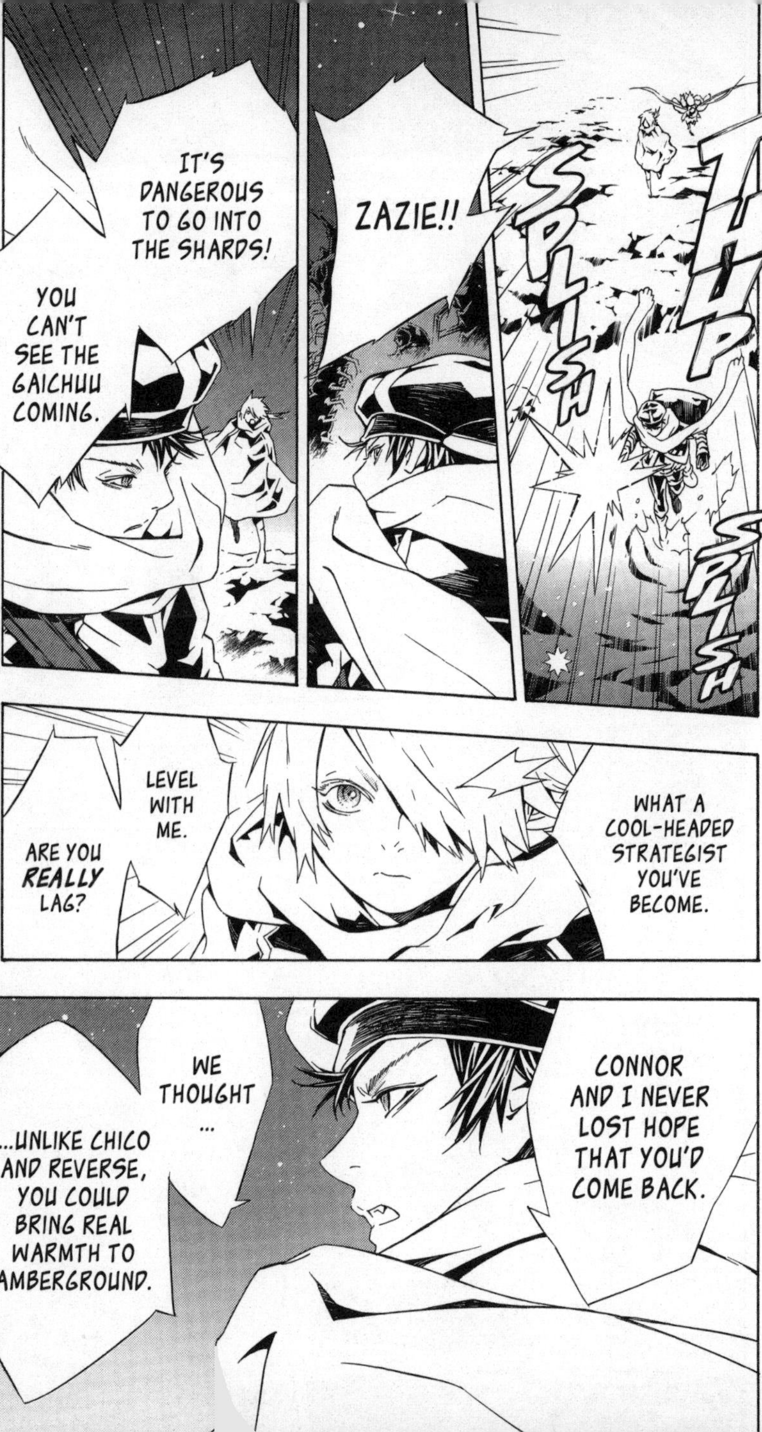
THUP
SPLISH
SPLISH
ZAZIE!!
IT'S DANGEROUS TO GO INTO THE SHARDS!
YOU CAN'T SEE THE GAICHUU COMING.
WHAT A COOL-HEADED STRATEGIST YOU'VE BECOME.
LEVEL WITH ME.
ARE YOU REALLY LAG?
CONNOR AND I NEVER LOST HOPE THAT YOU'D COME BACK.
WE THOUGHT ...
...UNLIKE CHICO AND REVERSE, YOU COULD BRING REAL WARMTH TO AMBERGROUND.

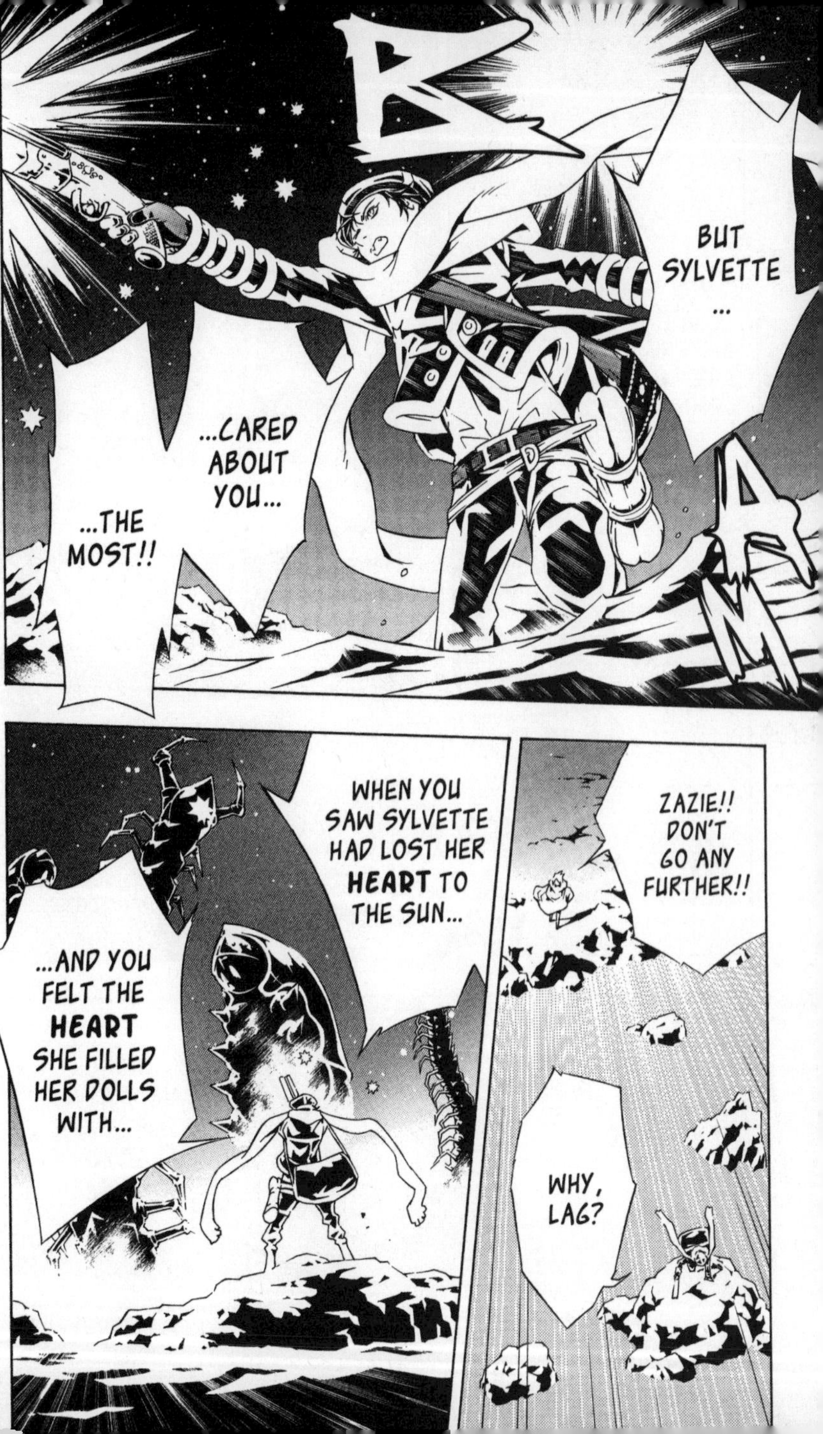
BUT SYLVETTE ...
...CARED ABOUT YOU...
...THE MOST!!
B
A
M
WHEN YOU SAW SYLVETTE HAD LOST HER **HEART** TO THE SUN...
...AND YOU FELT THE **HEART** SHE FILLED HER DOLLS WITH...
ZAZIE!! DON'T GO ANY FURTHER!!
WHY, LAG?

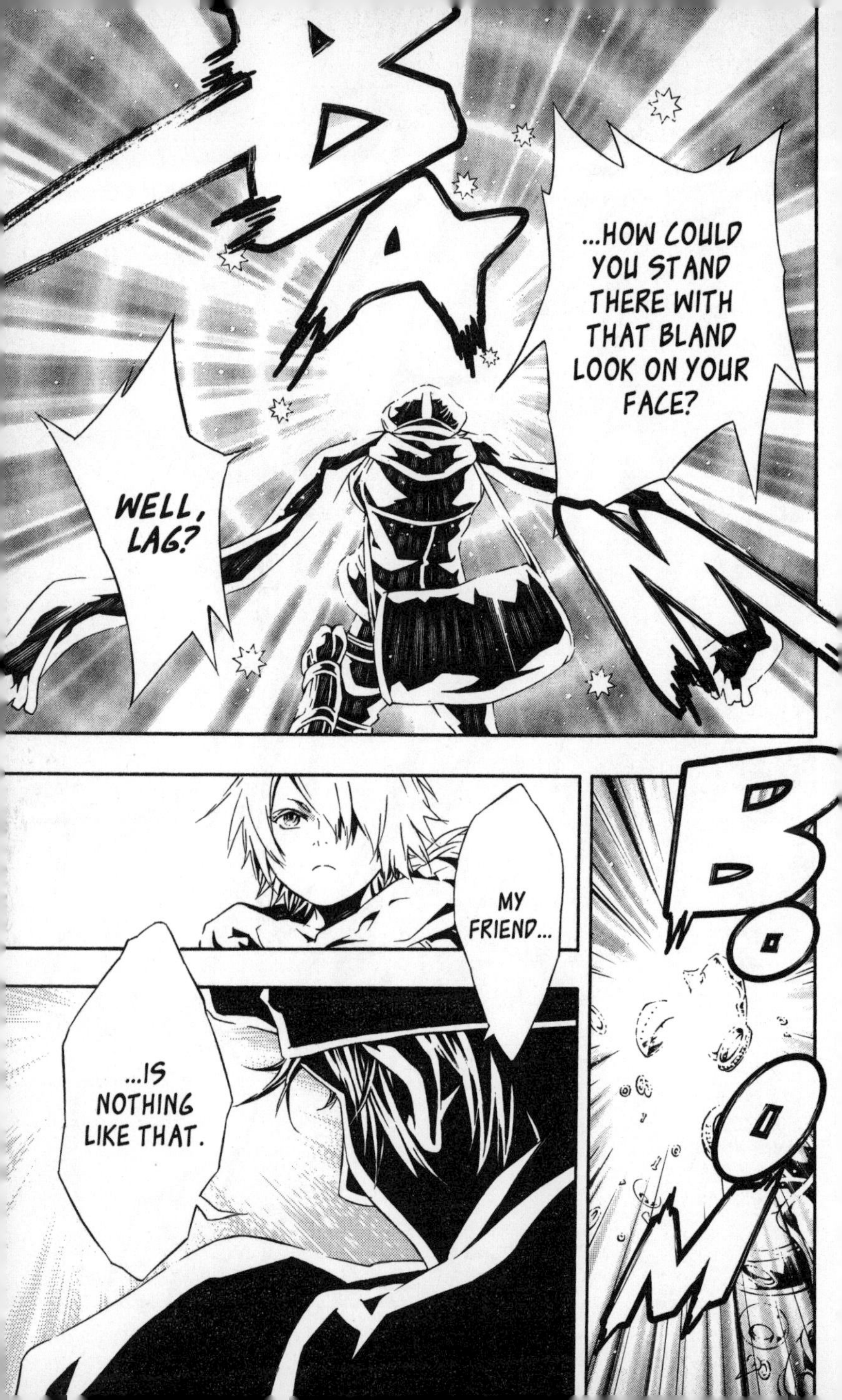
...HOW COULD YOU STAND THERE WITH THAT BLAND LOOK ON YOUR FACE?
WELL, LAG?
BOOOM
MY FRIEND...
...IS NOTHING LIKE THAT.

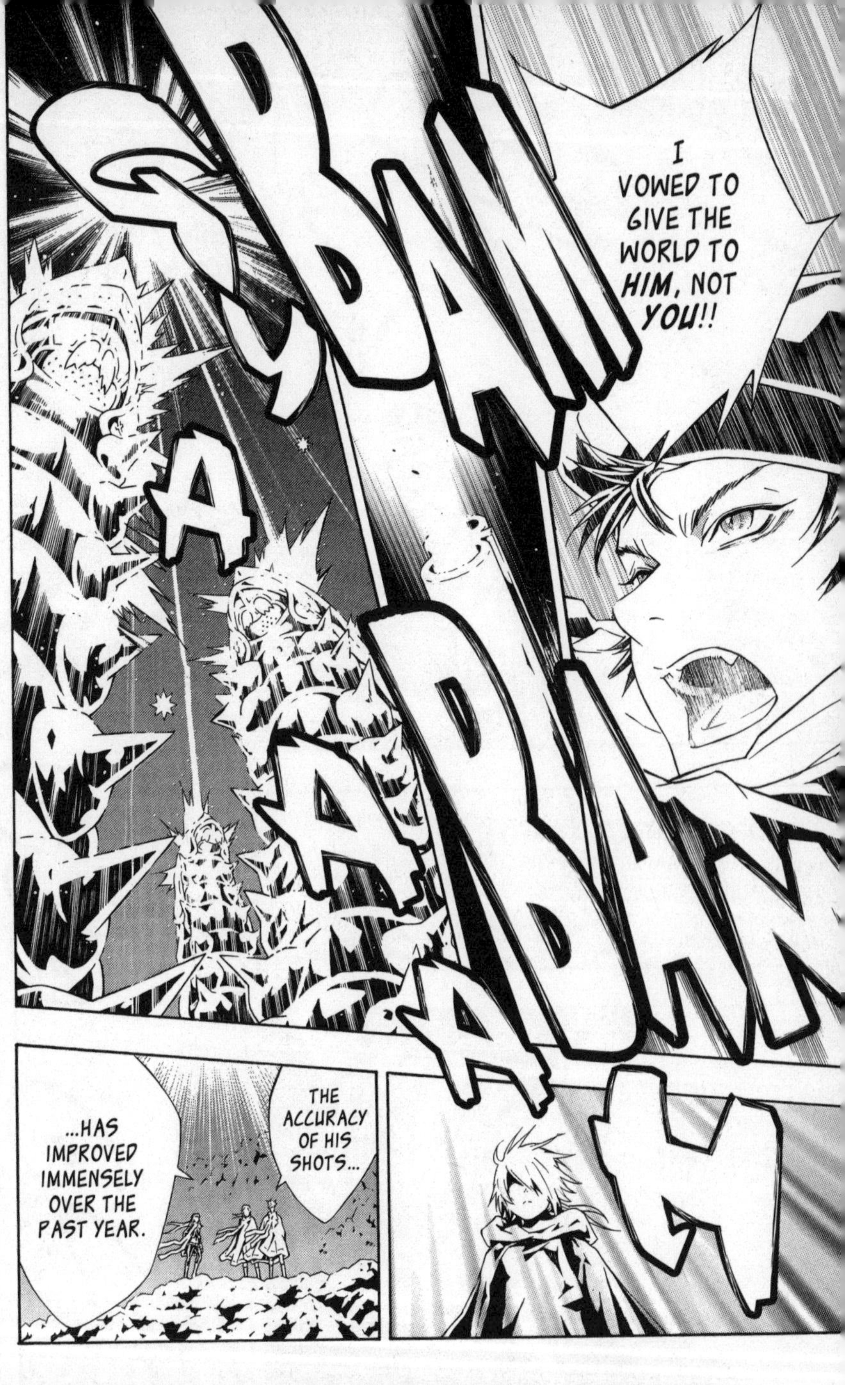
I VOWED TO GIVE THE WORLD TO *HIM*, NOT *YOU*!!
THE ACCURACY OF HIS SHOTS...
...HAS IMPROVED IMMENSELY OVER THE PAST YEAR.

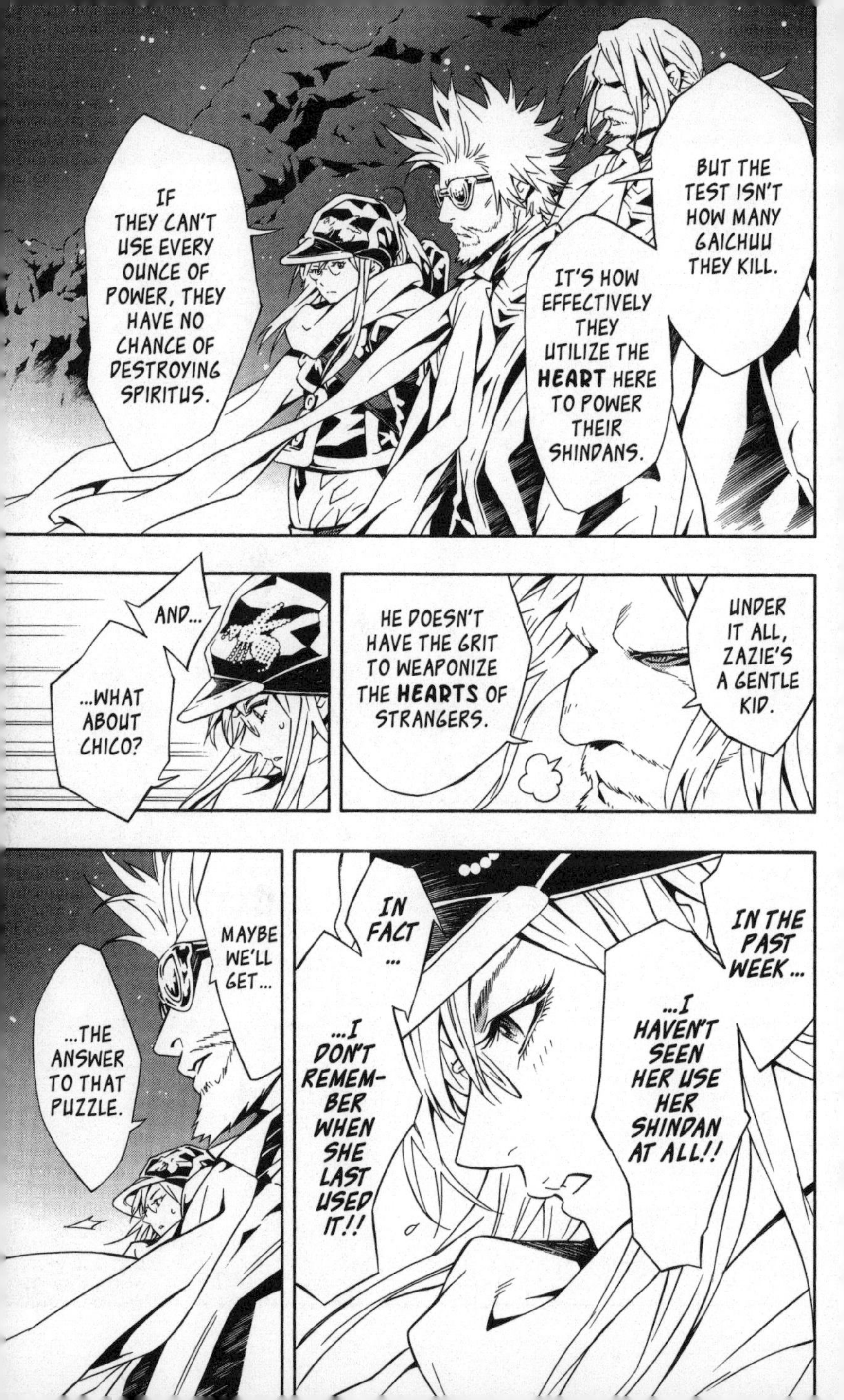
BUT THE TEST ISN'T HOW MANY GAICHUU THEY KILL.
IT'S HOW EFFECTIVELY THEY UTILIZE THE **HEART** HERE TO POWER THEIR SHINDANS.
IF THEY CAN'T USE EVERY OUNCE OF POWER, THEY HAVE NO CHANCE OF DESTROYING SPIRITUS.
UNDER IT ALL, ZAZIE'S A GENTLE KID.
HE DOESN'T HAVE THE GRIT TO WEAPONIZE THE **HEARTS** OF STRANGERS.
AND...
...WHAT ABOUT CHICO?
IN THE PAST WEEK...
...I HAVEN'T SEEN HER USE HER SHINDAN AT ALL!!
IN FACT...
...I DON'T REMEMBER WHEN SHE LAST USED IT!!
MAYBE WE'LL GET...
...THE ANSWER TO THAT PUZZLE.

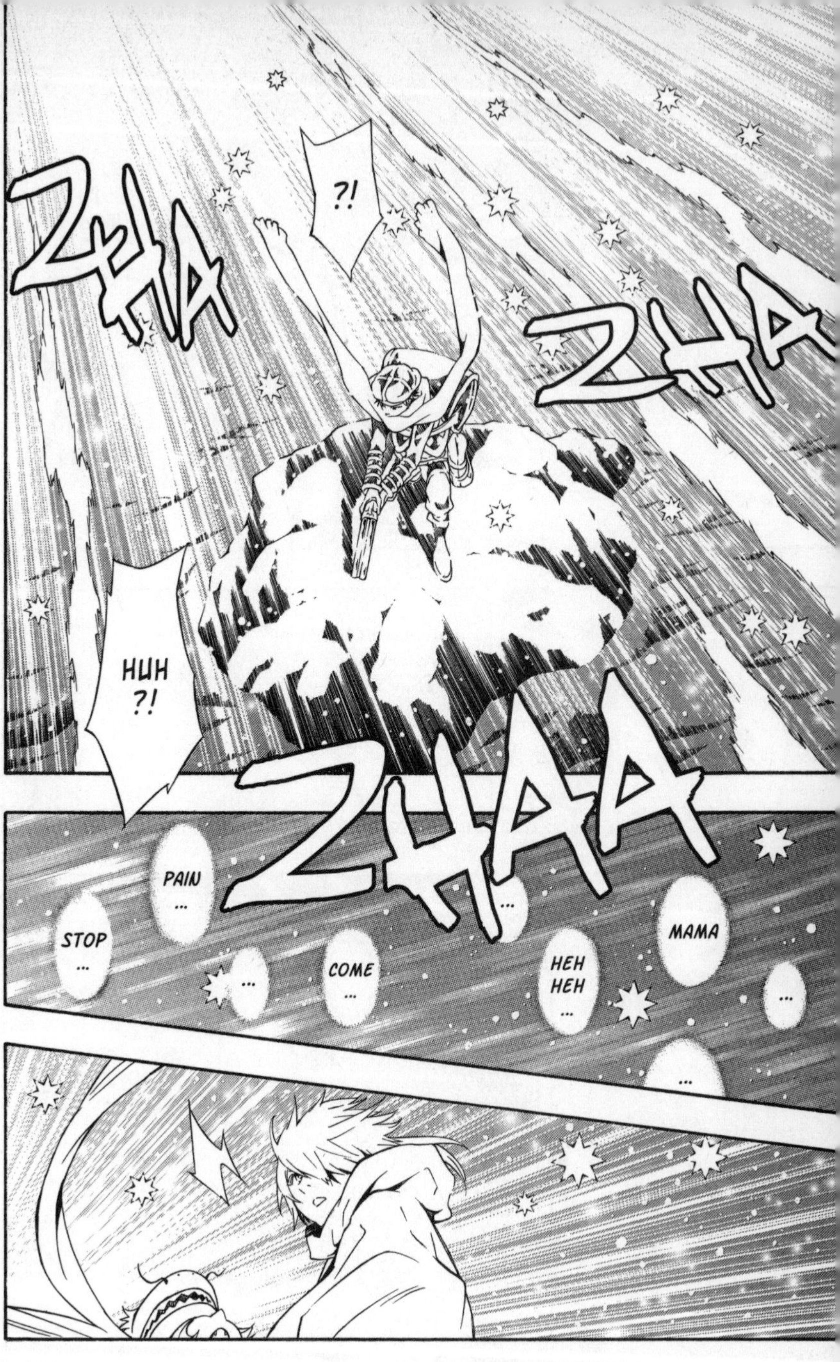
ZHA
?!
ZHA
HUH ?!
ZHAA
...
MAMA
HEH HEH ...
...
COME ...
...
PAIN ...
STOP ...
...

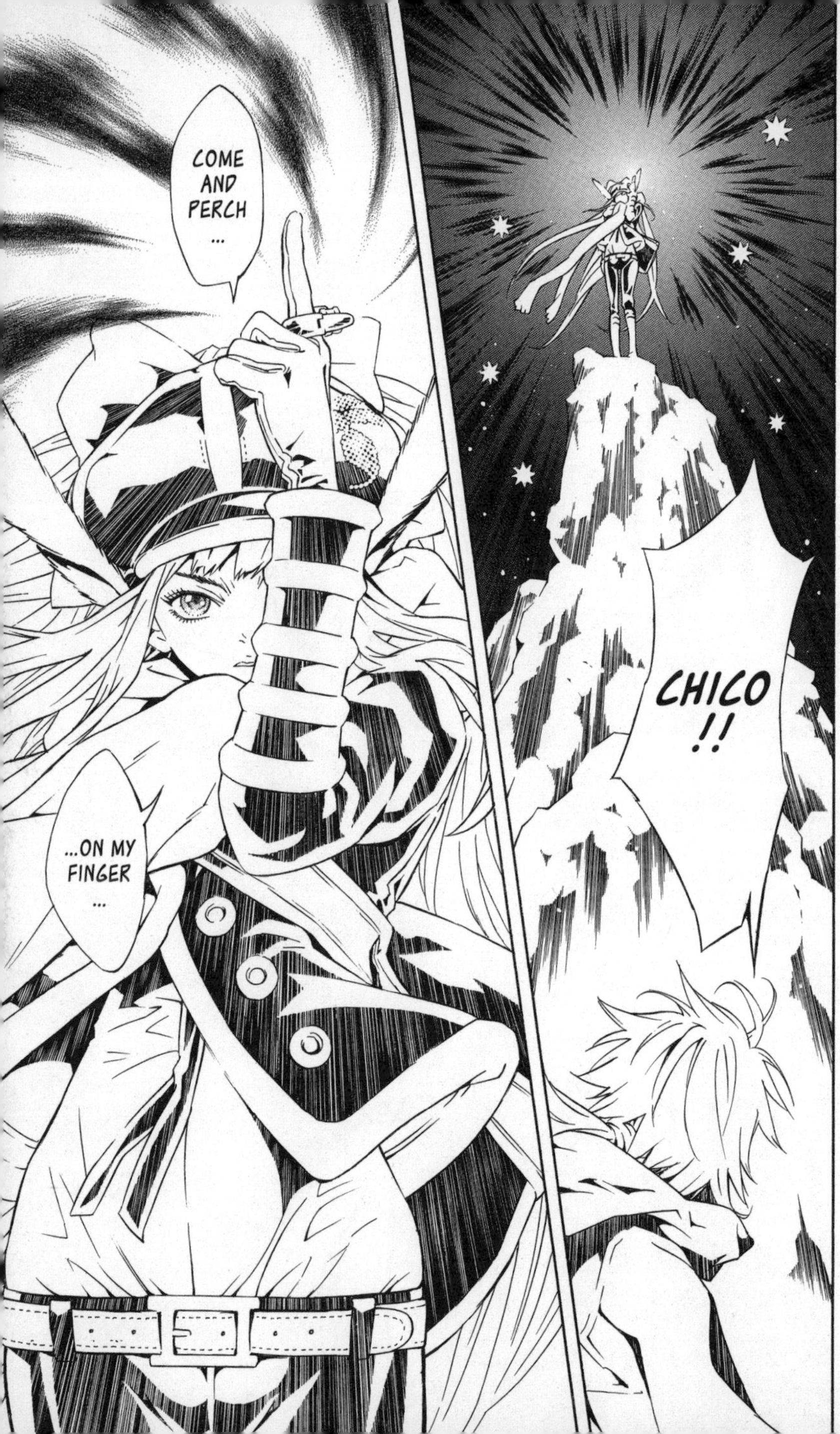
CHICO!!
COME AND PERCH...
...ON MY FINGER...

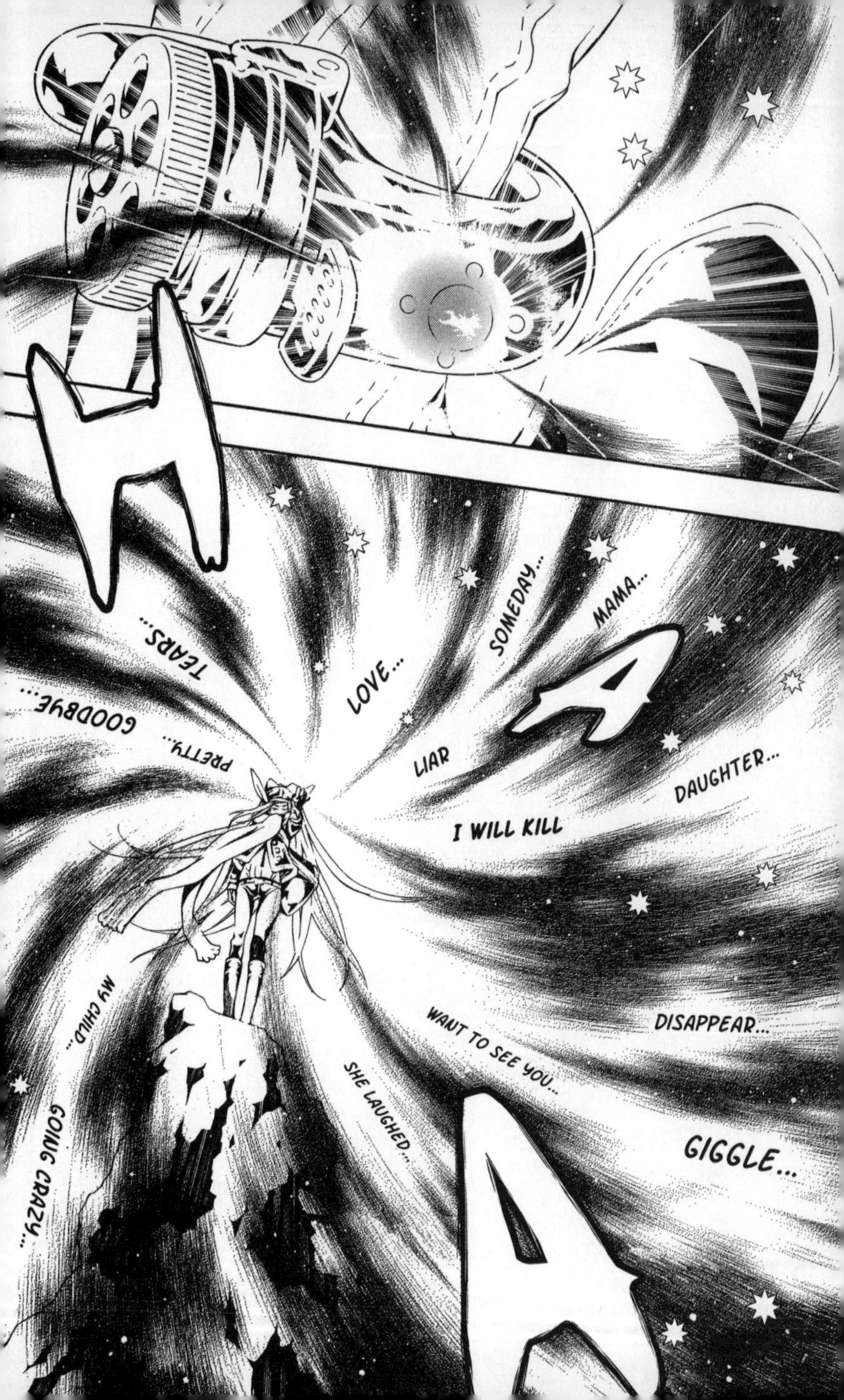
MAMA...
SOMEDAY...
LOVE...
TEARS...
GOODBYE...
PRETTY...
LIAR
DAUGHTER...
I WILL KILL
DISAPPEAR...
WANT TO SEE YOU...
SHE LAUGHED...
MY CHILD...
GOING CRAZY...
GIGGLE...

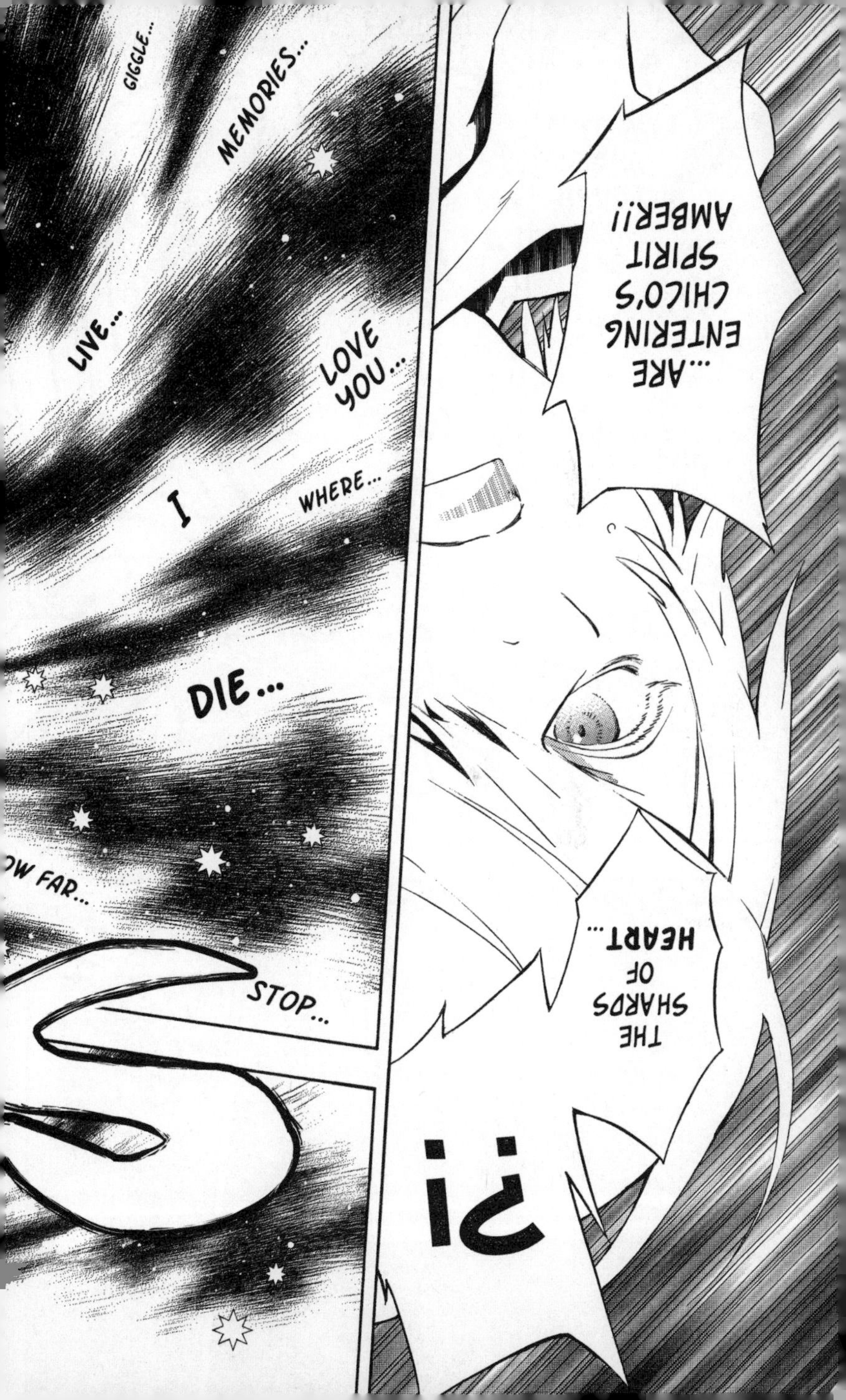
?!
THE SHARDS OF HEART...
...ARE ENTERING CHICO'S SPIRIT AMBER!!
MEMORIES...
GIGGLE...
LOVE YOU...
LIVE...
WHERE...
I
DIE...
STOP...
OW FAR...

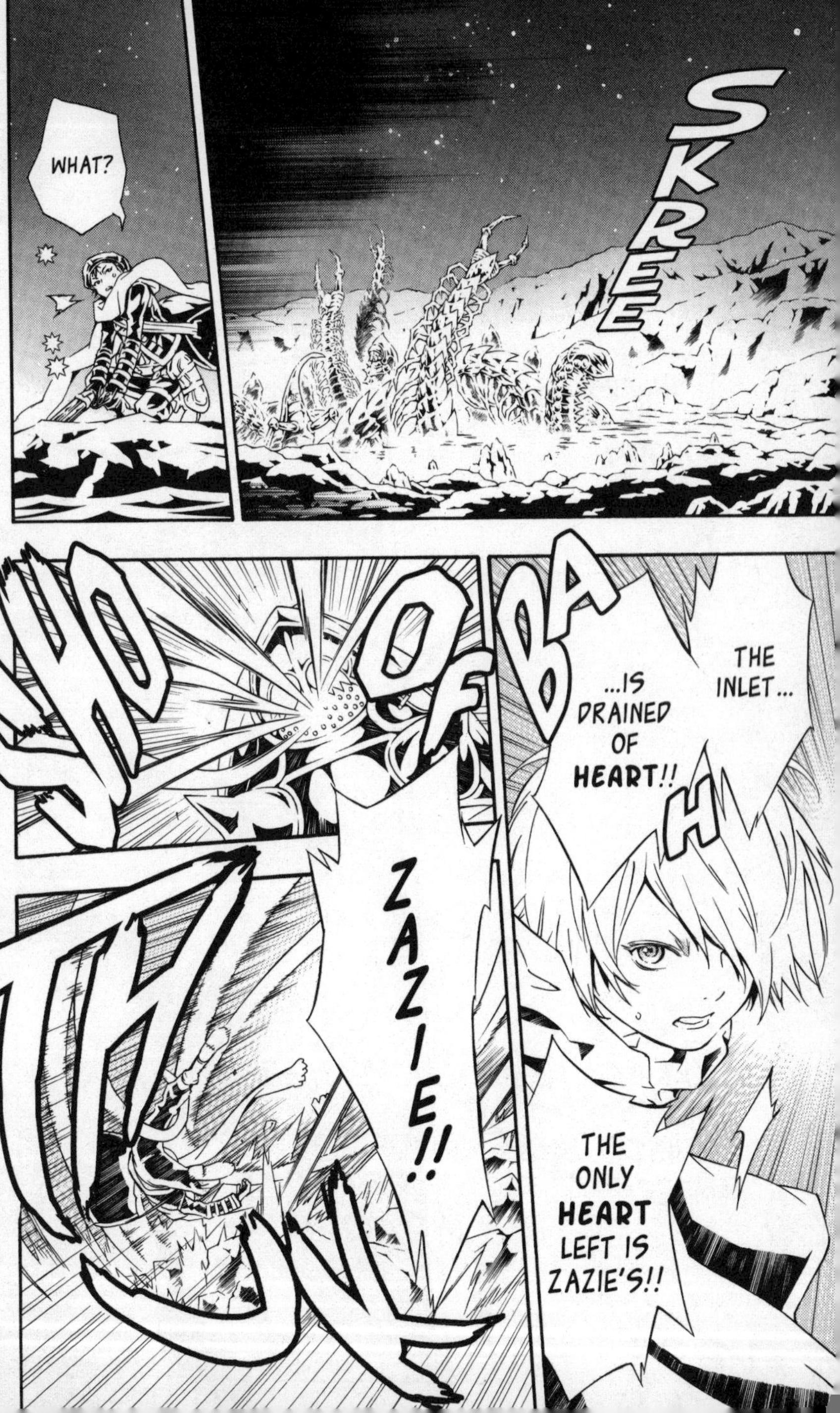
SKREE
WHAT?
BAH
THE INLET...
...IS DRAINED OF HEART!!
WHOOF
THE ONLY HEART LEFT IS ZAZIE'S!!
ZAZIE!!
THUK

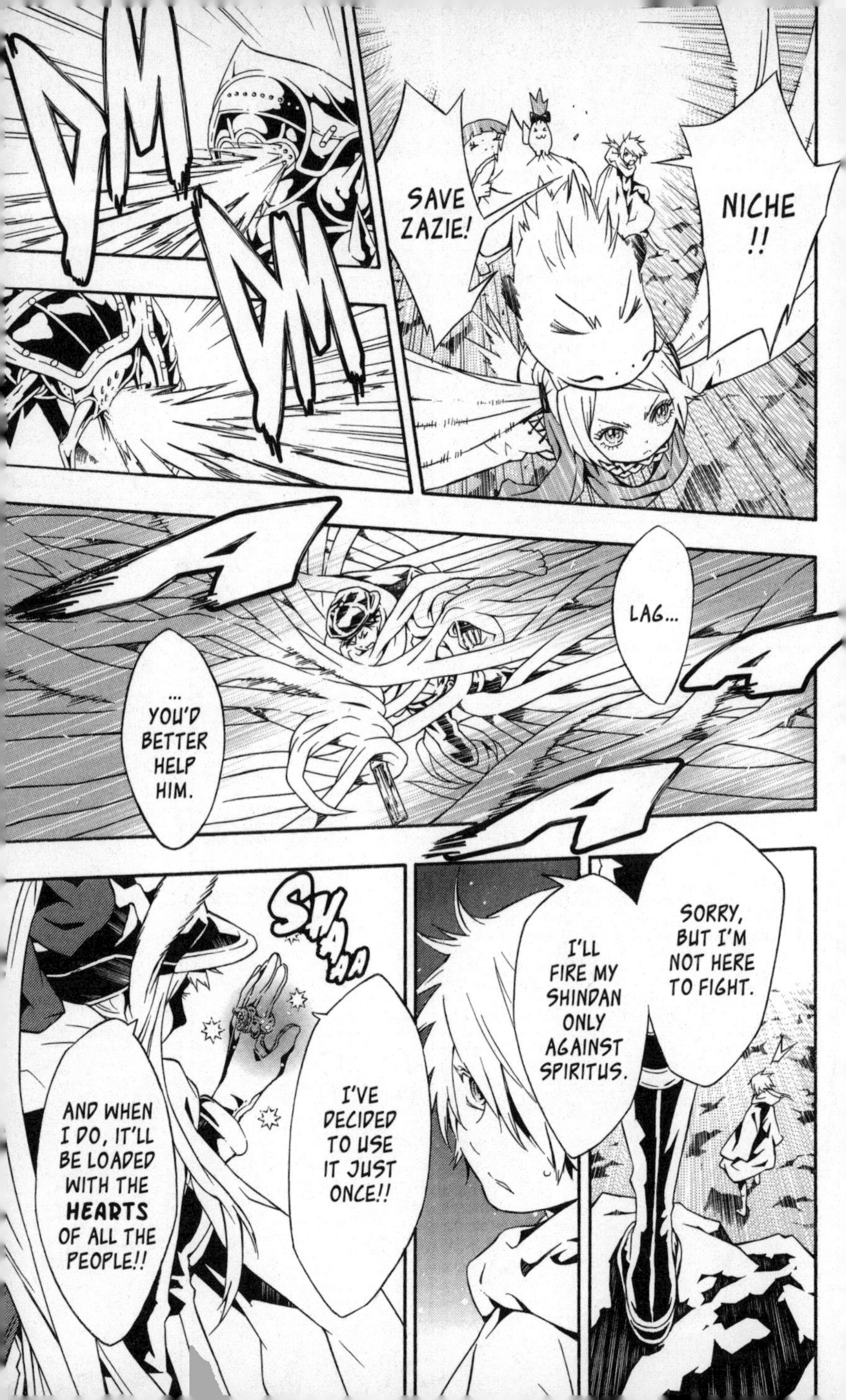
NICHE !!
SAVE ZAZIE!
DMM
DMM
LAG...
... YOU'D BETTER HELP HIM.
SORRY, BUT I'M NOT HERE TO FIGHT.
I'LL FIRE MY SHINDAN ONLY AGAINST SPIRITUS.
I'VE DECIDED TO USE IT JUST ONCE!!
SHAAA
AND WHEN I DO, IT'LL BE LOADED WITH THE HEARTS OF ALL THE PEOPLE!!

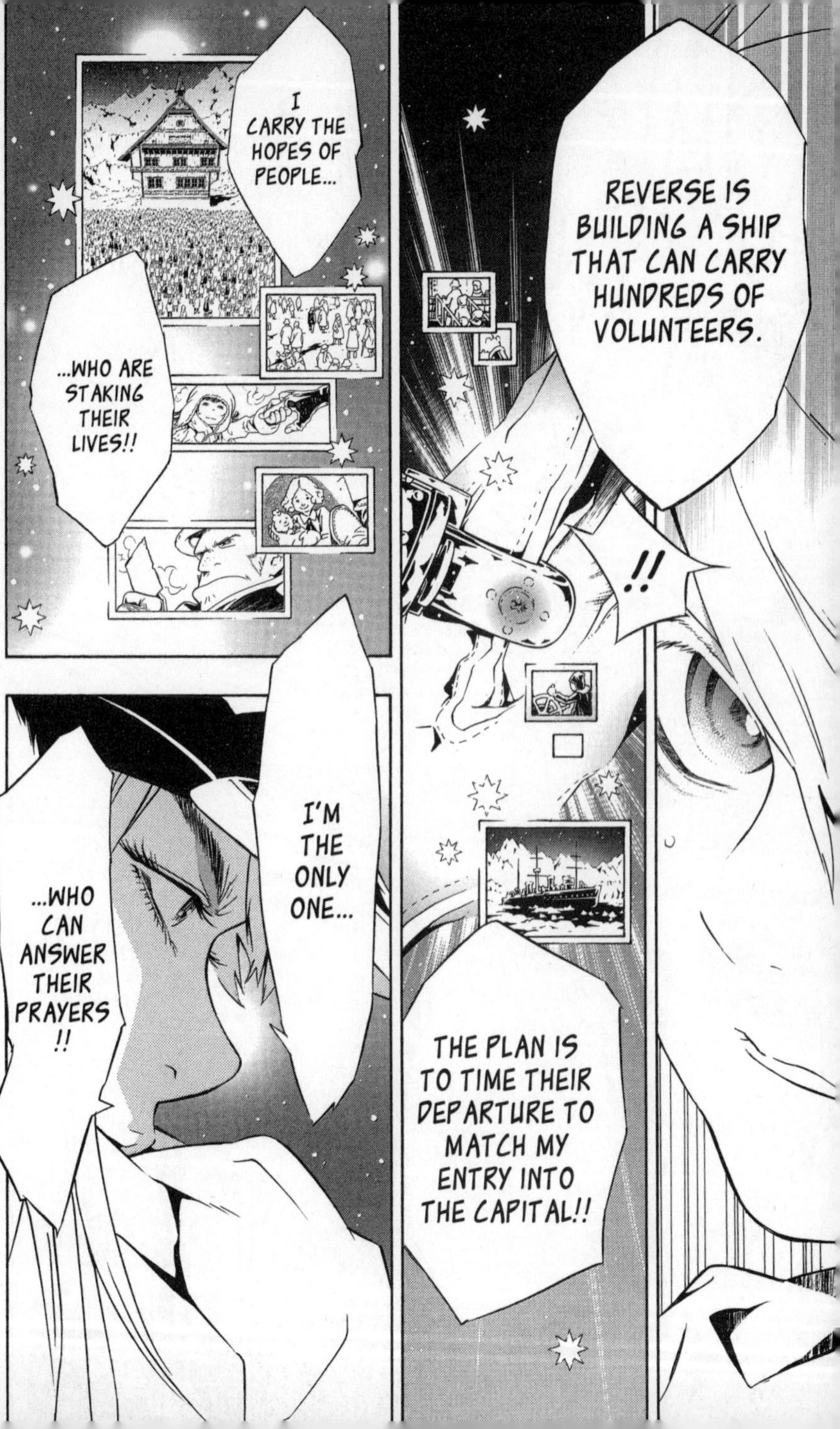
REVERSE IS BUILDING A SHIP THAT CAN CARRY HUNDREDS OF VOLUNTEERS.
!!
THE PLAN IS TO TIME THEIR DEPARTURE TO MATCH MY ENTRY INTO THE CAPITAL!!
I CARRY THE HOPES OF PEOPLE...
...WHO ARE STAKING THEIR LIVES!!
I'M THE ONLY ONE...
...WHO CAN ANSWER THEIR PRAYERS!!

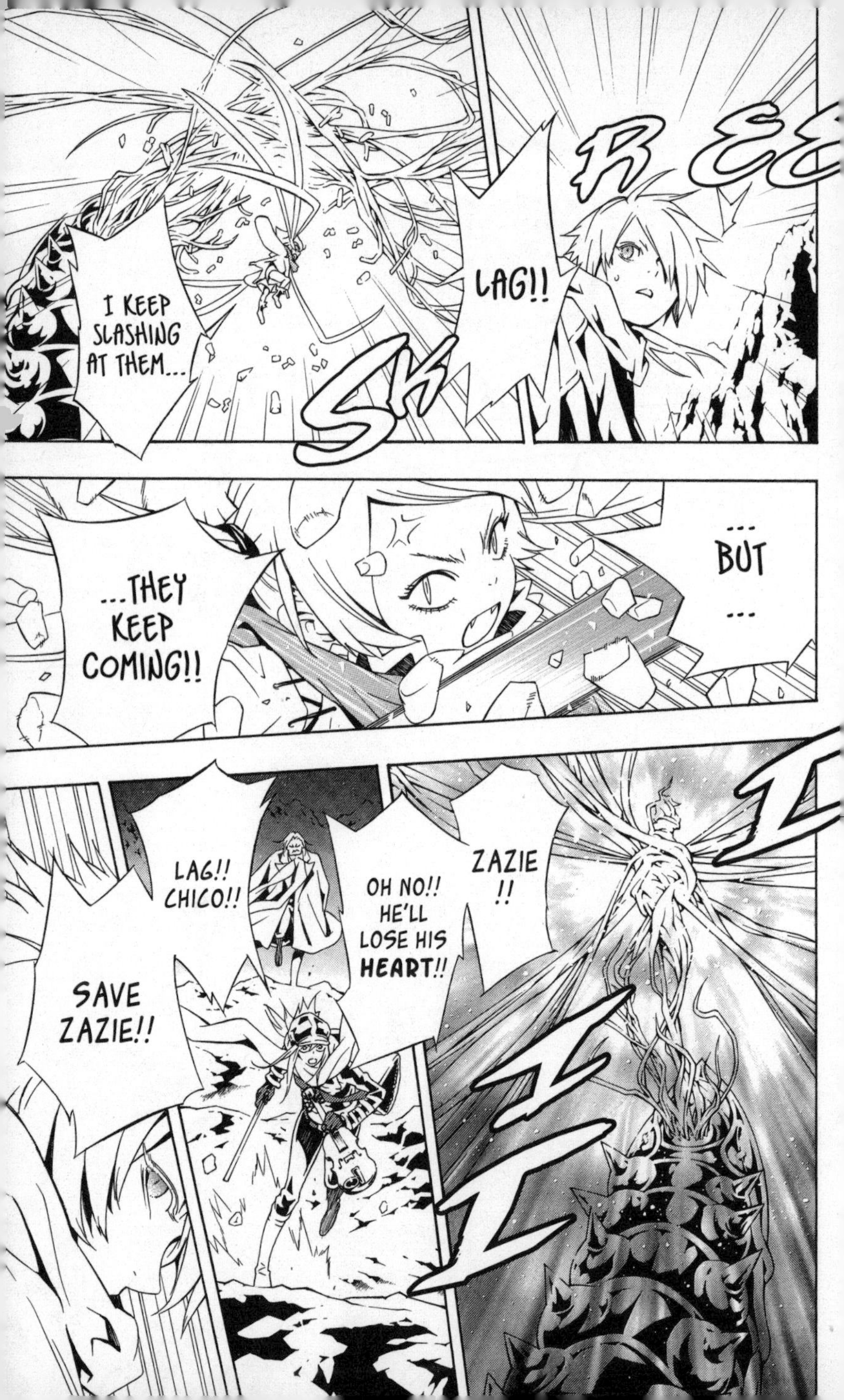
REE
LAG!!
SK
I KEEP SLASHING AT THEM...
...BUT...
...THEY KEEP COMING!!
ZAZIE!!
OH NO!! HE'LL LOSE HIS HEART!!
LAG!! CHICO!!
SAVE ZAZIE!!

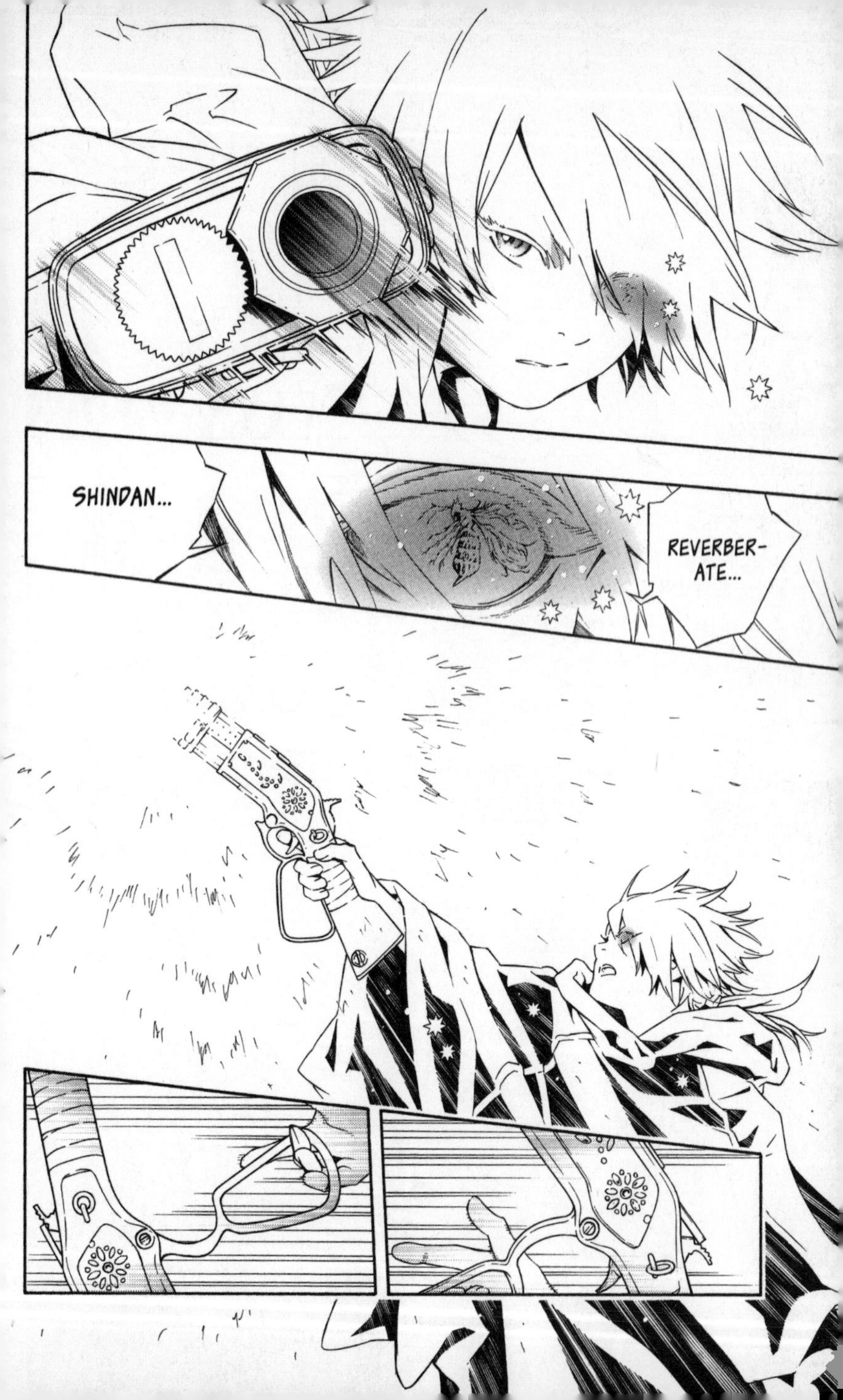
REVERBER-ATE...
SHINDAN...

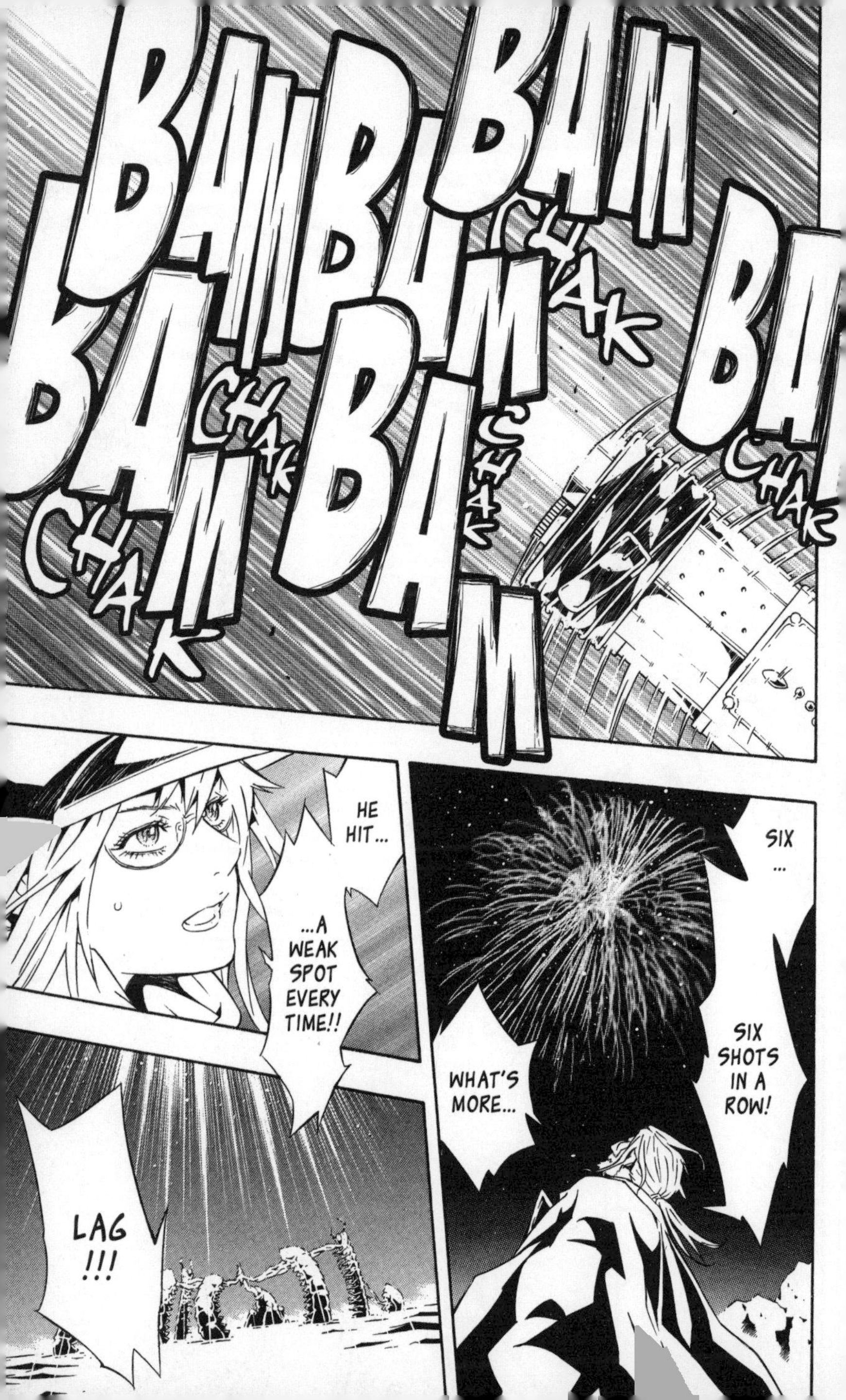
BAM
CHAK
BAM
BAM
CHAK
BAM
CHAK
BAM
CHAK
BAM
CHAK
SIX...
SIX SHOTS IN A ROW!
WHAT'S MORE...
HE HIT...
...A WEAK SPOT EVERY TIME!!
LAG!!!

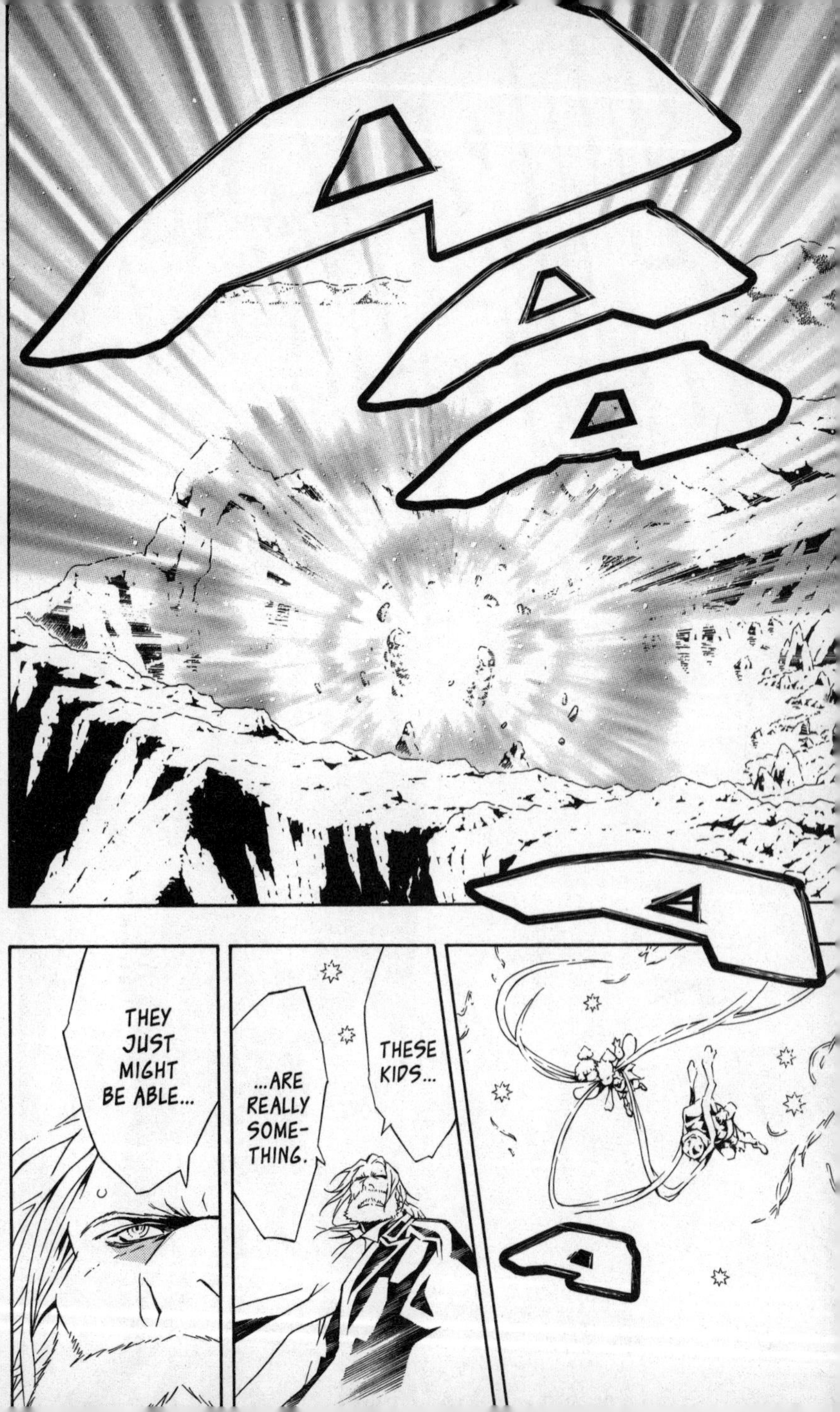
THESE KIDS...
...ARE REALLY SOME-THING.
THEY JUST MIGHT BE ABLE...

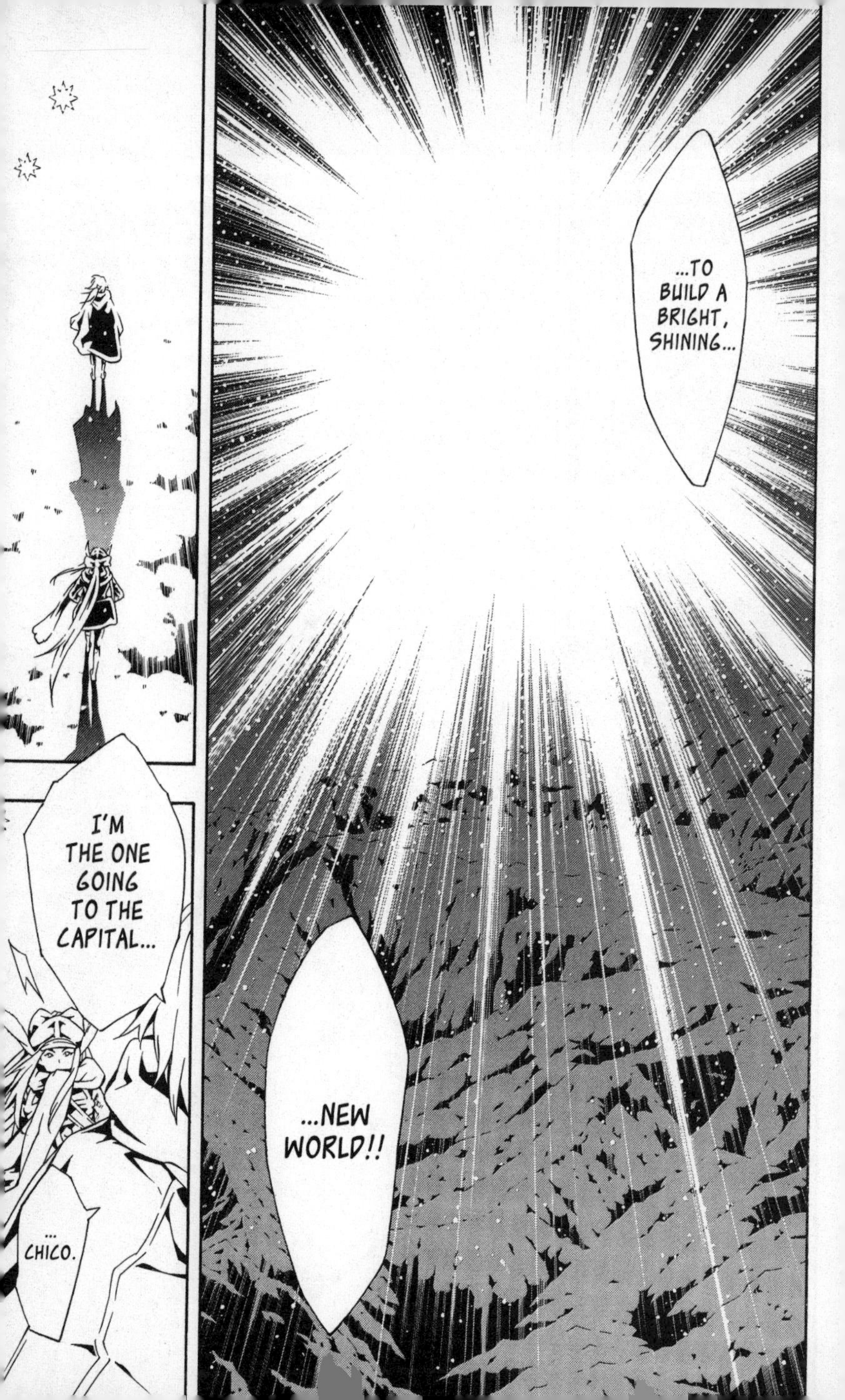
I'M THE ONE GOING TO THE CAPITAL...
...CHICO.
...TO BUILD A BRIGHT, SHINING...
...NEW WORLD!!

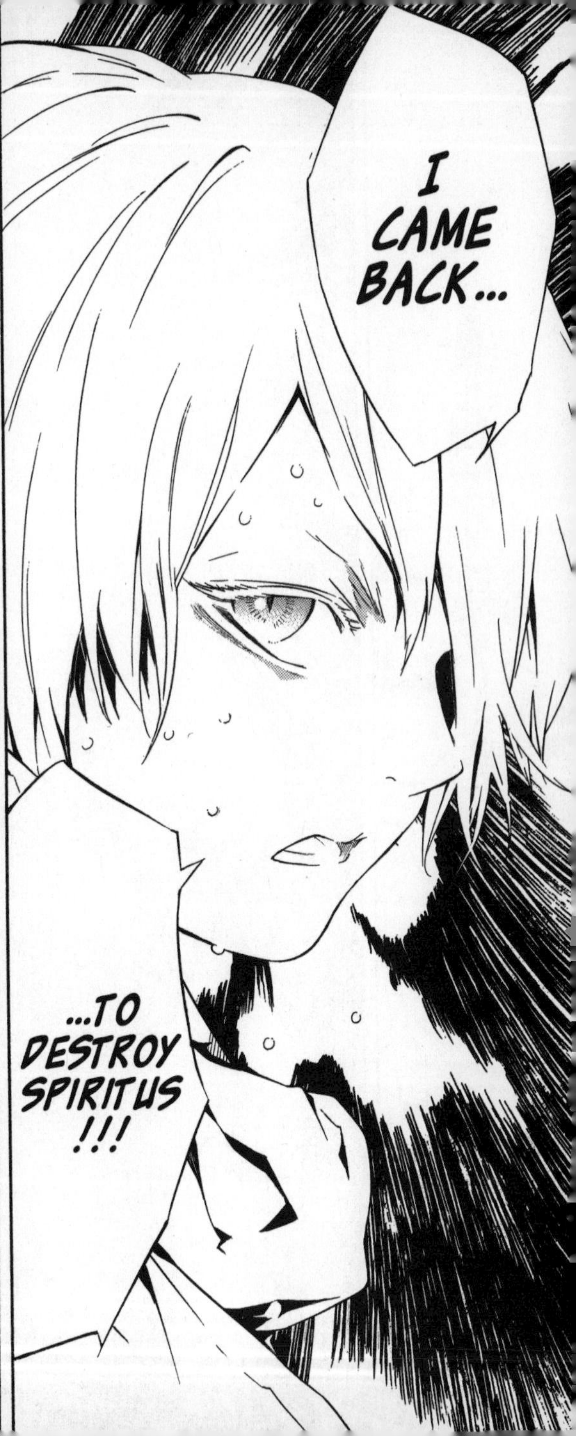
I CAME BACK...
...TO DESTROY SPIRITUS !!!

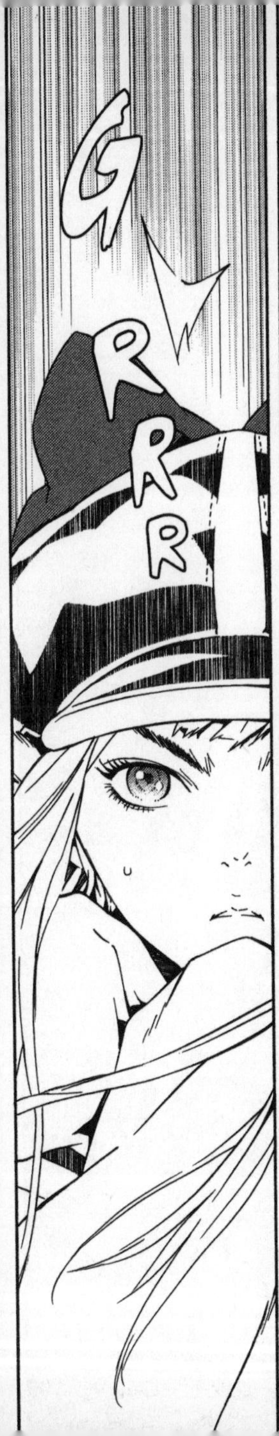
GRRR

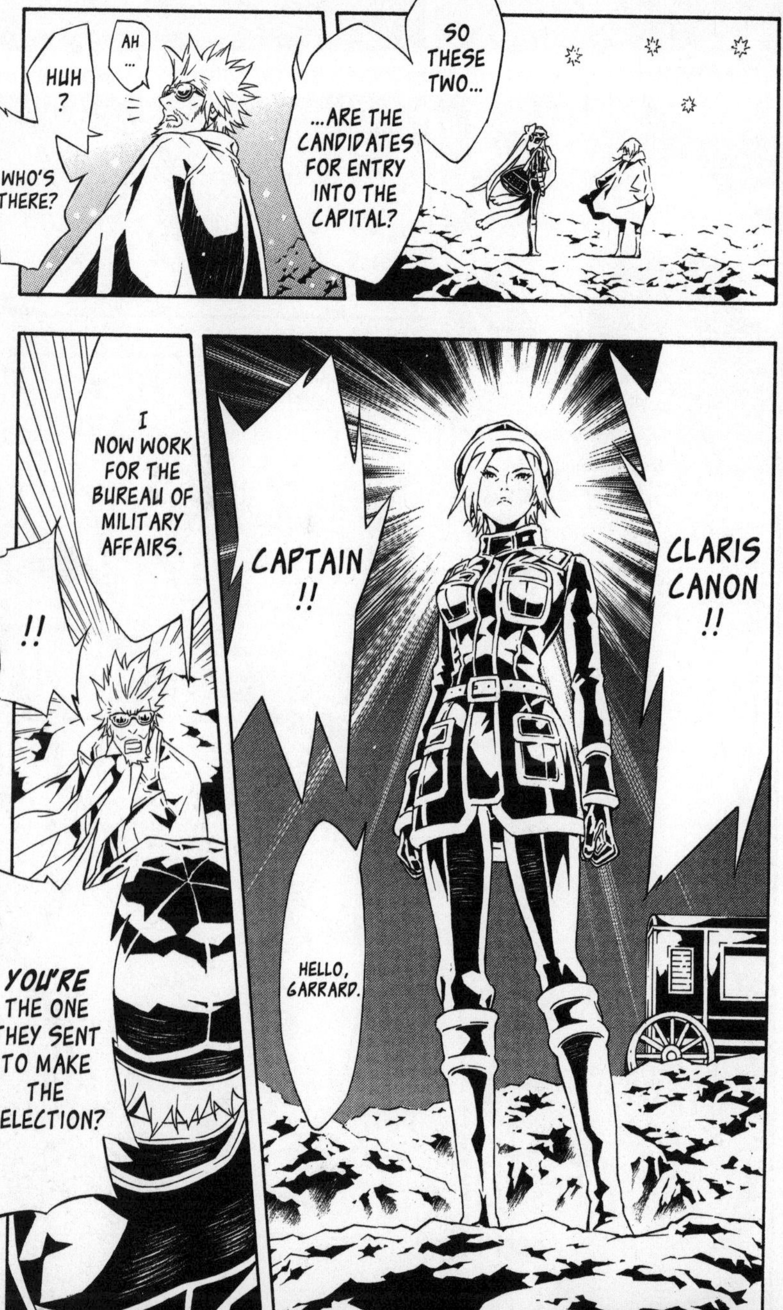
SO THESE TWO...
...ARE THE CANDIDATES FOR ENTRY INTO THE CAPITAL?
AH ...
HUH ?
WHO'S THERE?
CLARIS CANON !!
CAPTAIN !!
HELLO, GARRARD.
I NOW WORK FOR THE BUREAU OF MILITARY AFFAIRS.
!!
YOU'RE THE ONE THEY SENT TO MAKE THE SELECTION?

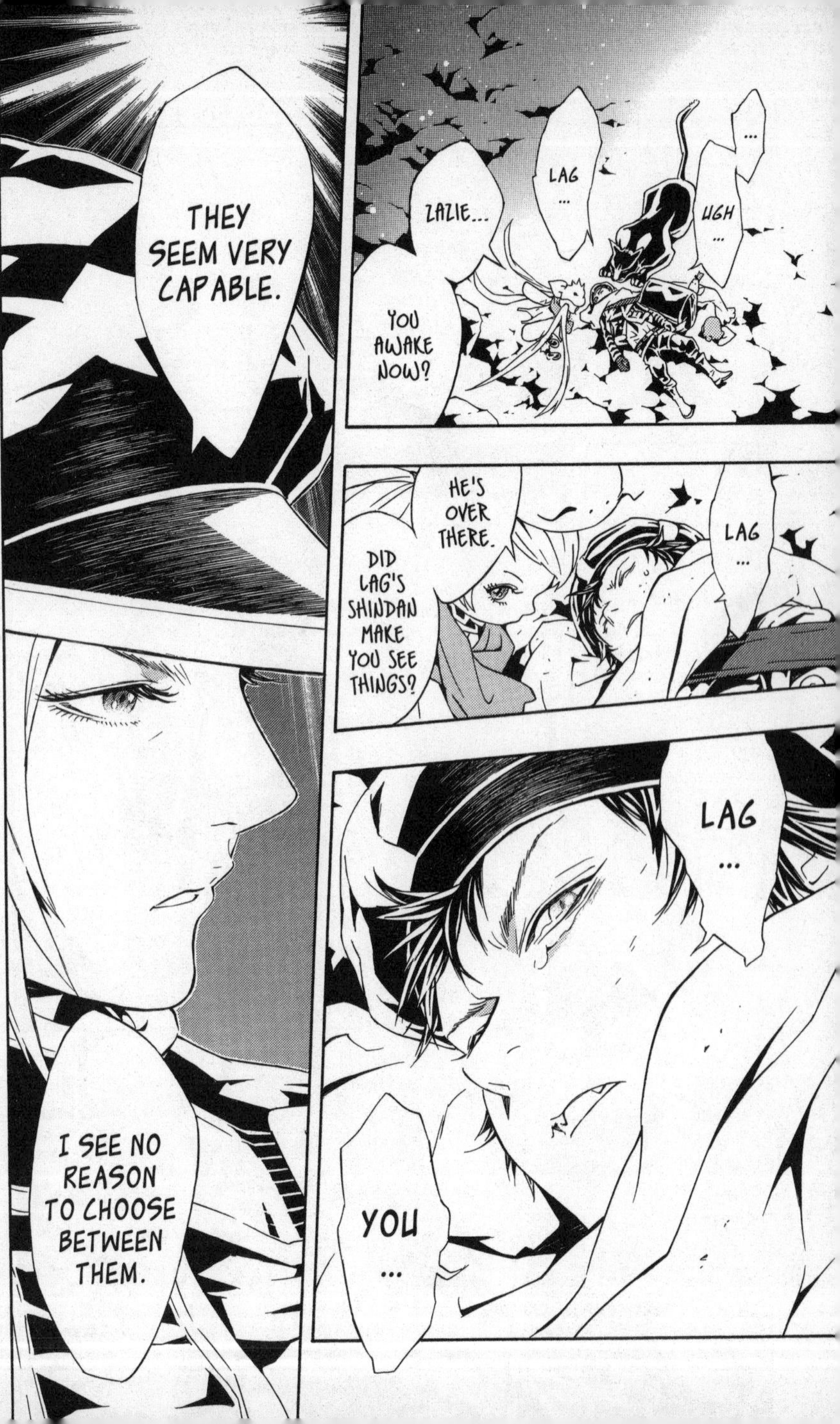
...
UGH ...
LAG ...
ZAZIE...
YOU AWAKE NOW?
LAG ...
HE'S OVER THERE.
DID LAG'S SHINDAN MAKE YOU SEE THINGS?
LAG ...
YOU ...
THEY SEEM VERY CAPABLE.
I SEE NO REASON TO CHOOSE BETWEEN THEM.

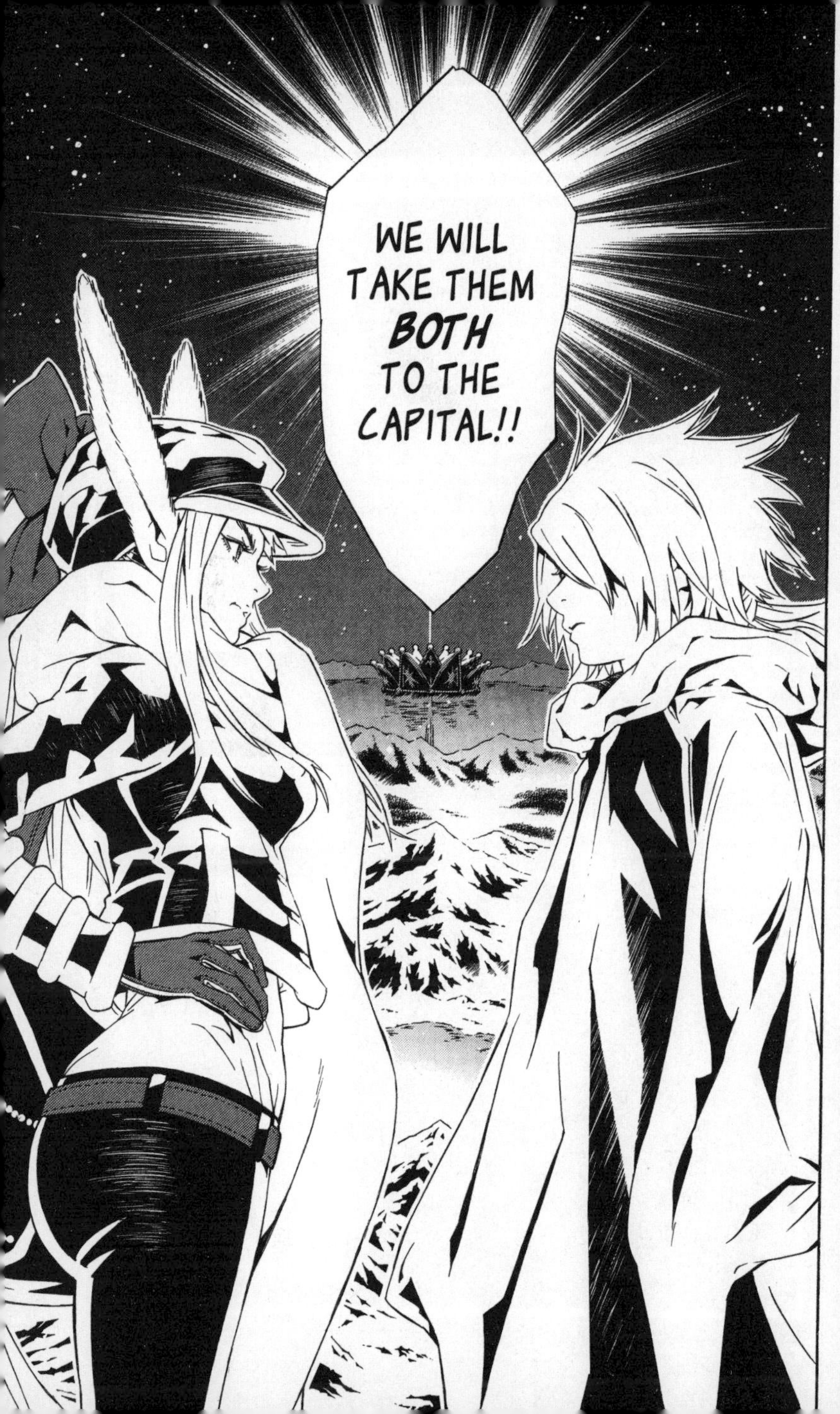
WE WILL TAKE THEM ***BOTH*** TO THE CAPITAL!!

■ THE 358TH DAY

My, my! Lag has grown quite manly! But while he always used to wear his emotions on his sleeve, now he acts so cool. As Zazie noted, something's up with that boy.

...I'LL SAVE THE WORLD!!
I SWEAR ...

And poor Sylvette, who had her *heart* stolen by Spiritus. (*Sob!*) Would they like me to take care of her? Nurse her? Bathe her? Definitely bathe her! What's that? You say soon I'll need a nurse myself? Hey...how old am I supposed to be, anyway? Does anyone know?

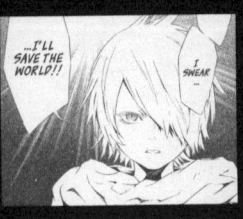

■ HIKARIBARI

Akabari was a gentle Shindan that allowed Lag's *heart* to bring forth the memories stored inside objects. Hikaribari seems to be a shindan that gathers *heart*, amplifies it and directs it at the target. It doesn't look like it replays memories like Akabari did. After seeing Akabari at work, I feel like Hikaribari is missing something, but its power is tremendous. In order to defeat Spiritus, he'll need Hikaribari...or me. Reverberate! **Washibari!** ("Geezer's needle!")

GRAAAH
HIKARI-BARI!!
PENE-TRATE!

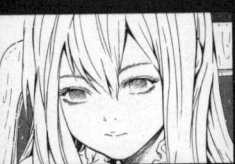

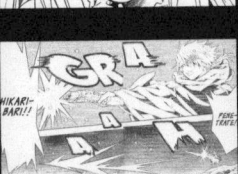

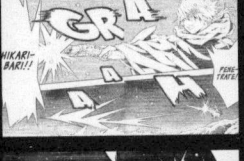

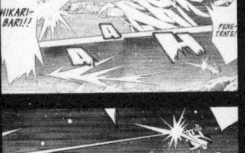

■ CHICO'S HAIR

Hey, her hair's turned white. She acts like it's no big deal, but is that true? Some animals' hair turns white with age. As Chico carries the hopes of the people and stores their *hearts* in her amber, she seems exhausted, body and soul. At least, that's the way it seems to me.

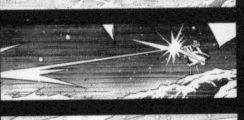

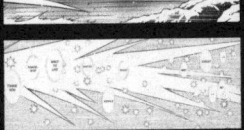

n.b.: Waltz for Debby / Title of an album by jazz pianist Bill Evans and his trio, recorded live in 1961 at the Village Vanguard. The title song was dedicated to his little niece Debby.

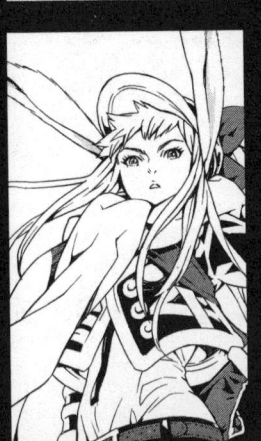

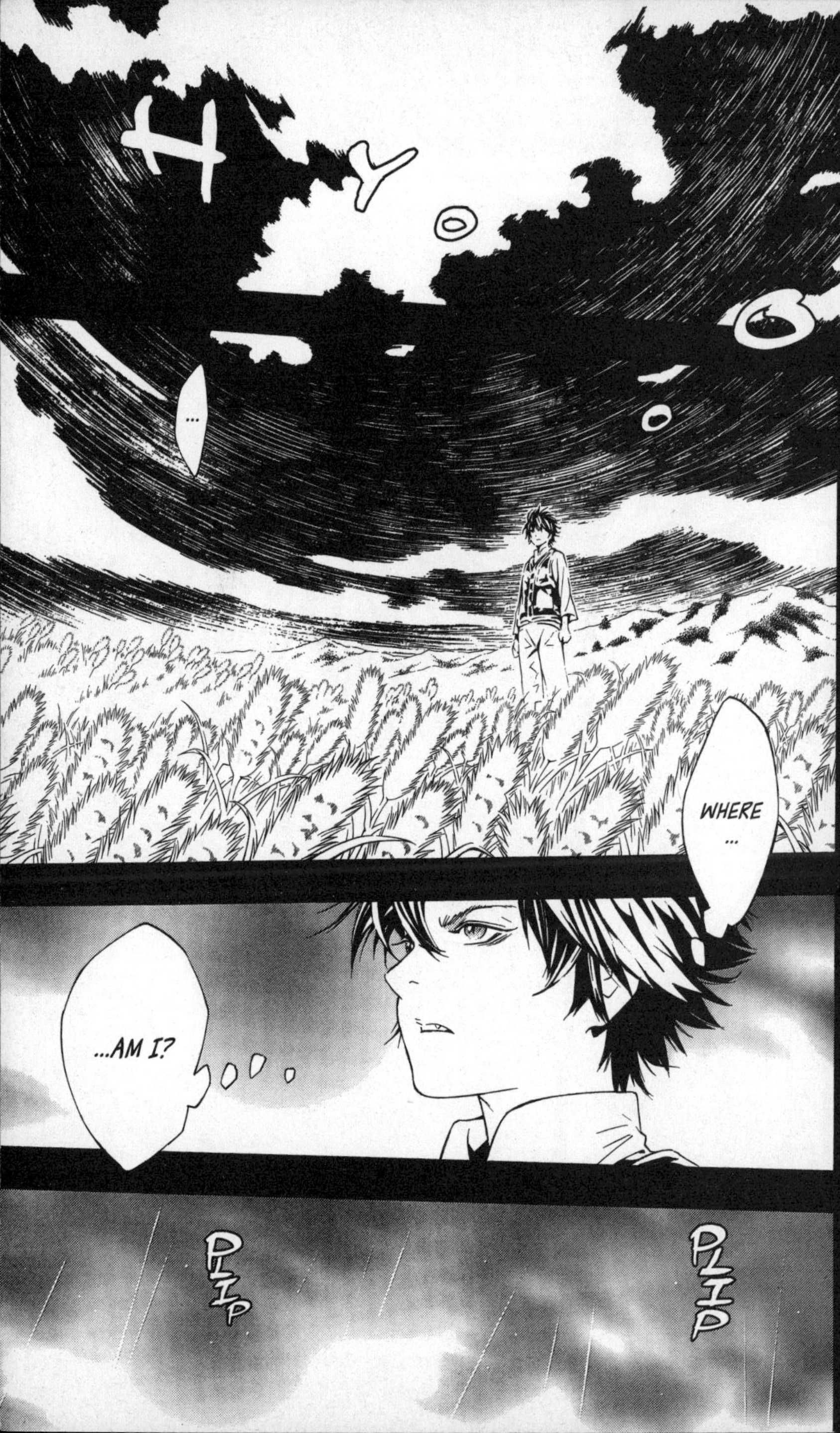
...
WHERE ...
...AM I?
PLIP
PLIP

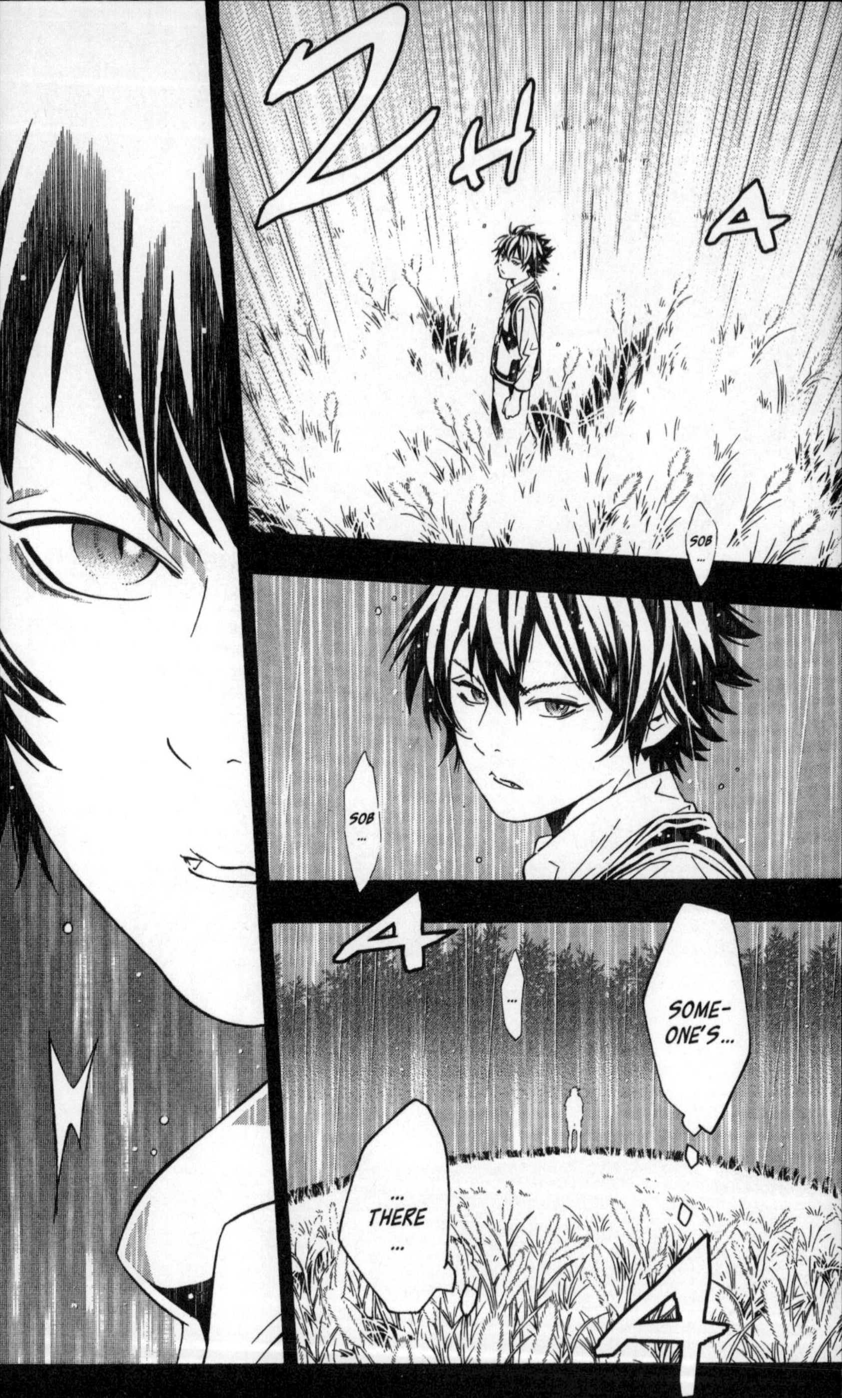
SOB...
SOB...
SOME-ONE'S...
...
...THERE...

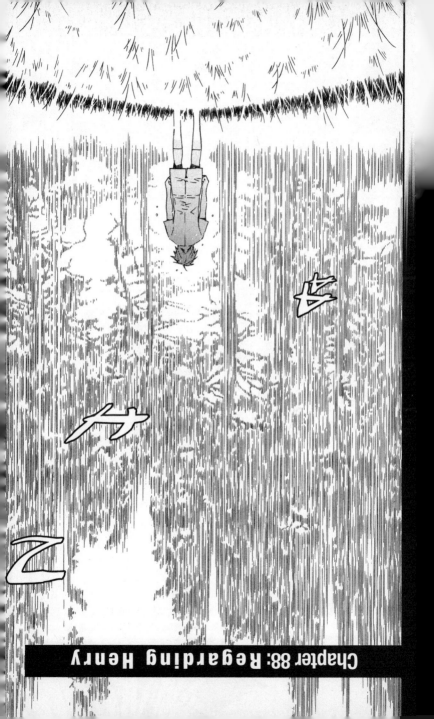

Chapter 88: Regarding Henry

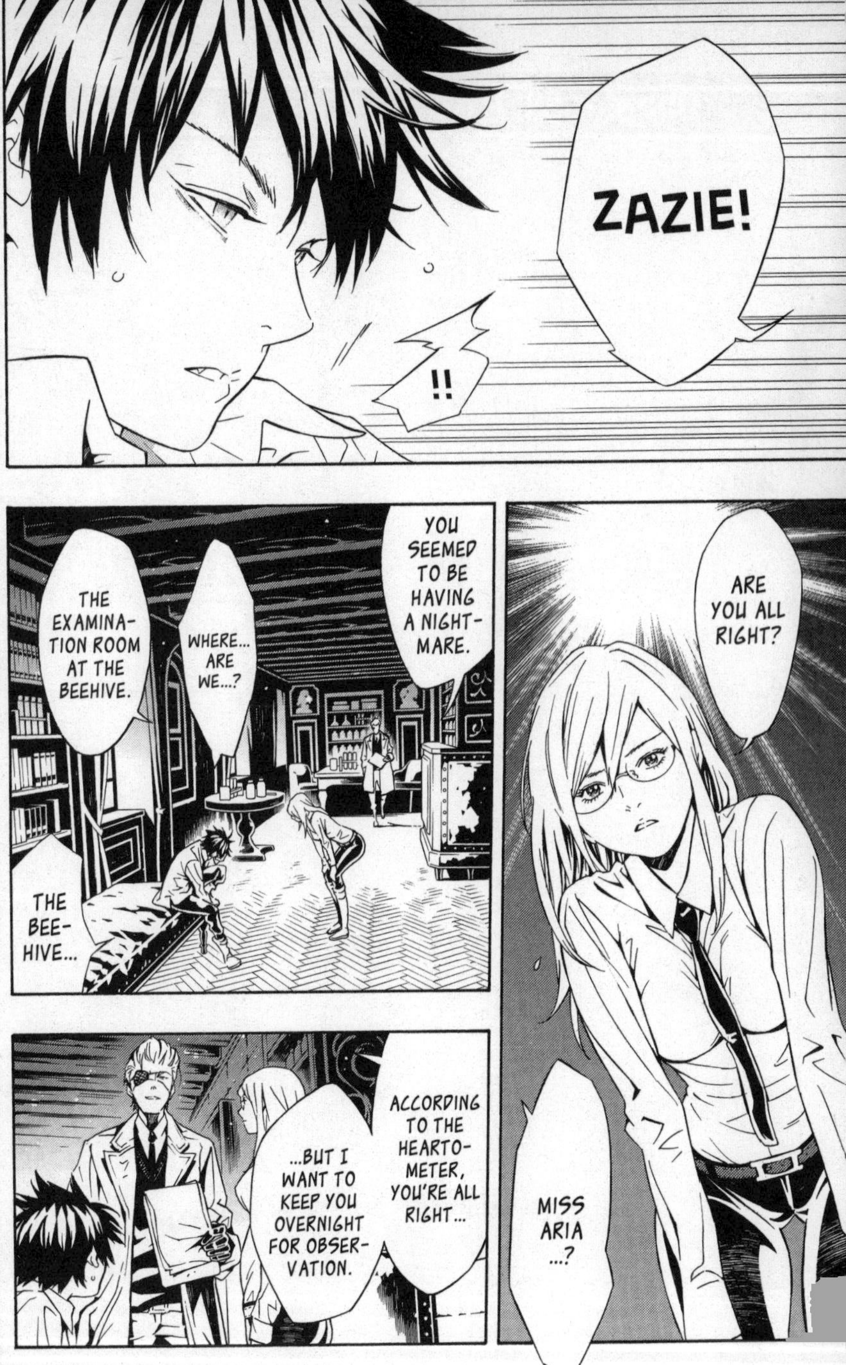
ZAZIE!
!!
ARE YOU ALL RIGHT?
MISS ARIA ...?
YOU SEEMED TO BE HAVING A NIGHT-MARE.
WHERE... ARE WE...?
THE EXAMINA-TION ROOM AT THE BEEHIVE.
THE BEE-HIVE...
ACCORDING TO THE HEARTO-METER, YOU'RE ALL RIGHT...
...BUT I WANT TO KEEP YOU OVERNIGHT FOR OBSER-VATION.

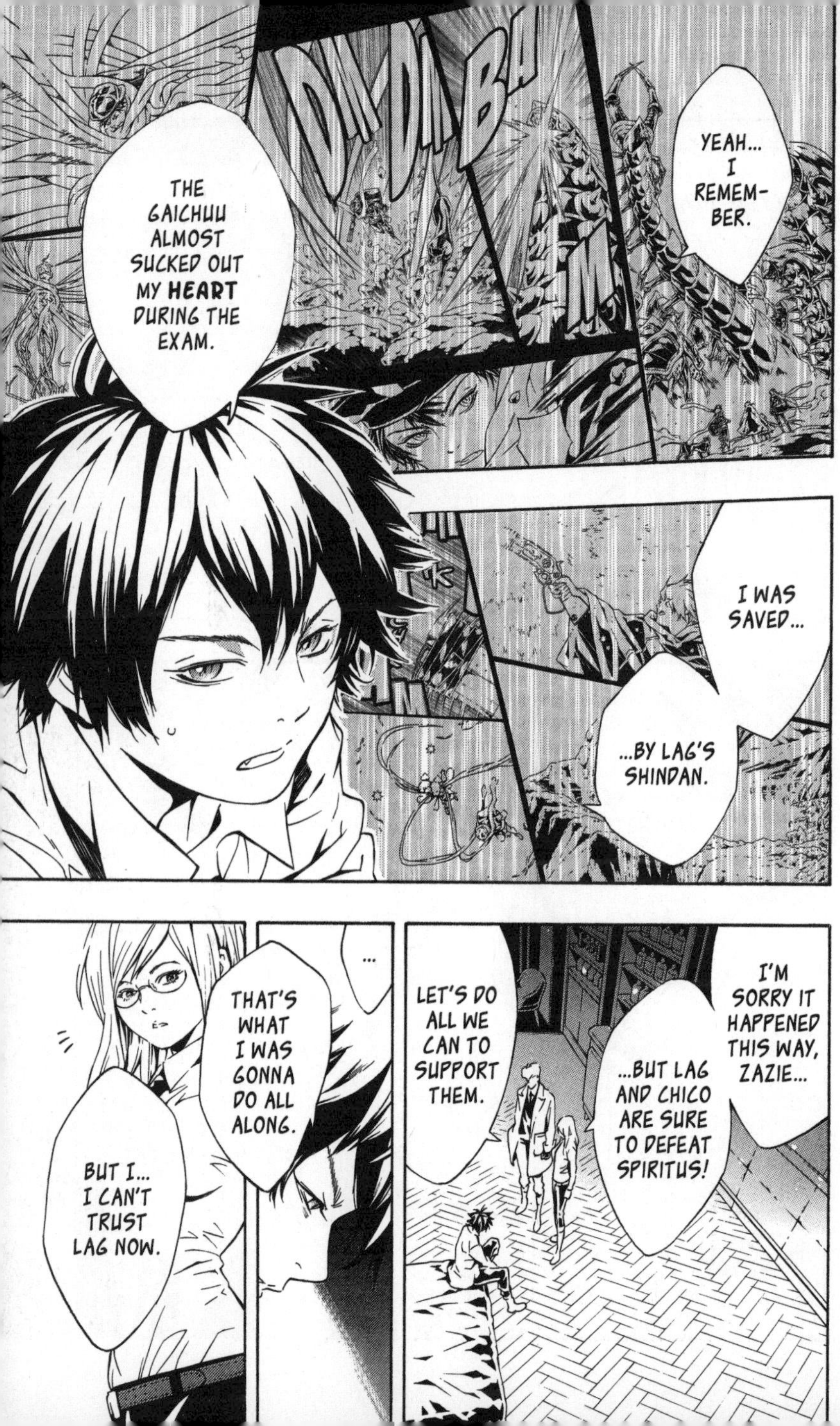
YEAH... I REMEMBER.
DM DM BA
I WAS SAVED...
...BY LAG'S SHINDAN.
THE GAICHUU ALMOST SUCKED OUT MY **HEART** DURING THE EXAM.
I'M SORRY IT HAPPENED THIS WAY, ZAZIE...
...BUT LAG AND CHICO ARE SURE TO DEFEAT SPIRITUS!
LET'S DO ALL WE CAN TO SUPPORT THEM.
...
THAT'S WHAT I WAS GONNA DO ALL ALONG.
BUT I... I CAN'T TRUST LAG NOW.

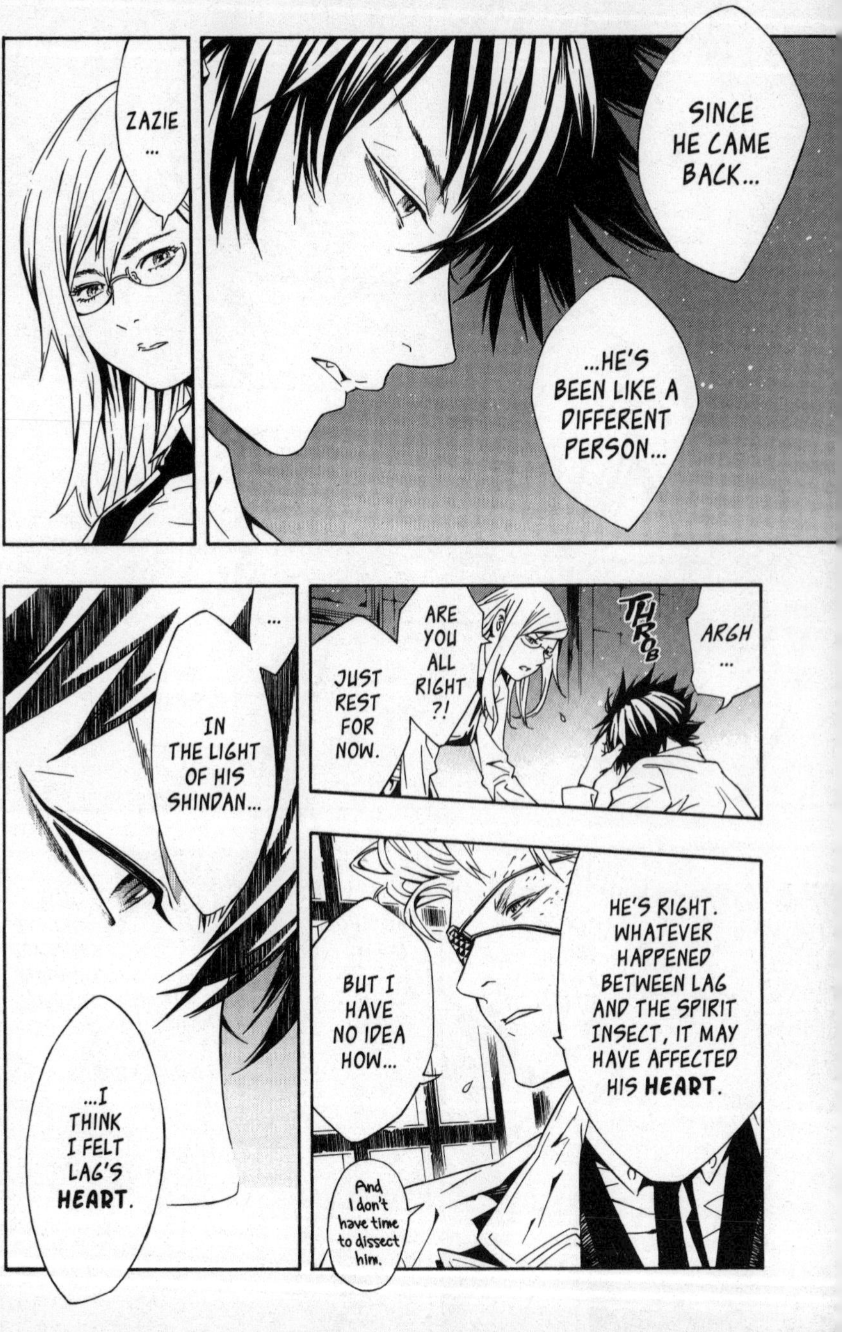
SINCE HE CAME BACK...
...HE'S BEEN LIKE A DIFFERENT PERSON...
ZAZIE ...
ARGH ...
THROB
ARE YOU ALL RIGHT ?!
JUST REST FOR NOW.
HE'S RIGHT. WHATEVER HAPPENED BETWEEN LAG AND THE SPIRIT INSECT, IT MAY HAVE AFFECTED HIS **HEART**.
BUT I HAVE NO IDEA HOW...
And I don't have time to dissect him.
...
IN THE LIGHT OF HIS SHINDAN...
...I THINK I FELT LAG'S **HEART**.

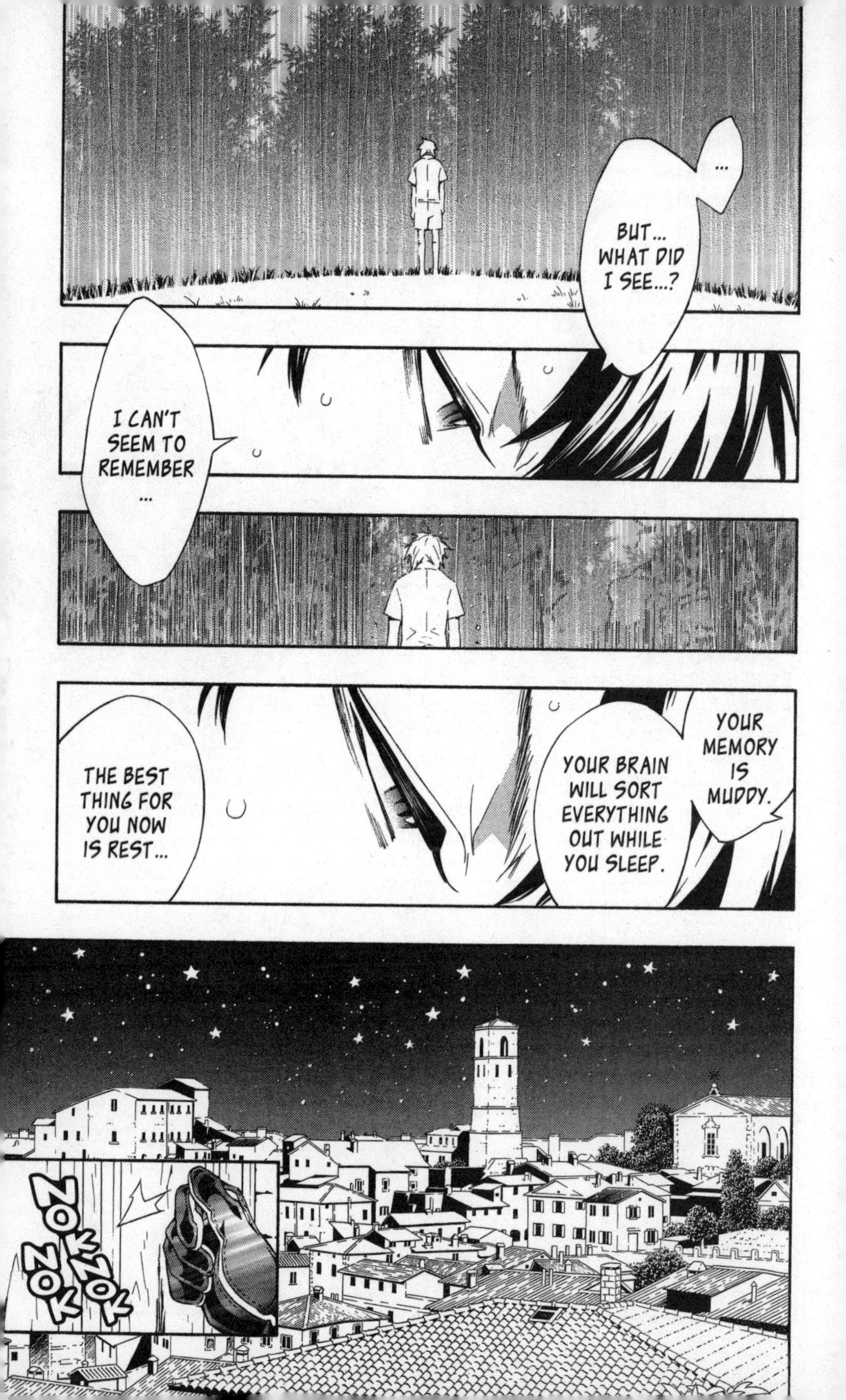
...
BUT... WHAT DID I SEE...?
I CAN'T SEEM TO REMEMBER ...
YOUR MEMORY IS MUDDY.
YOUR BRAIN WILL SORT EVERYTHING OUT WHILE YOU SLEEP.
THE BEST THING FOR YOU NOW IS REST...
ZOK ZOK ZOK

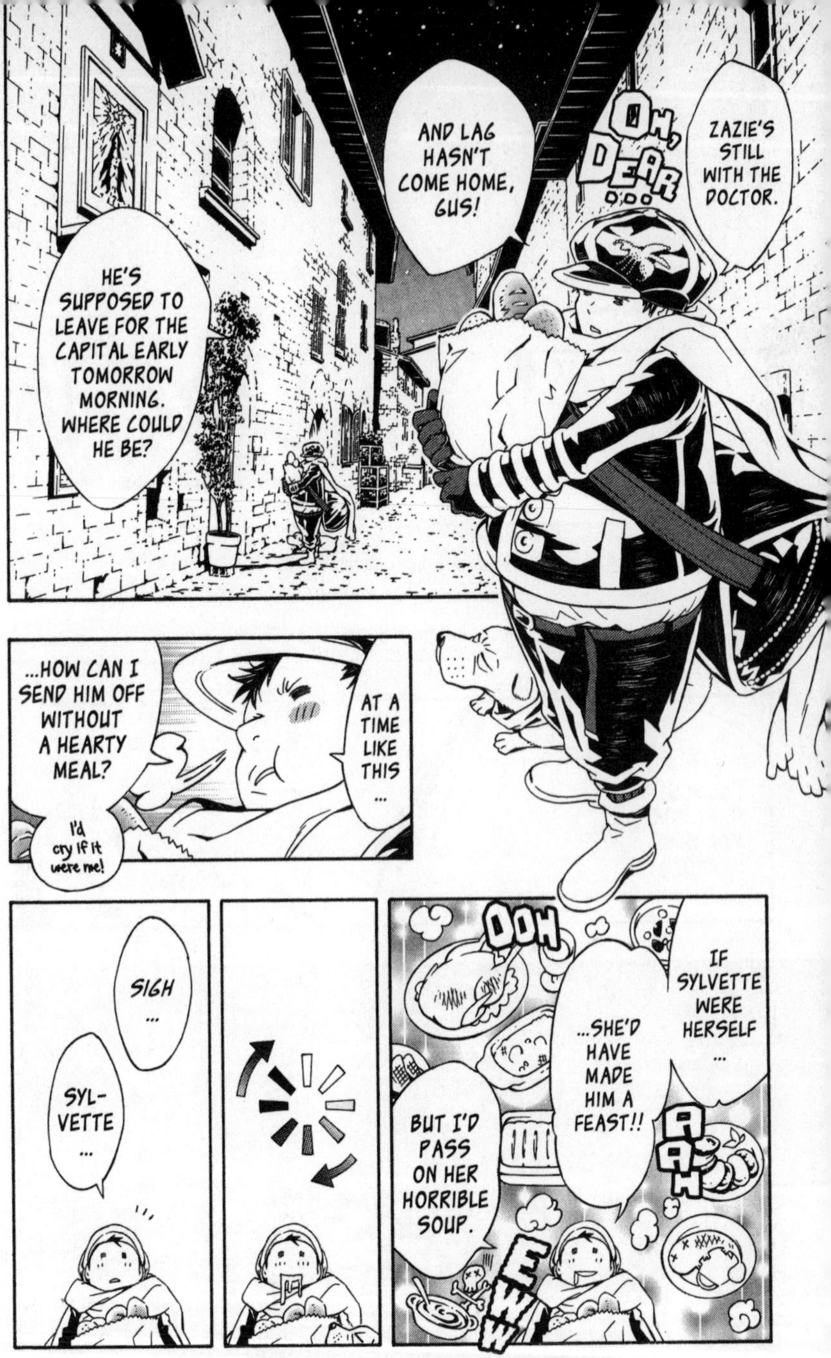
ZAZIE'S STILL WITH THE DOCTOR.
OH, DEAR...
AND LAG HASN'T COME HOME, GUS!
HE'S SUPPOSED TO LEAVE FOR THE CAPITAL EARLY TOMORROW MORNING. WHERE COULD HE BE?
AT A TIME LIKE THIS...
...HOW CAN I SEND HIM OFF WITHOUT A HEARTY MEAL?
I'd cry if it were me!
IF SYLVETTE WERE HERSELF...
...SHE'D HAVE MADE HIM A FEAST!!
OOH
AAH
BUT I'D PASS ON HER HORRIBLE SOUP.
EWW
SIGH...
SYL-VETTE...

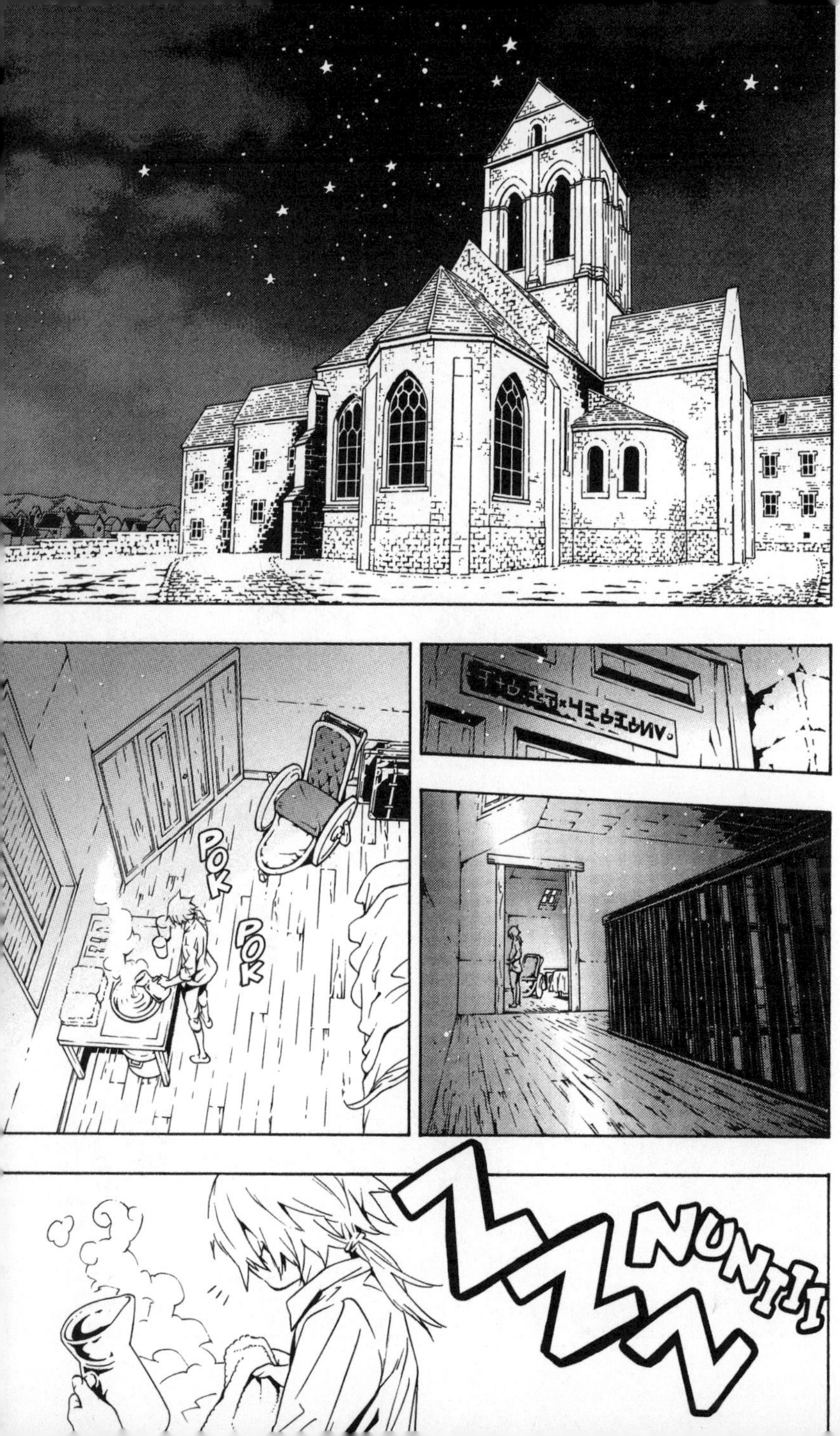
POK
POK
ZZZ
NUNTIII

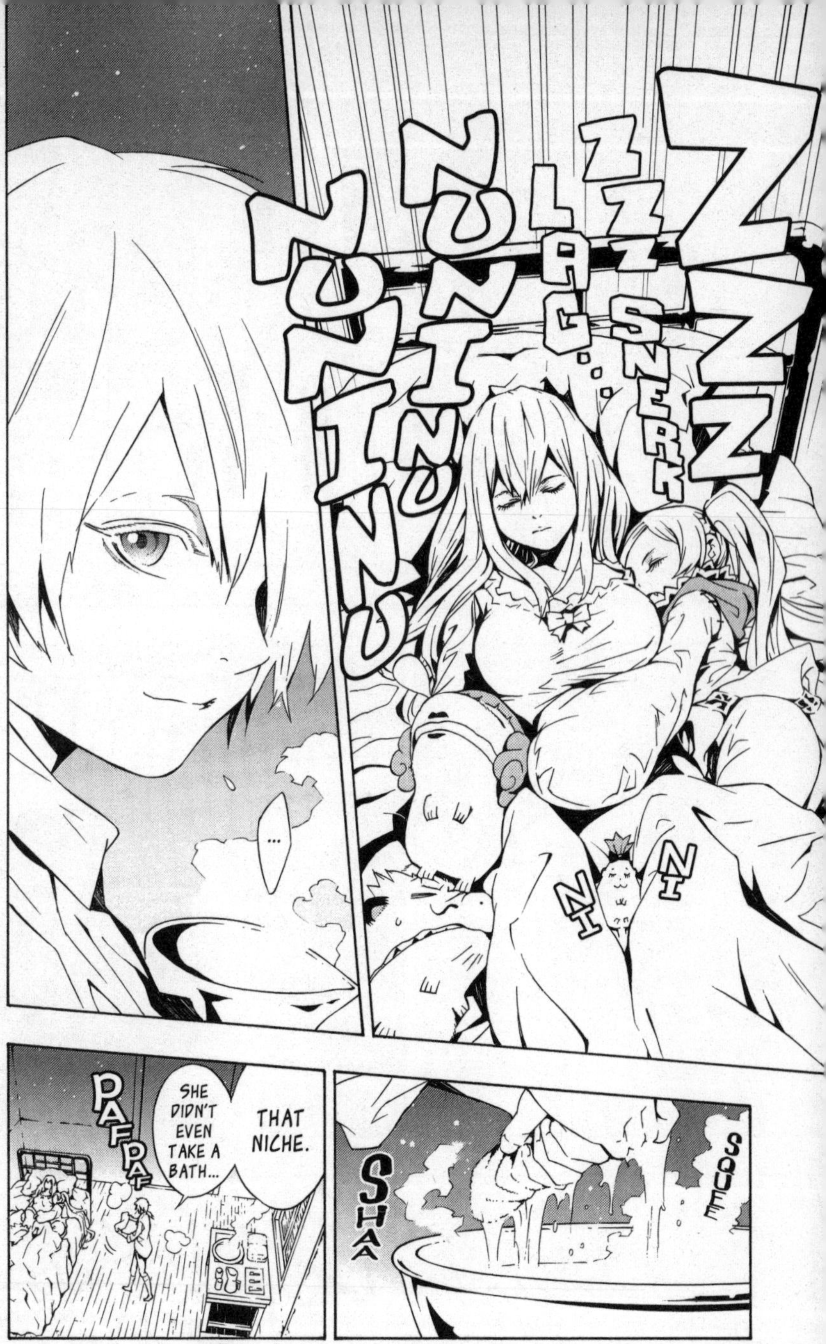
ZZZ
ZZZ SNERK
LAG...
NUNINU
YUNINU
NI NI
...
SQUEE
SHAA
PAFPAF
SHE DIDN'T EVEN TAKE A BATH...
THAT NICHE.

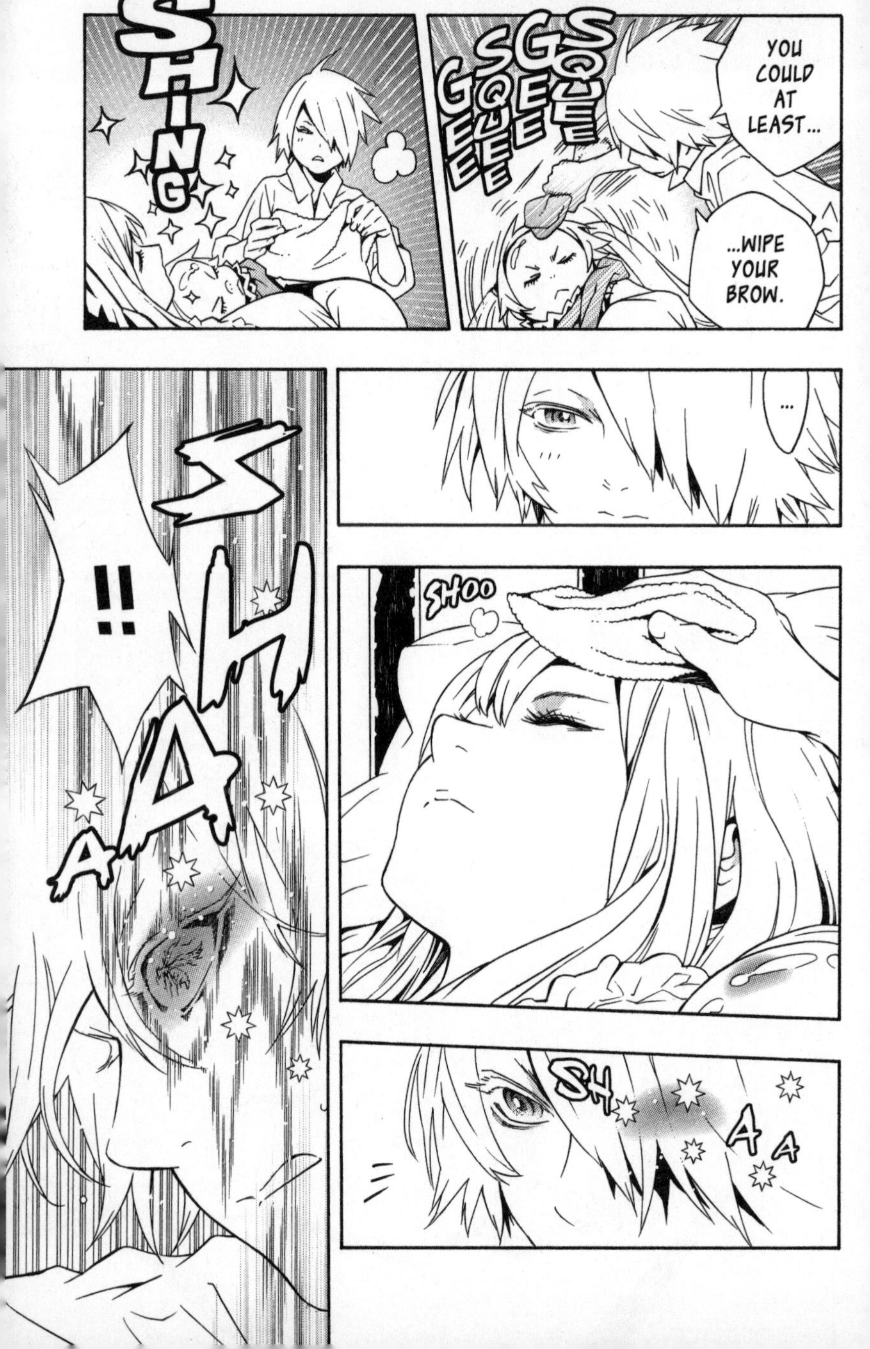
SQUEEE
GQUEEE
YOU COULD AT LEAST...
...WIPE YOUR BROW.
SHING
...
SHOO
SHAA
SHAA!!

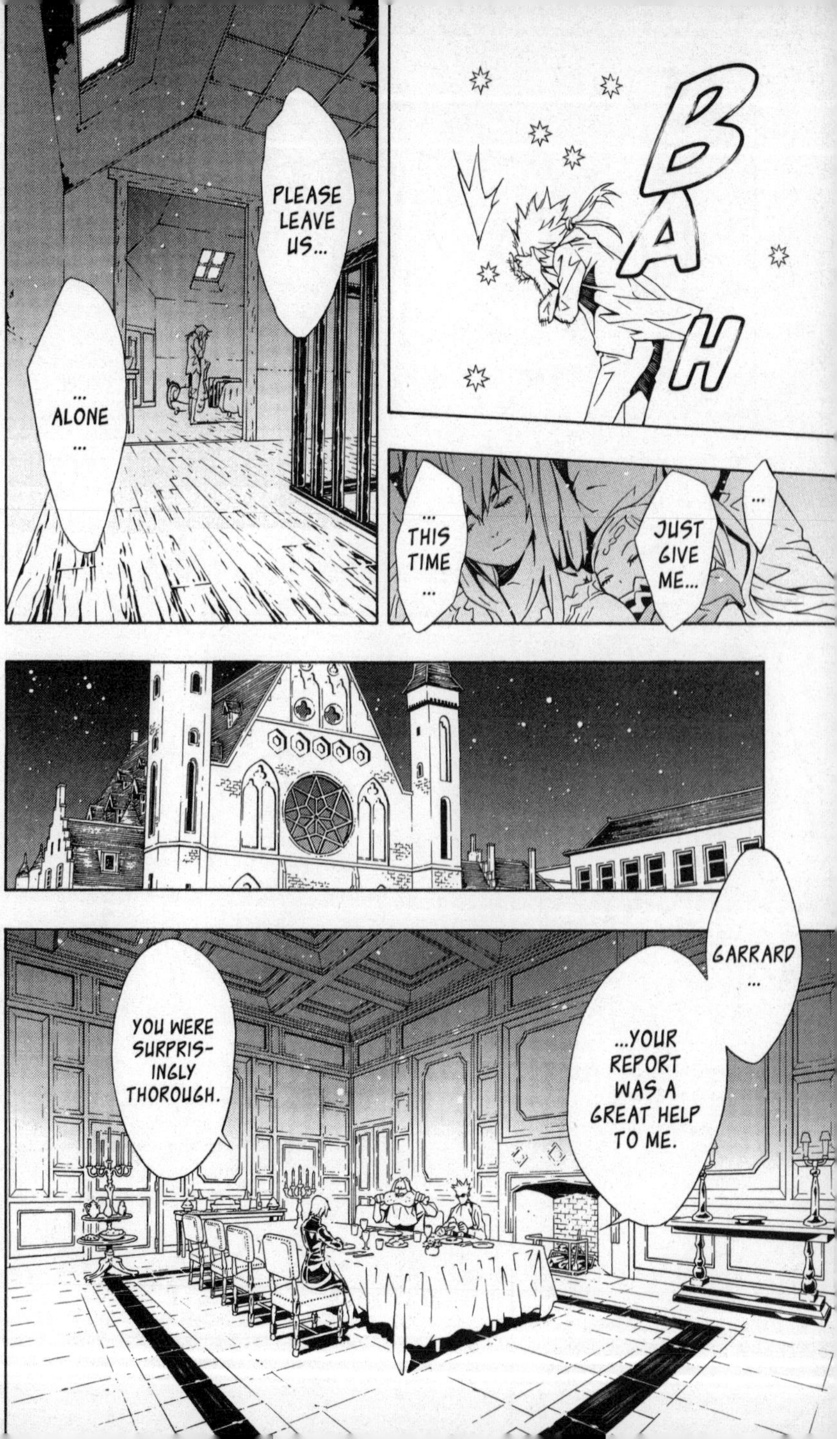
BAH
...
JUST GIVE ME...
...THIS TIME...
PLEASE LEAVE US...
...ALONE...
GARRARD...
...YOUR REPORT WAS A GREAT HELP TO ME.
YOU WERE SURPRIS-INGLY THOROUGH.

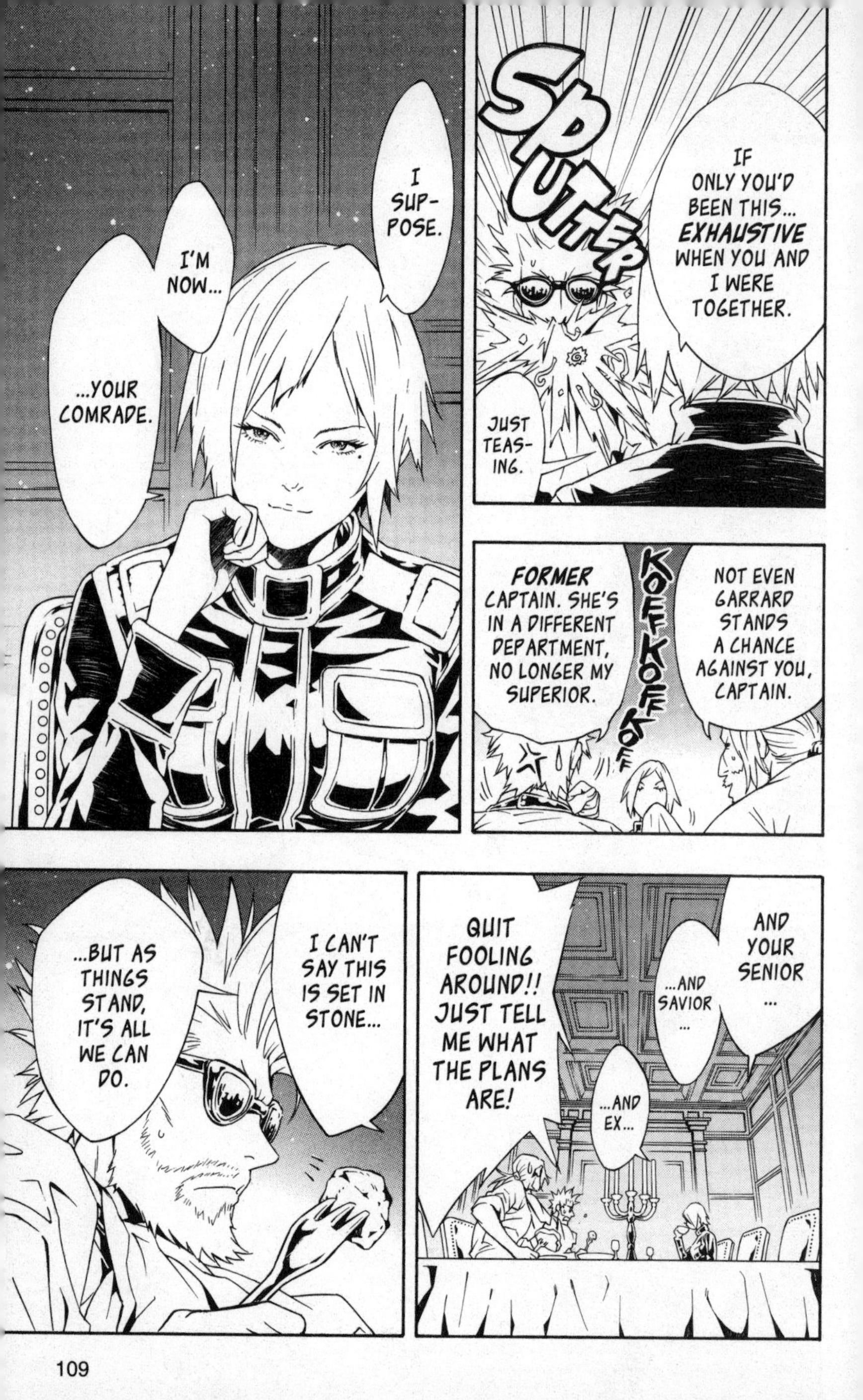
IF ONLY YOU'D BEEN THIS... EXHAUSTIVE WHEN YOU AND I WERE TOGETHER.
SPUTTER
JUST TEASING.
I SUPPOSE.
I'M NOW...
...YOUR COMRADE.
NOT EVEN GARRARD STANDS A CHANCE AGAINST YOU, CAPTAIN.
KOFF KOFF KOFF
FORMER CAPTAIN. SHE'S IN A DIFFERENT DEPARTMENT, NO LONGER MY SUPERIOR.
AND YOUR SENIOR ...
...AND SAVIOR ...
...AND EX...
QUIT FOOLING AROUND!! JUST TELL ME WHAT THE PLANS ARE!
I CAN'T SAY THIS IS SET IN STONE...
...BUT AS THINGS STAND, IT'S ALL WE CAN DO.

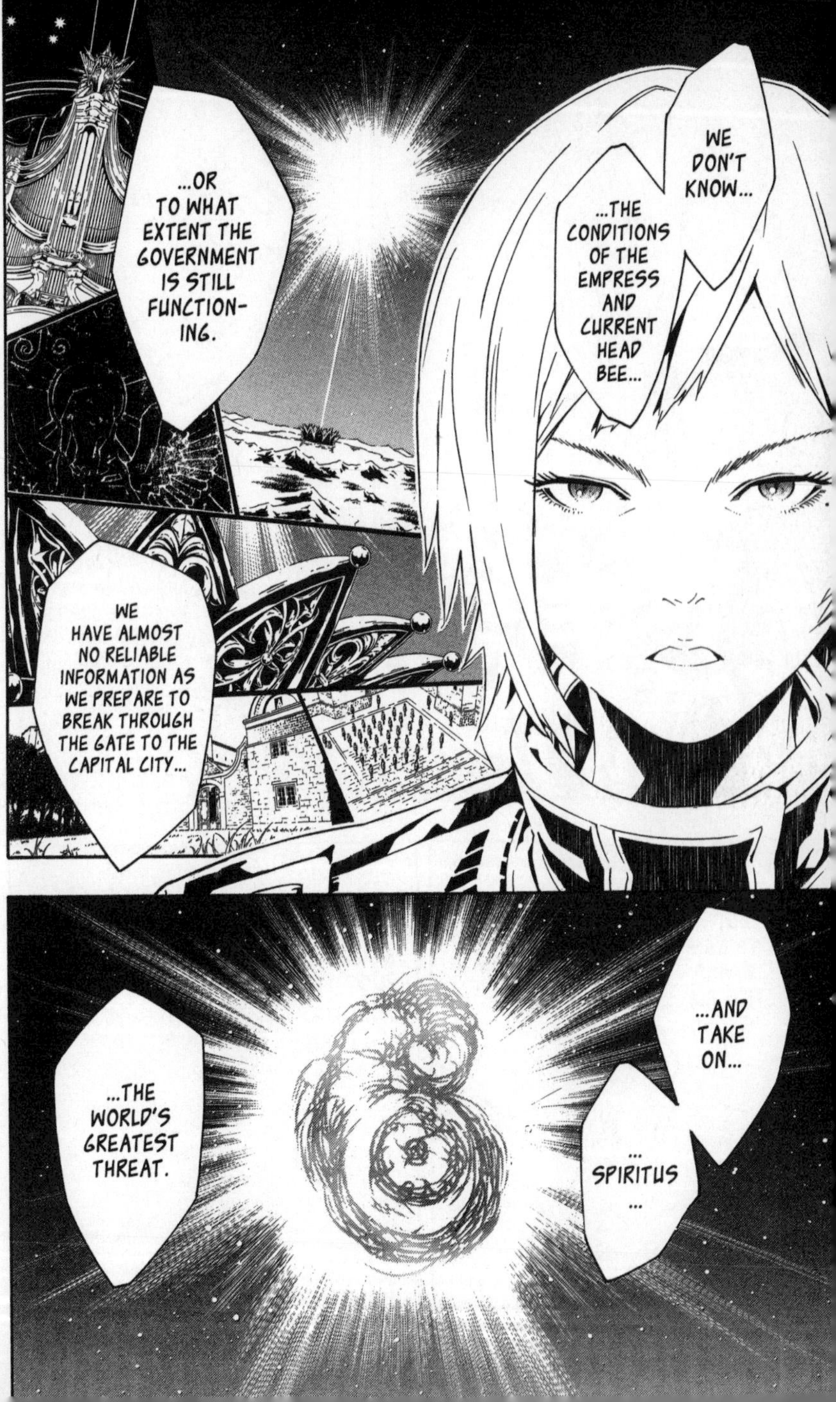
WE DON'T KNOW...
...THE CONDITIONS OF THE EMPRESS AND CURRENT HEAD BEE...
...OR TO WHAT EXTENT THE GOVERNMENT IS STILL FUNCTION-ING.
WE HAVE ALMOST NO RELIABLE INFORMATION AS WE PREPARE TO BREAK THROUGH THE GATE TO THE CAPITAL CITY...
...AND TAKE ON...
... SPIRITUS ...
...THE WORLD'S GREATEST THREAT.

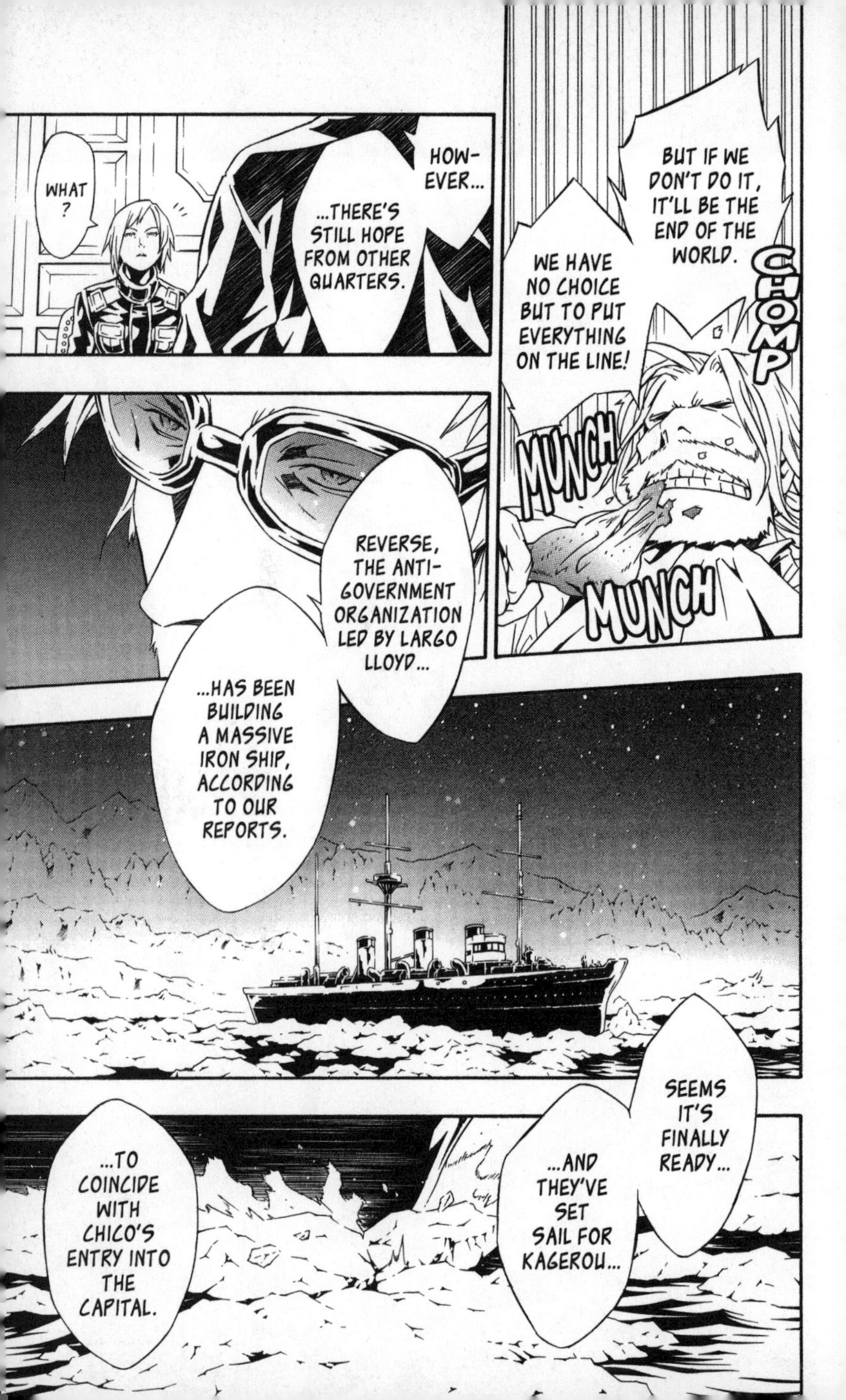
BUT IF WE DON'T DO IT, IT'LL BE THE END OF THE WORLD.
WE HAVE NO CHOICE BUT TO PUT EVERYTHING ON THE LINE!
CHOMP
MUNCH
MUNCH
HOW-EVER...
...THERE'S STILL HOPE FROM OTHER QUARTERS.
WHAT ?
REVERSE, THE ANTI-GOVERNMENT ORGANIZATION LED BY LARGO LLOYD...
...HAS BEEN BUILDING A MASSIVE IRON SHIP, ACCORDING TO OUR REPORTS.
SEEMS IT'S FINALLY READY...
...AND THEY'VE SET SAIL FOR KAGEROU...
...TO COINCIDE WITH CHICO'S ENTRY INTO THE CAPITAL.

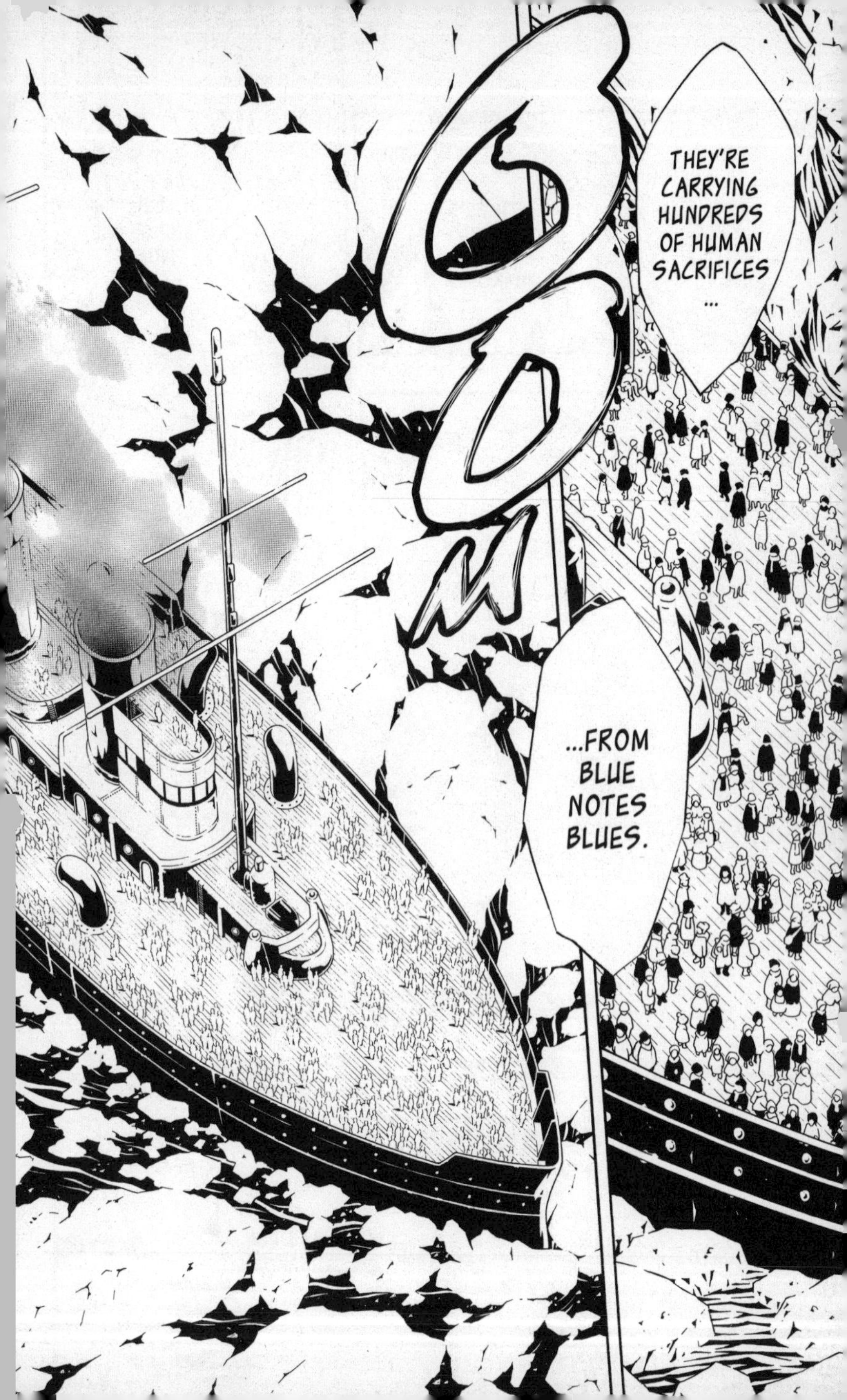
THEY'RE CARRYING HUNDREDS OF HUMAN SACRIFICES...
...FROM BLUE NOTES BLUES.
GOM

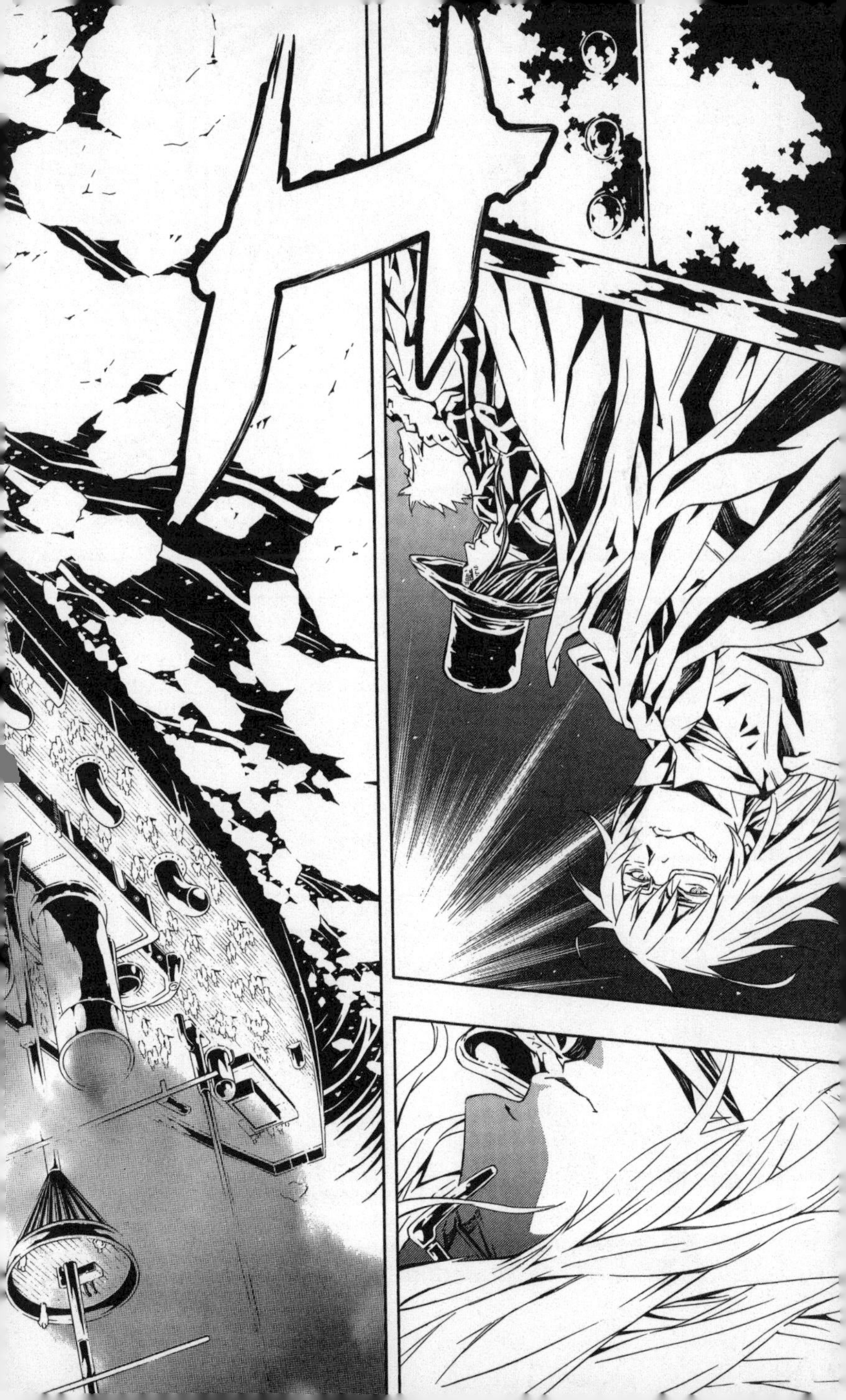

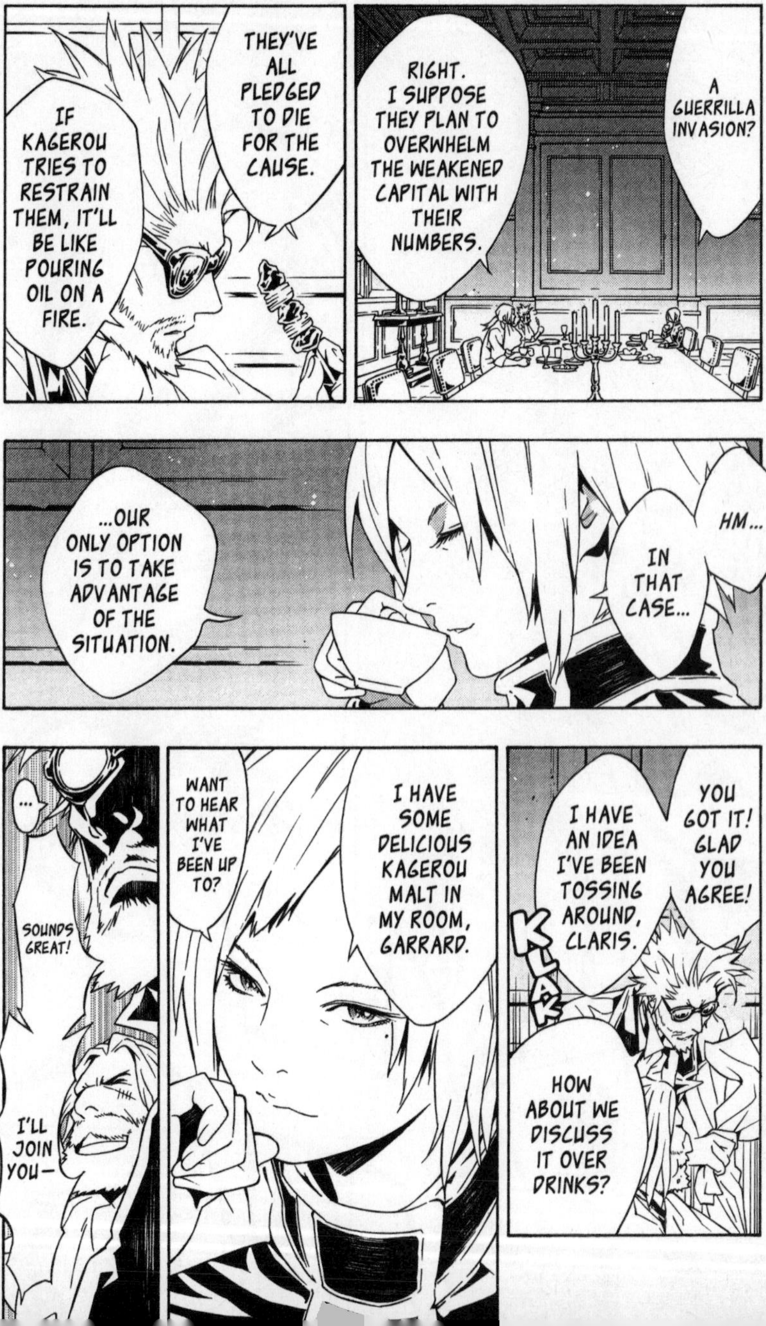
A GUERRILLA INVASION?
RIGHT. I SUPPOSE THEY PLAN TO OVERWHELM THE WEAKENED CAPITAL WITH THEIR NUMBERS.
THEY'VE ALL PLEDGED TO DIE FOR THE CAUSE.
IF KAGEROU TRIES TO RESTRAIN THEM, IT'LL BE LIKE POURING OIL ON A FIRE.
HM...
IN THAT CASE...
...OUR ONLY OPTION IS TO TAKE ADVANTAGE OF THE SITUATION.
YOU GOT IT! GLAD YOU AGREE!
I HAVE AN IDEA I'VE BEEN TOSSING AROUND, CLARIS.
KLAK
HOW ABOUT WE DISCUSS IT OVER DRINKS?
I HAVE SOME DELICIOUS KAGEROU MALT IN MY ROOM, GARRARD.
WANT TO HEAR WHAT I'VE BEEN UP TO?
...
SOUNDS GREAT!
I'LL JOIN YOU—

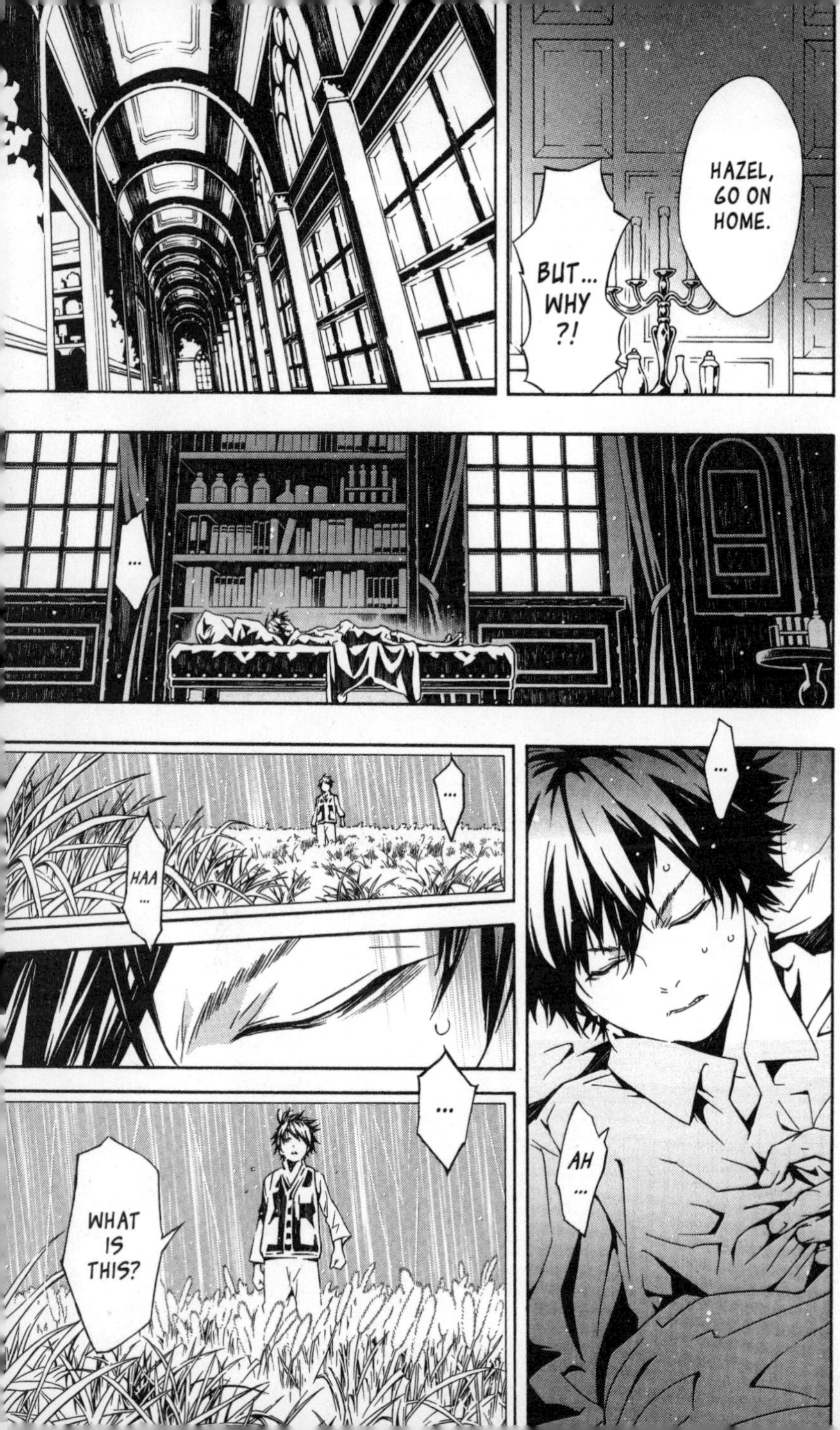
HAZEL, GO ON HOME.
BUT... WHY ?!
...
...
AH ...
...
HAA ...
...
WHAT IS THIS?

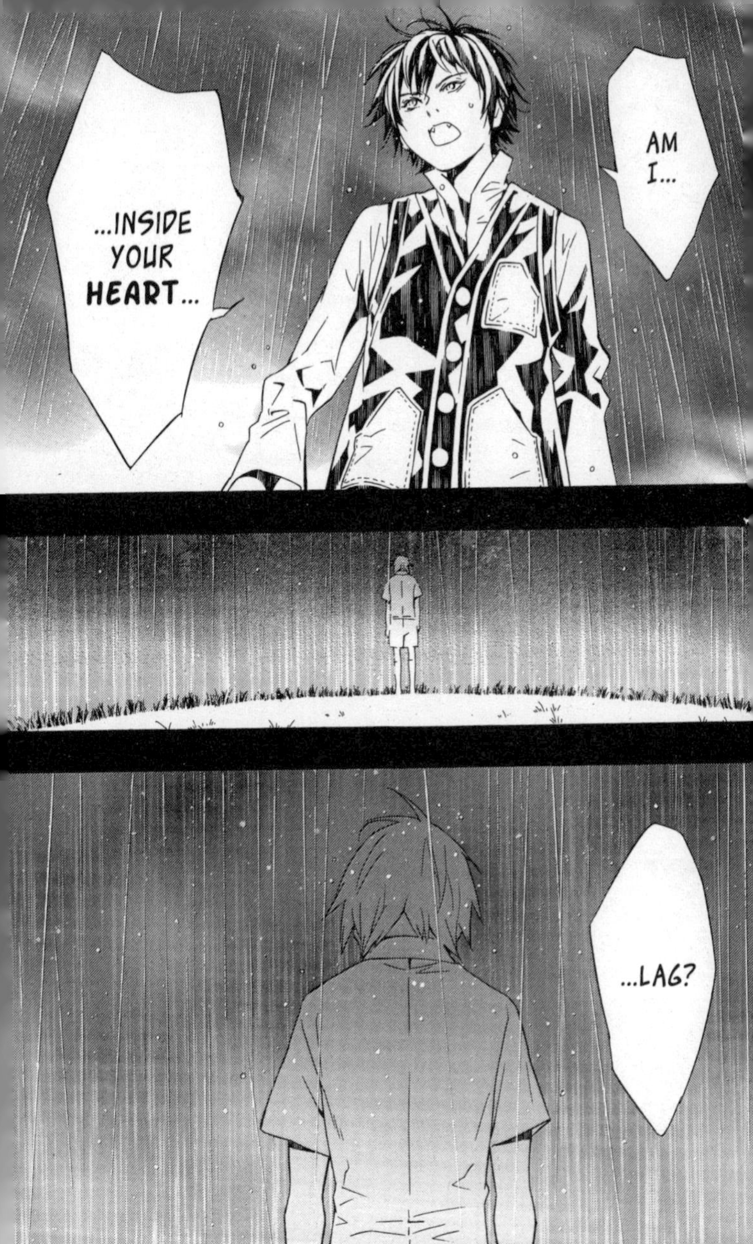
AM I...
...INSIDE YOUR HEART...
...LAG?

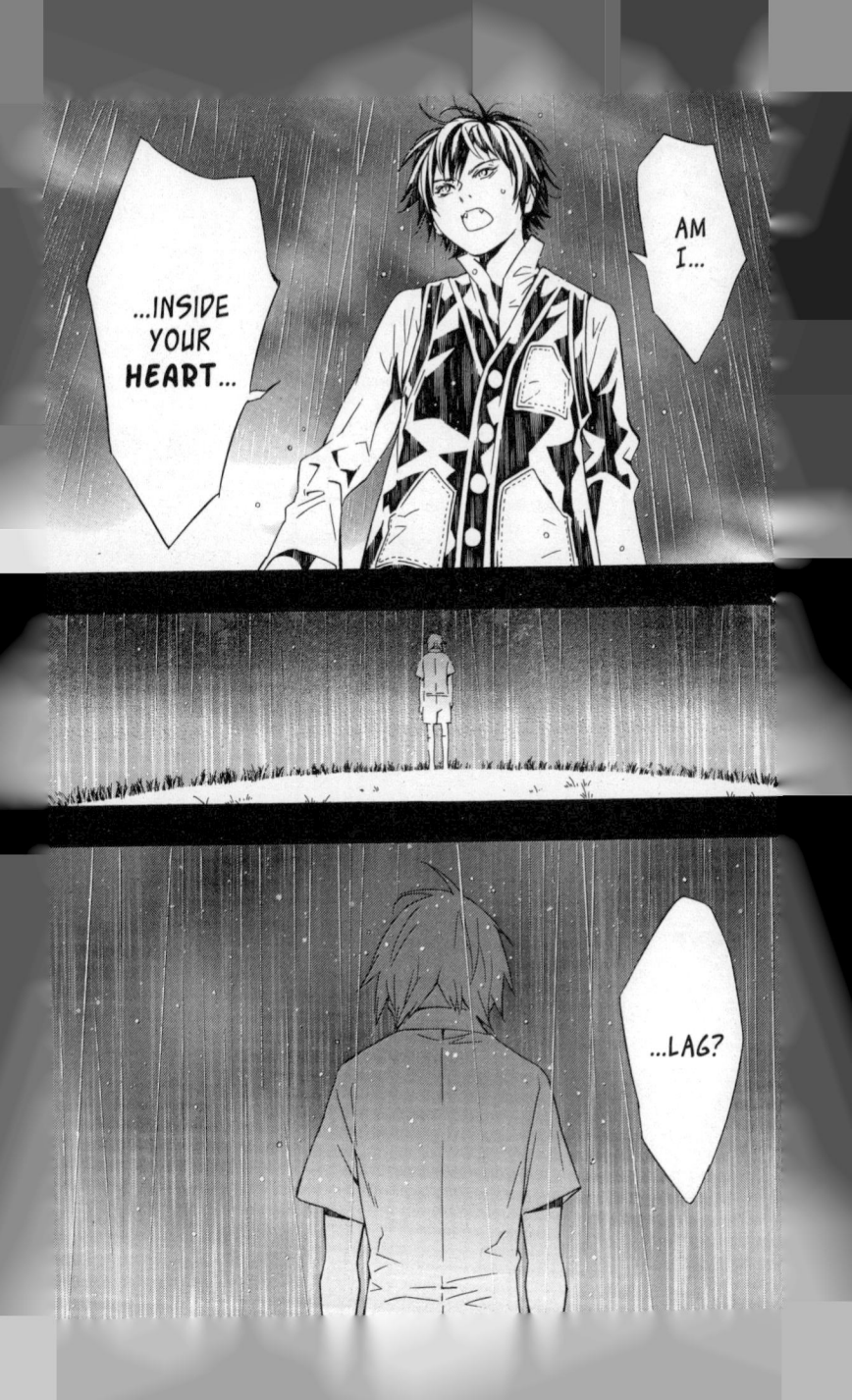

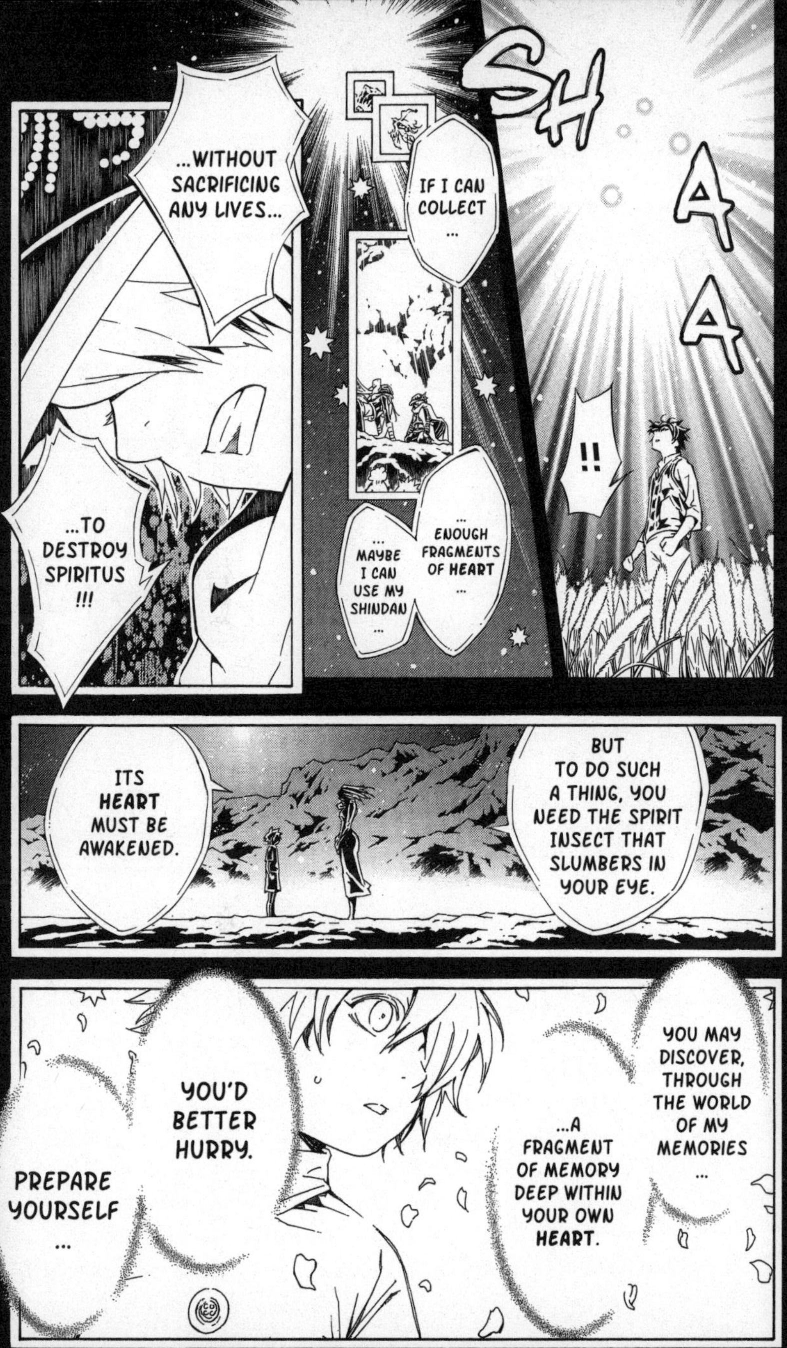
SHAA
!!
IF I CAN COLLECT ...
... ENOUGH FRAGMENTS OF HEART ...
... MAYBE I CAN USE MY SHINDAN ...
...WITHOUT SACRIFICING ANY LIVES...
...TO DESTROY SPIRITUS !!!
BUT TO DO SUCH A THING, YOU NEED THE SPIRIT INSECT THAT SLUMBERS IN YOUR EYE.
ITS HEART MUST BE AWAKENED.
YOU MAY DISCOVER, THROUGH THE WORLD OF MY MEMORIES ...
...A FRAGMENT OF MEMORY DEEP WITHIN YOUR OWN HEART.
YOU'D BETTER HURRY.
PREPARE YOURSELF ...

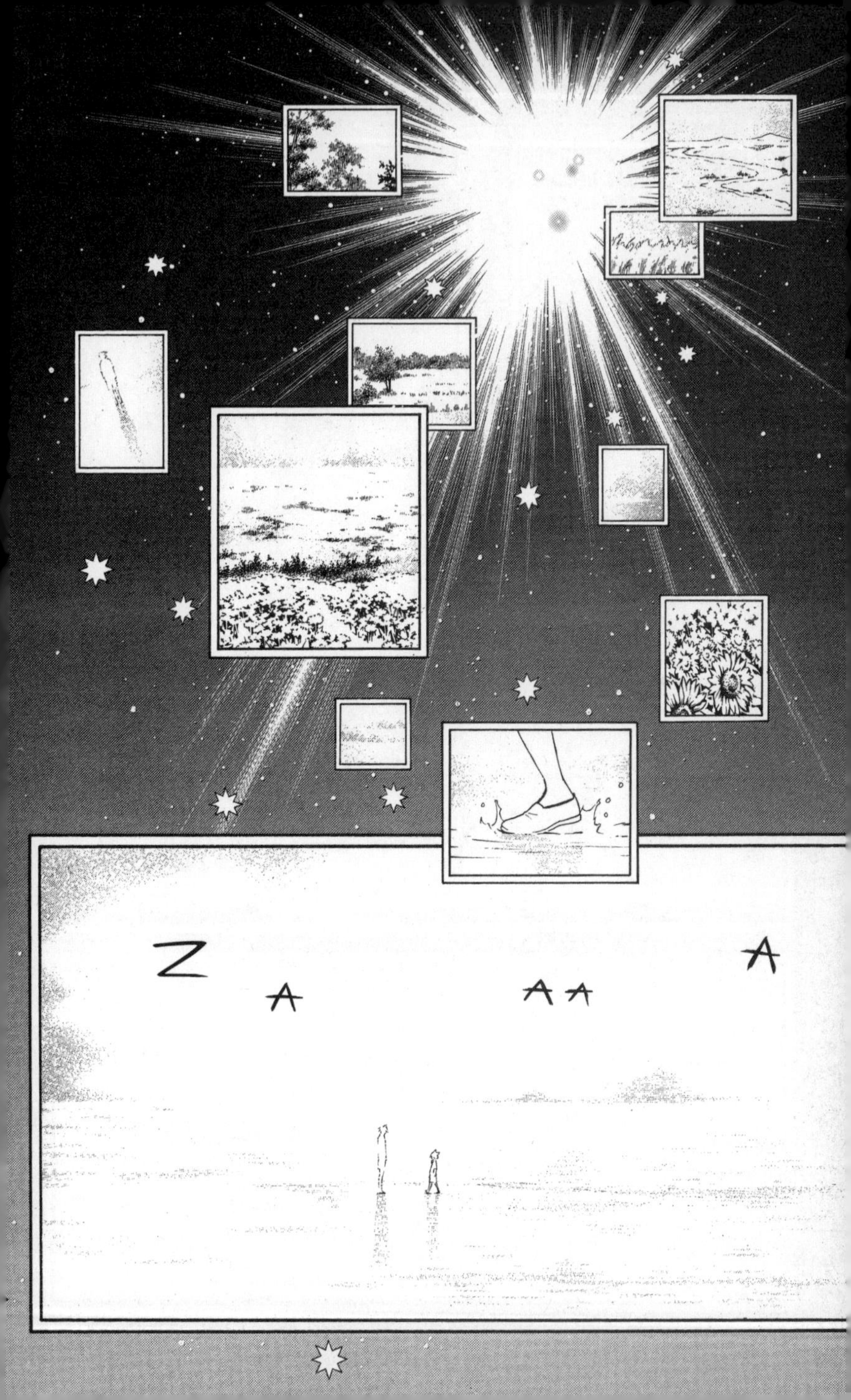
ZAAAA

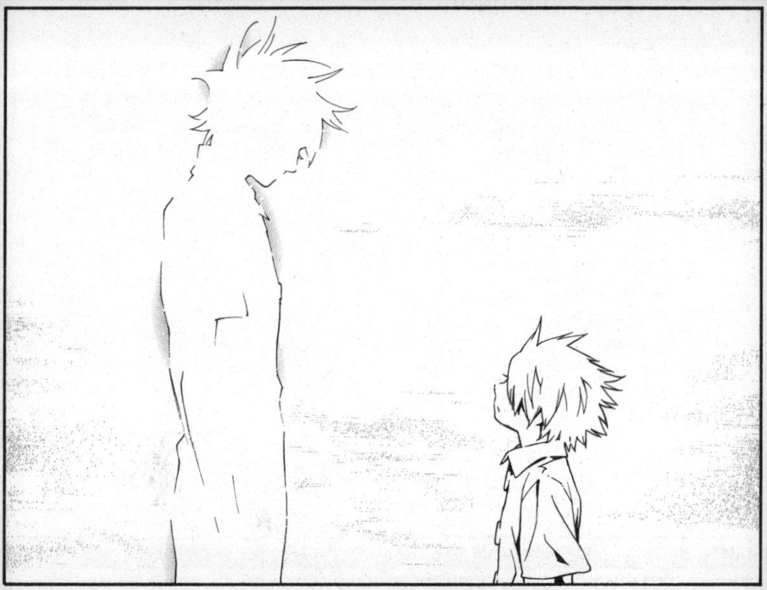
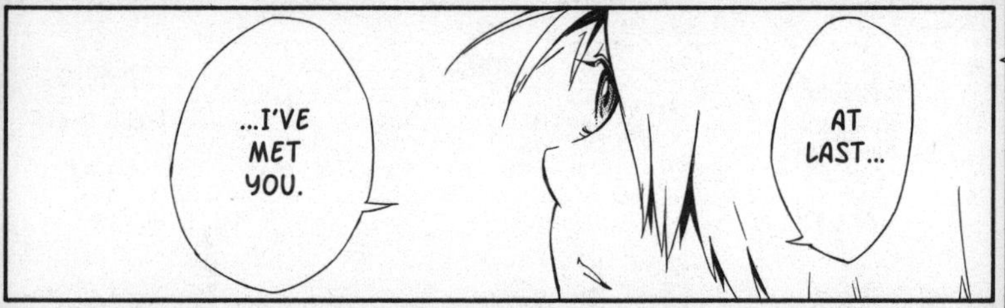
AT LAST...
...I'VE MET YOU.
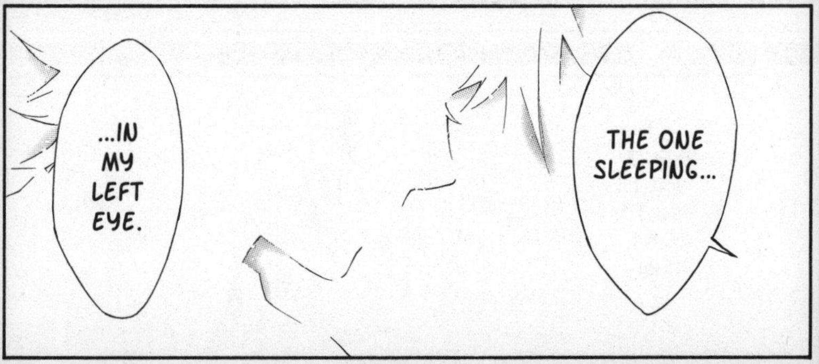
THE ONE SLEEPING...
...IN MY LEFT EYE.

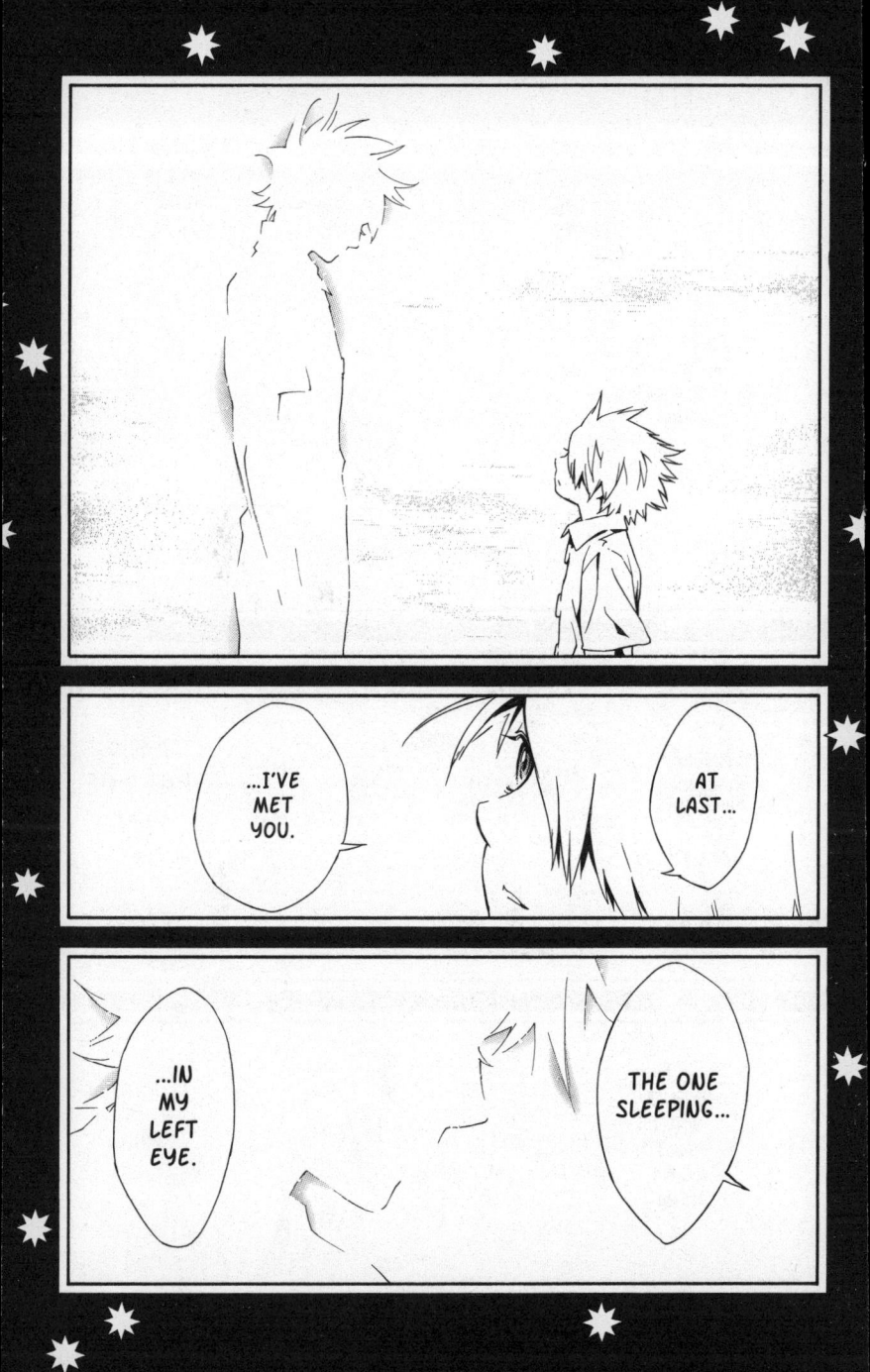

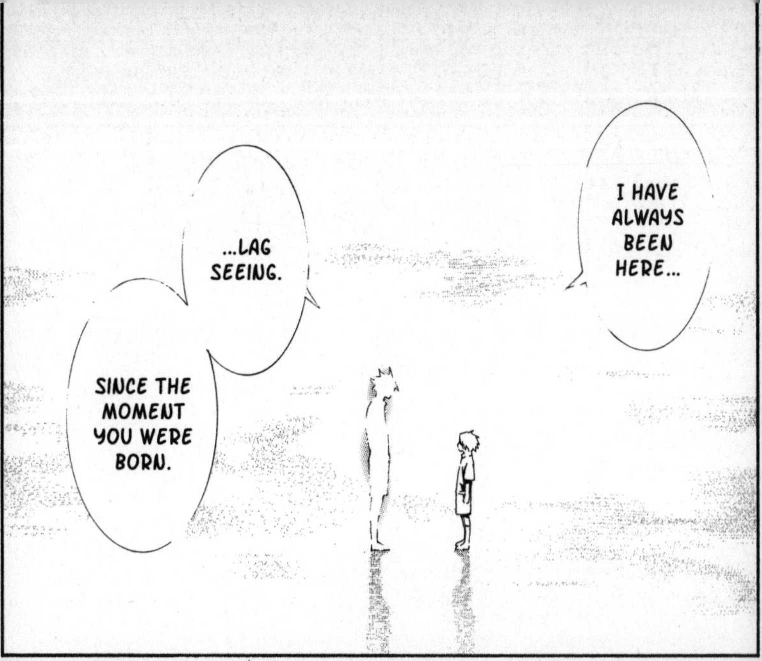
I HAVE ALWAYS BEEN HERE...
...LAG SEEING.
SINCE THE MOMENT YOU WERE BORN.

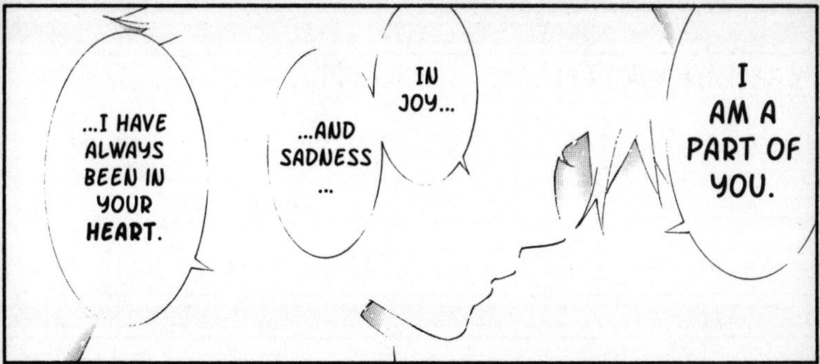
I AM A PART OF YOU.
IN JOY...
...AND SADNESS ...
...I HAVE ALWAYS BEEN IN YOUR HEART.

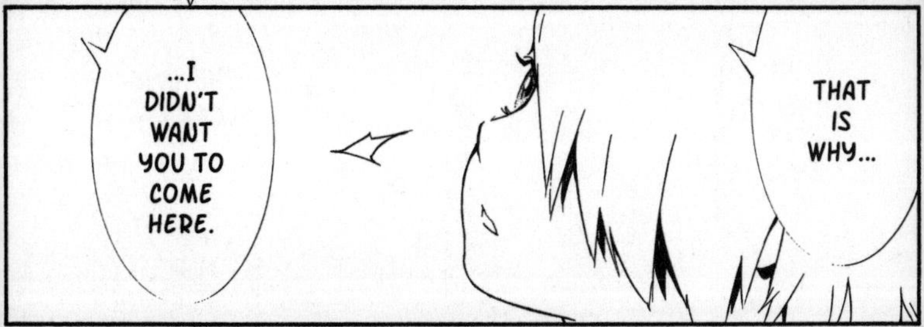
THAT IS WHY...
...I DIDN'T WANT YOU TO COME HERE.

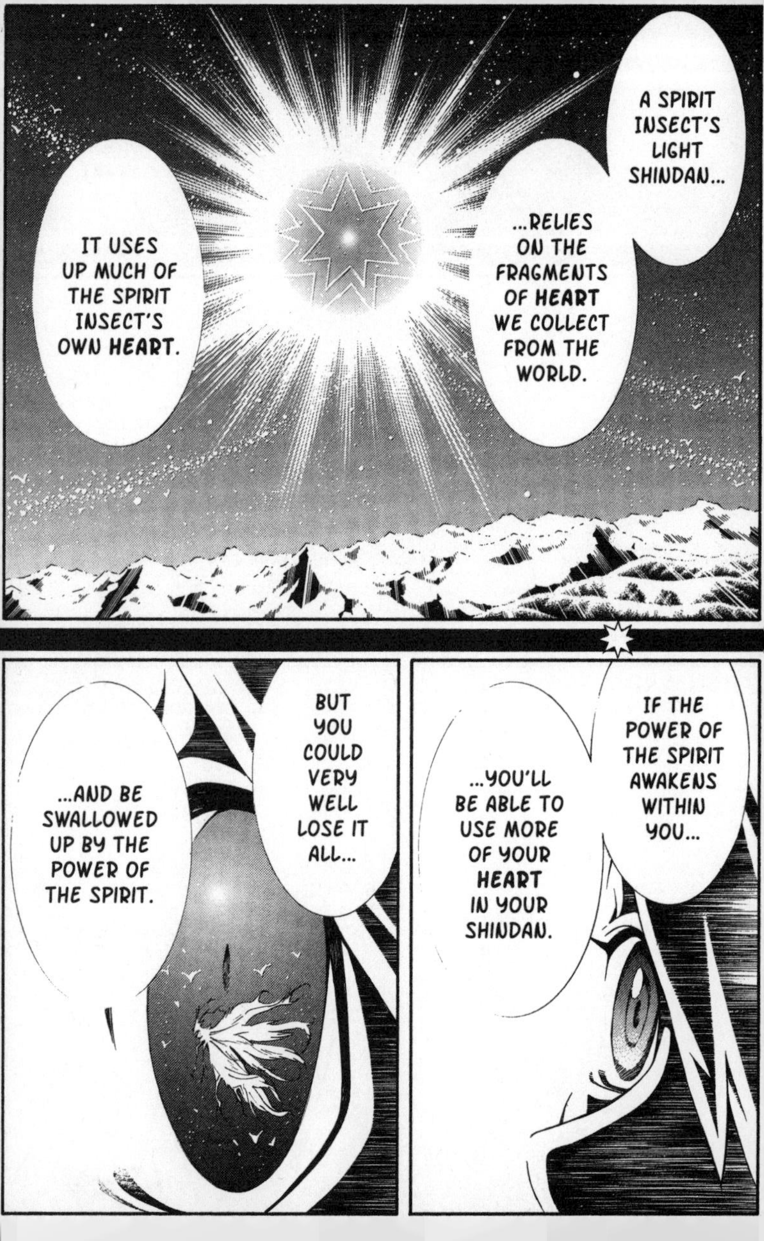
A SPIRIT INSECT'S LIGHT SHINDAN...
...RELIES ON THE FRAGMENTS OF HEART WE COLLECT FROM THE WORLD.
IT USES UP MUCH OF THE SPIRIT INSECT'S OWN HEART.
IF THE POWER OF THE SPIRIT AWAKENS WITHIN YOU...
...YOU'LL BE ABLE TO USE MORE OF YOUR HEART IN YOUR SHINDAN.
BUT YOU COULD VERY WELL LOSE IT ALL...
...AND BE SWALLOWED UP BY THE POWER OF THE SPIRIT.

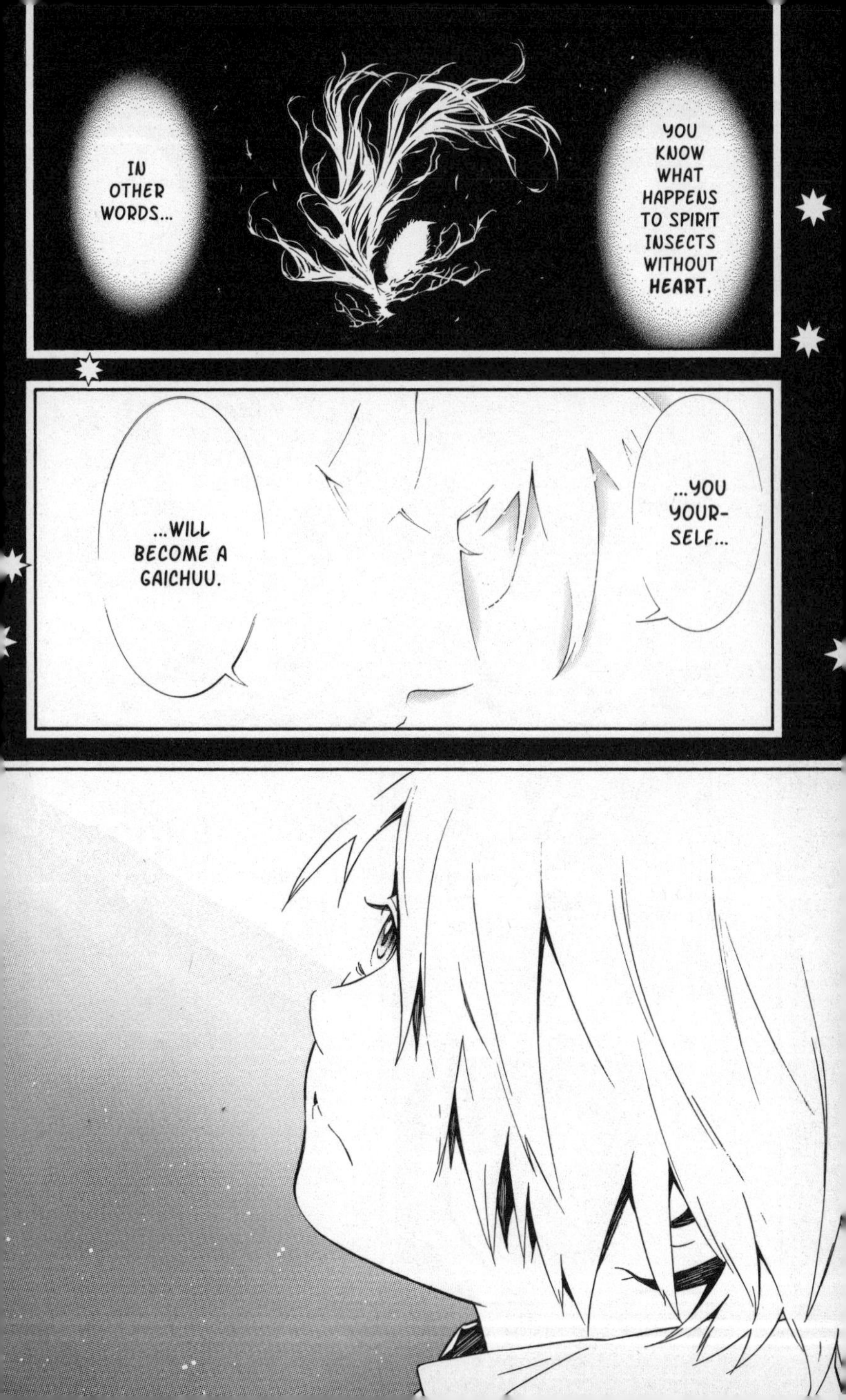
YOU KNOW WHAT HAPPENS TO SPIRIT INSECTS WITHOUT HEART.
IN OTHER WORDS...
...YOU YOURSELF...
...WILL BECOME A GAICHUU.

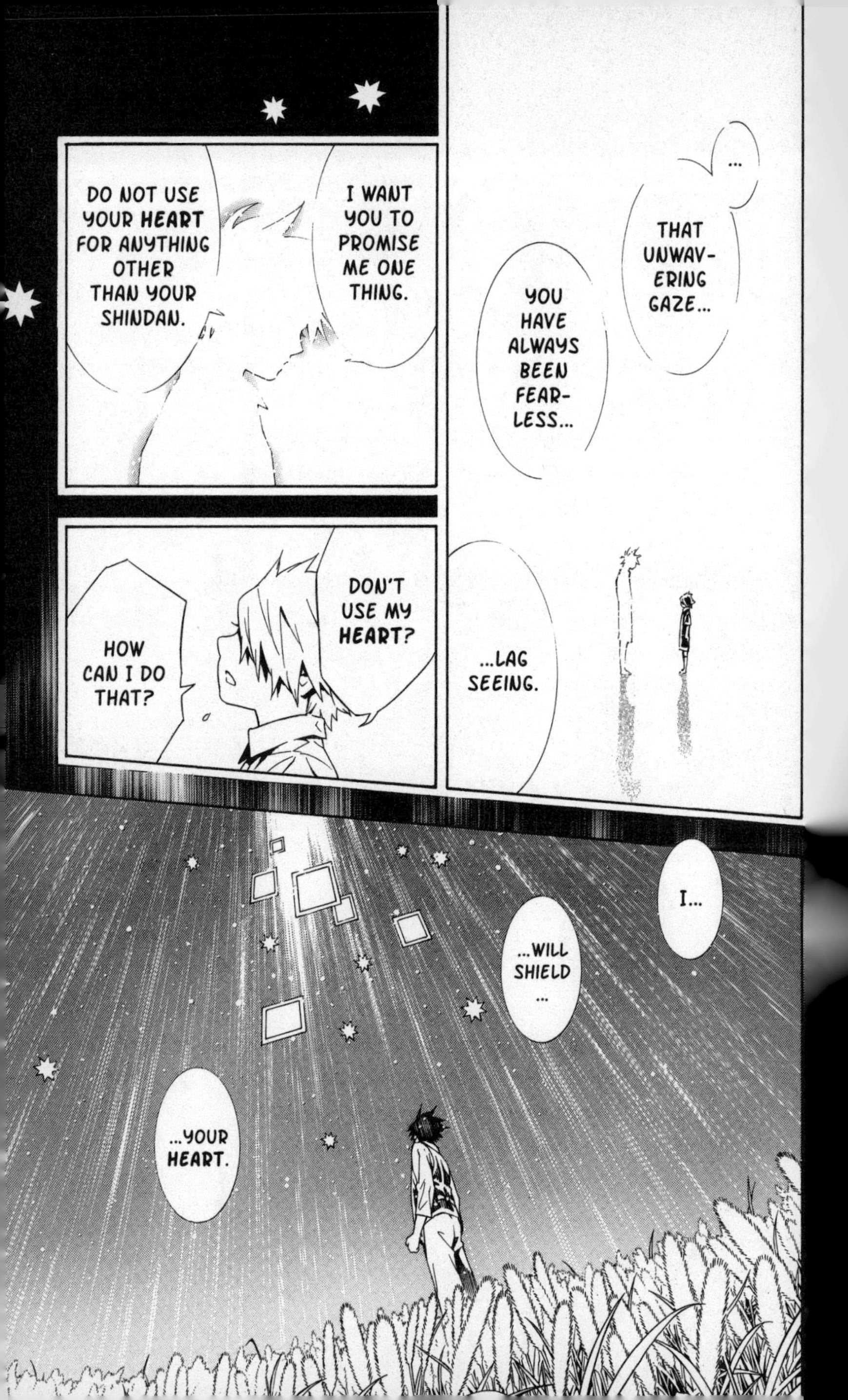
...
THAT UNWAV-ERING GAZE...
YOU HAVE ALWAYS BEEN FEAR-LESS...
...LAG SEEING.
I WANT YOU TO PROMISE ME ONE THING.
DO NOT USE YOUR **HEART** FOR ANYTHING OTHER THAN YOUR SHINDAN.
DON'T USE MY **HEART**?
HOW CAN I DO THAT?
I...
...WILL SHIELD ...
...YOUR **HEART**.

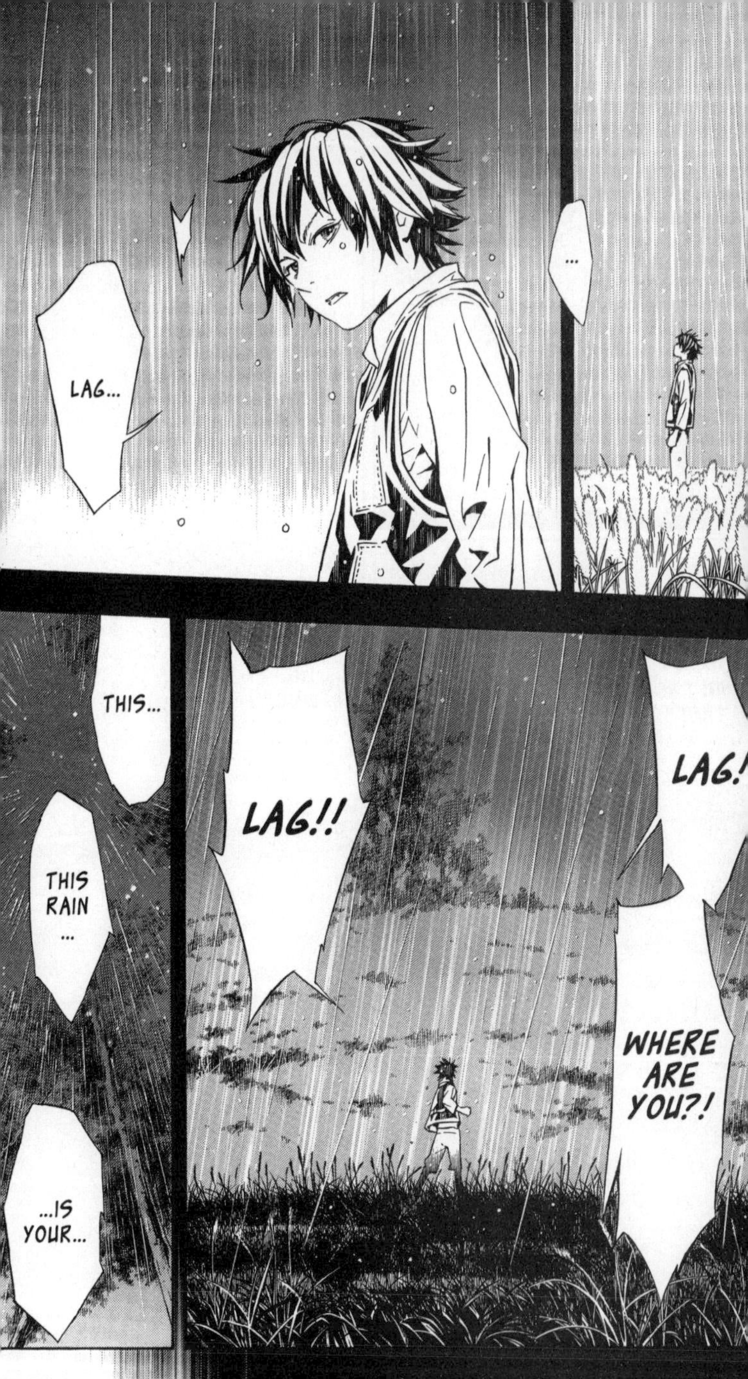
...
LAG...
LAG!
WHERE ARE YOU?!
LAG!!
THIS...
THIS RAIN...
...IS YOUR...

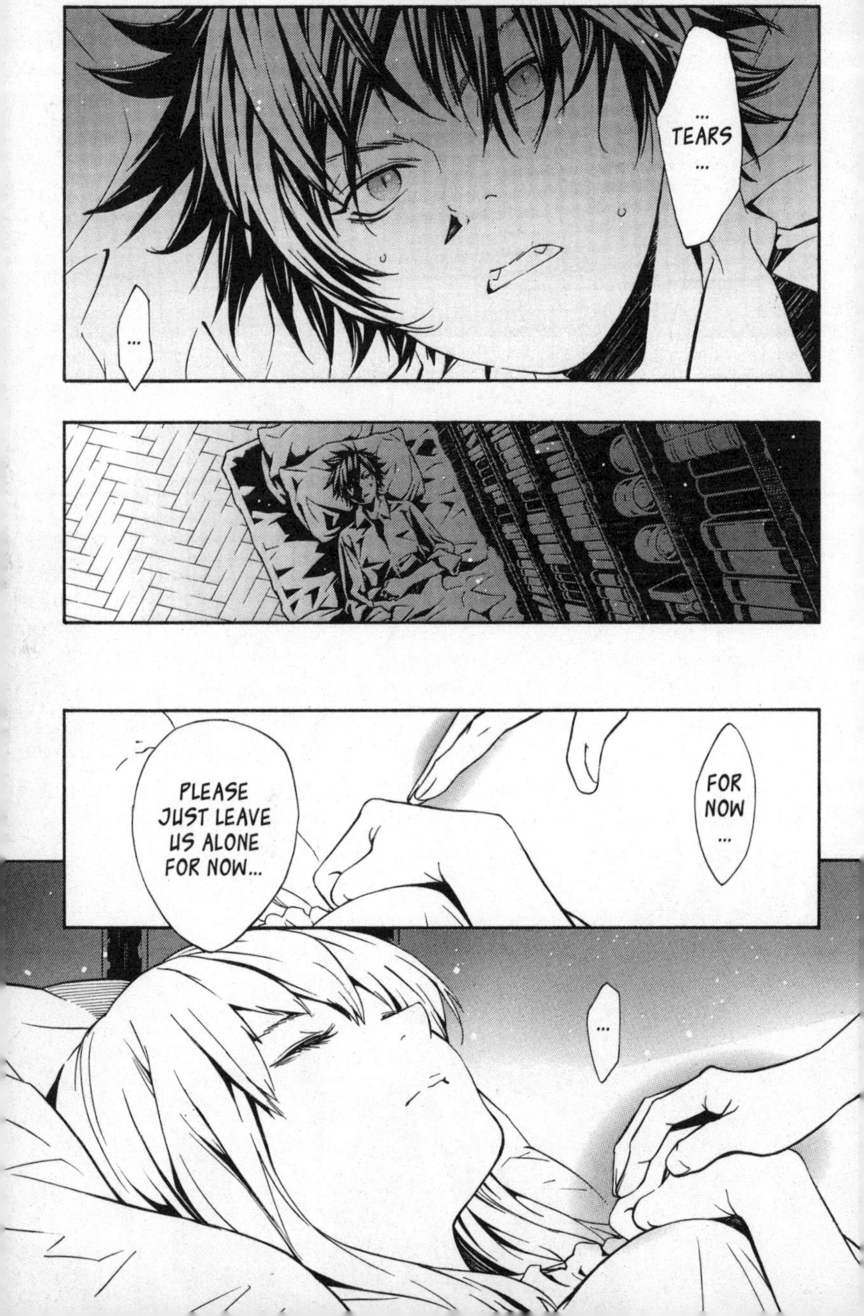
...TEARS...
...
FOR NOW...
PLEASE JUST LEAVE US ALONE FOR NOW...
...

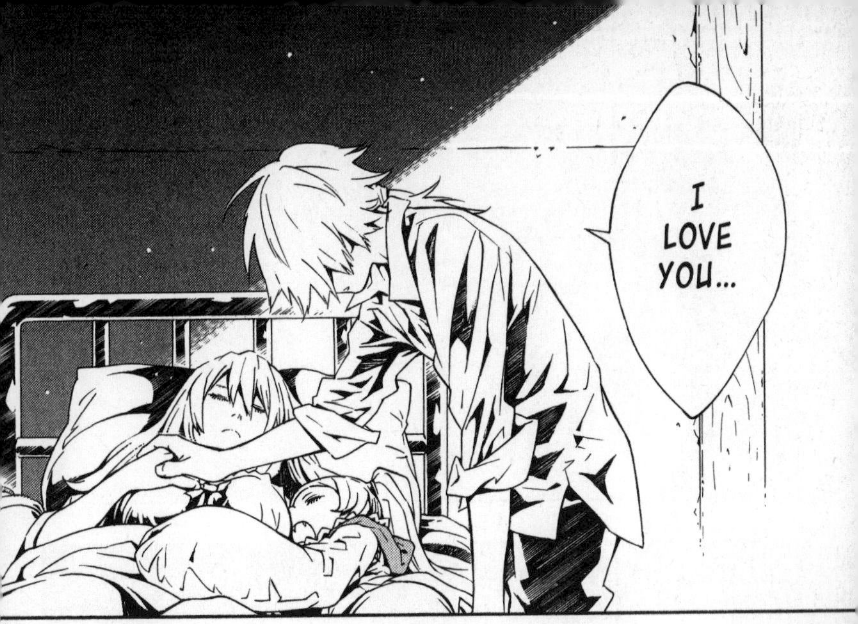
I LOVE YOU...
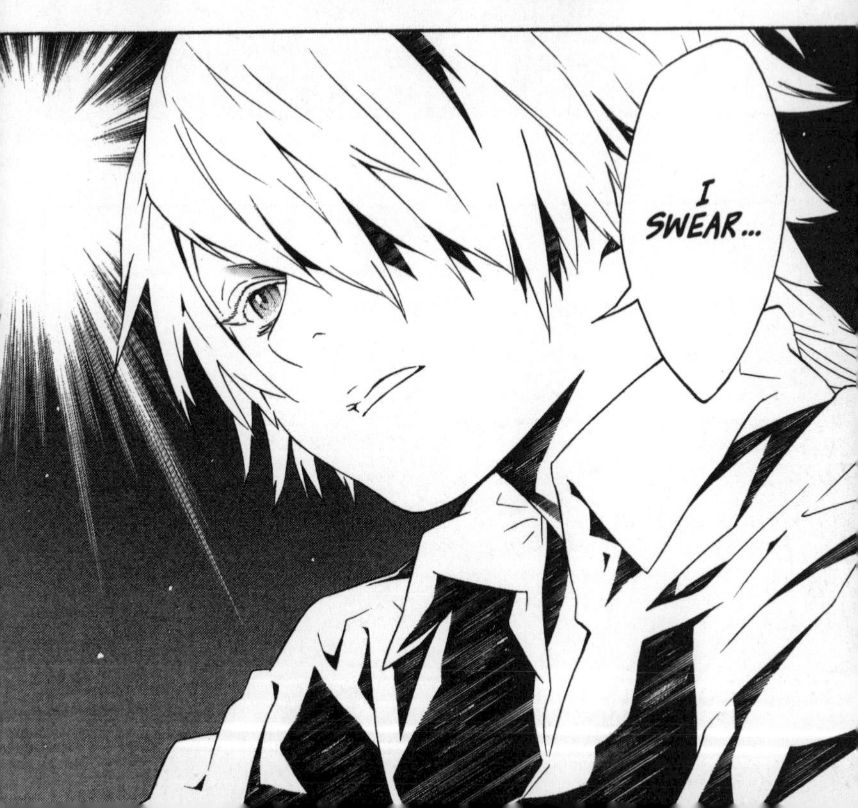
I SWEAR...

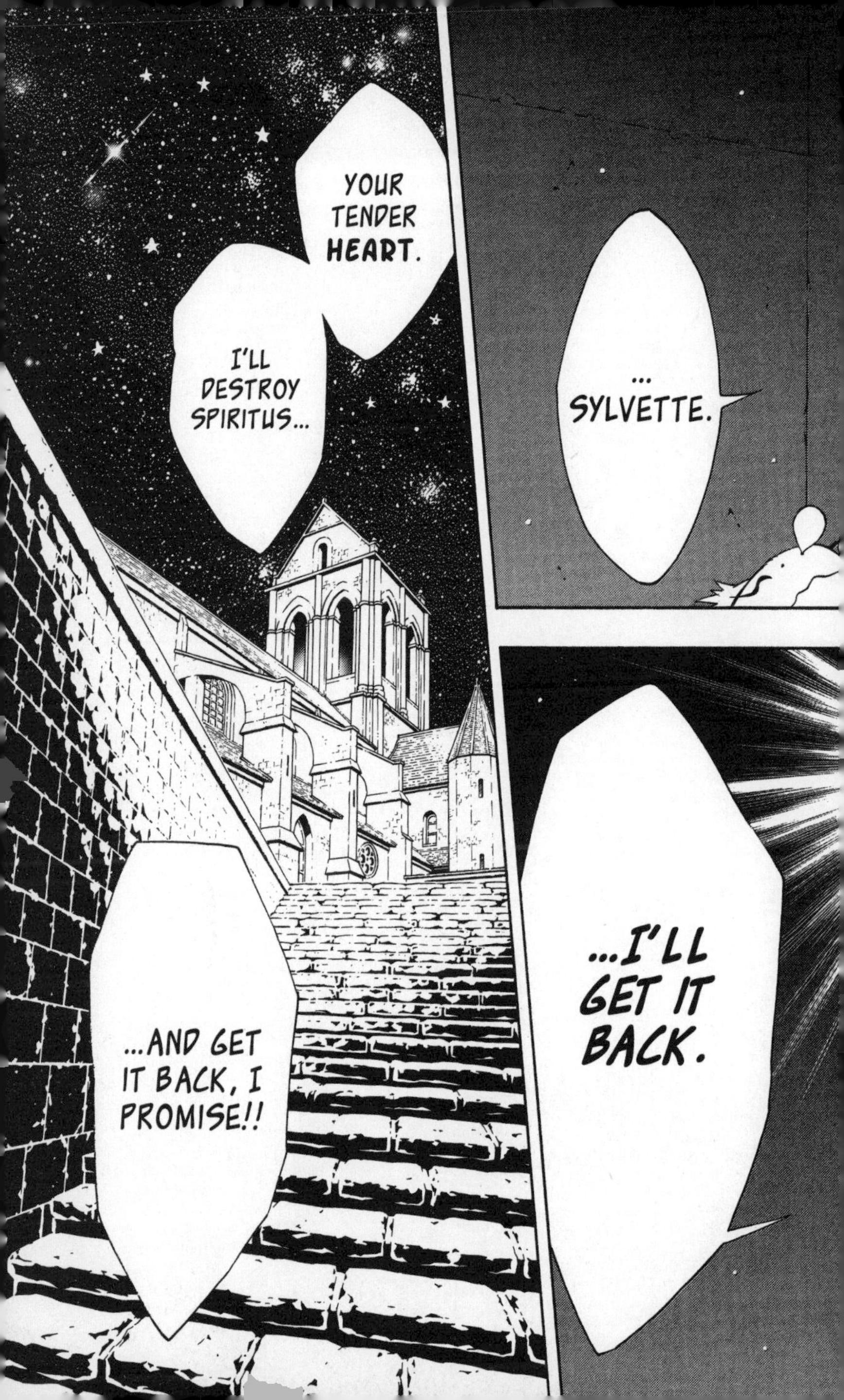
...
SYLVETTE.
...I'LL GET IT BACK.
YOUR TENDER HEART.
I'LL DESTROY SPIRITUS...
...AND GET IT BACK, I PROMISE!!

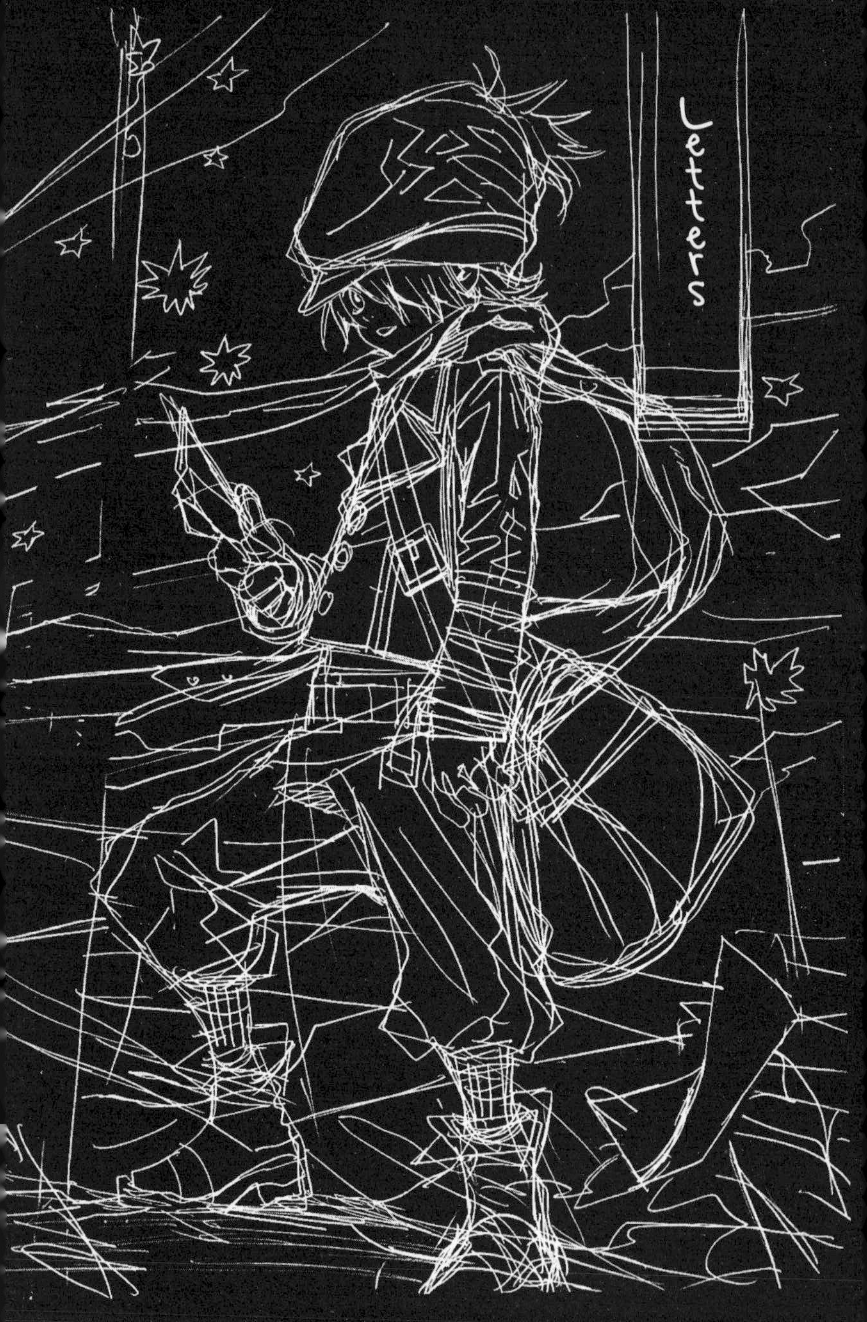
Letters

Rejected chapter 1 sketch.

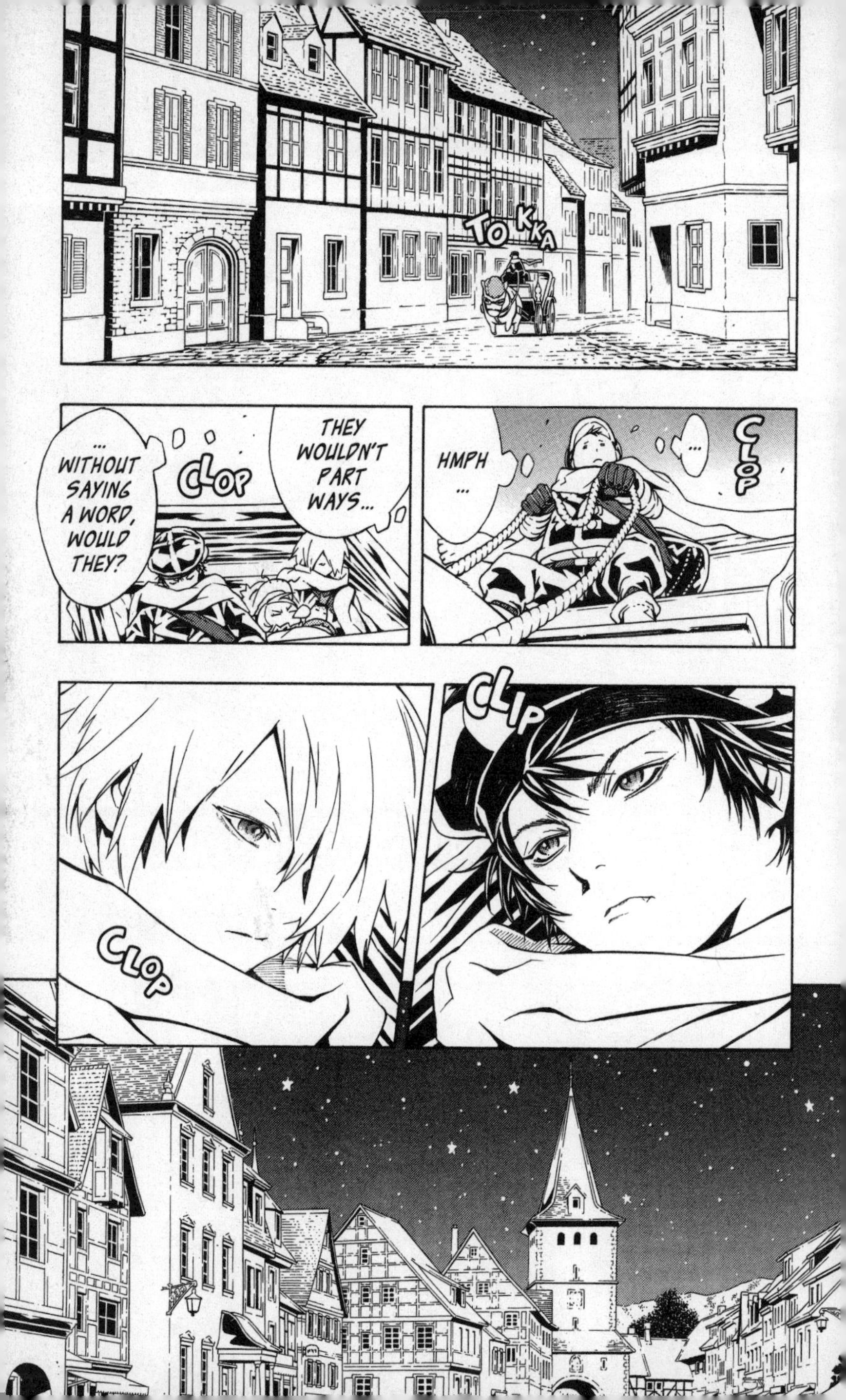
TOKKA
CLOP
...
HMPH
...
THEY WOULDN'T PART WAYS...
CLOP
... WITHOUT SAYING A WORD, WOULD THEY?
CLIP
CLOP

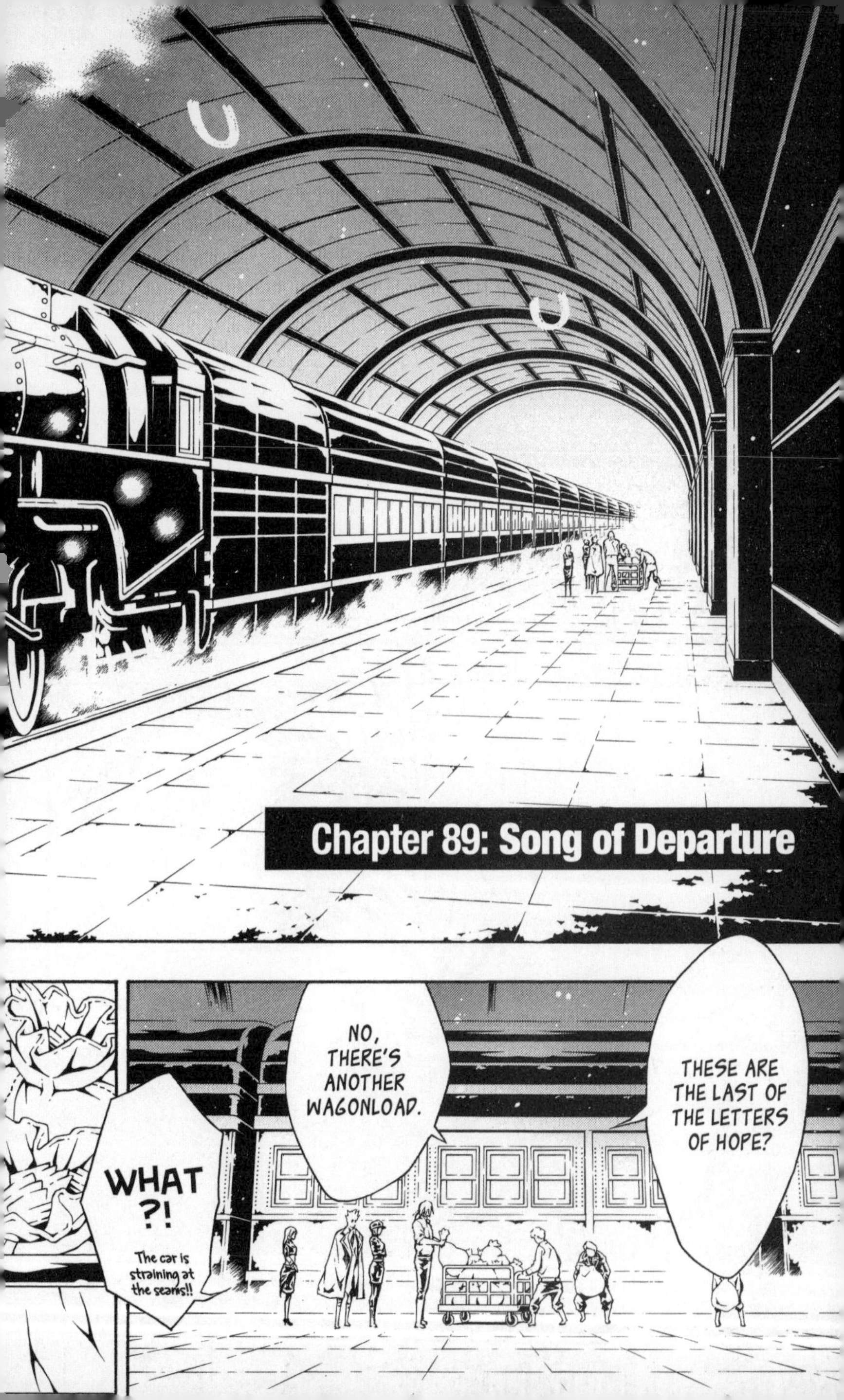
Chapter 89: Song of Departure
THESE ARE THE LAST OF THE LETTERS OF HOPE?
NO, THERE'S ANOTHER WAGONLOAD.
WHAT ?!
The car is straining at the seams!!

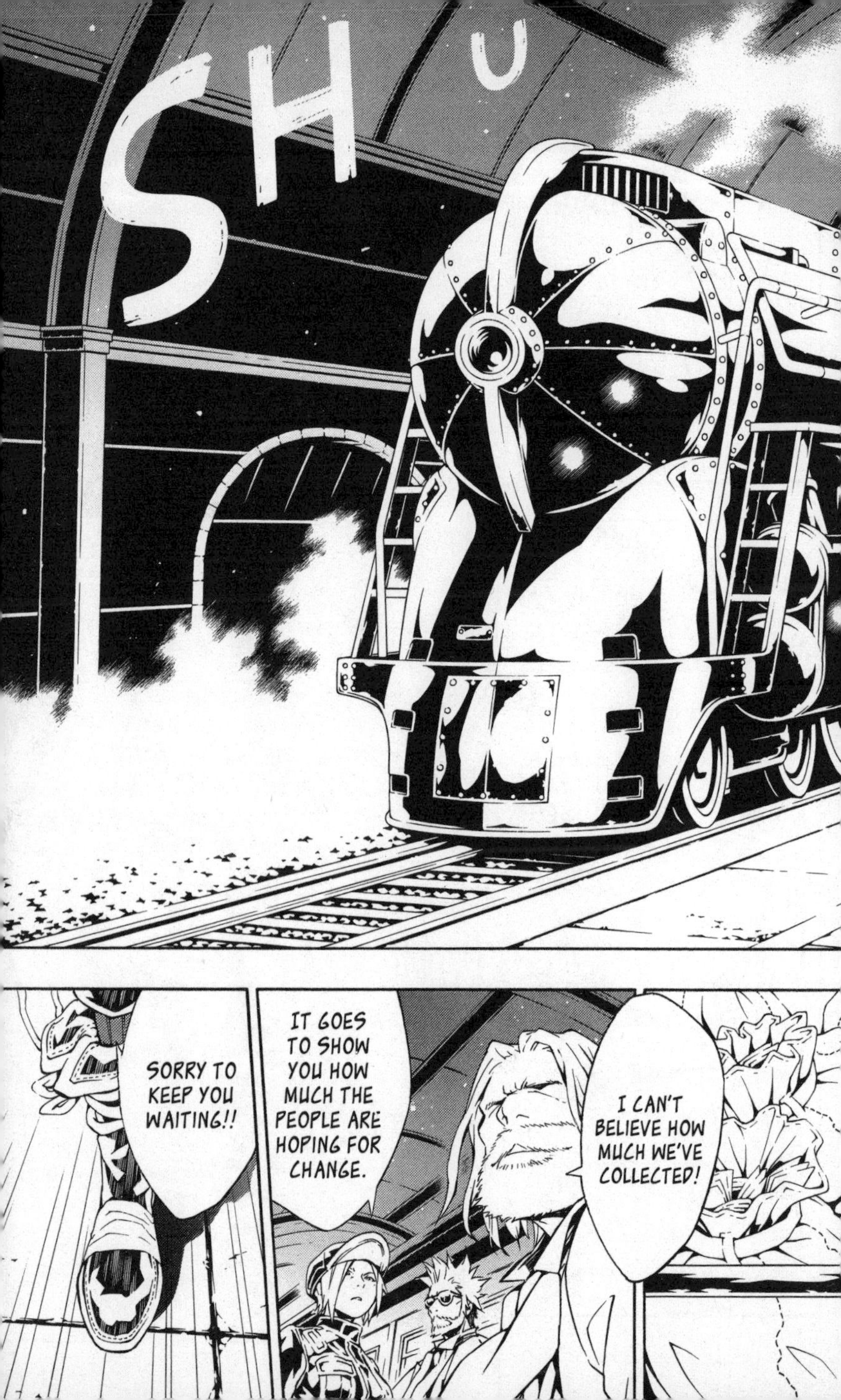
SHU
I CAN'T BELIEVE HOW MUCH WE'VE COLLECTED!
IT GOES TO SHOW YOU HOW MUCH THE PEOPLE ARE HOPING FOR CHANGE.
SORRY TO KEEP YOU WAITING!!

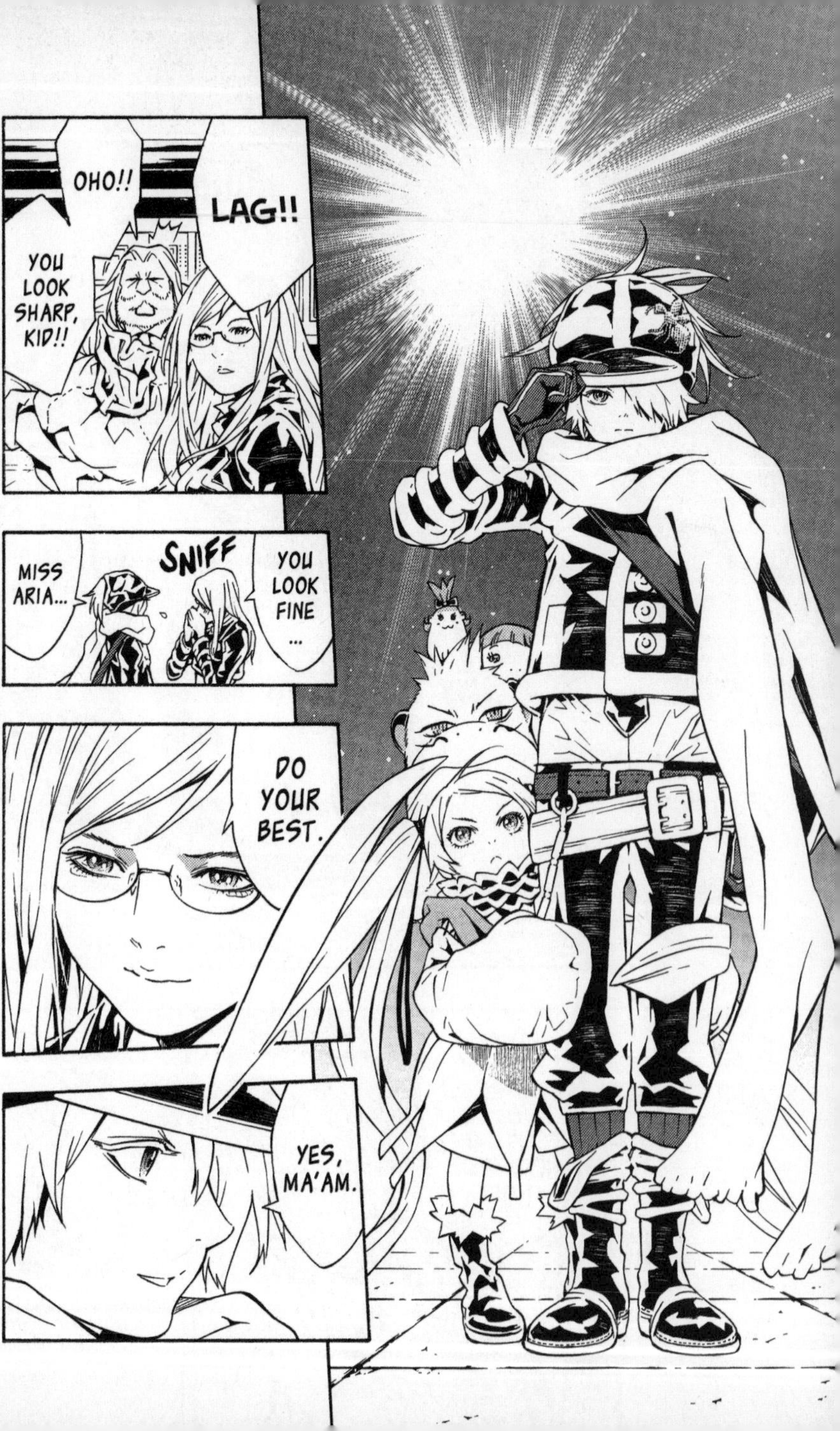
LAG!!
OHO!!
YOU LOOK SHARP, KID!!
YOU LOOK FINE ...
SNIFF
MISS ARIA...
DO YOUR BEST.
YES, MA'AM.

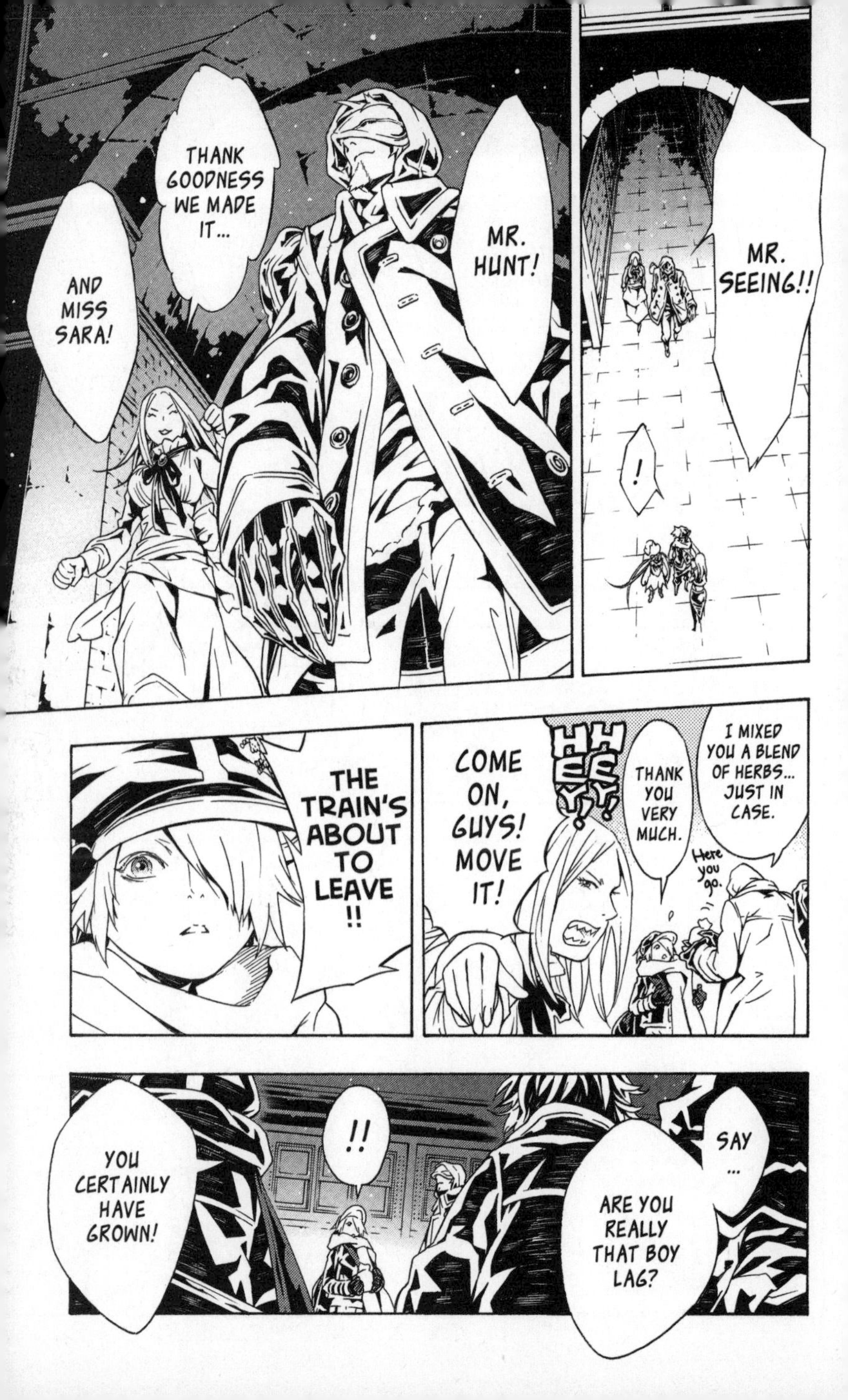
MR. SEEING!!
!
MR. HUNT!
THANK GOODNESS WE MADE IT...
AND MISS SARA!
I MIXED YOU A BLEND OF HERBS... JUST IN CASE.
Here you go.
THANK YOU VERY MUCH.
HHEEYY!
COME ON, GUYS! MOVE IT!
THE TRAIN'S ABOUT TO LEAVE!!
SAY...
ARE YOU REALLY THAT BOY LAG?
!!
YOU CERTAINLY HAVE GROWN!

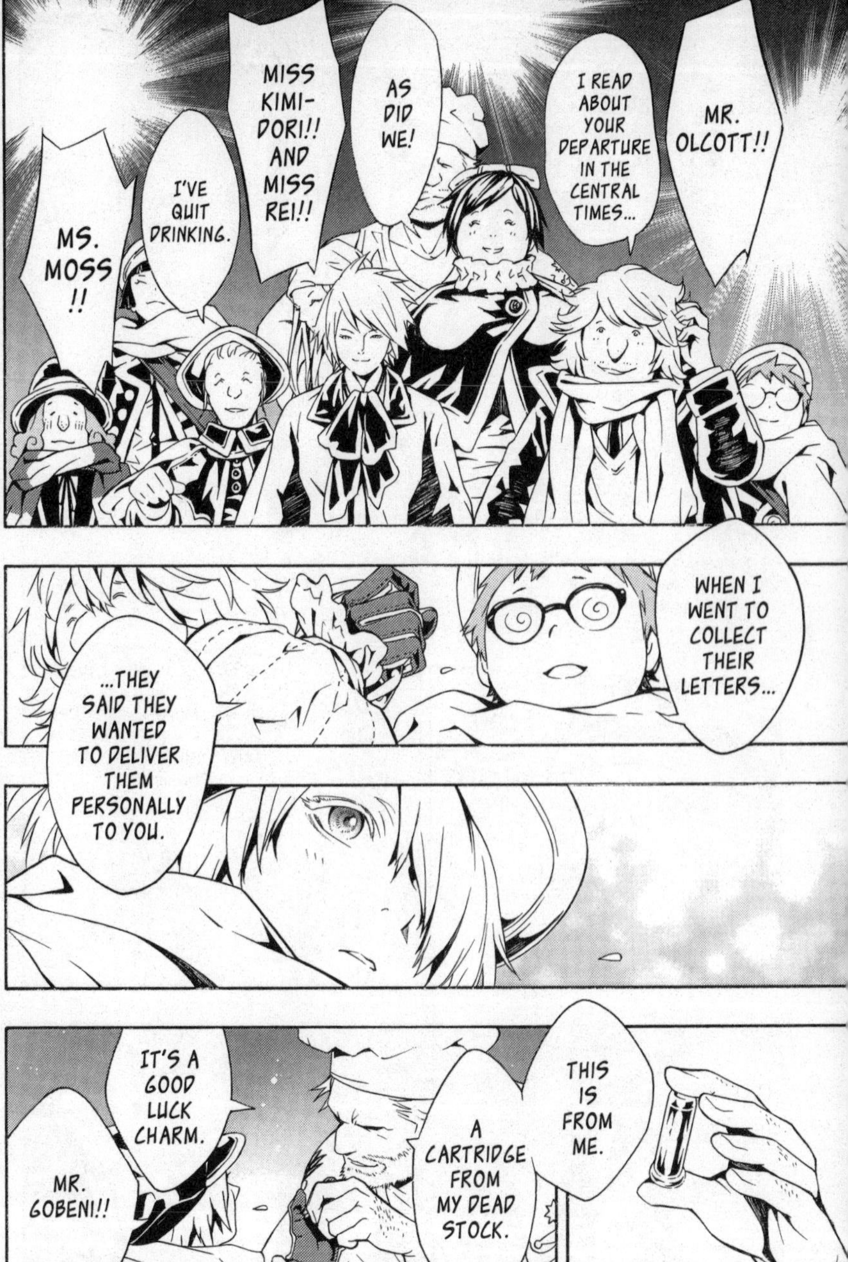
MR. OLCOTT!!
I READ ABOUT YOUR DEPARTURE IN THE CENTRAL TIMES...
AS DID WE!
MISS KIMI-DORI!! AND MISS REI!!
I'VE QUIT DRINKING.
MS. MOSS!!
WHEN I WENT TO COLLECT THEIR LETTERS...
...THEY SAID THEY WANTED TO DELIVER THEM PERSONALLY TO YOU.
THIS IS FROM ME.
A CARTRIDGE FROM MY DEAD STOCK.
IT'S A GOOD LUCK CHARM.
MR. GOBENI!!

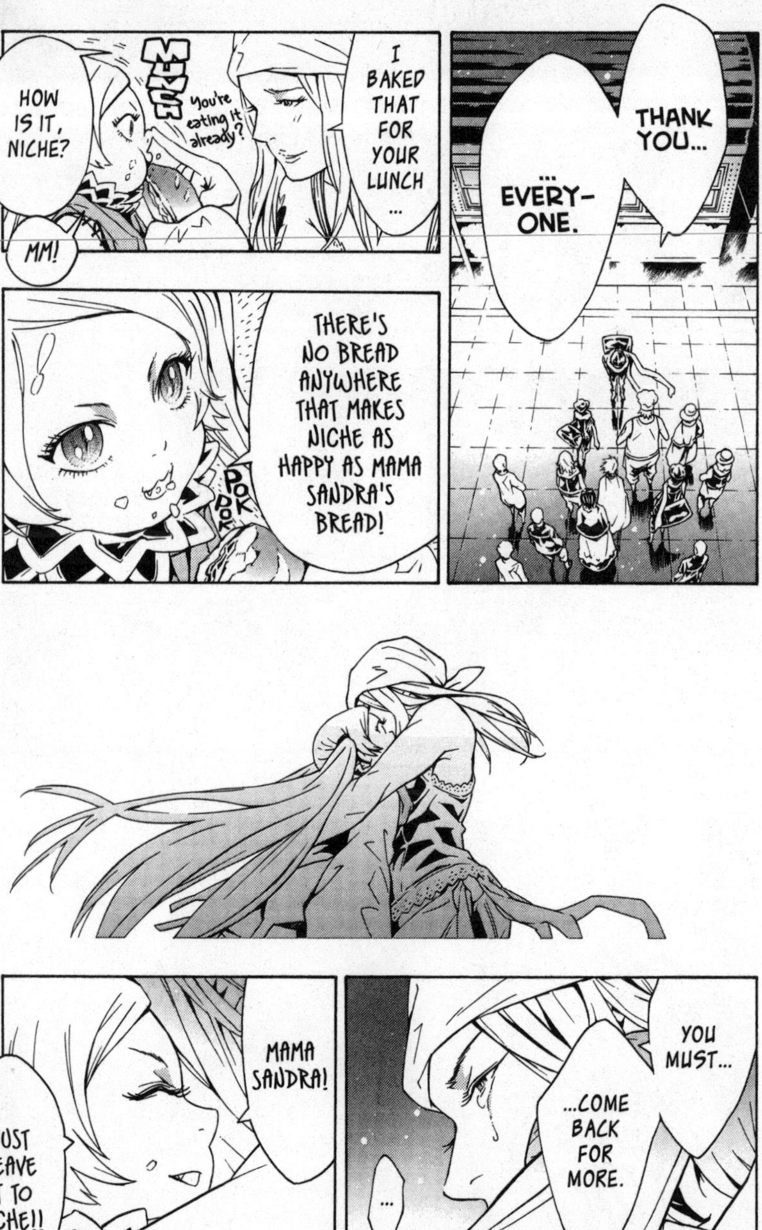
THANK YOU...
... EVERY-ONE.
I BAKED THAT FOR YOUR LUNCH ...
MUNCH
You're eating it already?
HOW IS IT, NICHE?
MM!
THERE'S NO BREAD ANYWHERE THAT MAKES NICHE AS HAPPY AS MAMA SANDRA'S BREAD!
POK POK
YOU MUST...
...COME BACK FOR MORE.
...
MAMA SANDRA!
JUST LEAVE IT TO NICHE!!

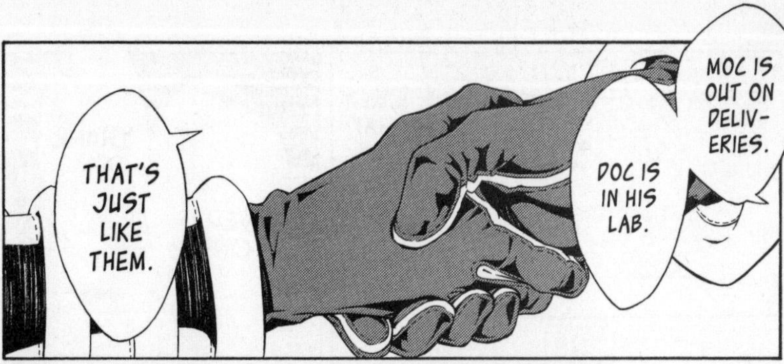
MOC IS OUT ON DELIV-ERIES.
DOC IS IN HIS LAB.
THAT'S JUST LIKE THEM.

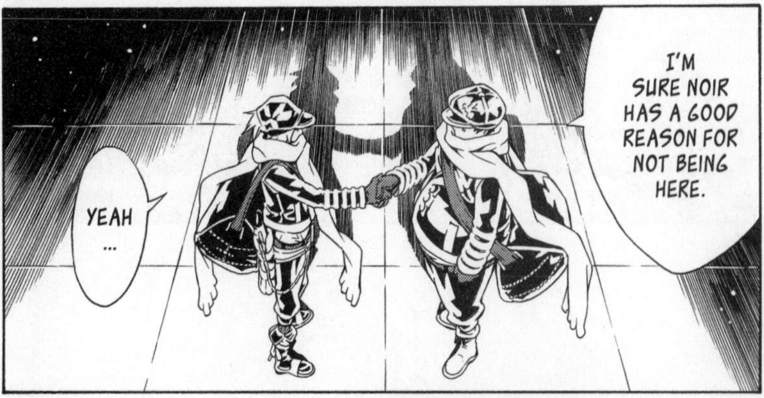
I'M SURE NOIR HAS A GOOD REASON FOR NOT BEING HERE.
YEAH ...

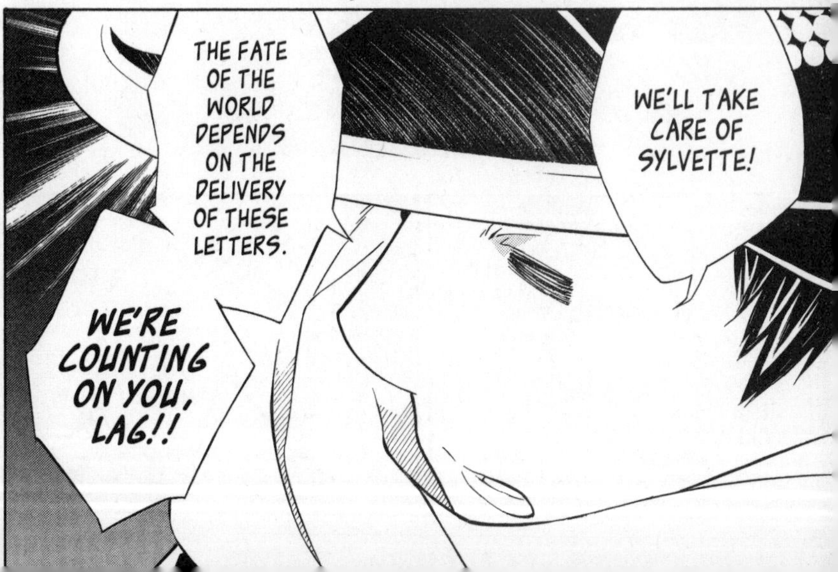
WE'LL TAKE CARE OF SYLVETTE!
THE FATE OF THE WORLD DEPENDS ON THE DELIVERY OF THESE LETTERS.
WE'RE COUNTING ON YOU, LAG!!

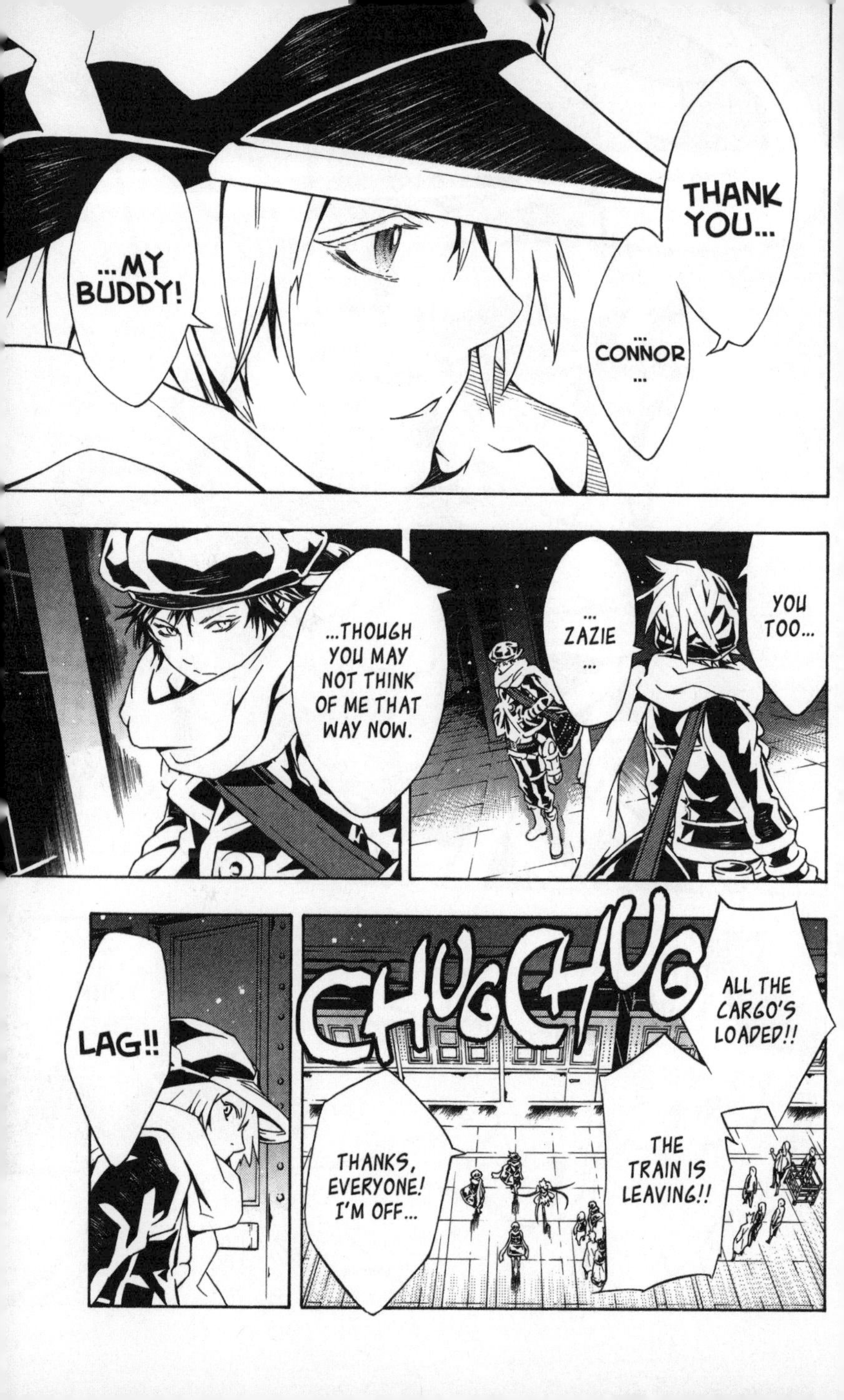
THANK YOU...
... CONNOR ...
...MY BUDDY!
YOU TOO...
... ZAZIE ...
...THOUGH YOU MAY NOT THINK OF ME THAT WAY NOW.
ALL THE CARGO'S LOADED!!
CHUG CHUG
THE TRAIN IS LEAVING!!
THANKS, EVERYONE! I'M OFF...
LAG!!

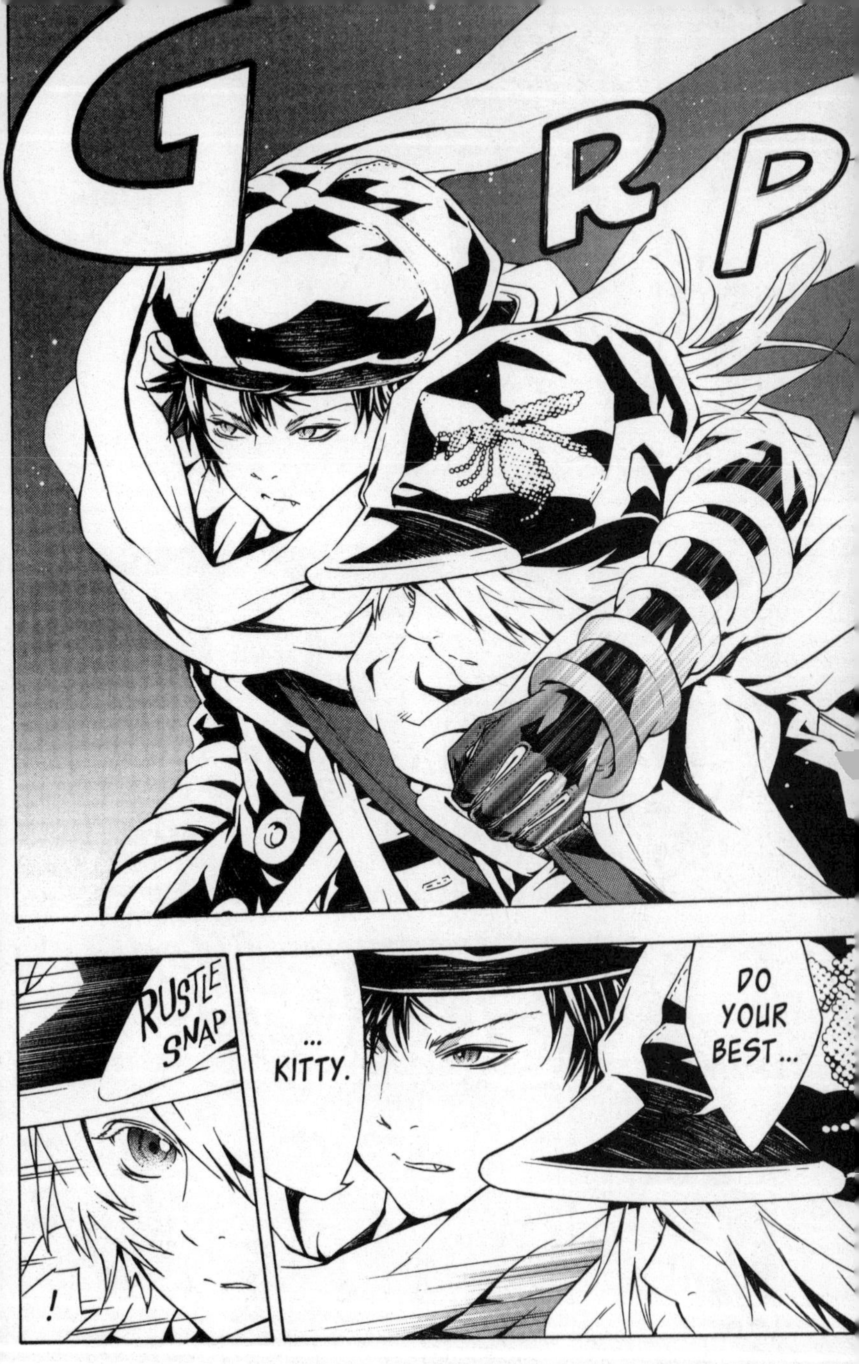
GRP
DO YOUR BEST...
... KITTY.
RUSTLE SNAP
!

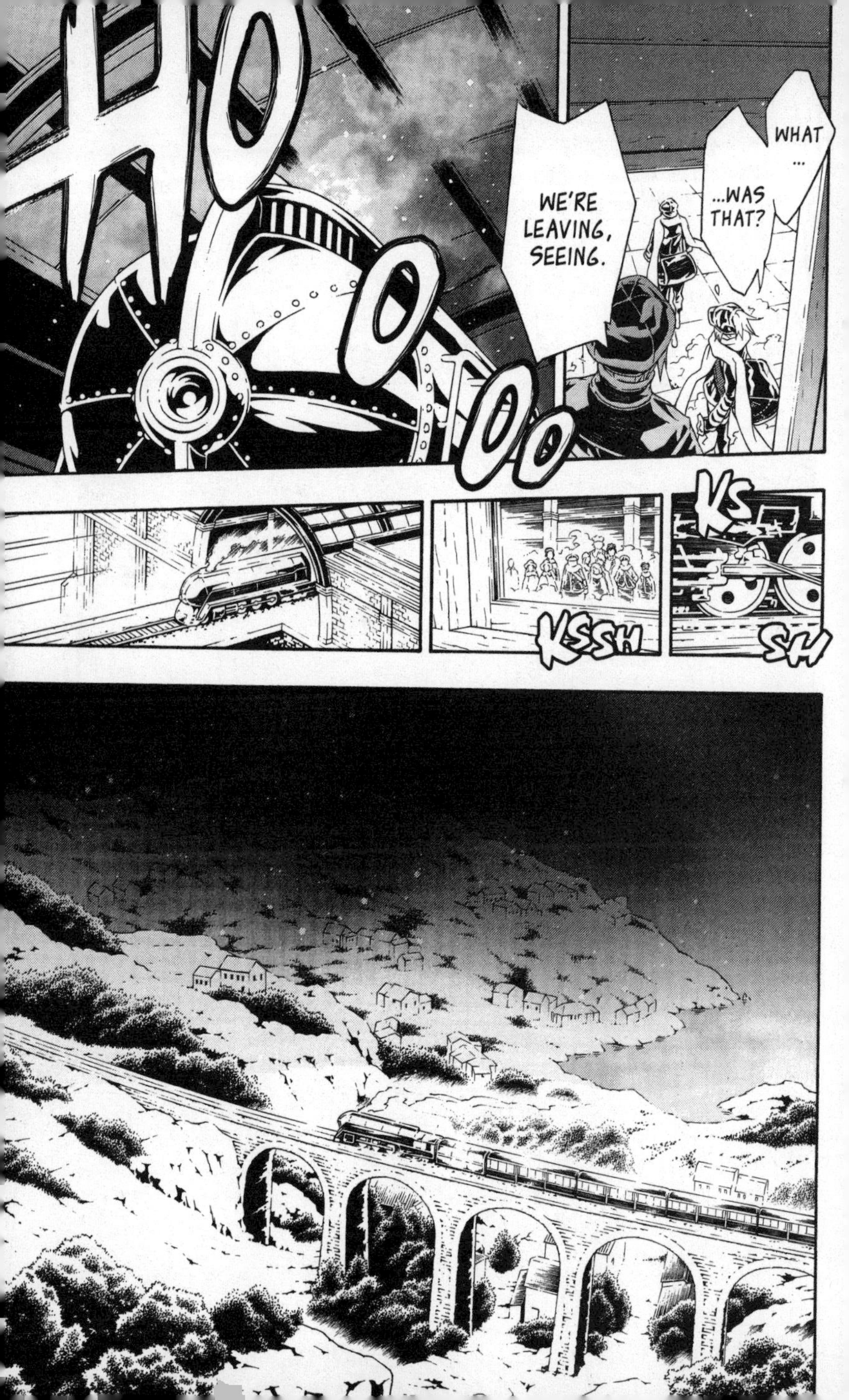
WHAT ...
...WAS THAT?
WE'RE LEAVING, SEEING.
HOOOOO
VSSH
KSSH

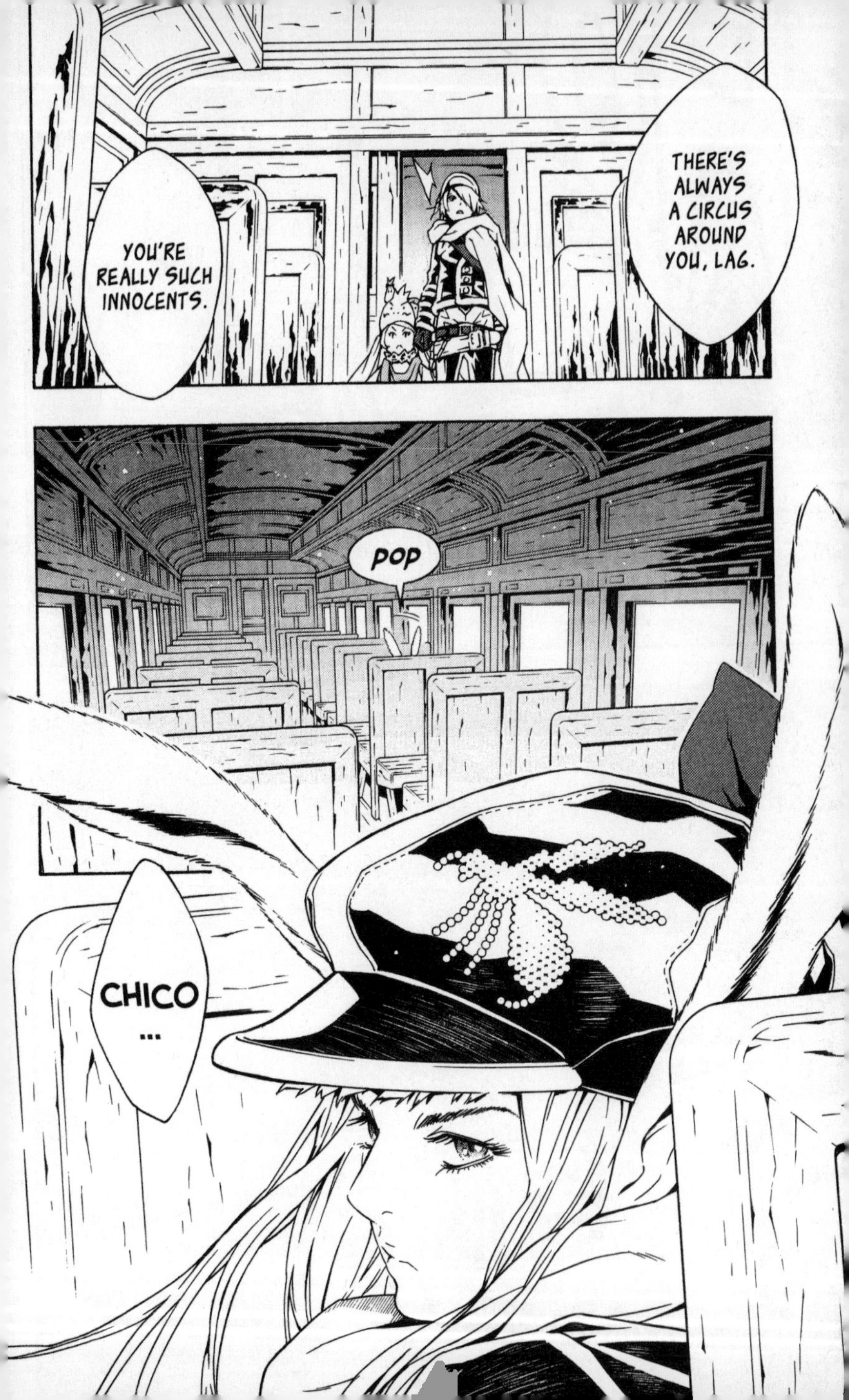
THERE'S ALWAYS A CIRCUS AROUND YOU, LAG.
YOU'RE REALLY SUCH INNOCENTS.
POP
CHICO ...

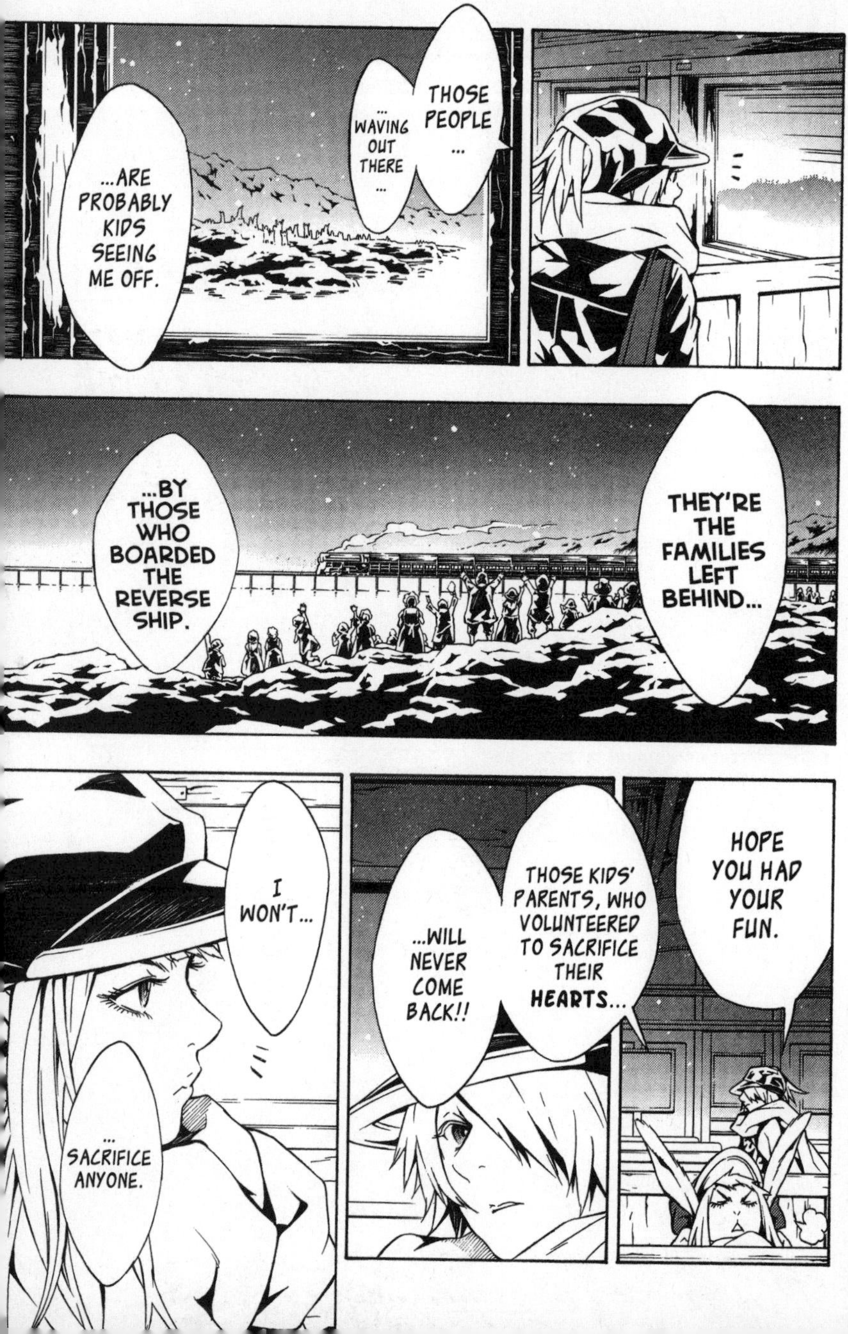
THOSE PEOPLE ...
... WAVING OUT THERE ...
...ARE PROBABLY KIDS SEEING ME OFF.
THEY'RE THE FAMILIES LEFT BEHIND...
...BY THOSE WHO BOARDED THE REVERSE SHIP.
HOPE YOU HAD YOUR FUN.
THOSE KIDS' PARENTS, WHO VOLUNTEERED TO SACRIFICE THEIR HEARTS...
...WILL NEVER COME BACK!!
I WON'T...
... SACRIFICE ANYONE.

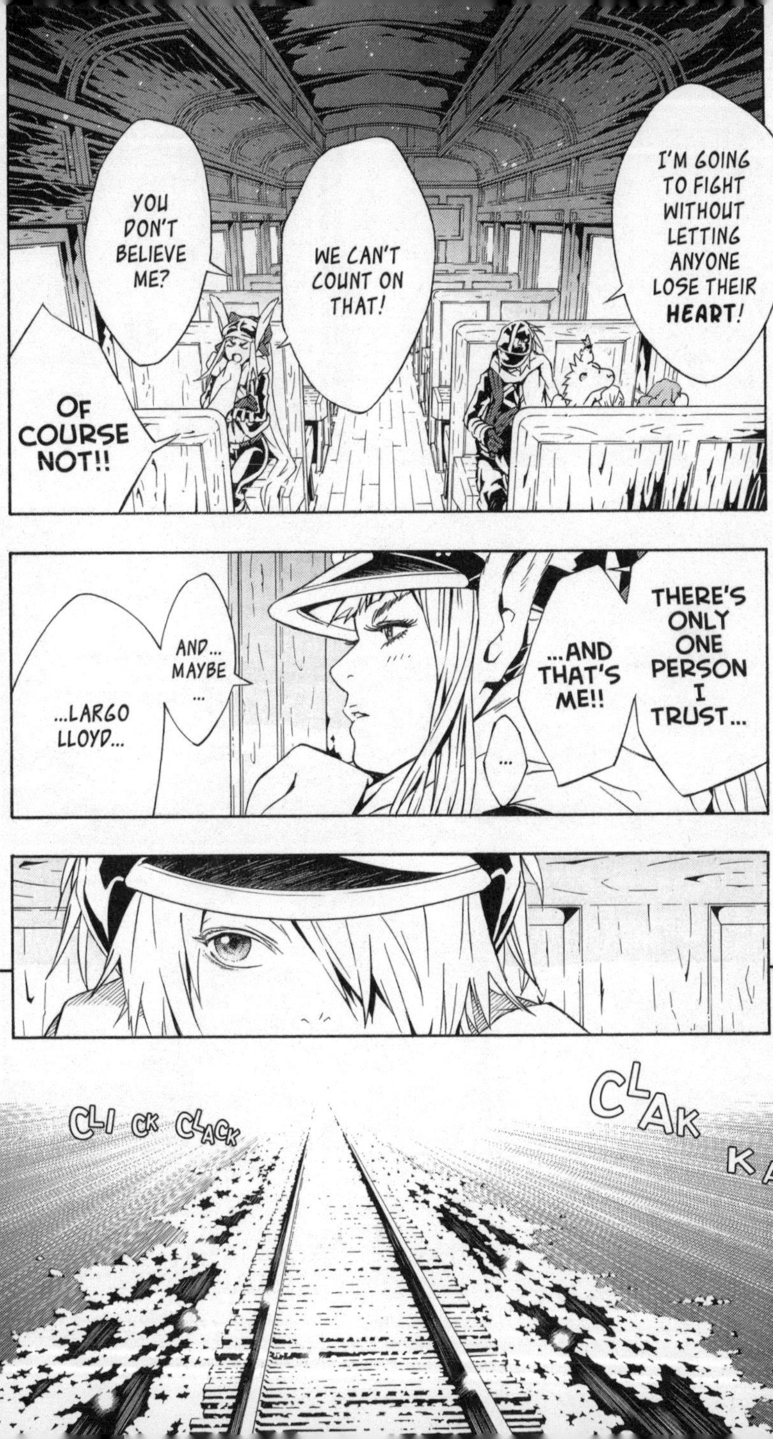
I'M GOING TO FIGHT WITHOUT LETTING ANYONE LOSE THEIR HEART!
WE CAN'T COUNT ON THAT!
YOU DON'T BELIEVE ME?
OF COURSE NOT!!
THERE'S ONLY ONE PERSON I TRUST...
...AND THAT'S ME!!
...
AND... MAYBE ...
...LARGO LLOYD...
CLAK KA
CLI CK CLACK

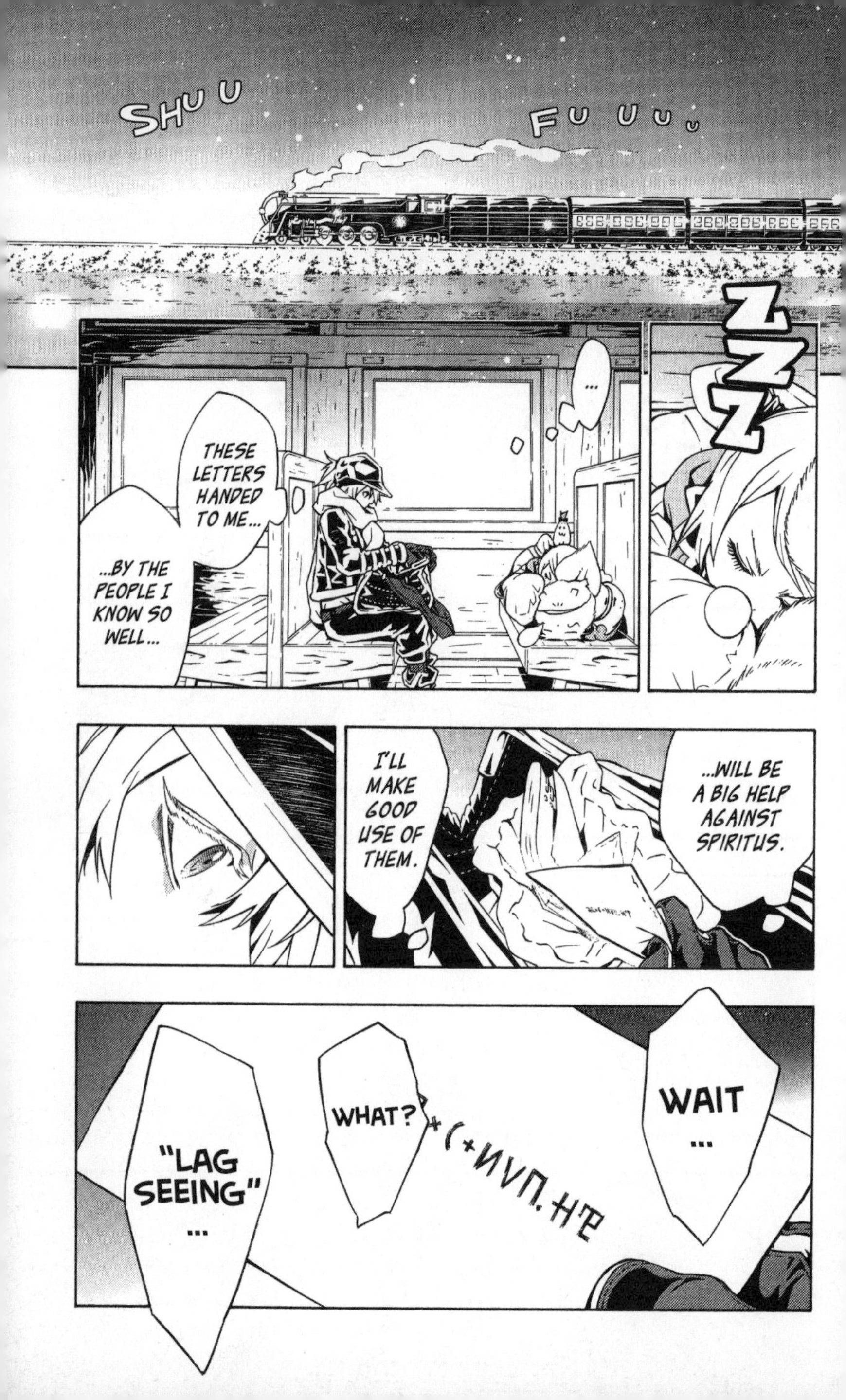
SHUU
FUUUU
ZZZ
THESE LETTERS HANDED TO ME...
...BY THE PEOPLE I KNOW SO WELL...
...
...WILL BE A BIG HELP AGAINST SPIRITUS.
I'LL MAKE GOOD USE OF THEM.
WAIT ...
WHAT?
"LAG SEEING" ...

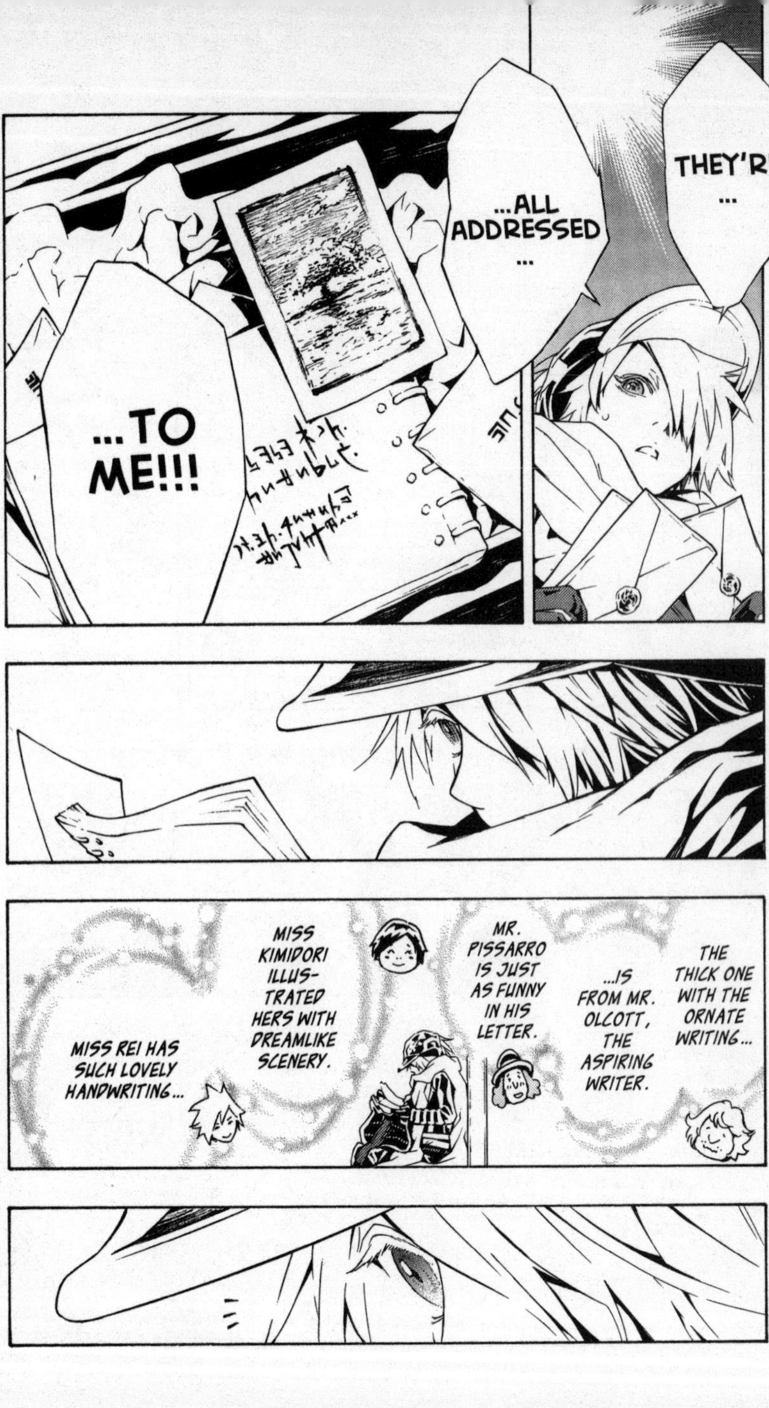
THEY'RE ...
...ALL ADDRESSED ...
...TO ME!!!
THE THICK ONE WITH THE ORNATE WRITING...
...IS FROM MR. OLCOTT, THE ASPIRING WRITER.
MR. PISSARRO IS JUST AS FUNNY IN HIS LETTER.
MISS KIMIDORI ILLUS-TRATED HERS WITH DREAMLIKE SCENERY.
MISS REI HAS SUCH LOVELY HANDWRITING...

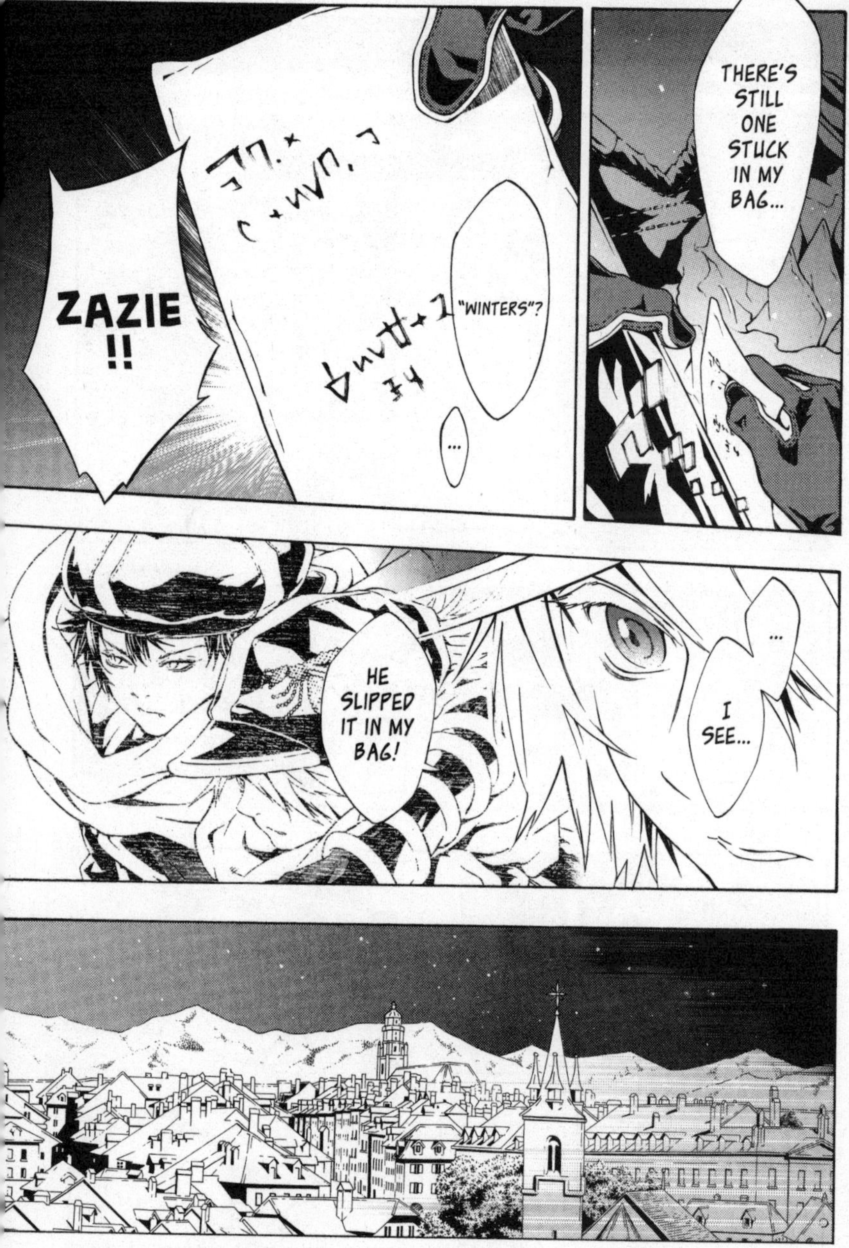
THERE'S STILL ONE STUCK IN MY BAG...
"WINTERS"?
...
ZAZIE!!
...
I SEE...
HE SLIPPED IT IN MY BAG!

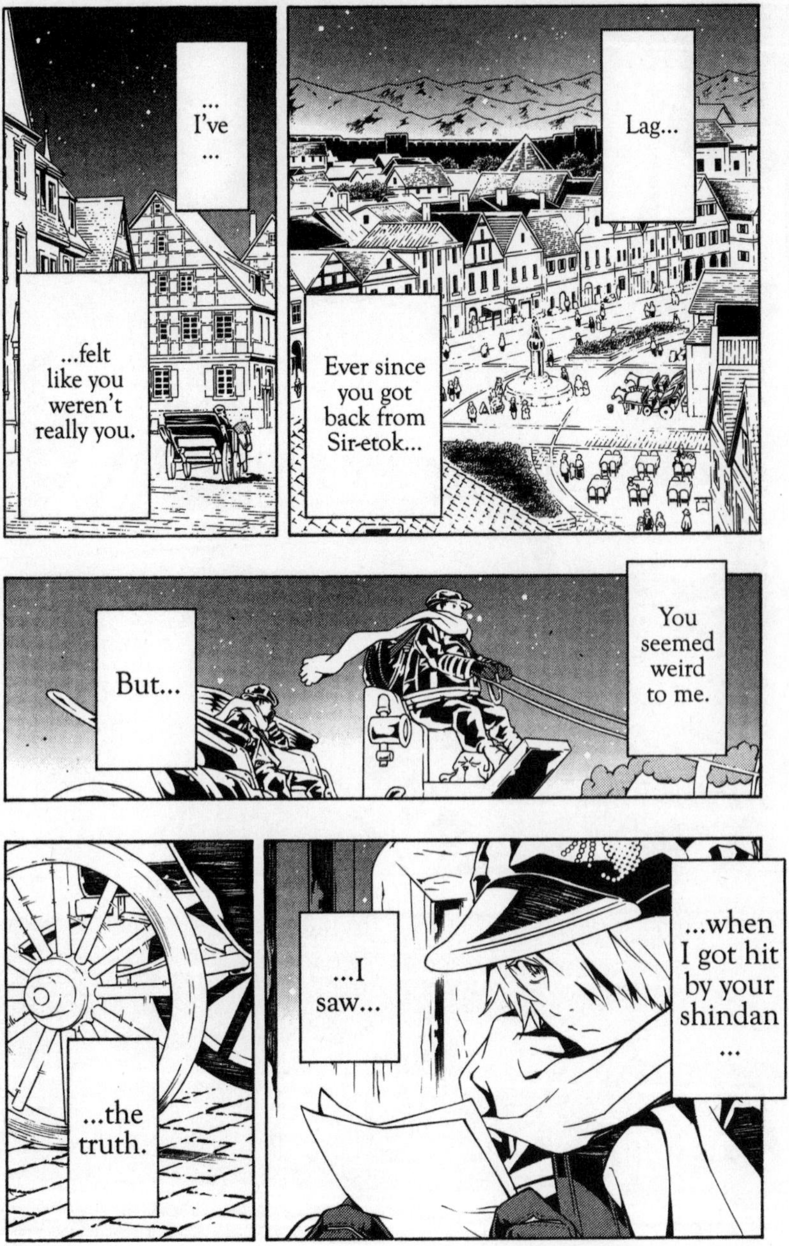
Lag...
Ever since you got back from Sir-etok...
... I've ...
...felt like you weren't really you.
You seemed weird to me.
But...
...when I got hit by your shindan ...
...I saw...
...the truth.

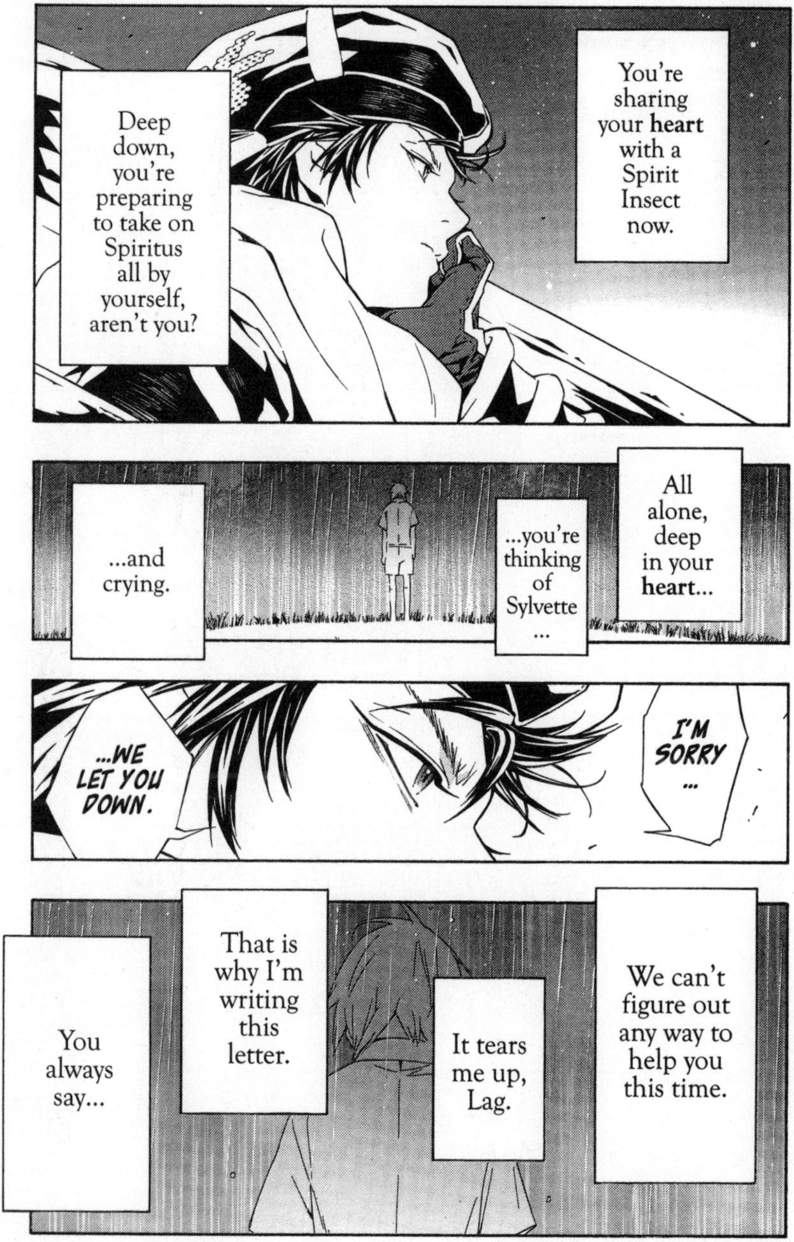
You're sharing your **heart** with a Spirit Insect now.
Deep down, you're preparing to take on Spiritus all by yourself, aren't you?
All alone, deep in your **heart**...
...you're thinking of Sylvette ...
...and crying.
I'M SORRY ...
...WE LET YOU DOWN.
We can't figure out any way to help you this time.
It tears me up, Lag.
That is why I'm writing this letter.
You always say...

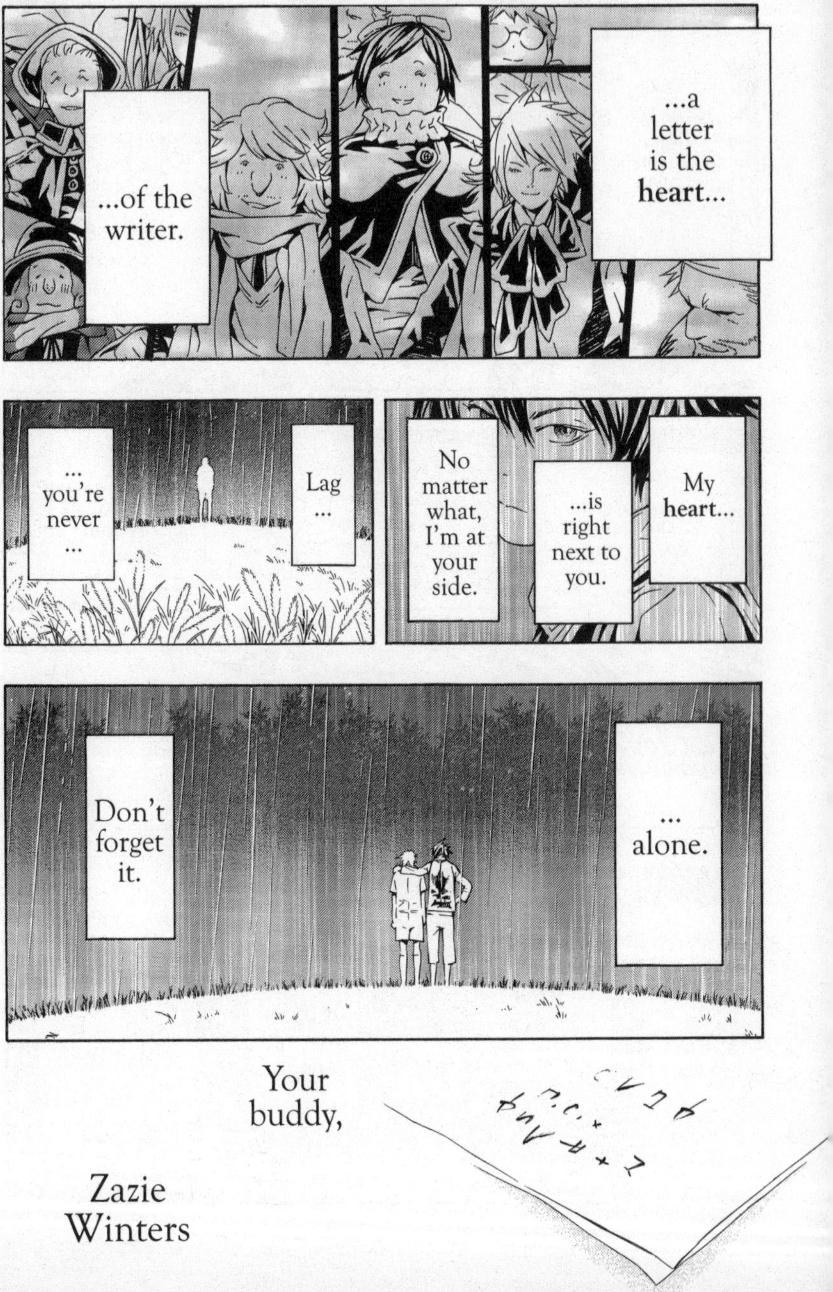
...a letter is the heart...
...of the writer.
My heart...
...is right next to you.
No matter what, I'm at your side.
Lag...
...you're never...
...alone.
Don't forget it.
Your buddy,
Zazie Winters

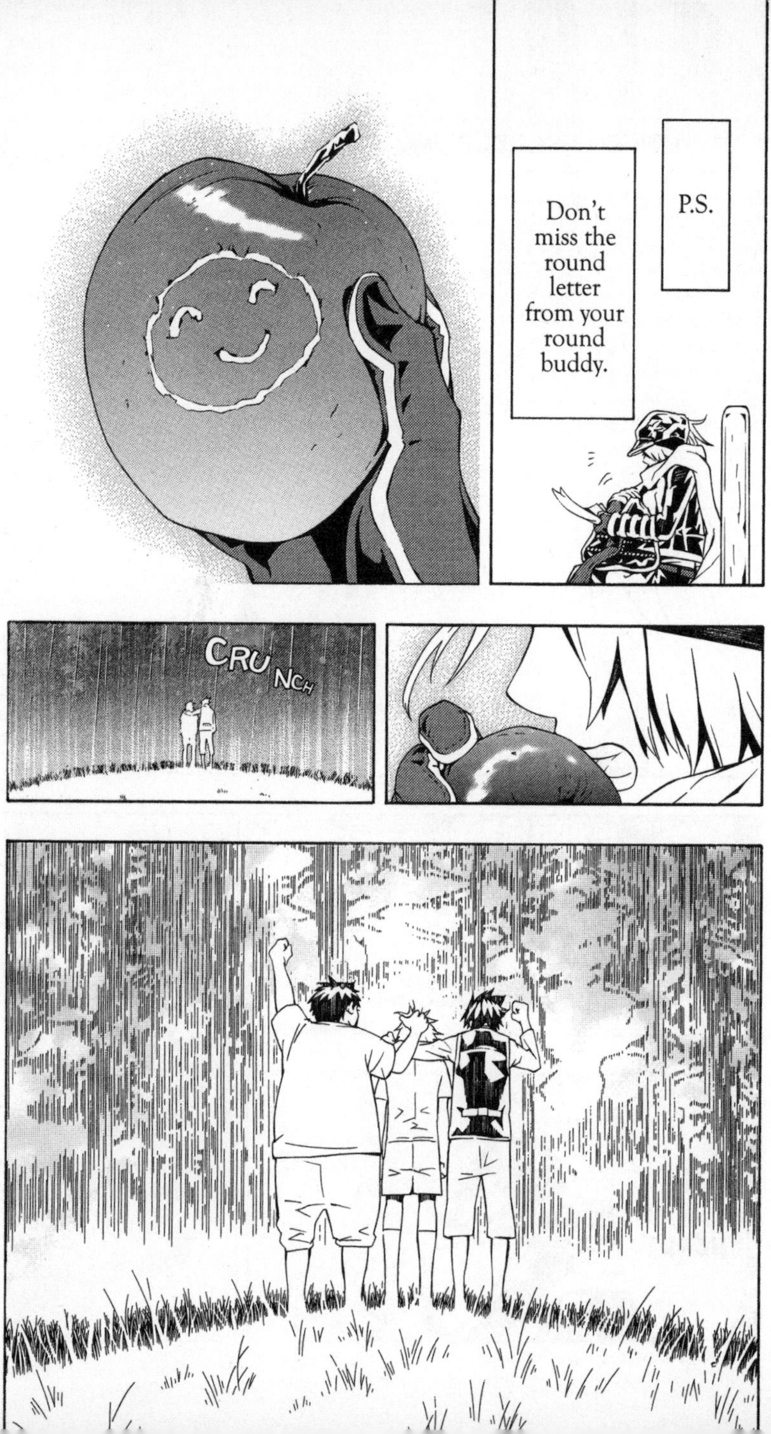
P.S.
Don't miss the round letter from your round buddy.
CRUNCH

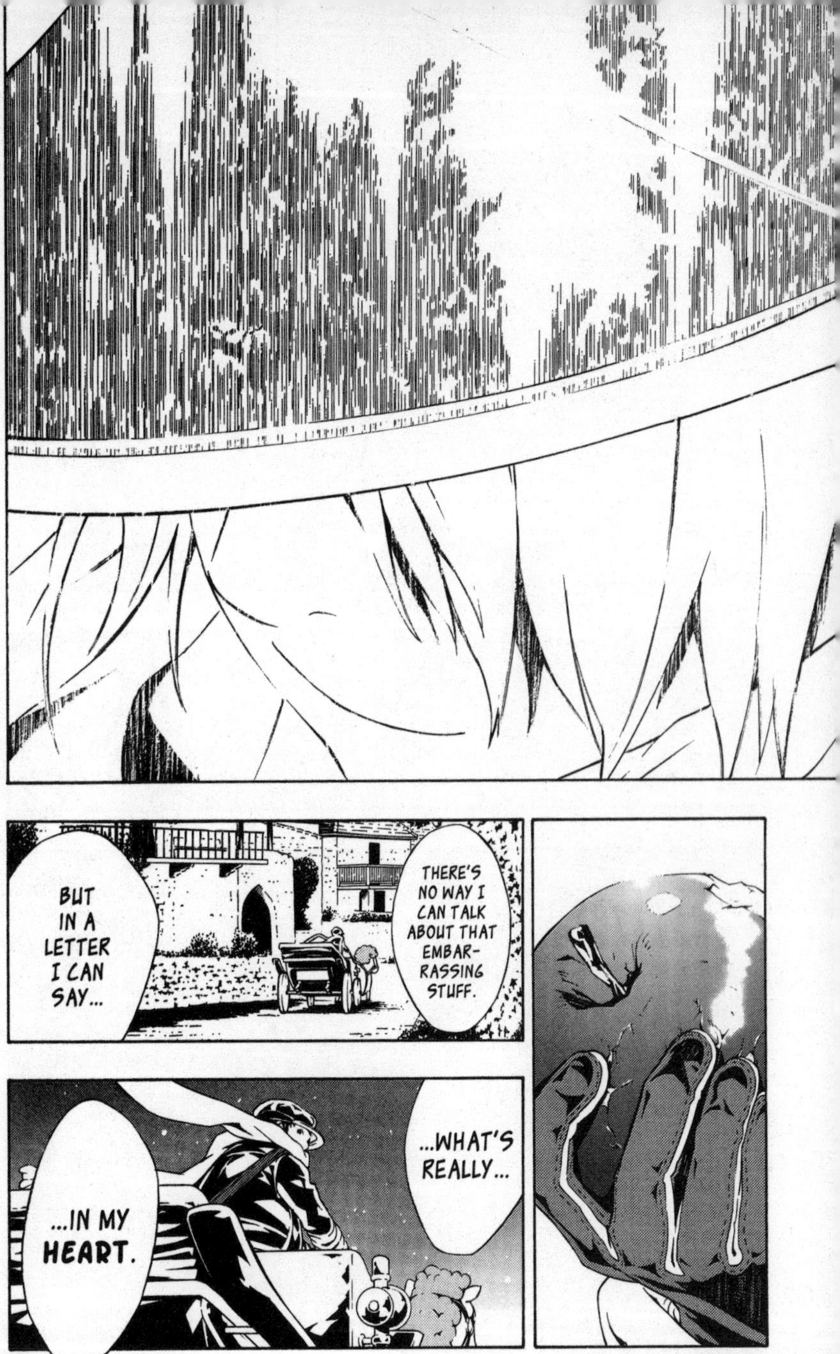
THERE'S NO WAY I CAN TALK ABOUT THAT EMBAR-RASSING STUFF.
BUT IN A LETTER I CAN SAY...
...WHAT'S REALLY...
...IN MY HEART.

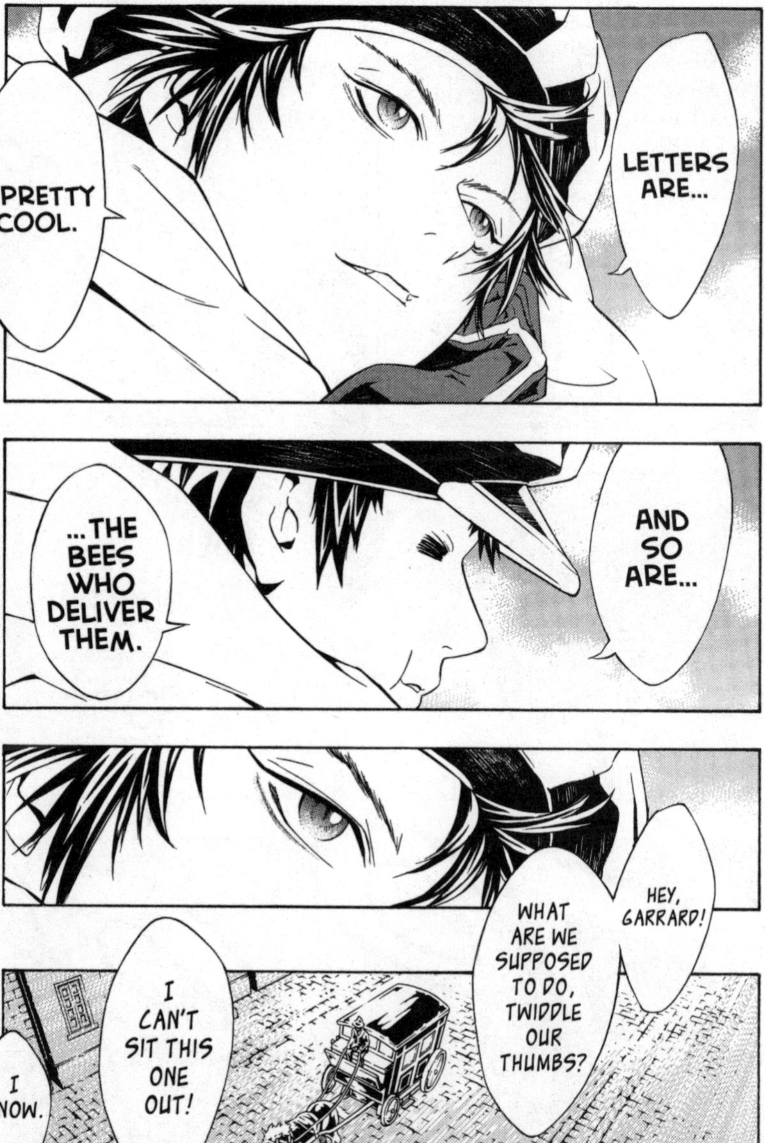
LETTERS ARE...
...PRETTY COOL.
AND SO ARE...
...THE BEES WHO DELIVER THEM.
HEY, GARRARD!
WHAT ARE WE SUPPOSED TO DO, TWIDDLE OUR THUMBS?
I CAN'T SIT THIS ONE OUT!
I KNOW.

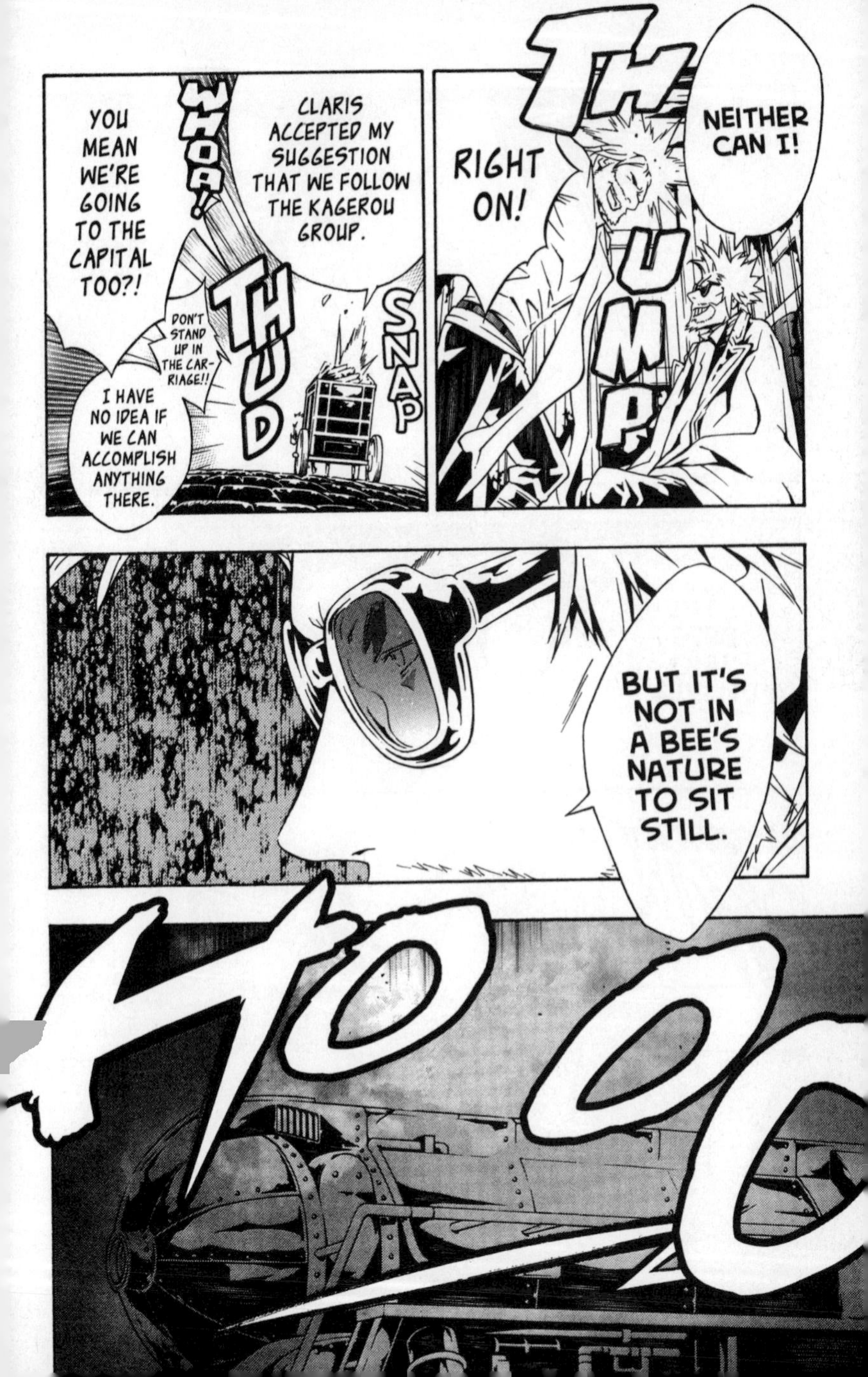
NEITHER CAN I!
THUMP
RIGHT ON!
CLARIS ACCEPTED MY SUGGESTION THAT WE FOLLOW THE KAGEROU GROUP.
WHOA!
YOU MEAN WE'RE GOING TO THE CAPITAL TOO?!
SNAP
THUD
DON'T STAND UP IN THE CAR-RIAGE!!
I HAVE NO IDEA IF WE CAN ACCOMPLISH ANYTHING THERE.
BUT IT'S NOT IN A BEE'S NATURE TO SIT STILL.
TOOO

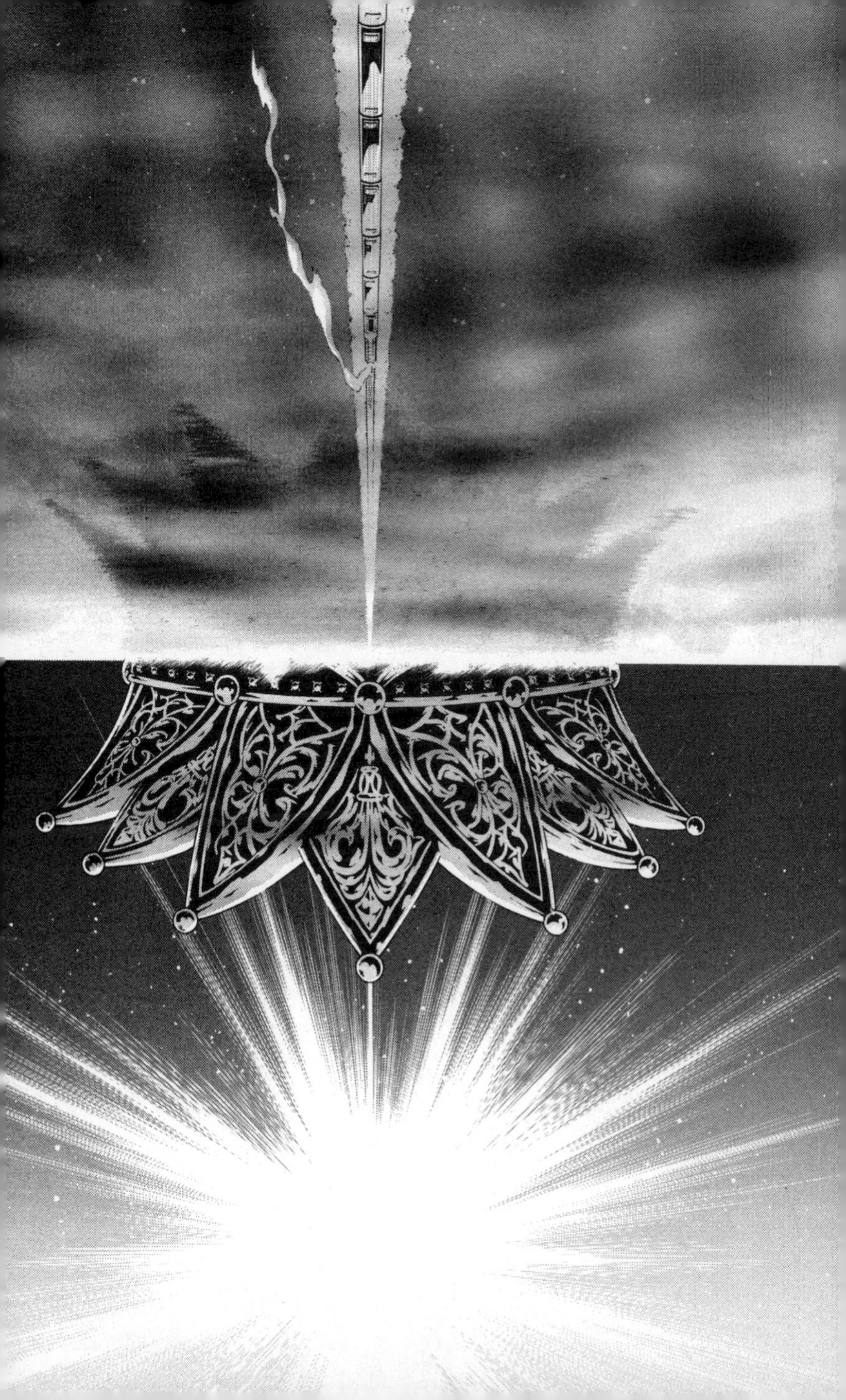

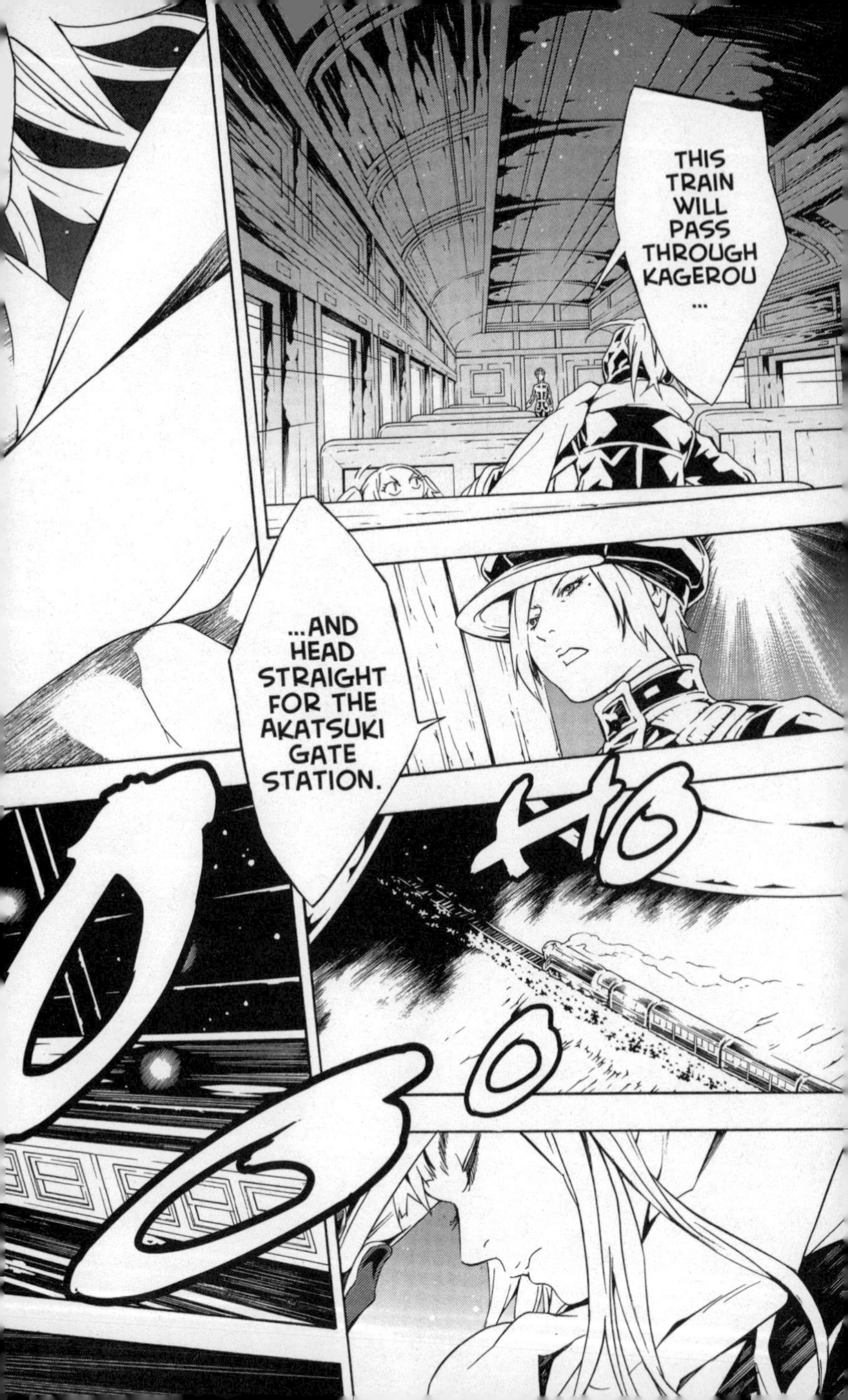
THIS TRAIN WILL PASS THROUGH KAGEROU ...
...AND HEAD STRAIGHT FOR THE AKATSUKI GATE STATION.

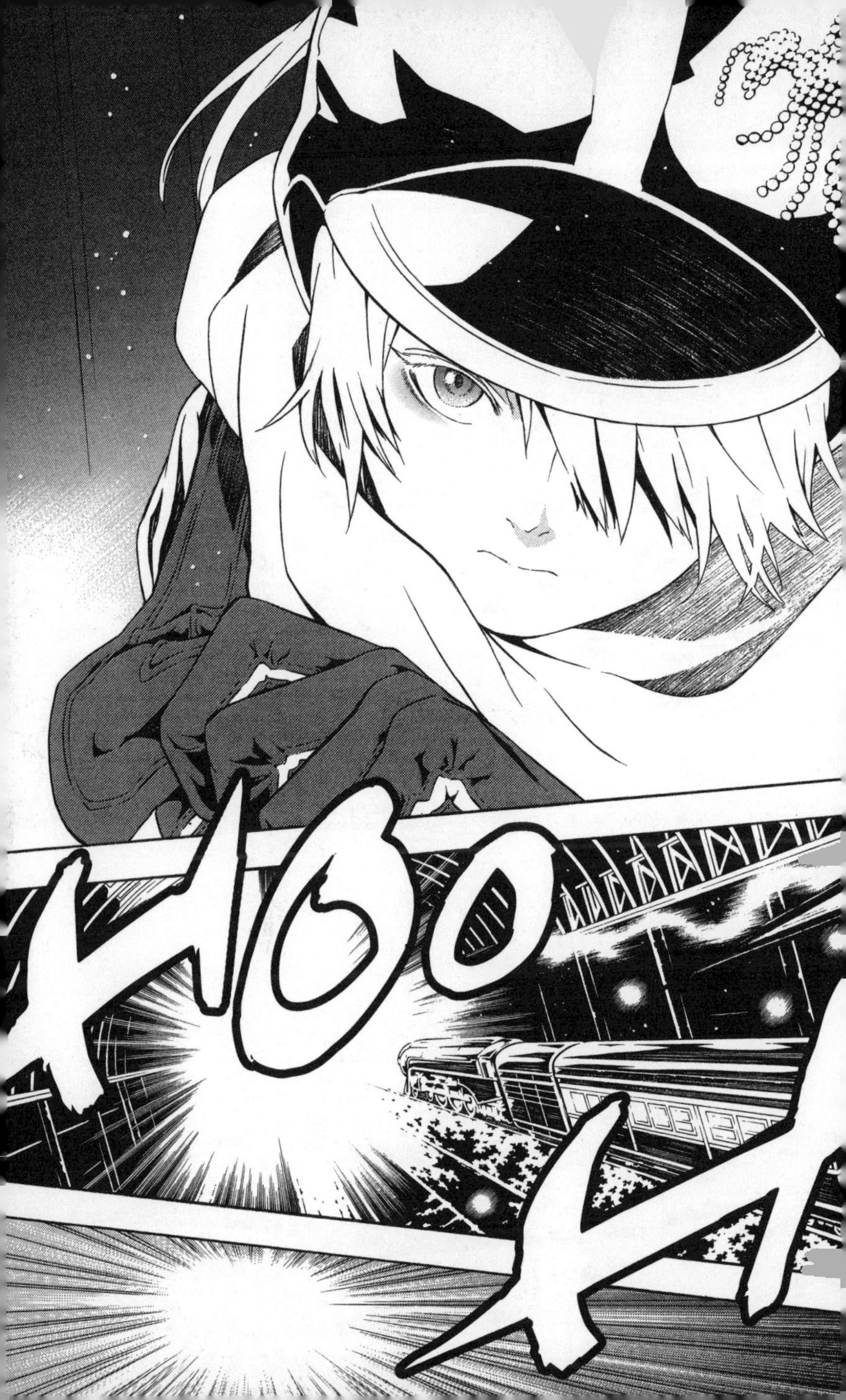

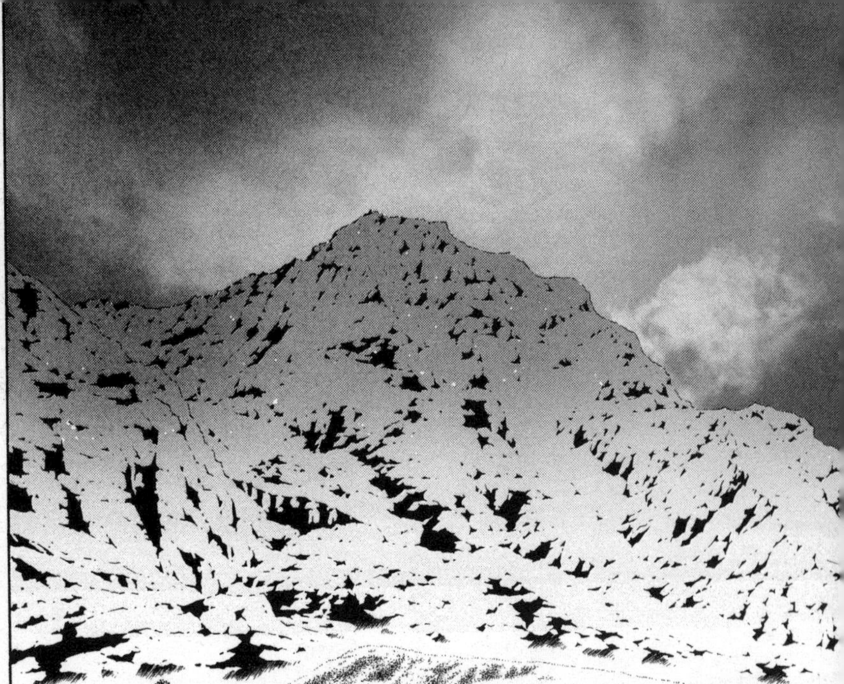

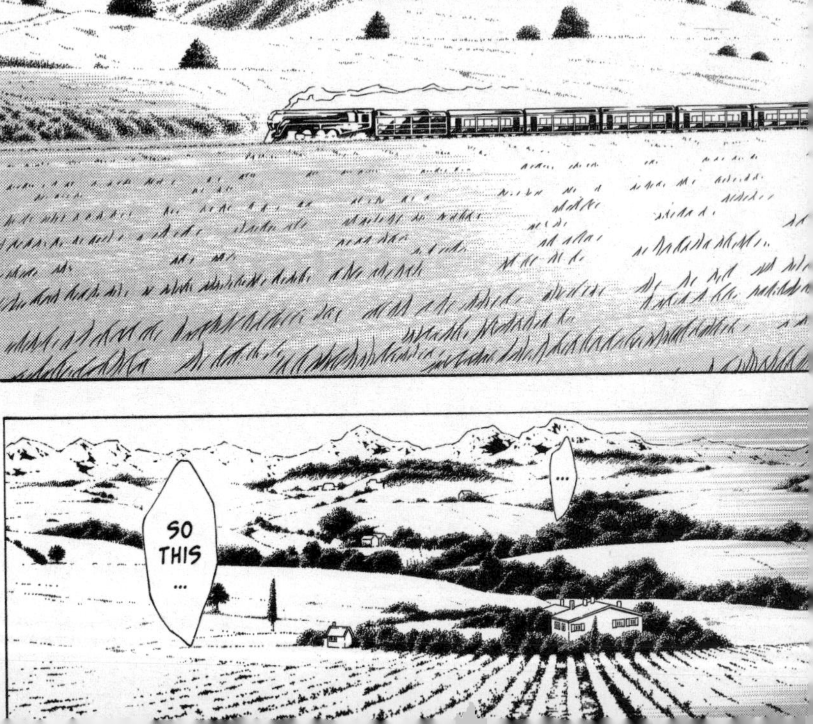
...
SO THIS ...

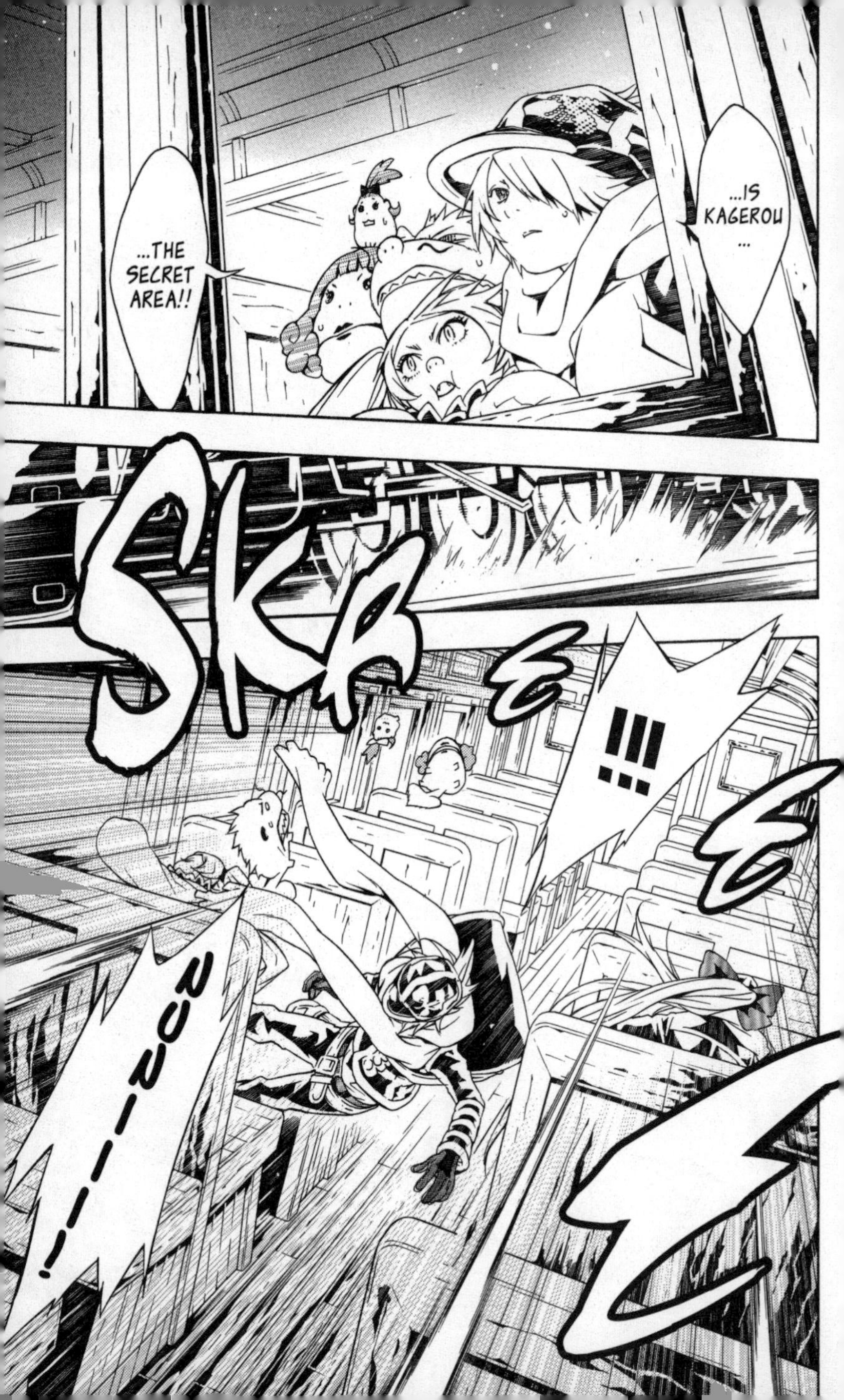
...IS KAGEROU ...
...THE SECRET AREA!!
SKR
EEE
!!!...
RUUN---!

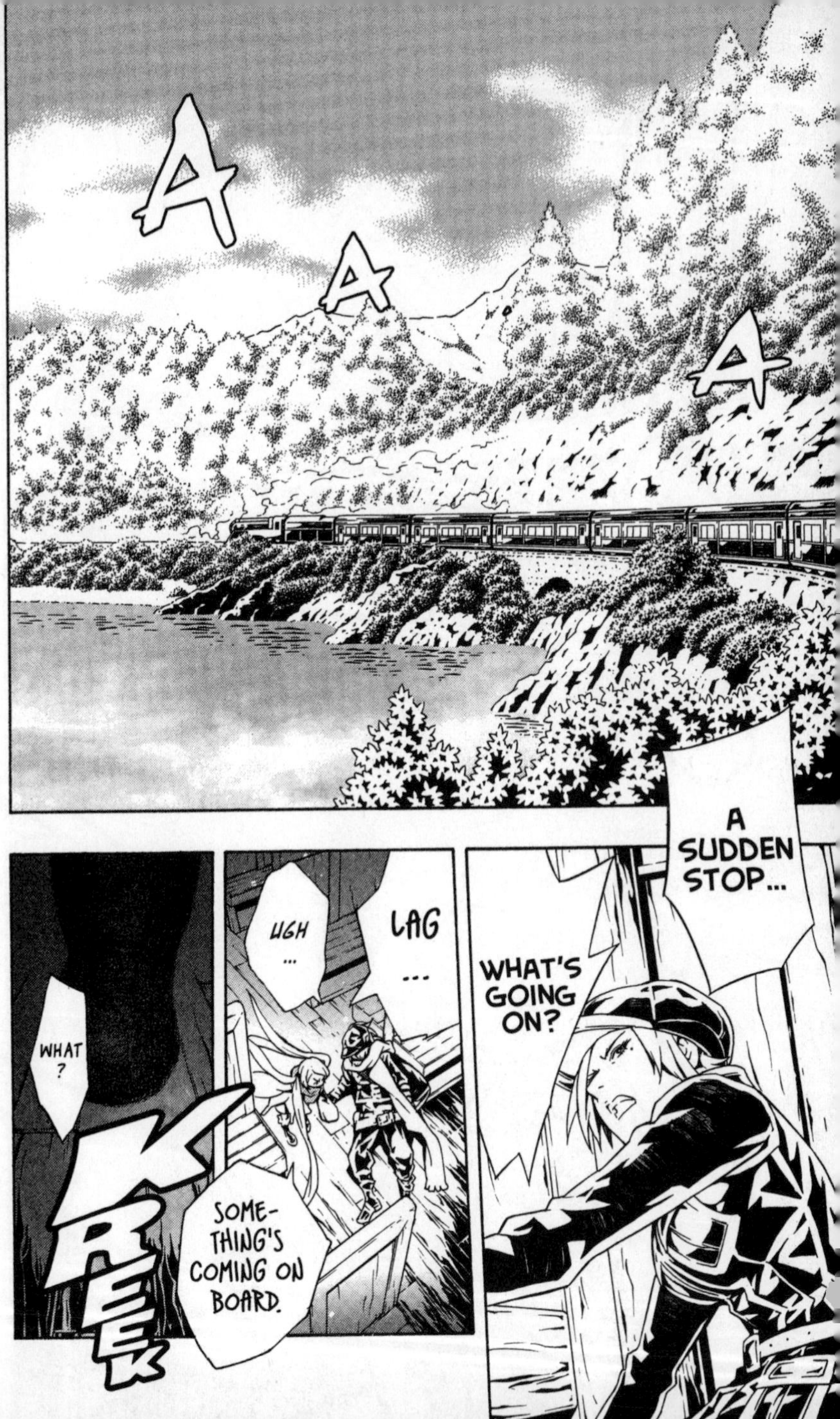
A
A
A
A SUDDEN STOP...
WHAT'S GOING ON?
LAG...
UGH...
SOME-THING'S COMING ON BOARD.
WHAT?
KREEK

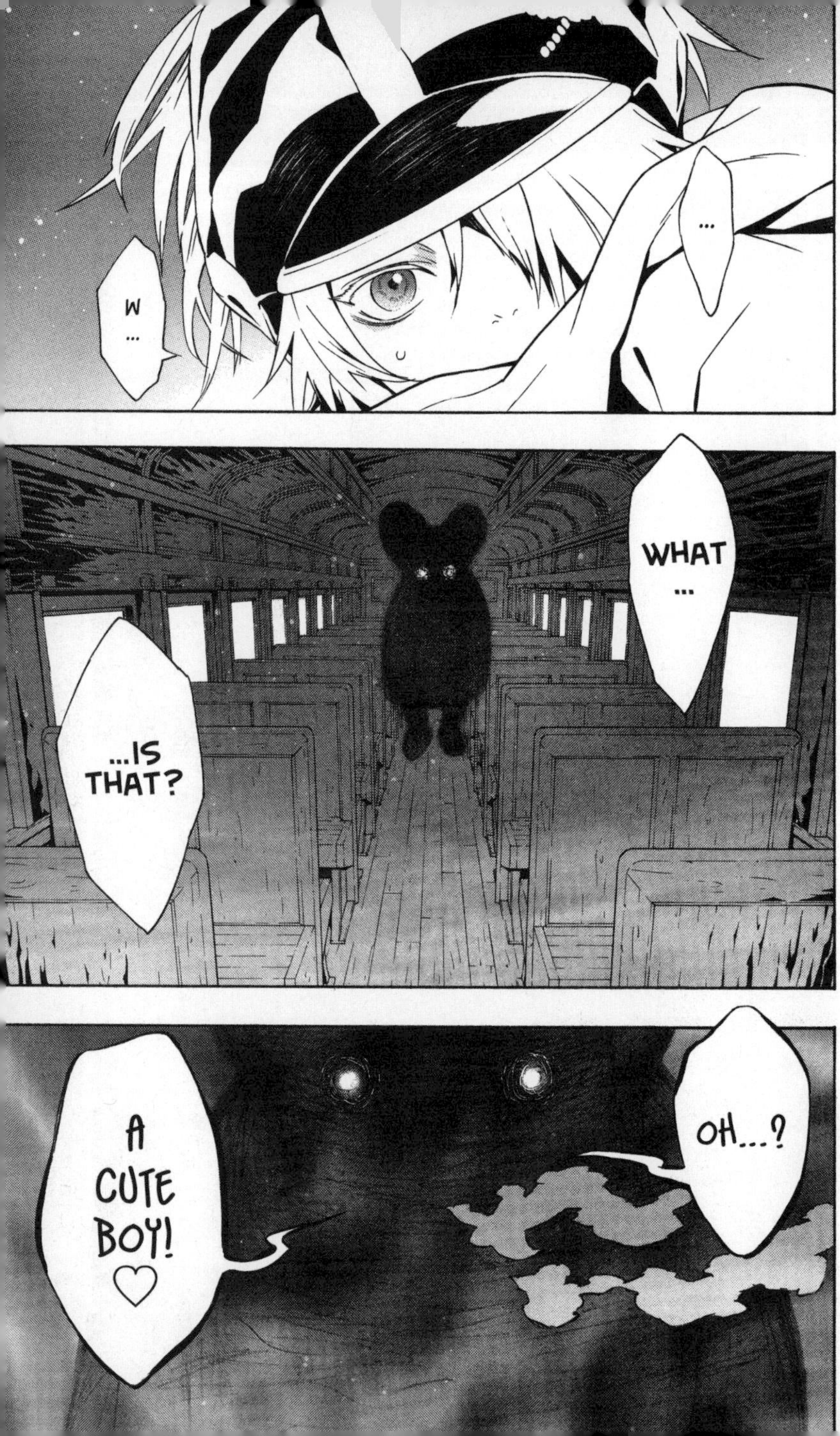
...
W ...
WHAT ...
...IS THAT?
OH...?
A CUTE BOY! ♡

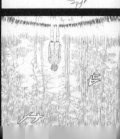

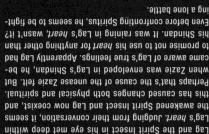

LAG'S HEART

Lag and the Spirit Insect in his eye met deep within Lag's *heart*. Judging from their conversation, it seems the awakened Spirit Insect and Lag now coexist, and this has caused changes both physical and spiritual. Perhaps that's the cause of the unease Zazie felt. But when Zazie was enveloped in Lag's Shindan, he became aware of Lag's true feelings. Apparently Lag had to promise not to use his *heart* for anything other than his Shindan. It was raining in Lag's *heart*, wasn't it? Even before confronting Spiritus, he seems to be fighting a lone battle.

Speaking of Lag's Shindan...it used to be Akabari, right? But it's different now. And he fired six shots in a row. We've never seen that before. This new Shindan must have been created when the *hearts* of Lag and the Spirit Insect converged.

Lag said he would defeat Spiritus and retrieve Sylvette's *heart*. Does that mean her *heart* is still whole? Perhaps awakening his Spirit Insect has allowed Lag to sense certain things.

Hrrmmph!! That does it! I'm going too! I'll defeat Spiritus! Let me fight! My Washibari must burst forth! I'll load it with my desires!! Shindan, loaded! Resonate Washibari! Now's the time!! Watch me jump to the left page just like Mario! in chapter 90, I'll hijack the train. You'd like to see that, right? Very well!! Here goes! Jump! Jump! Jump! Jump! Squaree!!

n.b.: Malt / Traditional whiskey made from germinated barley.

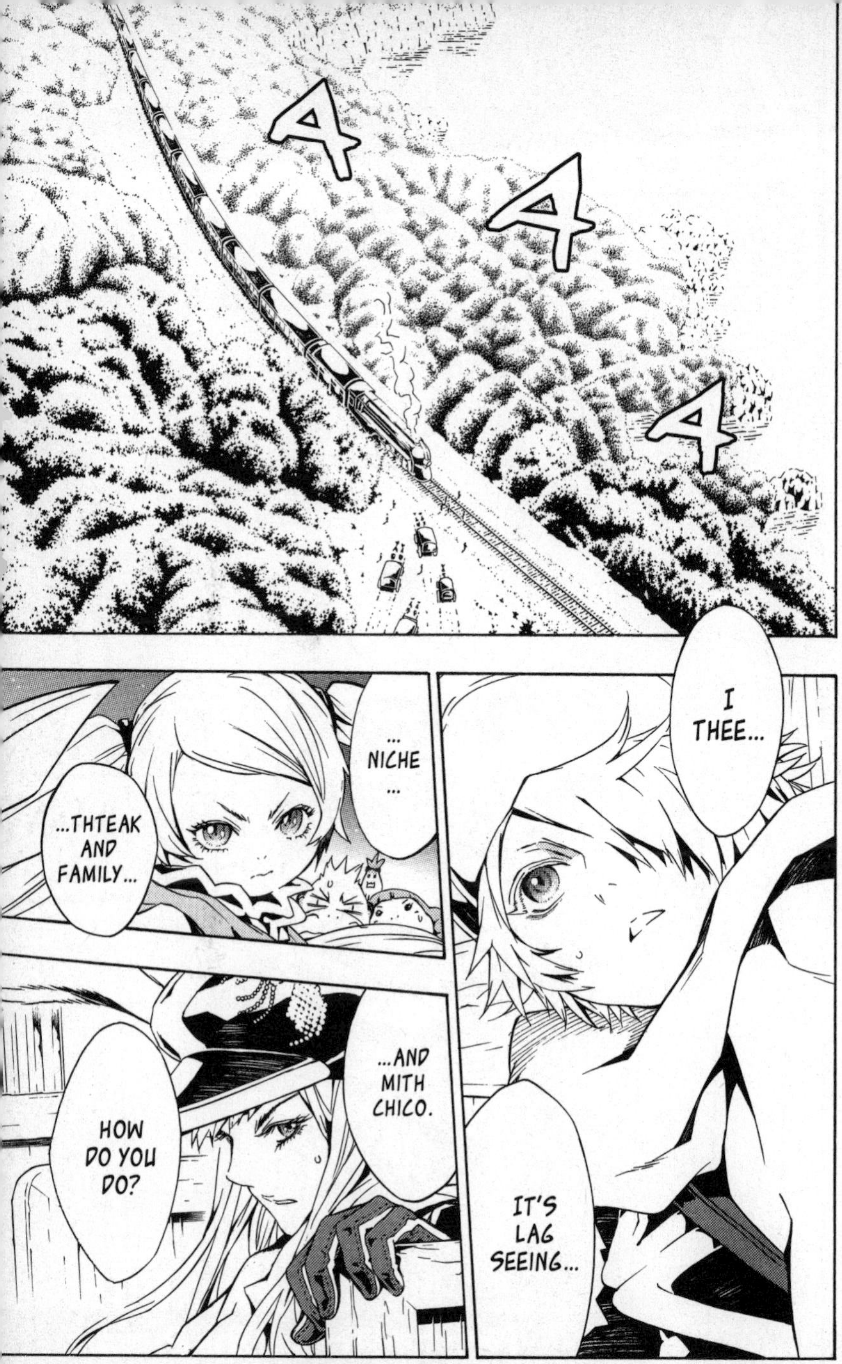
4
4
4
I THEE...
IT'S LAG SEEING...
... NICHE ...
...THTEAK AND FAMILY...
...AND MITH CHICO.
HOW DO YOU DO?

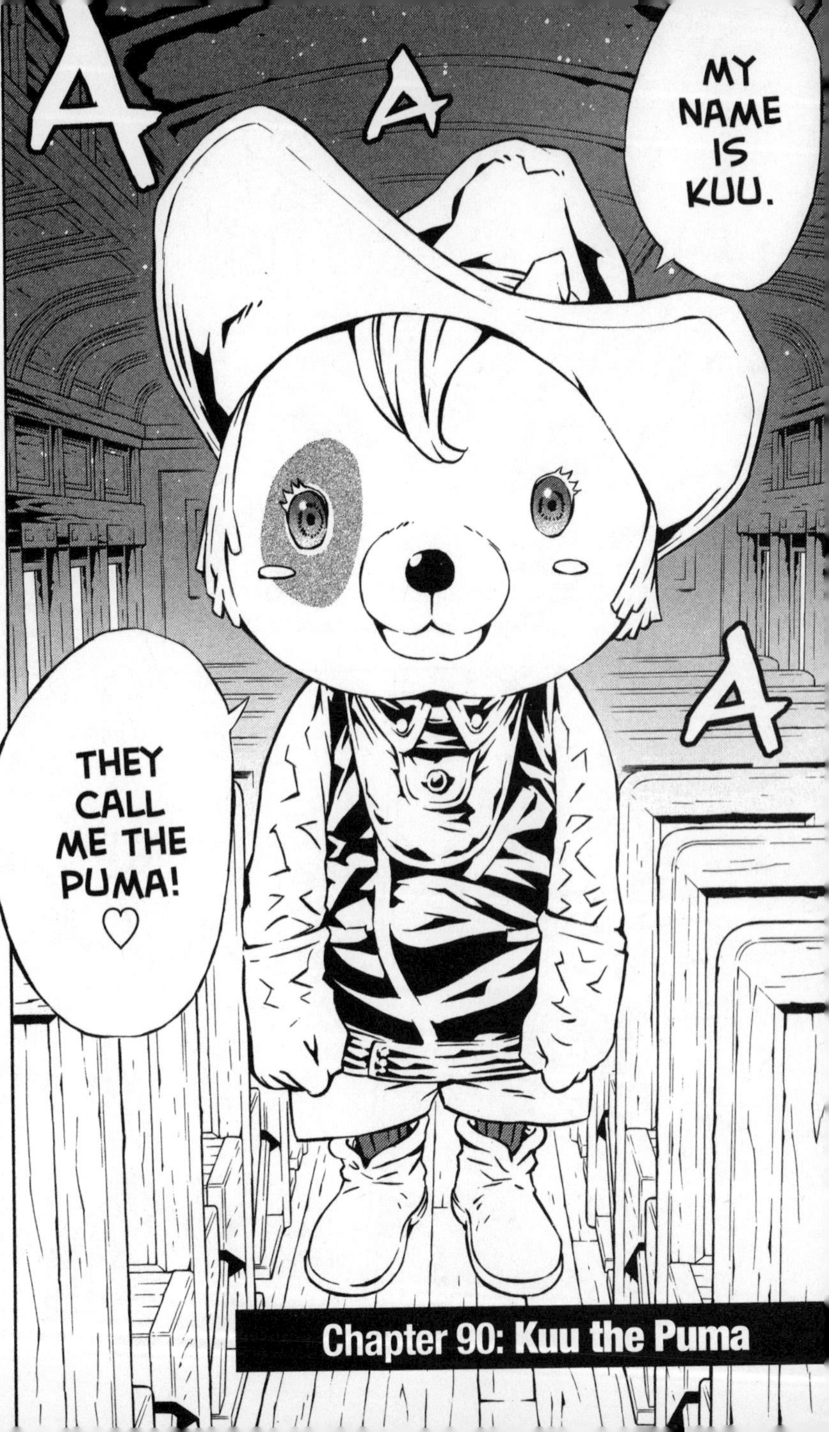
MY NAME IS KUU.
A
A
A
THEY CALL ME THE PUMA! ♡

Chapter 90: Kuu the Puma

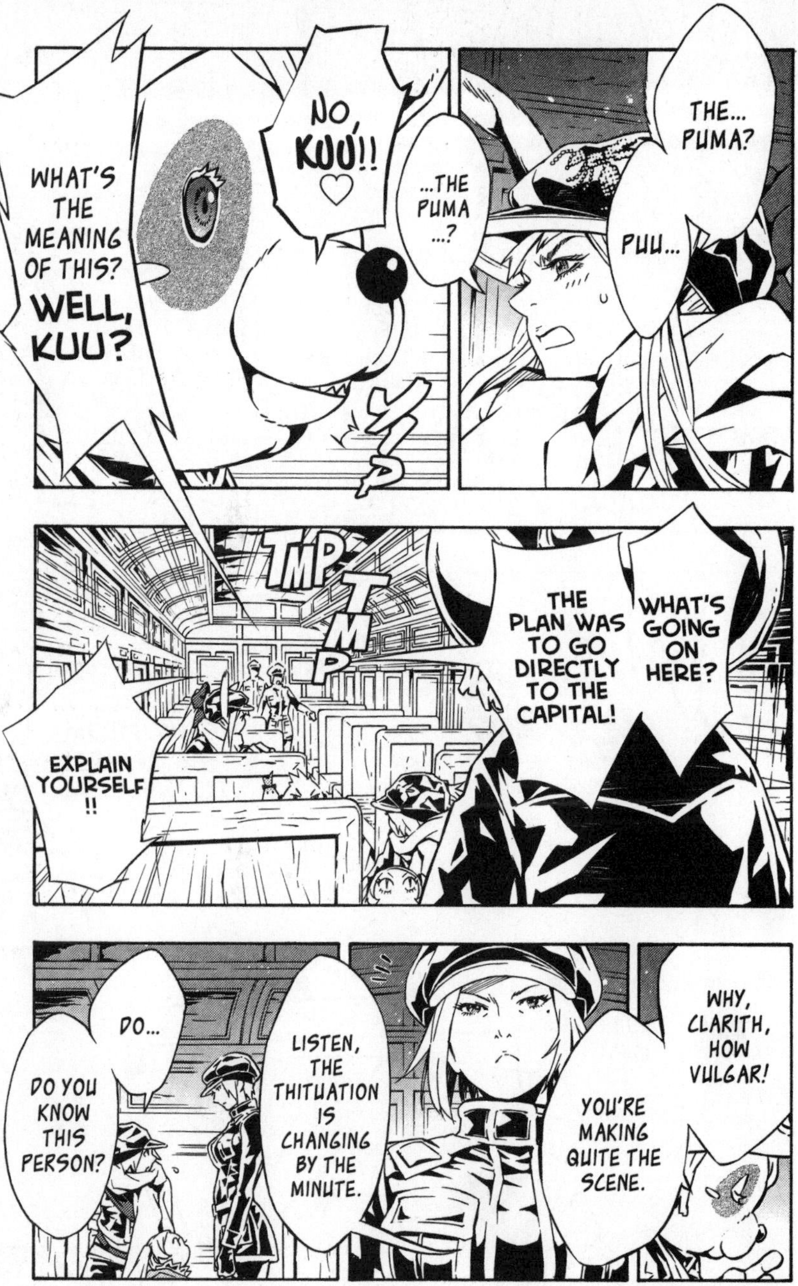
THE... PUMA?
PUU...
...THE PUMA ...?
NO, KUU!! ♡
YIP
WHAT'S THE MEANING OF THIS? WELL, KUU?
TMP TMP
WHAT'S GOING ON HERE?
THE PLAN WAS TO GO DIRECTLY TO THE CAPITAL!
EXPLAIN YOURSELF !!
WHY, CLARITH, HOW VULGAR!
YOU'RE MAKING QUITE THE SCENE.
LISTEN, THE THITUATION IS CHANGING BY THE MINUTE.
DO...
DO YOU KNOW THIS PERSON?

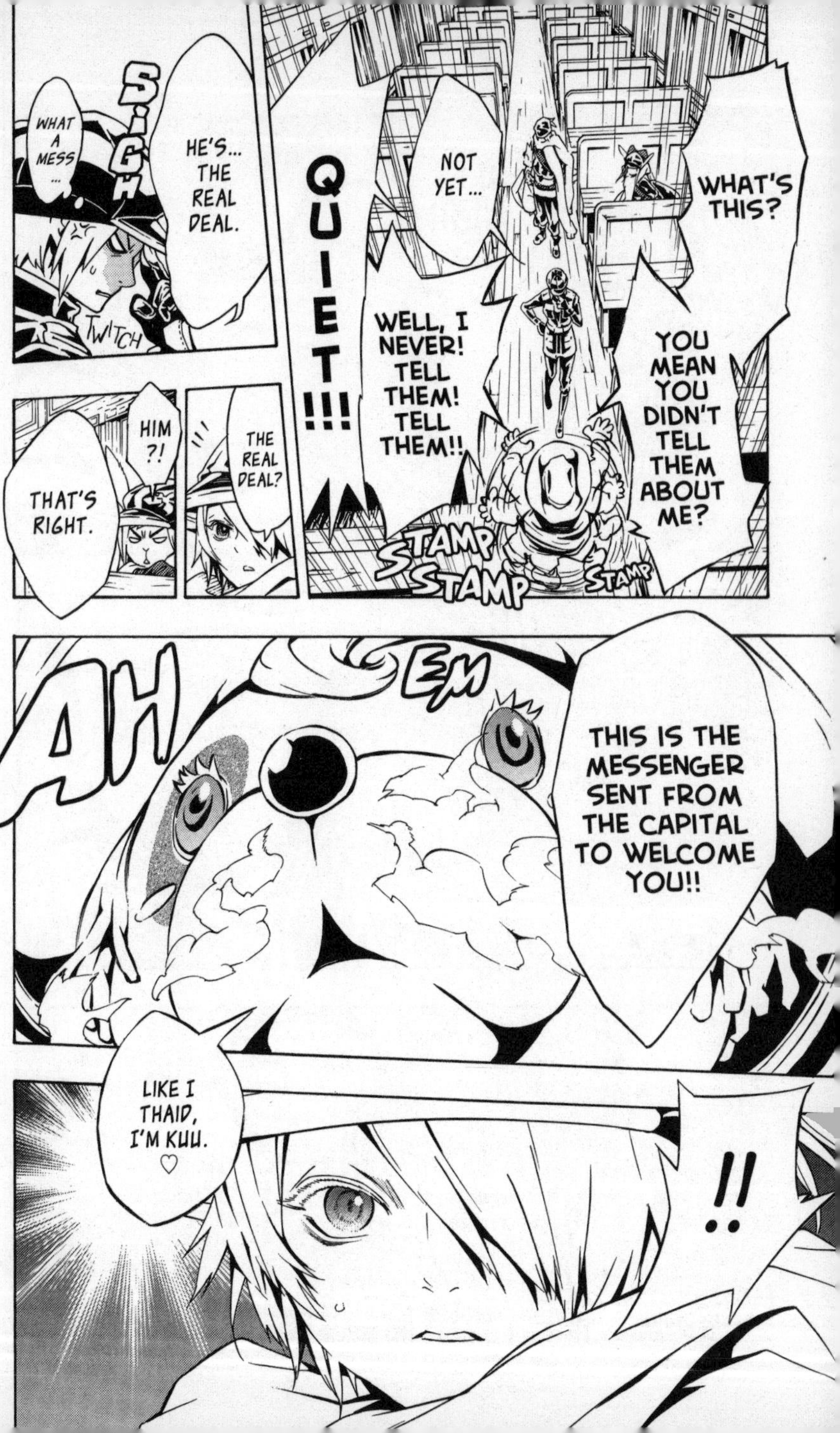
WHAT'S THIS?
YOU MEAN YOU DIDN'T TELL THEM ABOUT ME?
STAMP STAMP STAMP
NOT YET...
WELL, I NEVER! TELL THEM! TELL THEM!!
QUIET!!!
HE'S... THE REAL DEAL.
SIGH
WHAT A MESS...
TWITCH
THE REAL DEAL?
HIM ?!
THAT'S RIGHT.
THIS IS THE MESSENGER SENT FROM THE CAPITAL TO WELCOME YOU!!
AHEM
LIKE I THAID, I'M KUU. ♡
!!

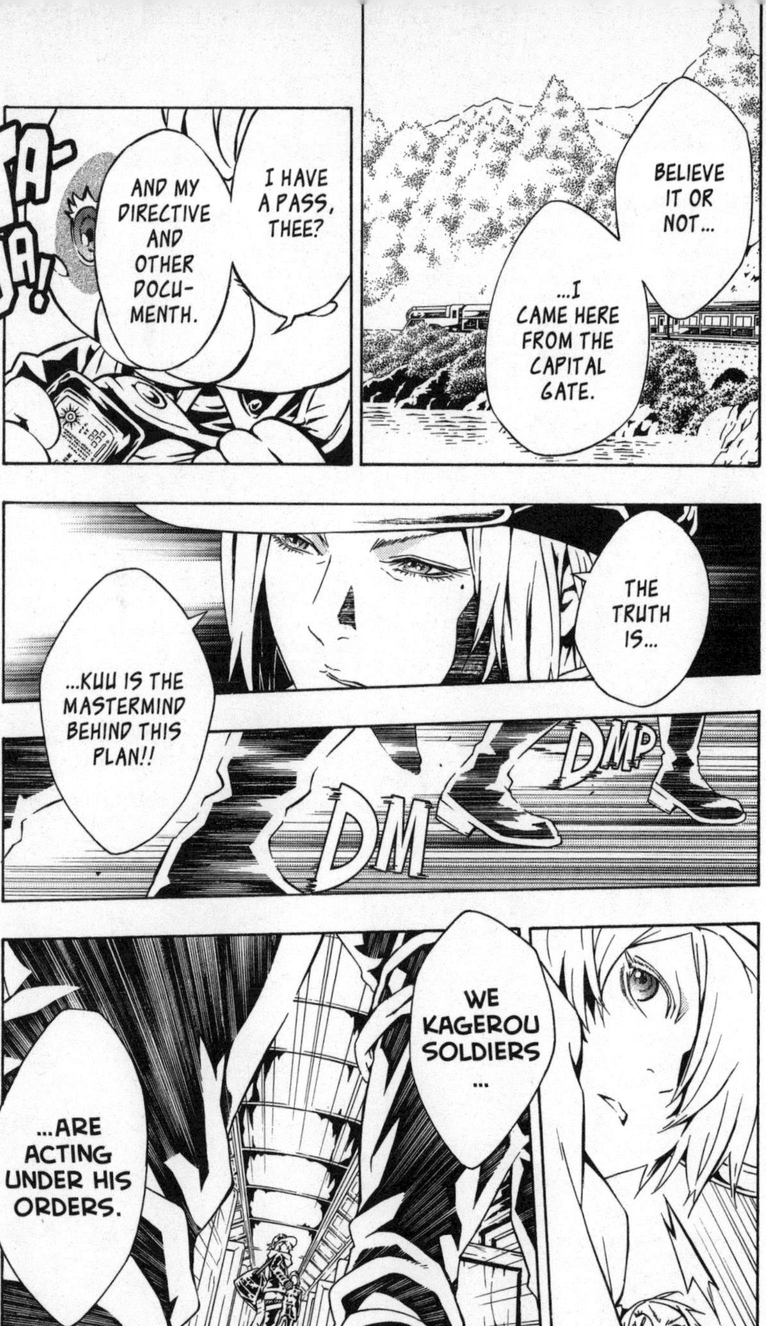
BELIEVE IT OR NOT...
...I CAME HERE FROM THE CAPITAL GATE.
I HAVE A PASS, THEE?
AND MY DIRECTIVE AND OTHER DOCU-MENTH.
TA-DA!
THE TRUTH IS...
...KUU IS THE MASTERMIND BEHIND THIS PLAN!!
DMP
DM
WE KAGEROU SOLDIERS...
...ARE ACTING UNDER HIS ORDERS.

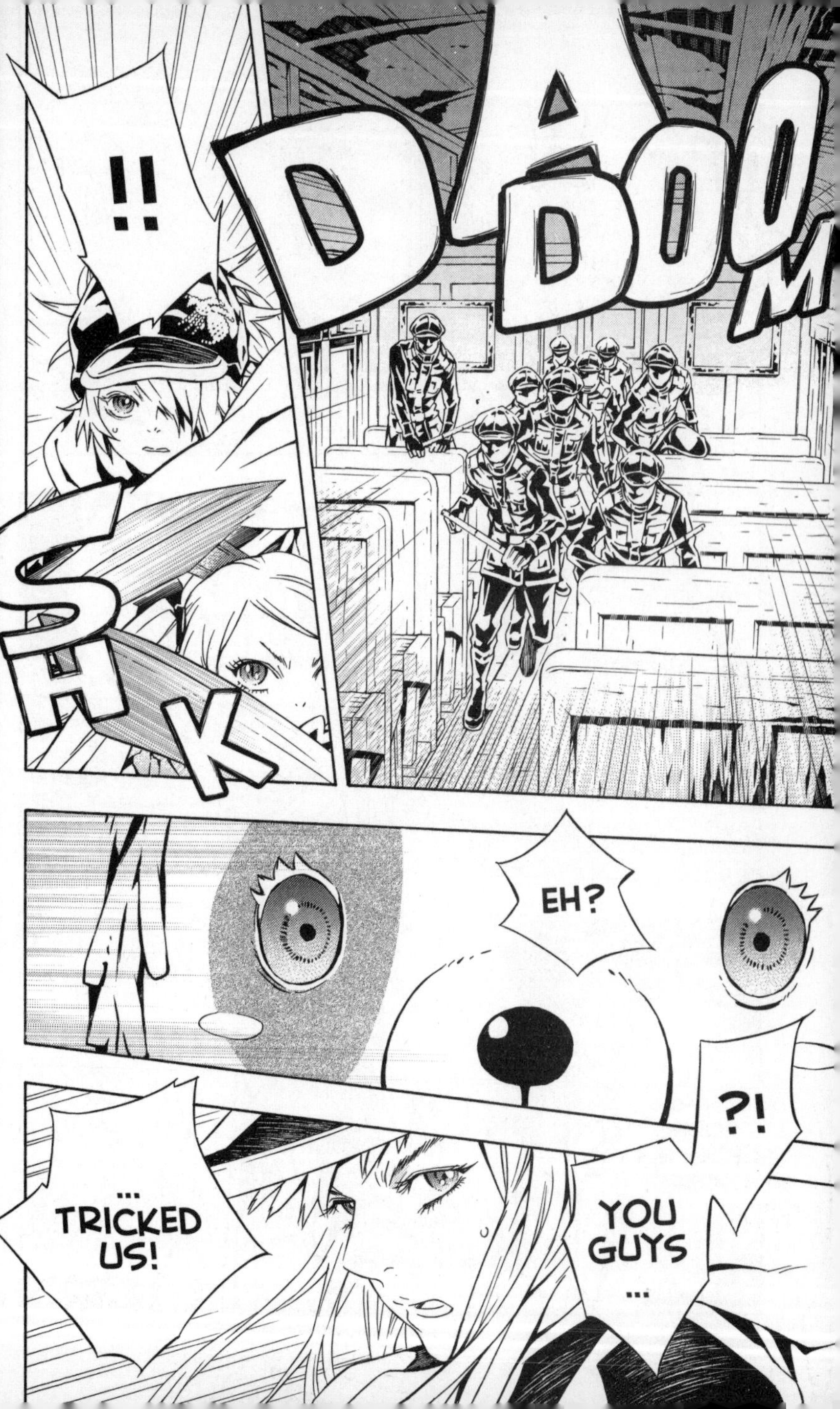
D-DOOM
!!
SHK
EH?
?!
YOU GUYS ...
... TRICKED US!

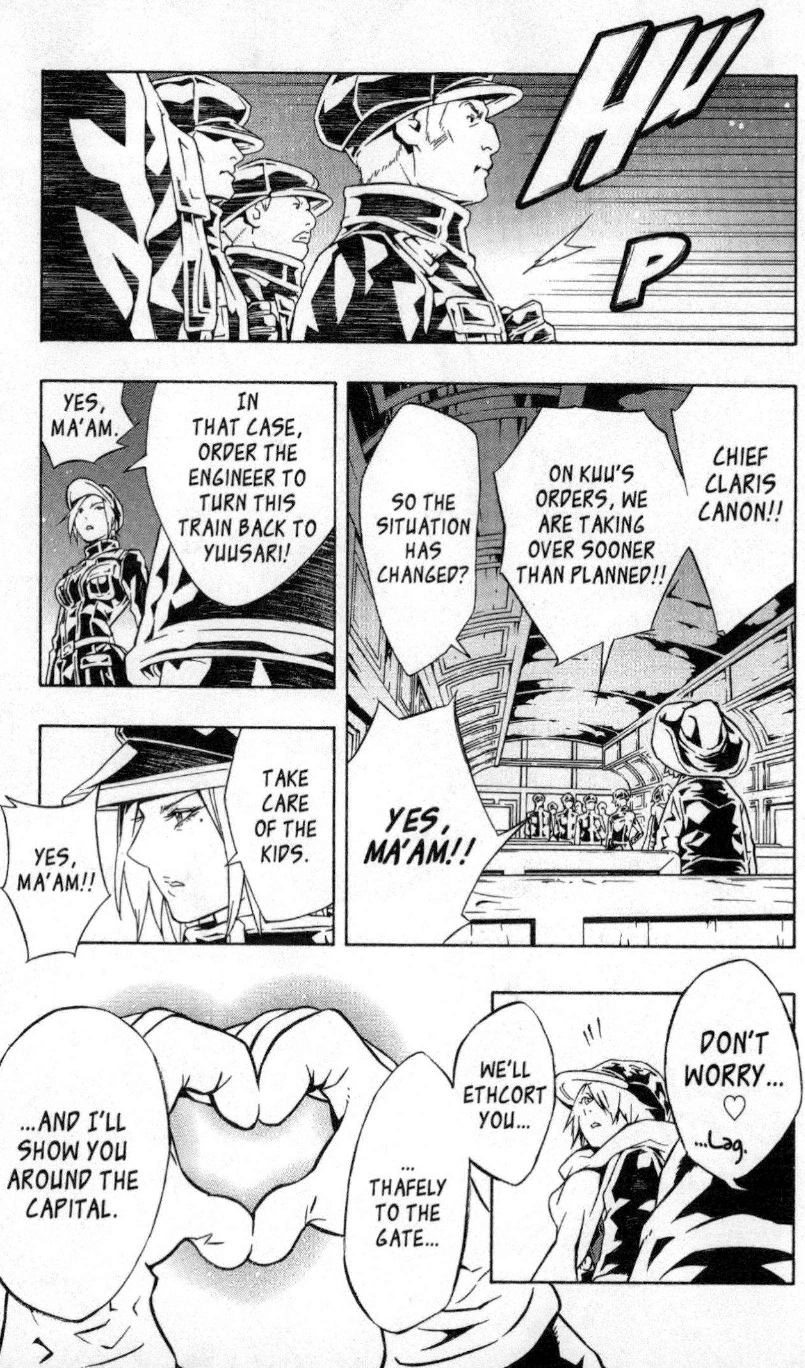
HUP
CHIEF CLARIS CANON!!
ON KUU'S ORDERS, WE ARE TAKING OVER SOONER THAN PLANNED!!
SO THE SITUATION HAS CHANGED?
YES, MA'AM!!
IN THAT CASE, ORDER THE ENGINEER TO TURN THIS TRAIN BACK TO YUUSARI!
YES, MA'AM.
TAKE CARE OF THE KIDS.
YES, MA'AM!!
DON'T WORRY... ♡ ...Lag.
WE'LL ETHCORT YOU...
...THAFELY TO THE GATE...
...AND I'LL SHOW YOU AROUND THE CAPITAL.

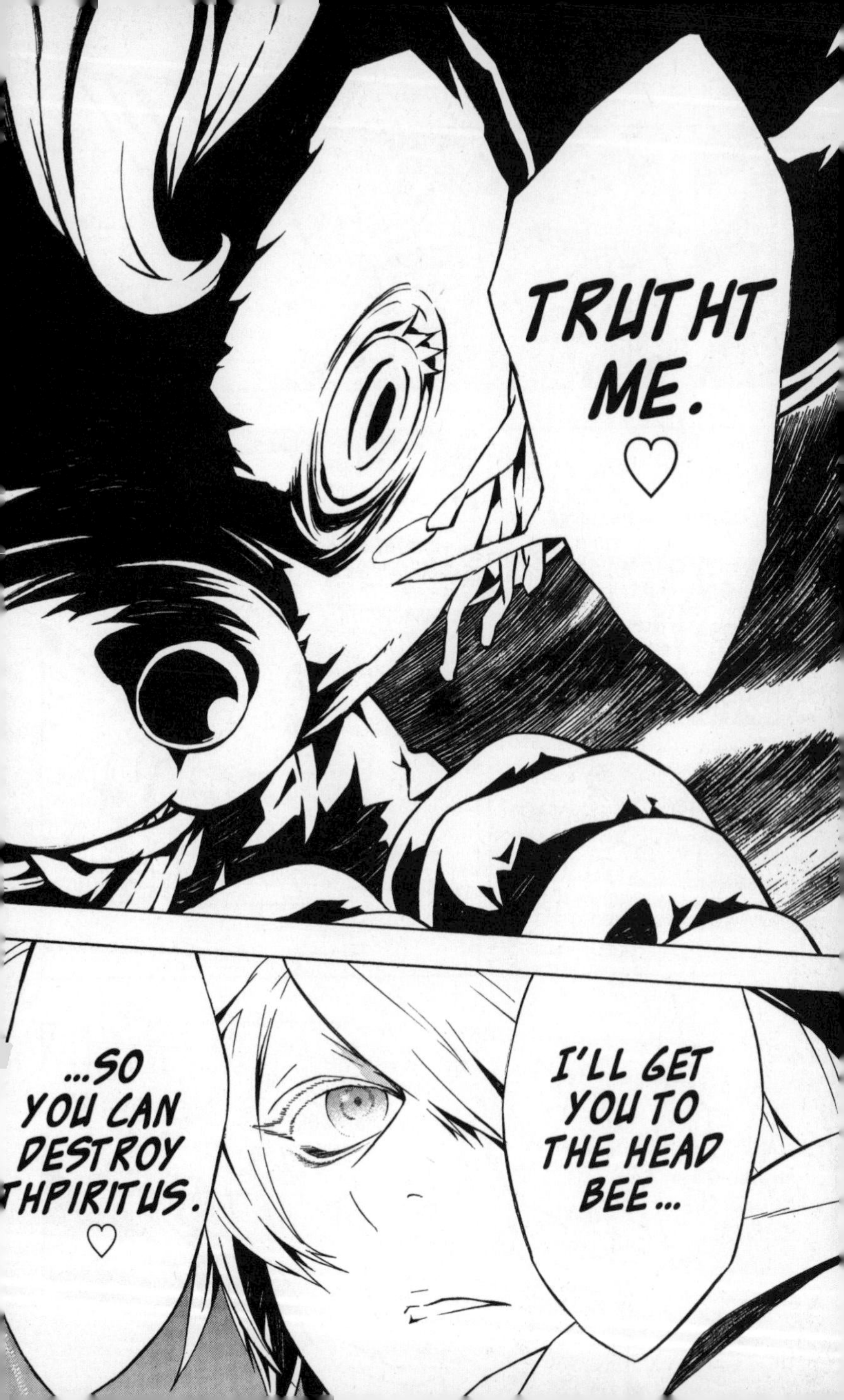
TRUTHT ME. ♡
I'LL GET YOU TO THE HEAD BEE...
...SO YOU CAN DESTROY THPIRITUS. ♡

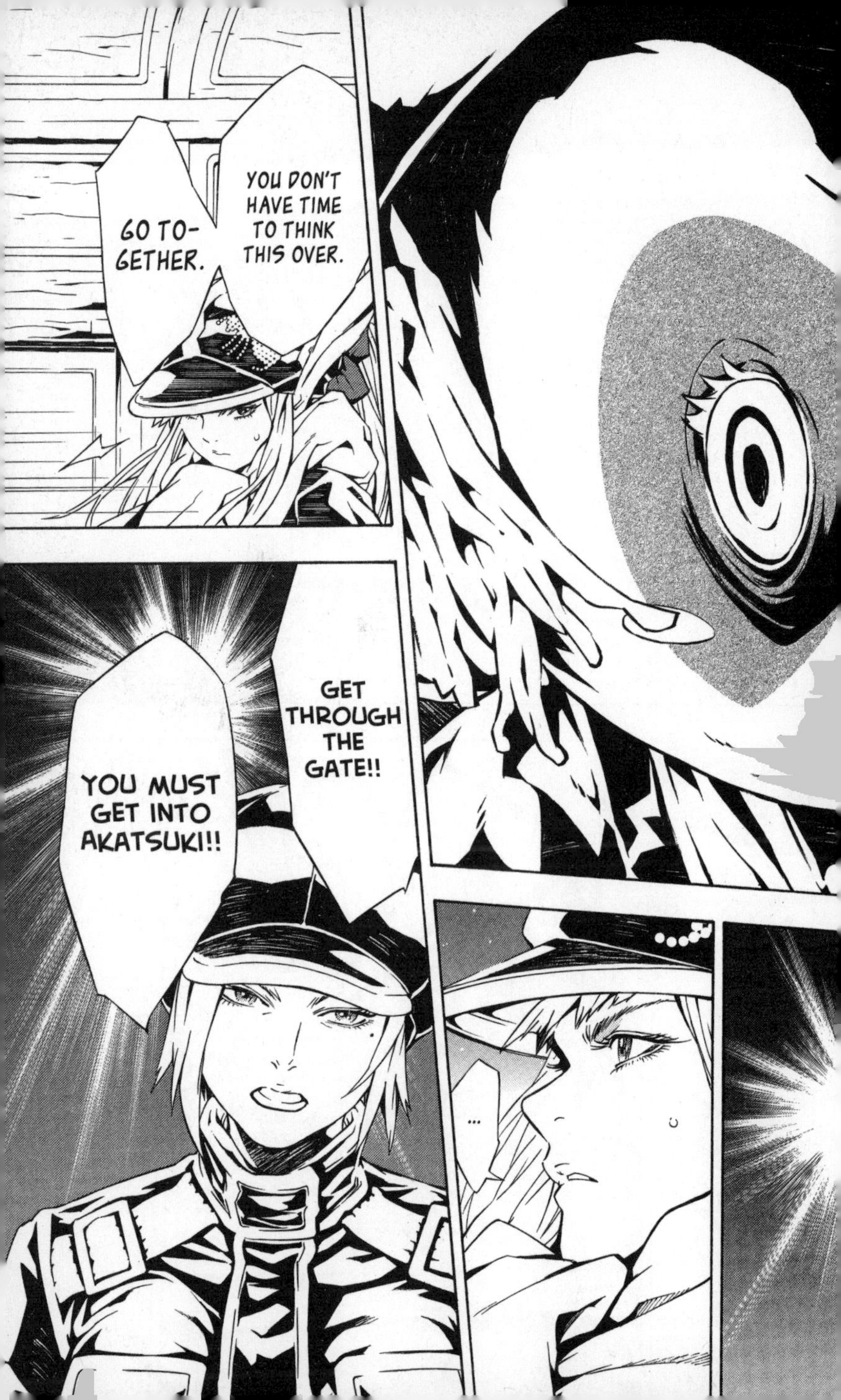
YOU DON'T HAVE TIME TO THINK THIS OVER.
GO TO-GETHER.
GET THROUGH THE GATE!!
YOU MUST GET INTO AKATSUKI!!
...

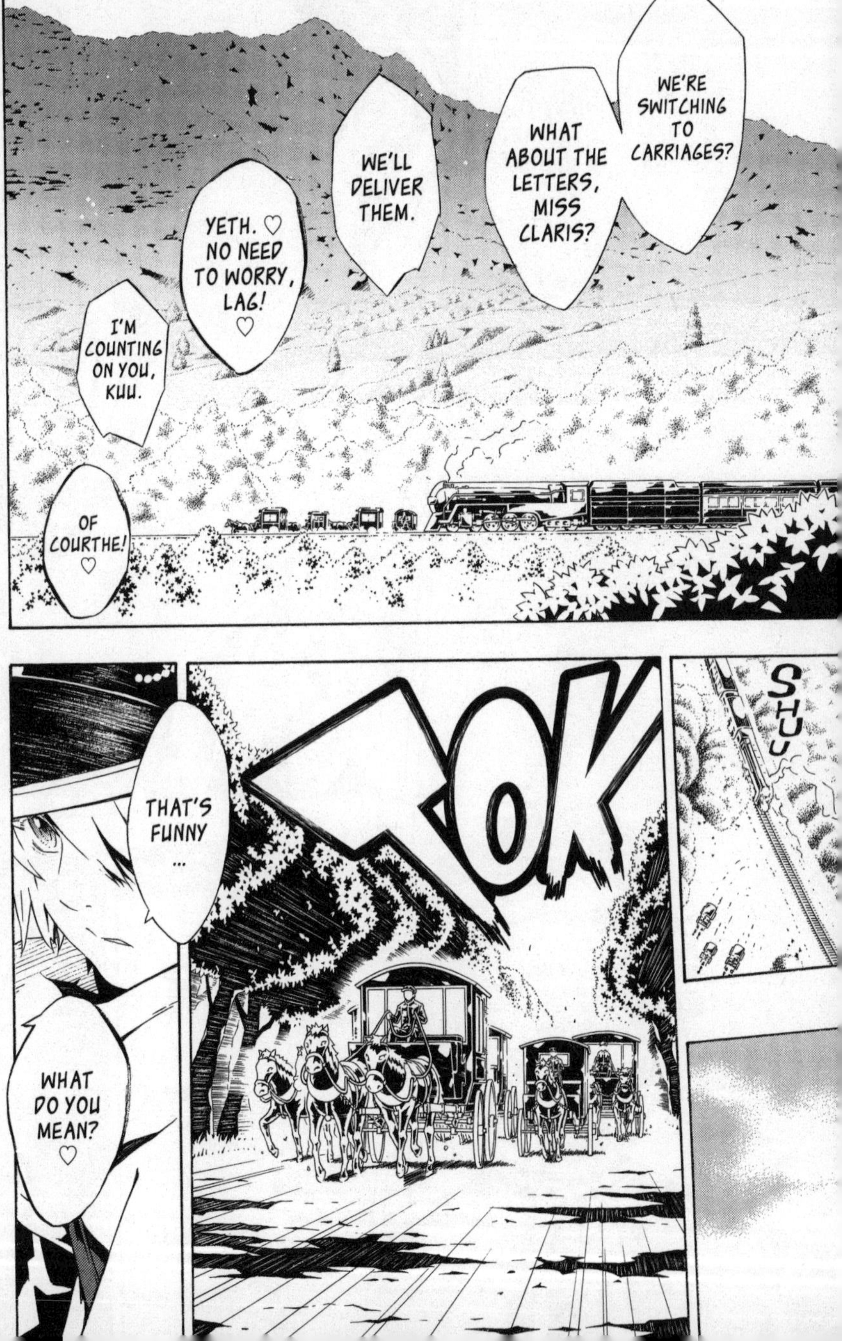
WE'RE SWITCHING TO CARRIAGES?
WHAT ABOUT THE LETTERS, MISS CLARIS?
WE'LL DELIVER THEM.
YETH. ♡ NO NEED TO WORRY, LAG! ♡
I'M COUNTING ON YOU, KUU.
OF COURTHE! ♡
SHUU
TOK
THAT'S FUNNY...
WHAT DO YOU MEAN? ♡

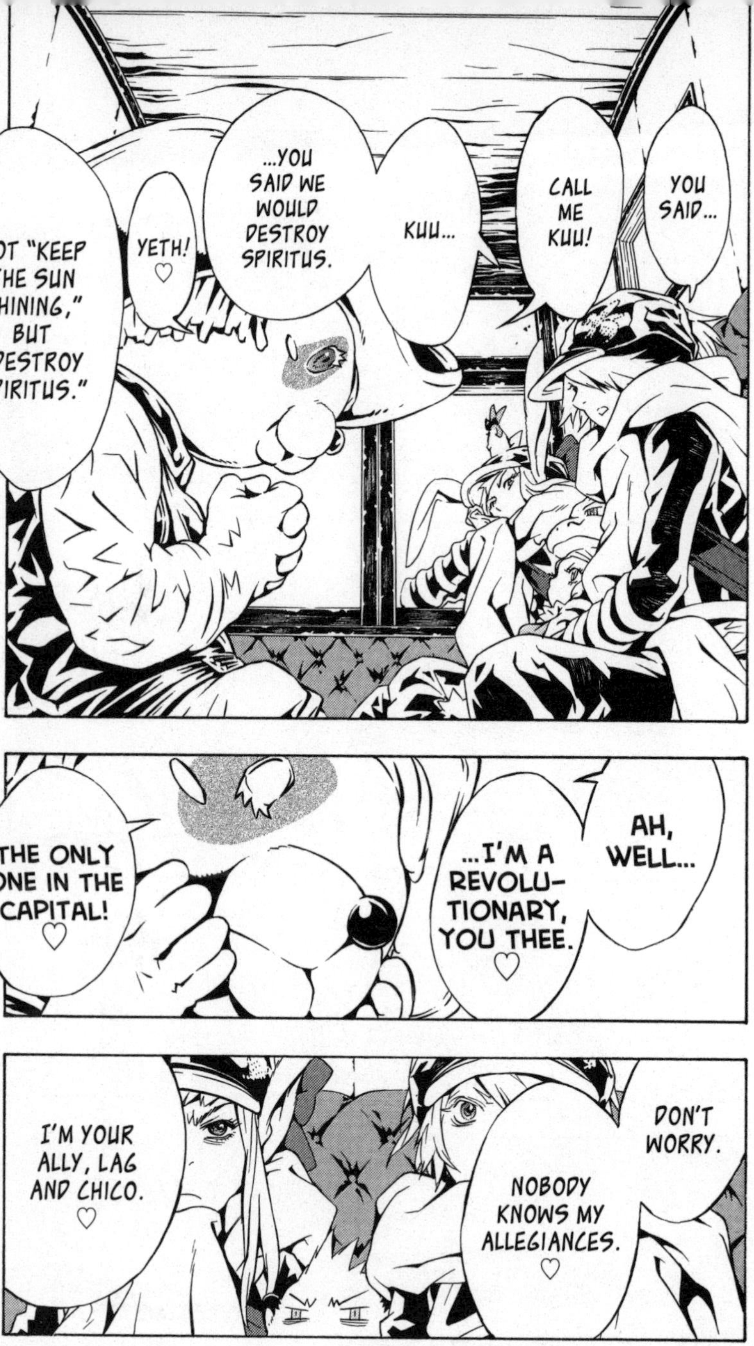
YOU SAID...
CALL ME KUU!
KUU...
...YOU SAID WE WOULD DESTROY SPIRITUS.
YETH! ♡
NOT "KEEP THE SUN SHINING," BUT "DESTROY SPIRITUS."
AH, WELL...
...I'M A REVOLUTIONARY, YOU THEE. ♡
THE ONLY ONE IN THE CAPITAL! ♡
DON'T WORRY.
NOBODY KNOWS MY ALLEGIANCES. ♡
I'M YOUR ALLY, LAG AND CHICO. ♡

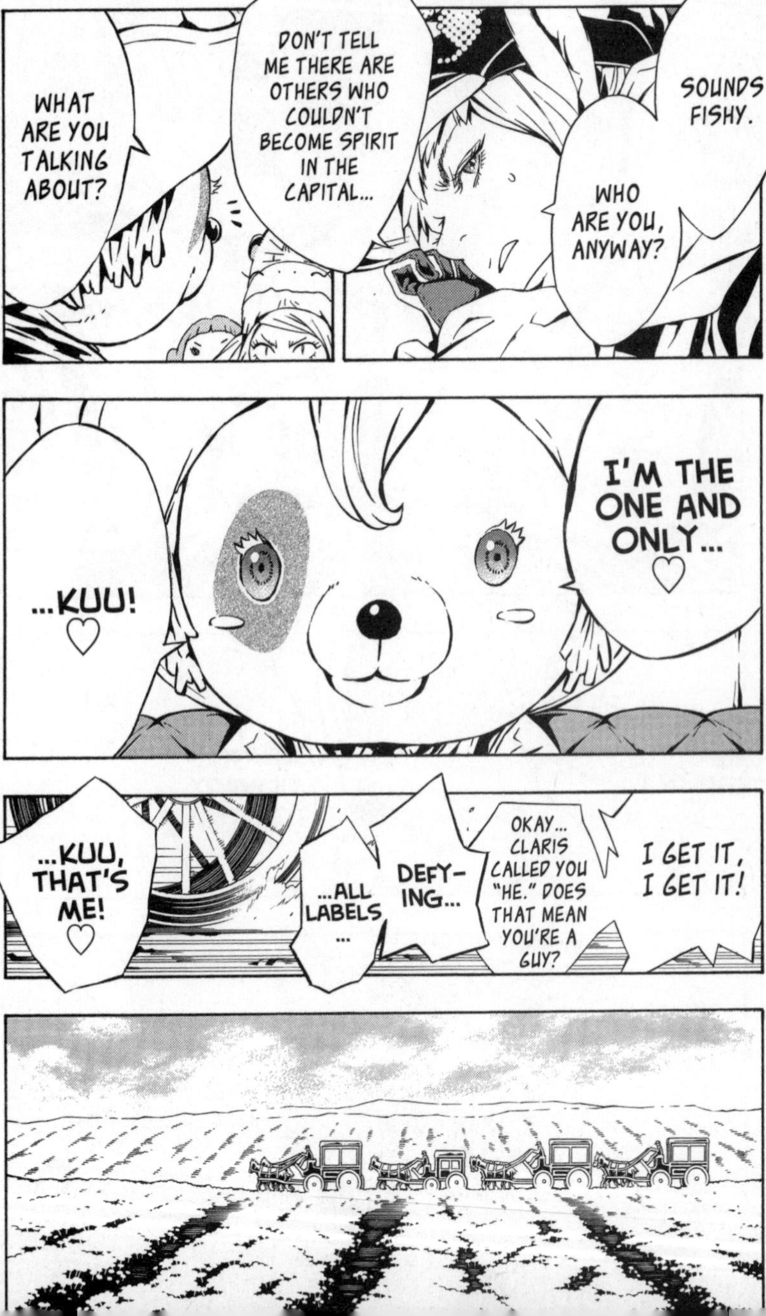
SOUNDS FISHY.
WHO ARE YOU, ANYWAY?
DON'T TELL ME THERE ARE OTHERS WHO COULDN'T BECOME SPIRIT IN THE CAPITAL...
WHAT ARE YOU TALKING ABOUT?
I'M THE ONE AND ONLY... ♡
...KUU! ♡
I GET IT, I GET IT!
OKAY... CLARIS CALLED YOU "HE." DOES THAT MEAN YOU'RE A GUY?
DEFY-ING...
...ALL LABELS ...
...KUU, THAT'S ME! ♡

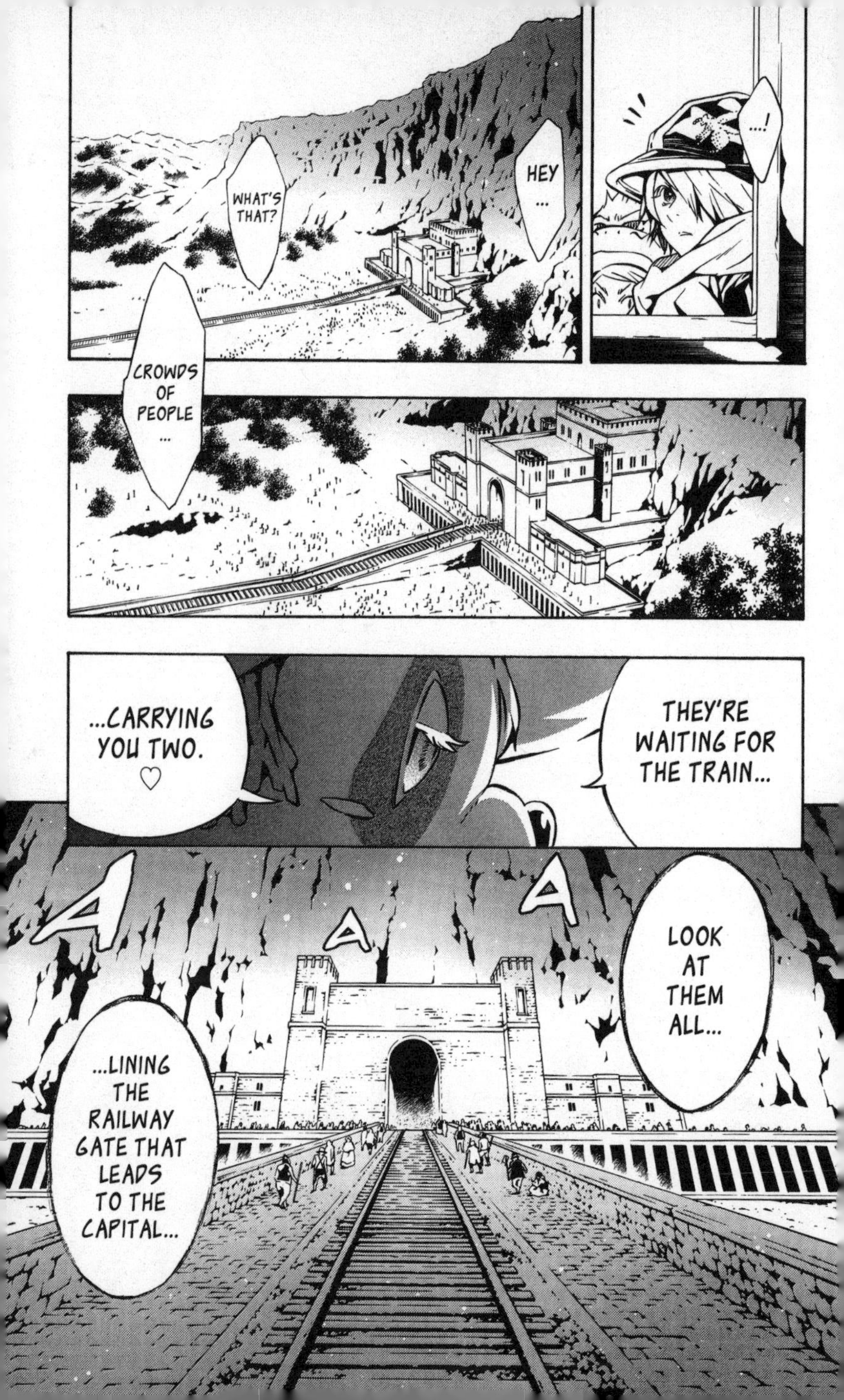
...!
HEY ...
WHAT'S THAT?
CROWDS OF PEOPLE ...
THEY'RE WAITING FOR THE TRAIN...
...CARRYING YOU TWO. ♡
LOOK AT THEM ALL...
...LINING THE RAILWAY GATE THAT LEADS TO THE CAPITAL...
A A A

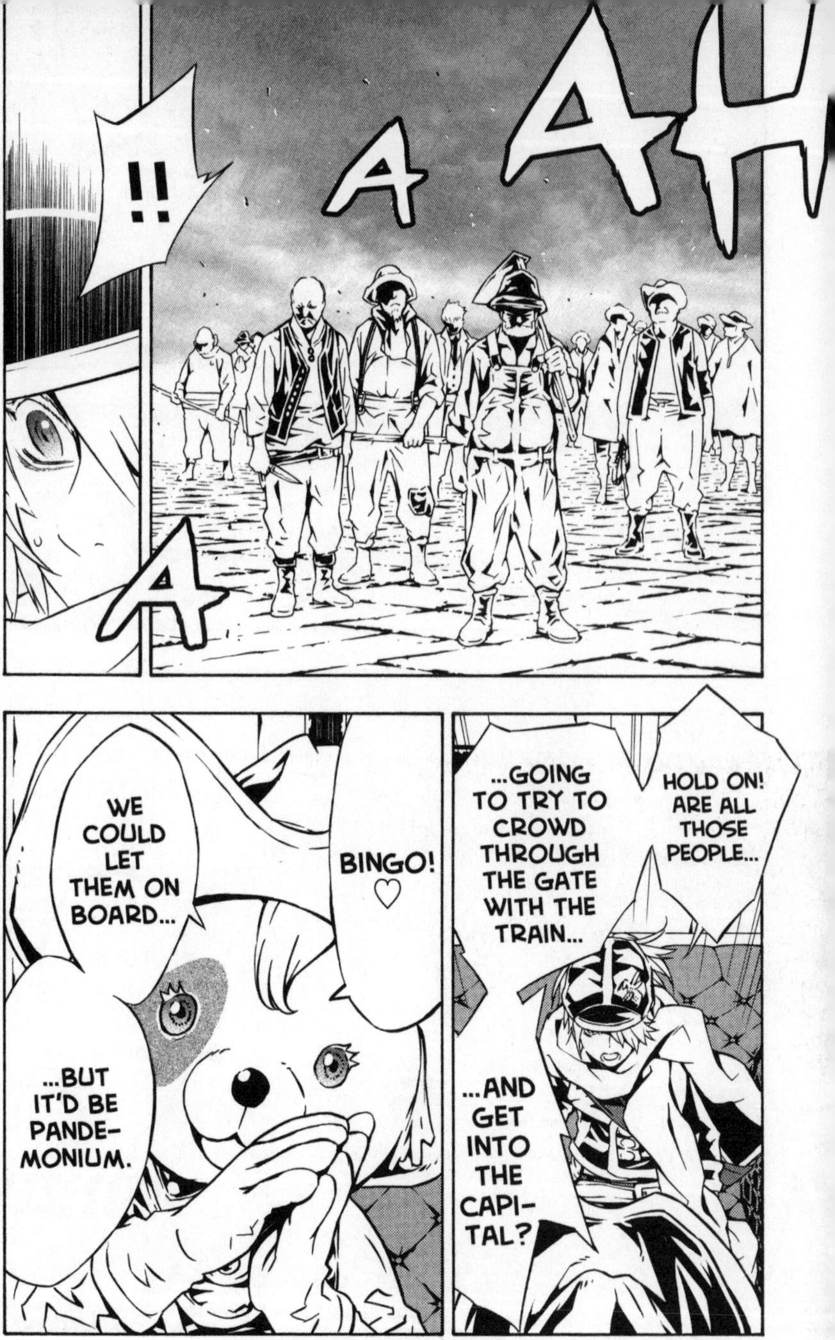
A A AH
!!
HOLD ON! ARE ALL THOSE PEOPLE...
...GOING TO TRY TO CROWD THROUGH THE GATE WITH THE TRAIN...
...AND GET INTO THE CAPI-TAL?
BINGO! ♡
WE COULD LET THEM ON BOARD...
...BUT IT'D BE PANDE-MONIUM.

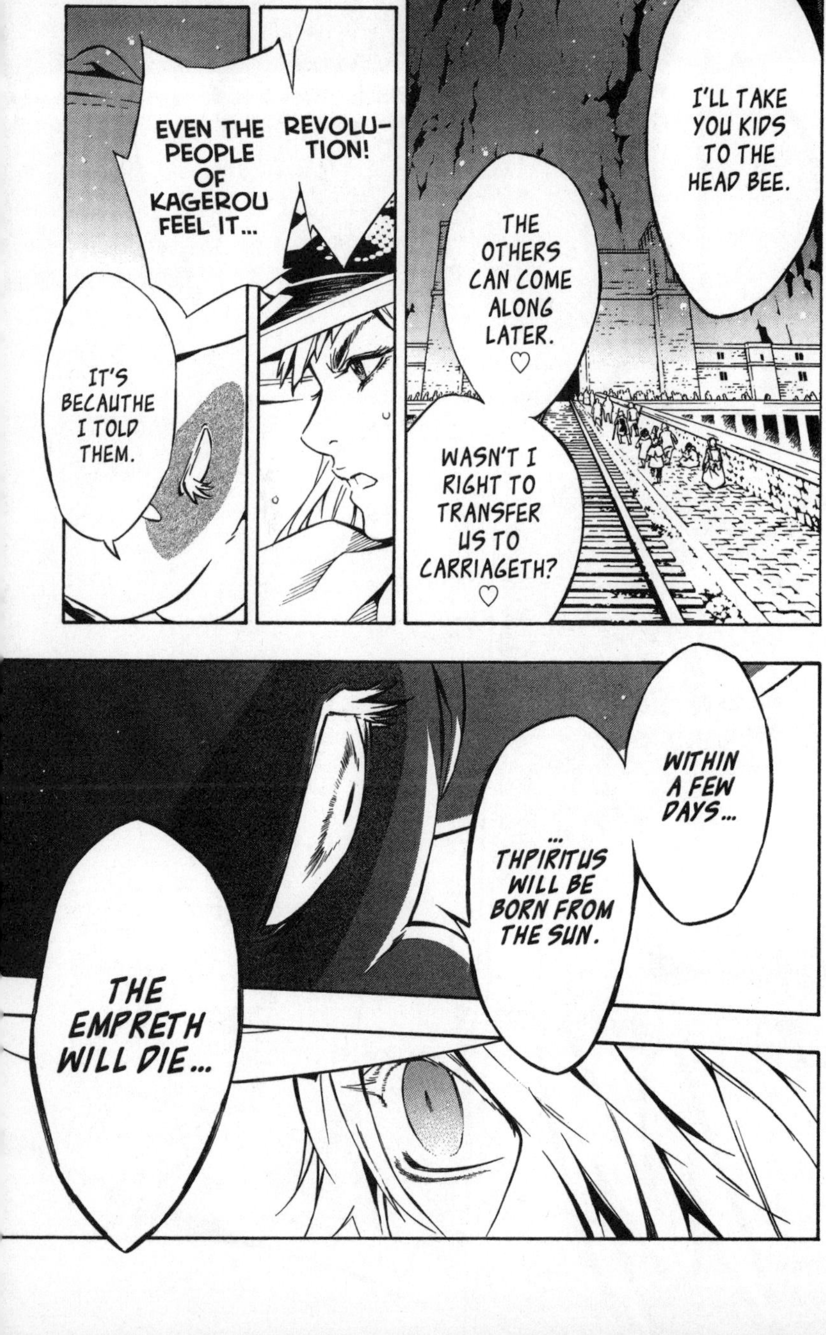
I'LL TAKE YOU KIDS TO THE HEAD BEE.
THE OTHERS CAN COME ALONG LATER. ♡
WASN'T I RIGHT TO TRANSFER US TO CARRIAGETH? ♡
REVOLU-TION!
EVEN THE PEOPLE OF KAGEROU FEEL IT...
IT'S BECAUTHE I TOLD THEM.
WITHIN A FEW DAYS...
...THPIRITUS WILL BE BORN FROM THE SUN.
THE EMPRETH WILL DIE...

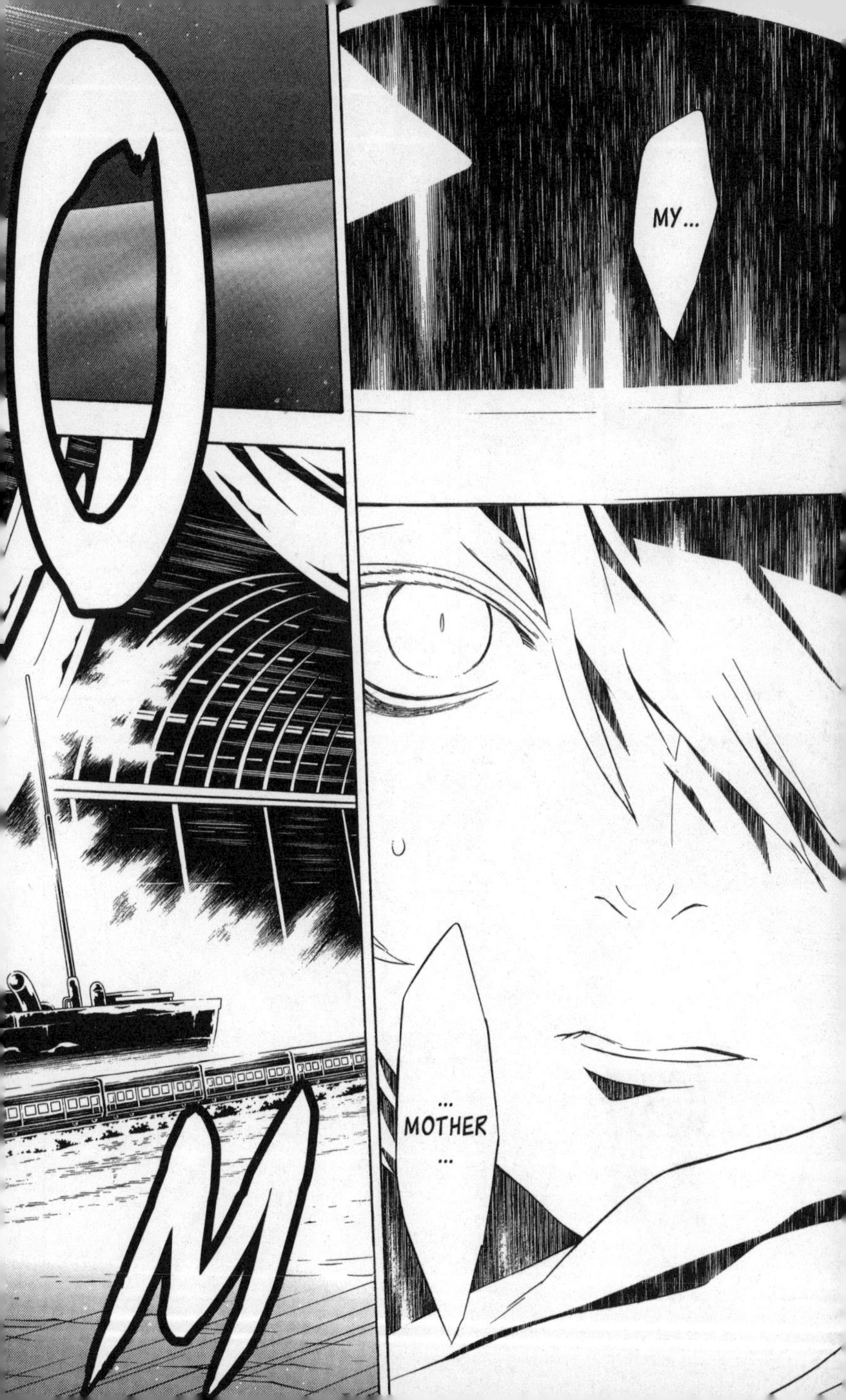
MY...
...MOTHER...
OM

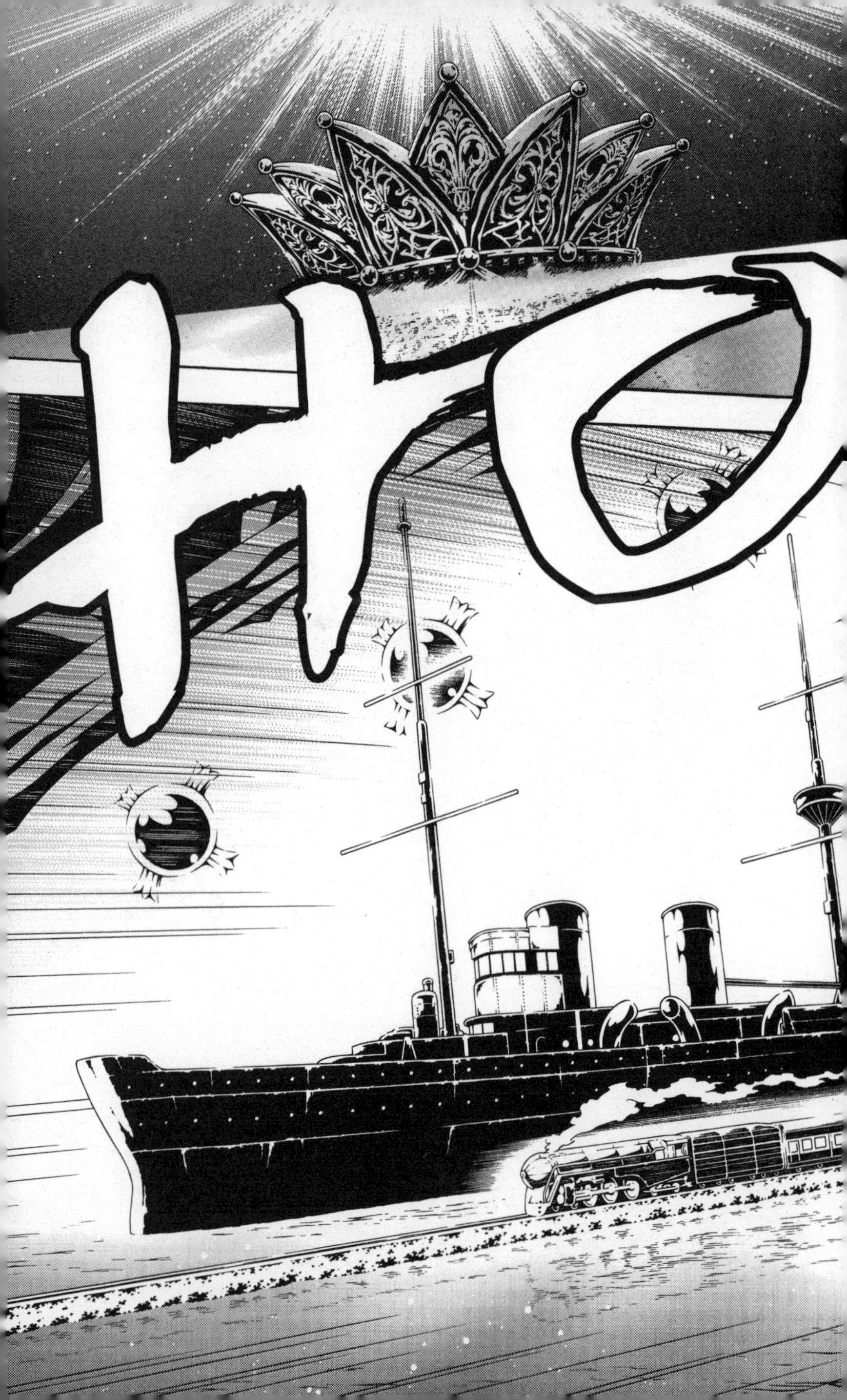
HO

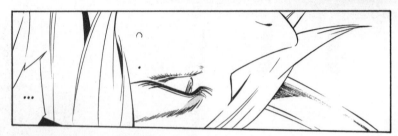

...

LOOK AT THAT CROWD!

RE-VERSE!

THERE IT IS!

THE IRON SHIP!!

!!

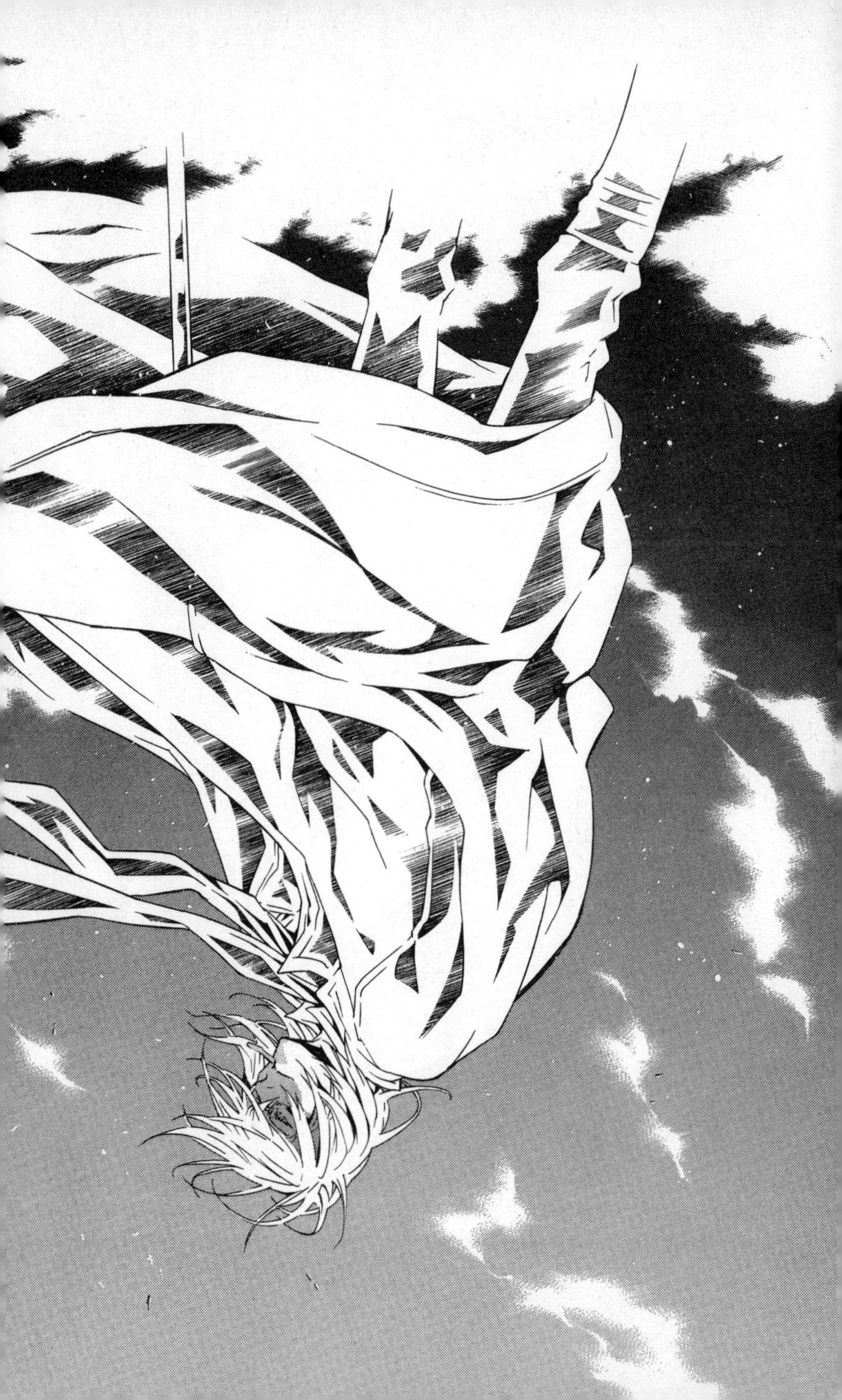

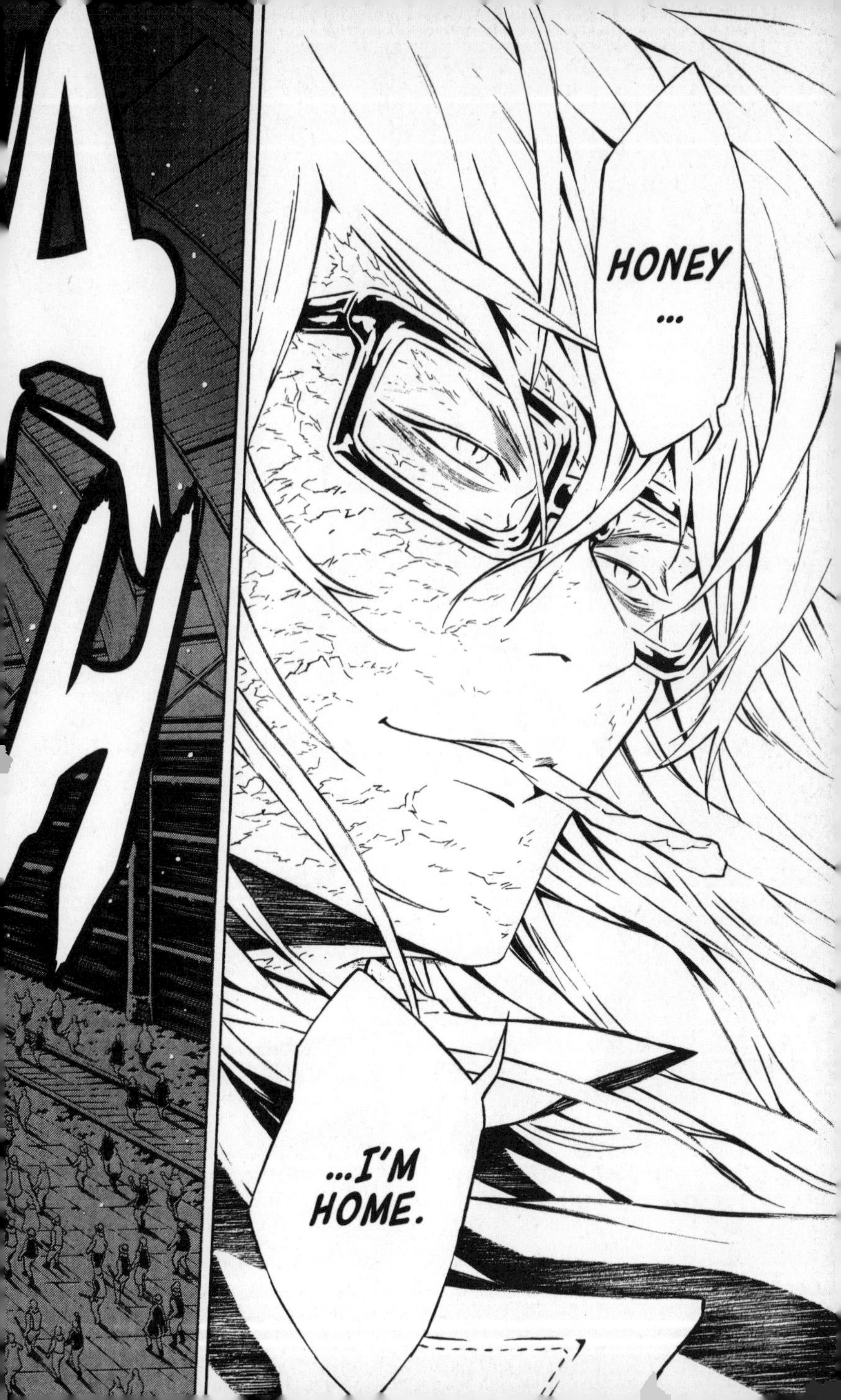
HONEY ...
...I'M HOME.

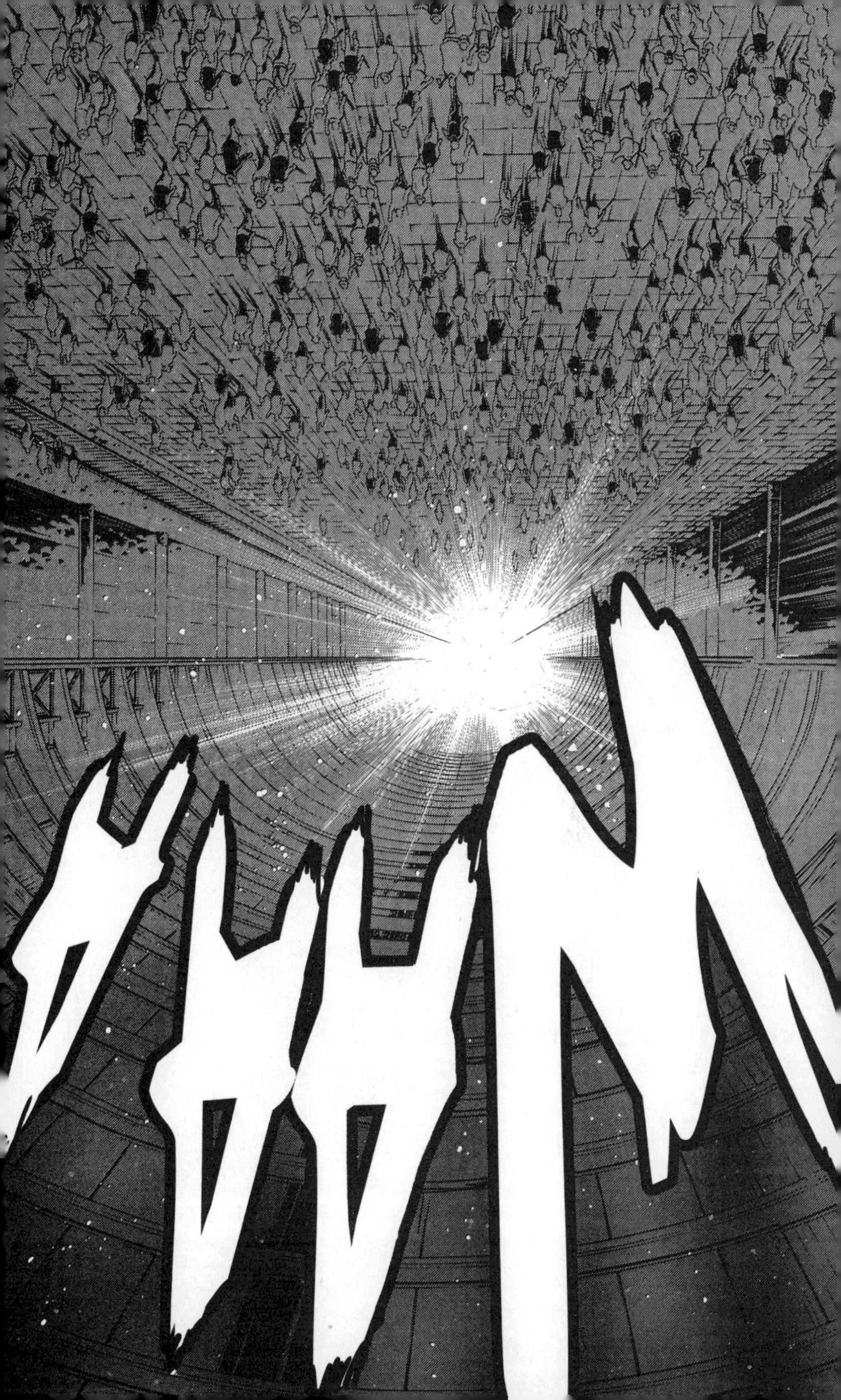

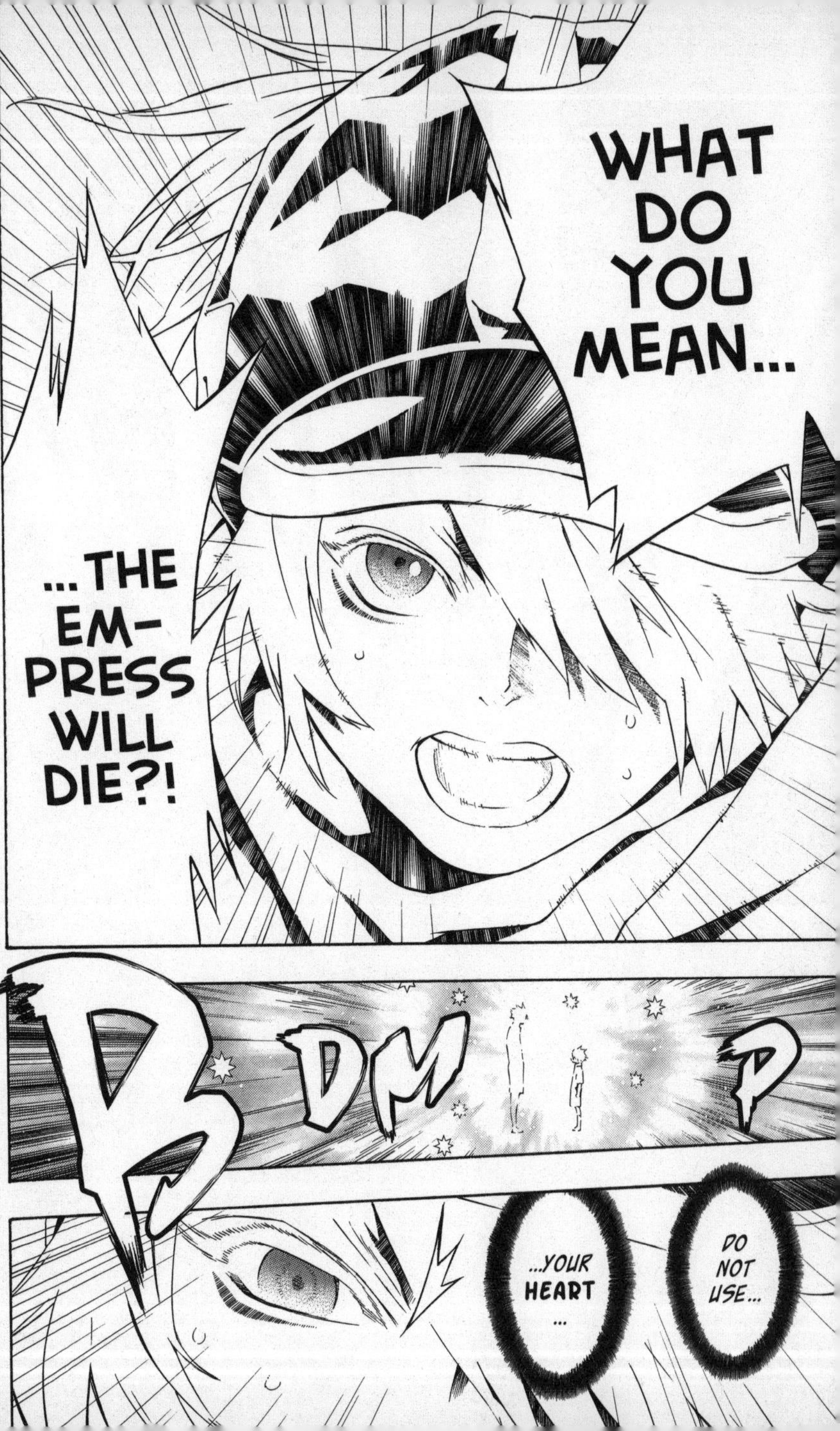
WHAT DO YOU MEAN...
...THE EM-PRESS WILL DIE?!
BDMP
DO NOT USE...
...YOUR HEART...

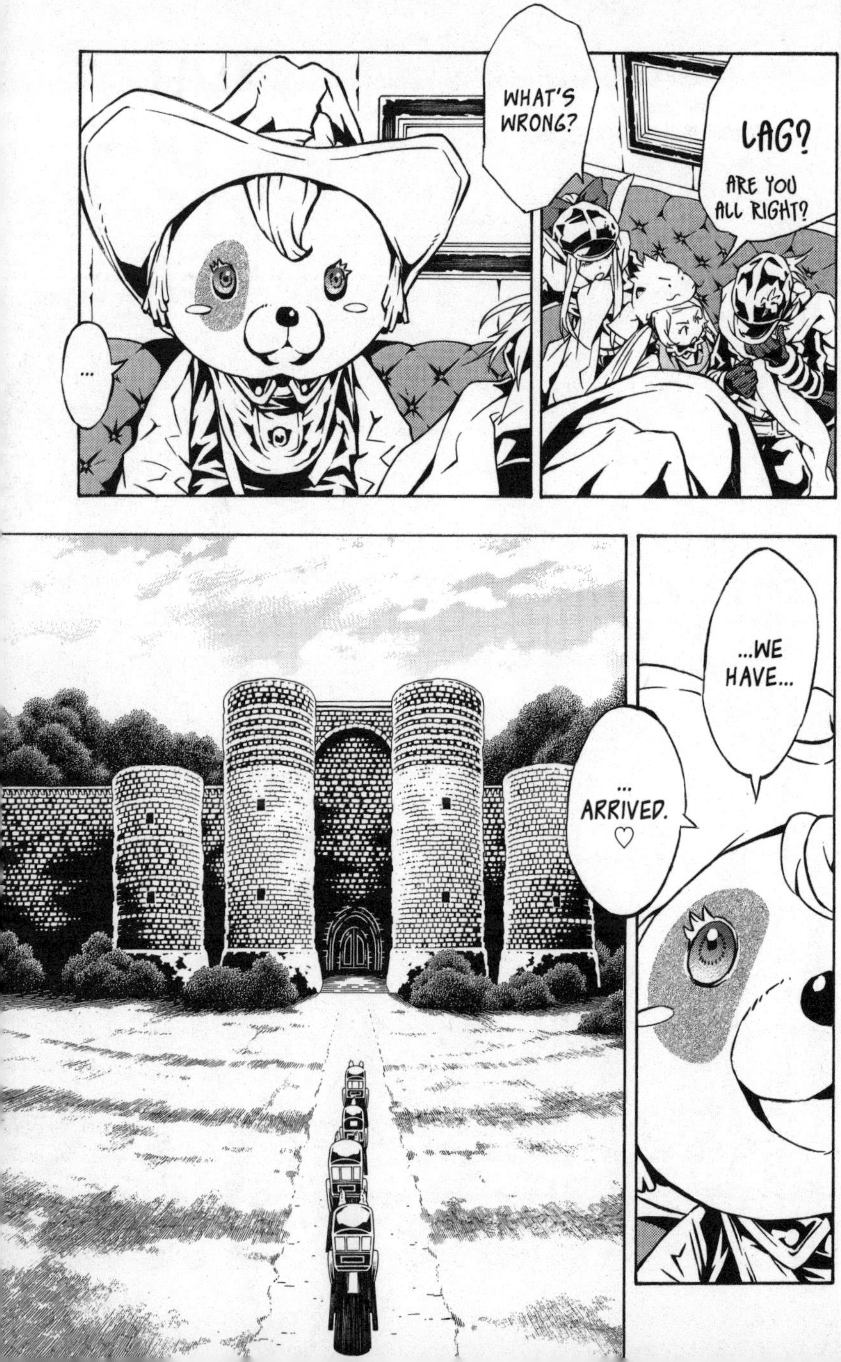
LAG?
ARE YOU ALL RIGHT?
WHAT'S WRONG?
...
...WE HAVE...
...ARRIVED. ♡

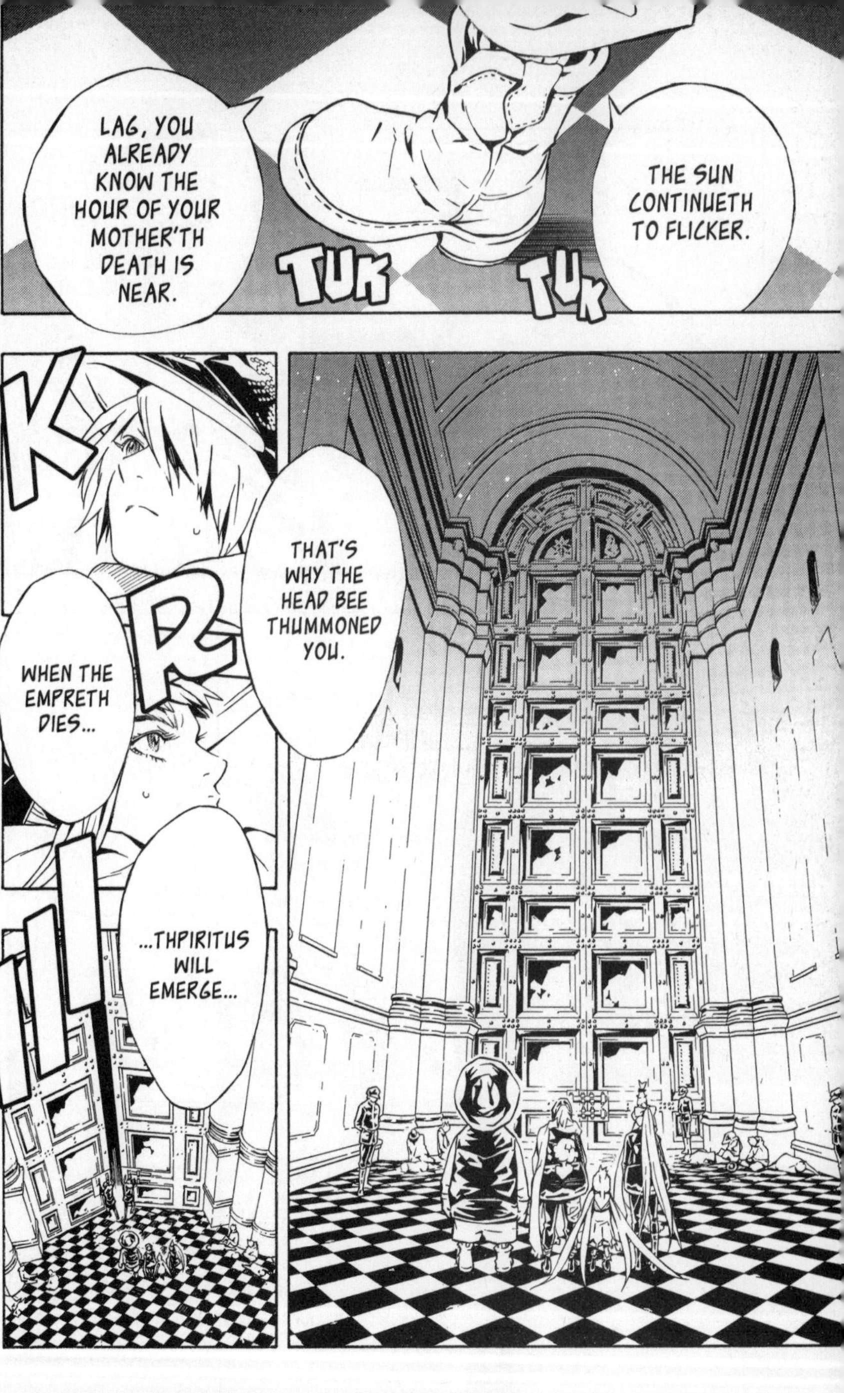
THE SUN CONTINUETH TO FLICKER.
LAG, YOU ALREADY KNOW THE HOUR OF YOUR MOTHER'TH DEATH IS NEAR.
TUK
TUK
THAT'S WHY THE HEAD BEE THUMMONED YOU.
KRII
WHEN THE EMPRETH DIES...
...THPIRITUS WILL EMERGE...

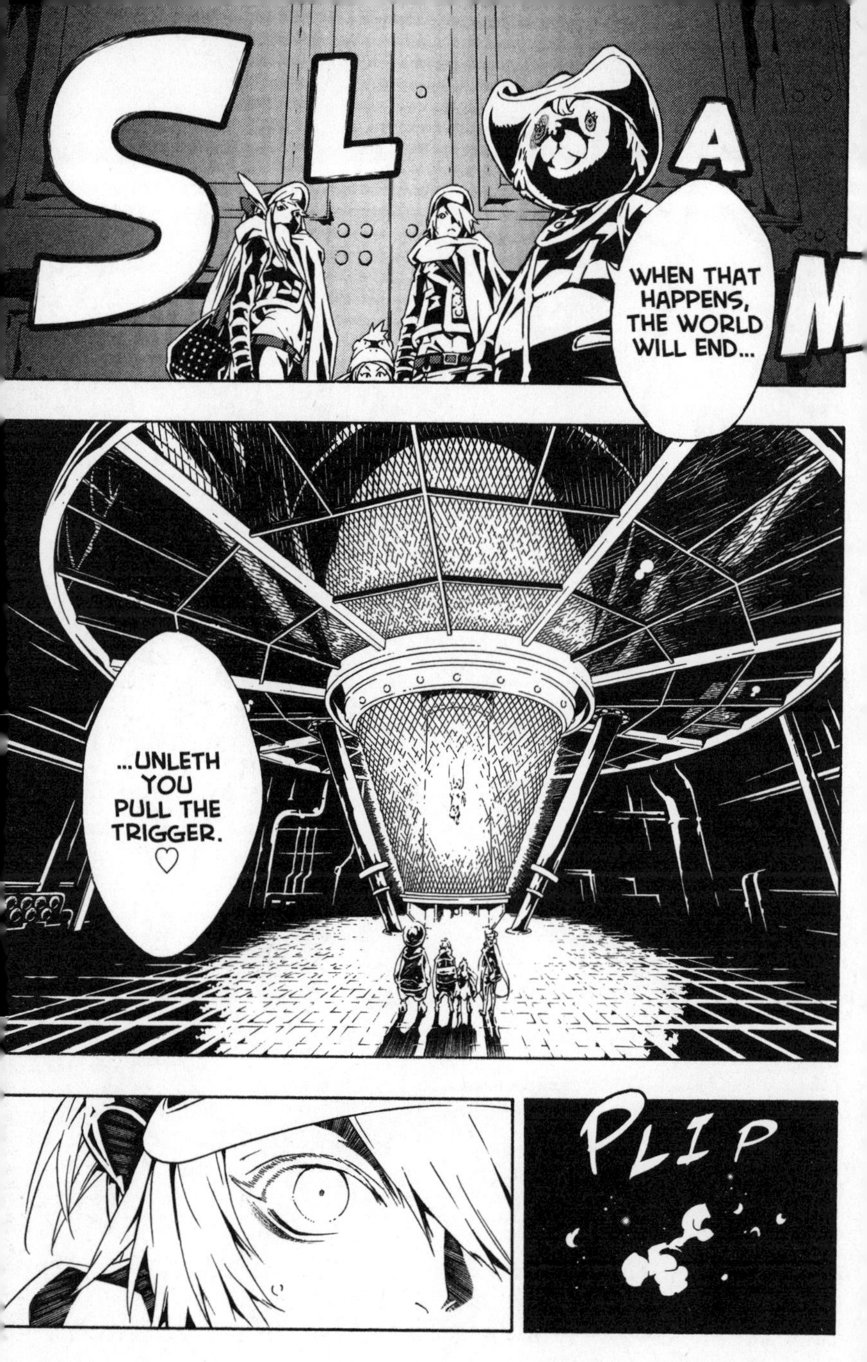
SLAM
WHEN THAT HAPPENS, THE WORLD WILL END...
...UNLETH YOU PULL THE TRIGGER. ♡
PLIP

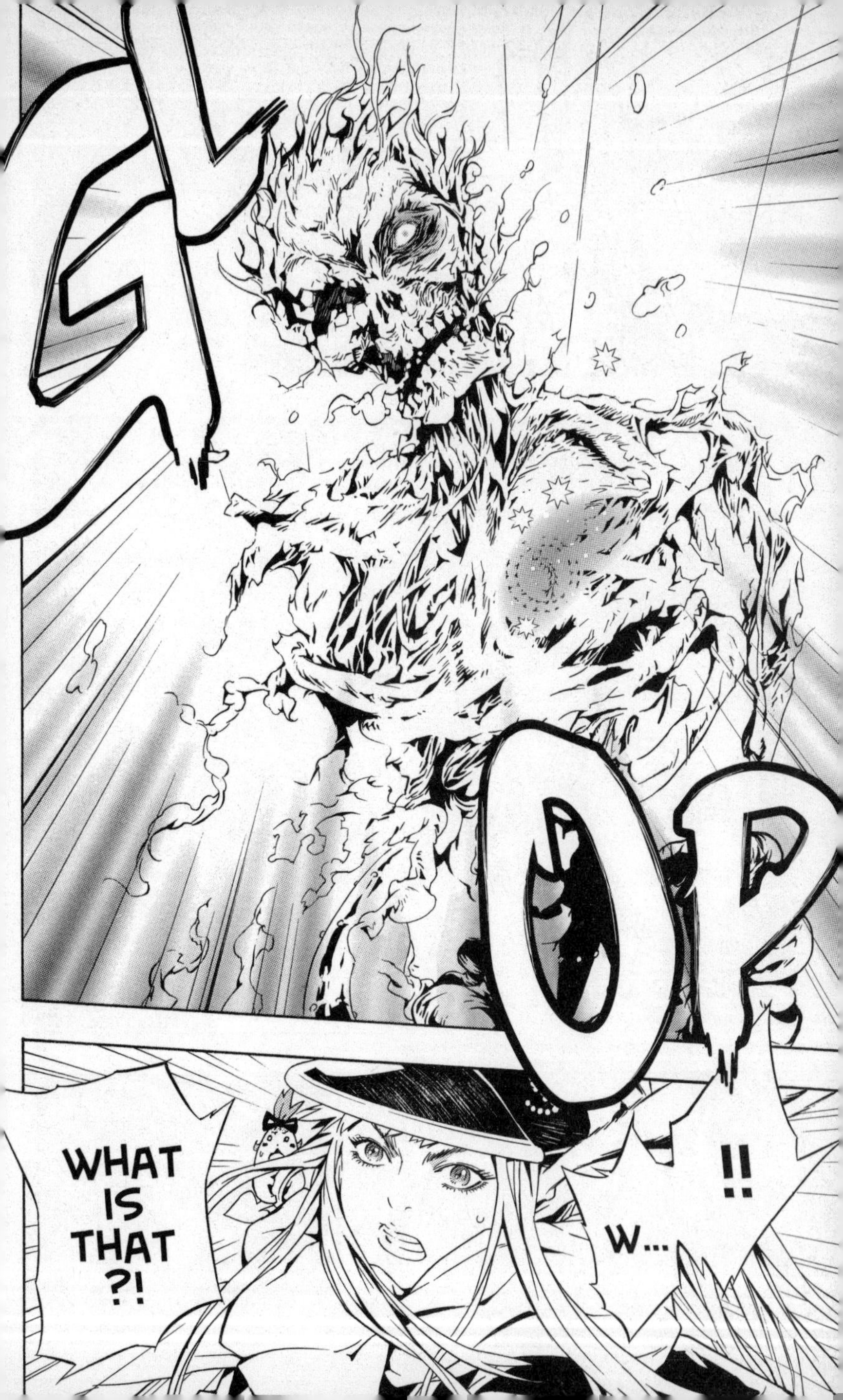
OP
!!
W...
WHAT IS THAT ?!

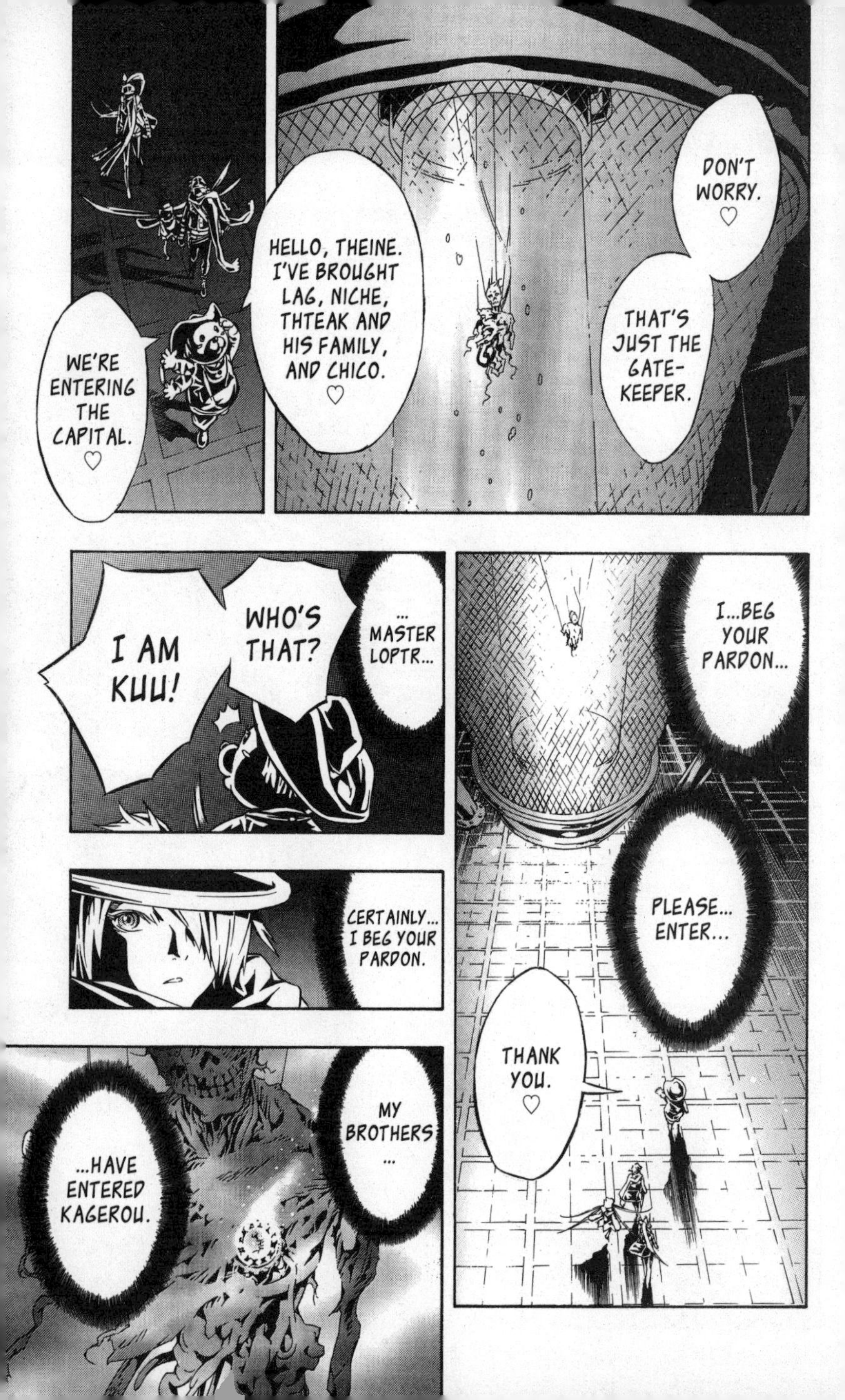
DON'T WORRY. ♡
THAT'S JUST THE GATE-KEEPER.
HELLO, THEINE. I'VE BROUGHT LAG, NICHE, THTEAK AND HIS FAMILY, AND CHICO. ♡
WE'RE ENTERING THE CAPITAL. ♡
I...BEG YOUR PARDON...
PLEASE... ENTER...
THANK YOU. ♡
... MASTER LOPTR...
WHO'S THAT?
I AM KUU!
CERTAINLY... I BEG YOUR PARDON.
MY BROTHERS ...
...HAVE ENTERED KAGEROU.

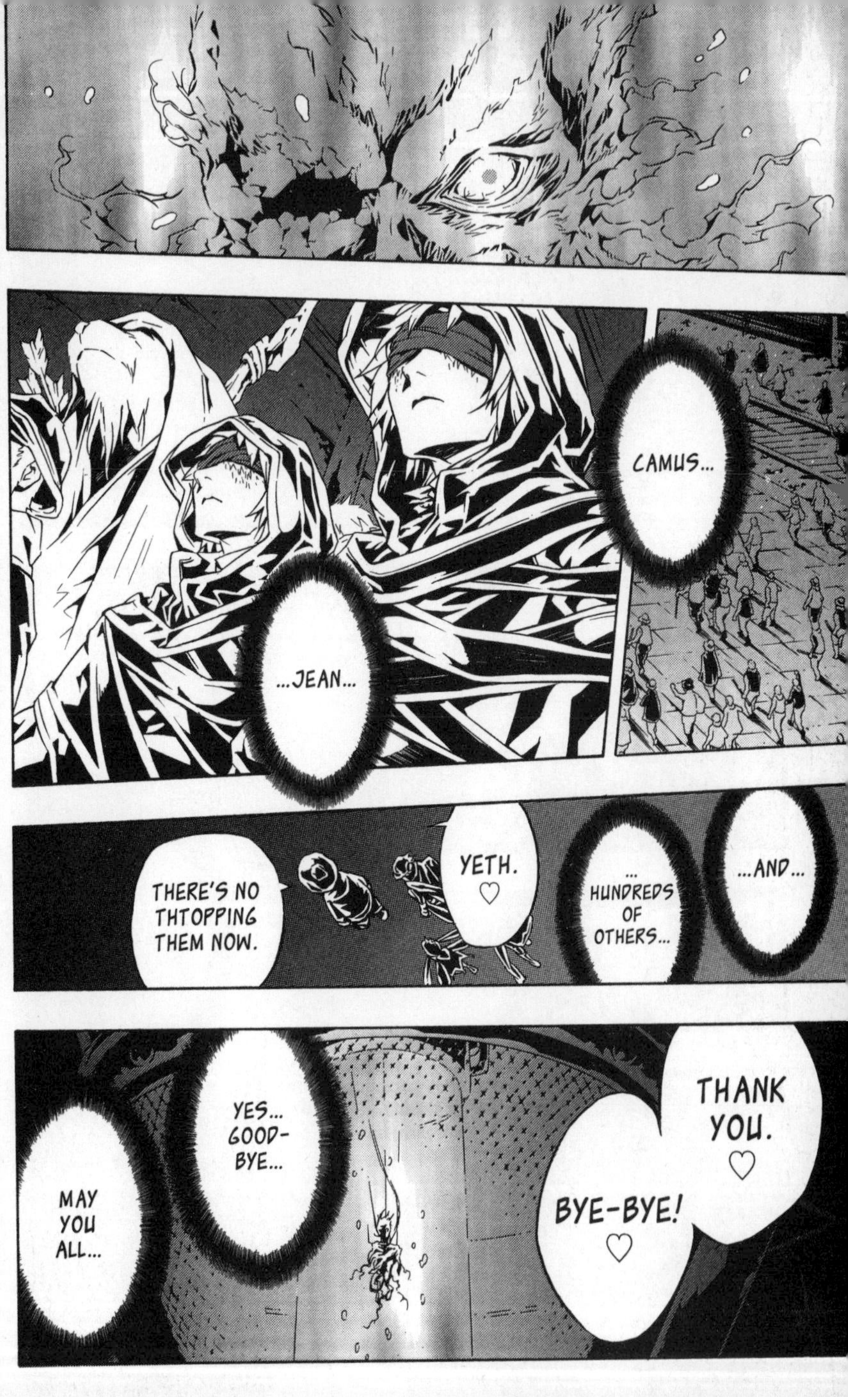
CAMUS...
...JEAN...
...AND...
... HUNDREDS OF OTHERS...
YETH. ♡
THERE'S NO THTOPPING THEM NOW.
THANK YOU. ♡
BYE-BYE! ♡
YES... GOOD-BYE...
MAY YOU ALL...

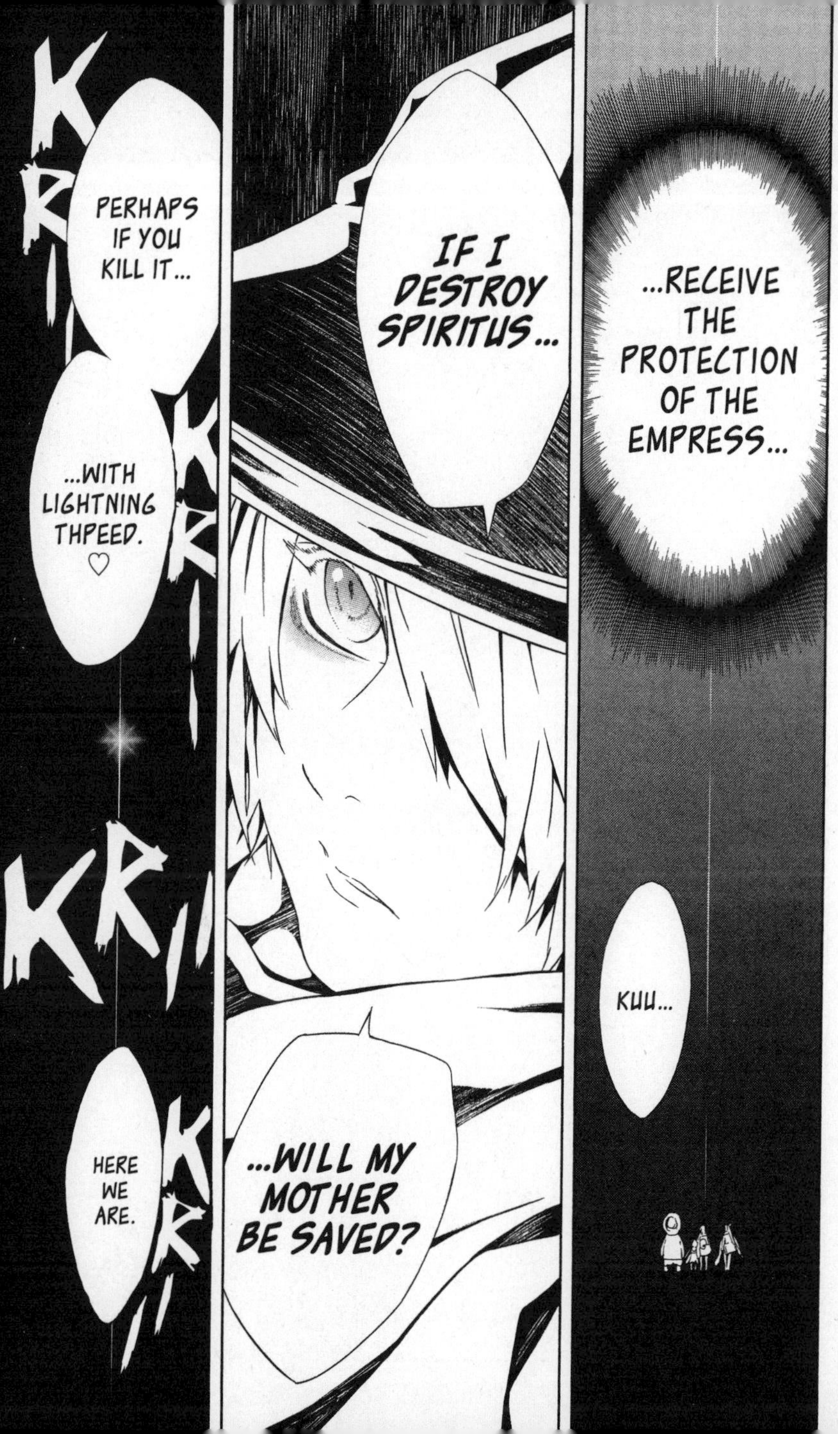
...RECEIVE THE PROTECTION OF THE EMPRESS...
KUU...
IF I DESTROY SPIRITUS...
...WILL MY MOTHER BE SAVED?
PERHAPS IF YOU KILL IT...
...WITH LIGHTNING THPEED. ♡
KRII
KRII
KRI
HERE WE ARE.
KR

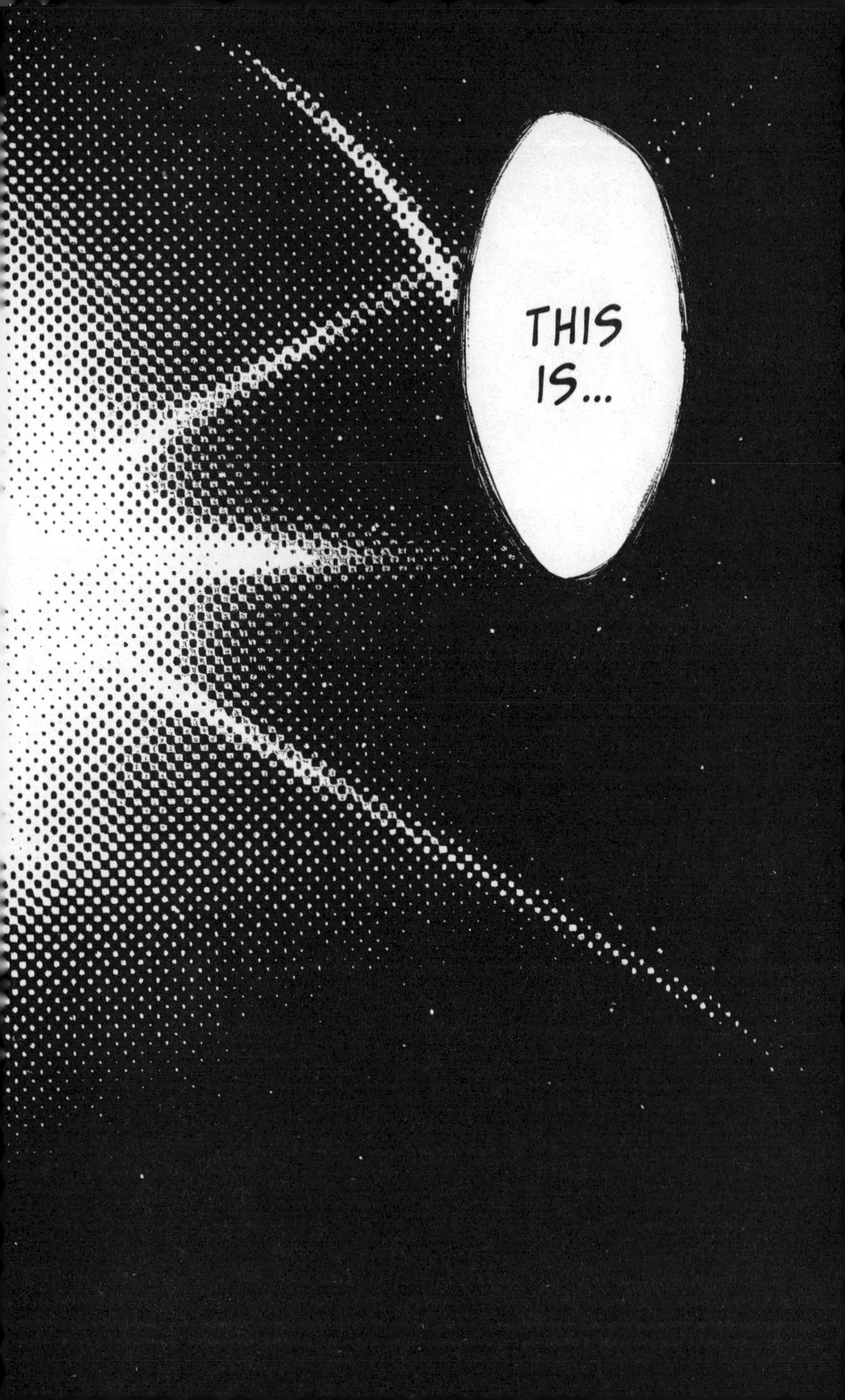
THIS IS...

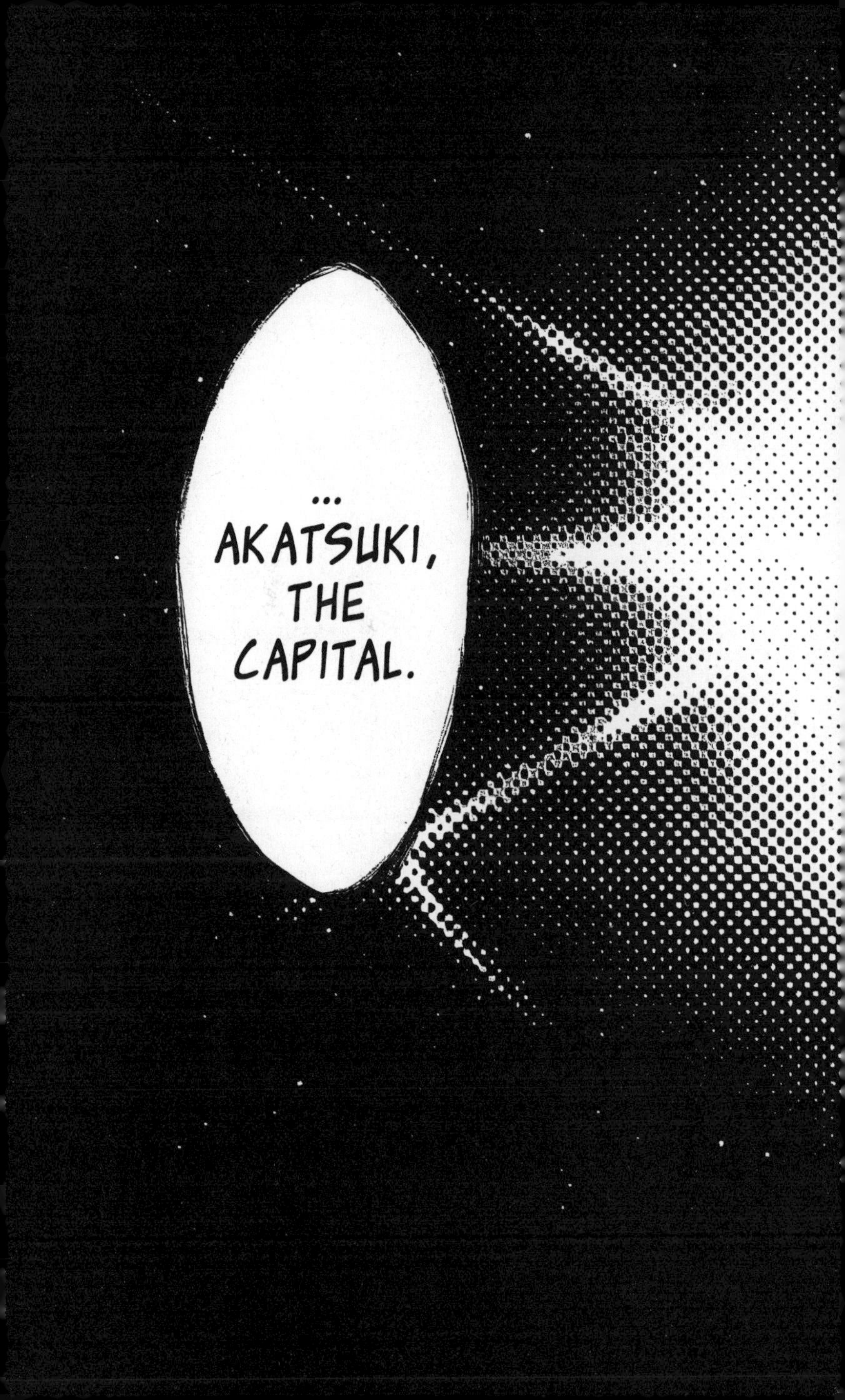
... AKATSUKI, THE CAPITAL.

Reverse has finally reached Kagerou! They're here! Even Signal and Signales! The three brothers are together again!

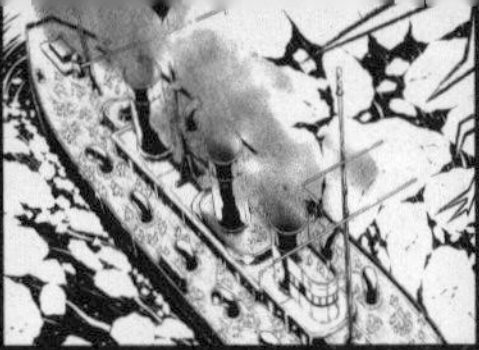

Looking carefully, you can see crowds of locals lining both the gates to the capital. Perhaps they were stopped by the military police or hindered by Seine's mental powers. I wonder if they tried to force their way in. The whole area is in chaos. And it seems this mysterious character Kuu is behind it all…

■ KUU THE PUMA
Is he a boy? A girl? An animal? Or somebody in a suit? He calls himself a revolutionary, but there's no telling what the truth is. Still, he does seem to know a lot about the capital and the government. According to Claris, Kuu planned the whole uprising. As the wheels start turning, all the people of Kagerou are getting involved. Is he the puppet master behind it all?

■ LOPTR
Oh yes! I didn't miss it, you know. I heard Gatekeeper Seine call him "Loptr." So his name isn't really Kuu. Who in the world is he? Kuu the Puma…Puma… Say, what's a puma?

■ THOSE WHO COULD NOT BECOME SPIRIT
Largo Lloyd doesn't look so good. What's up with that? He did once say that the government's test subjects didn't live as long as humans. Perhaps, considering the way they were created, they're destined for a short life. I wonder if Chico's white hair has something to do with that…

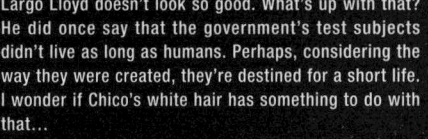

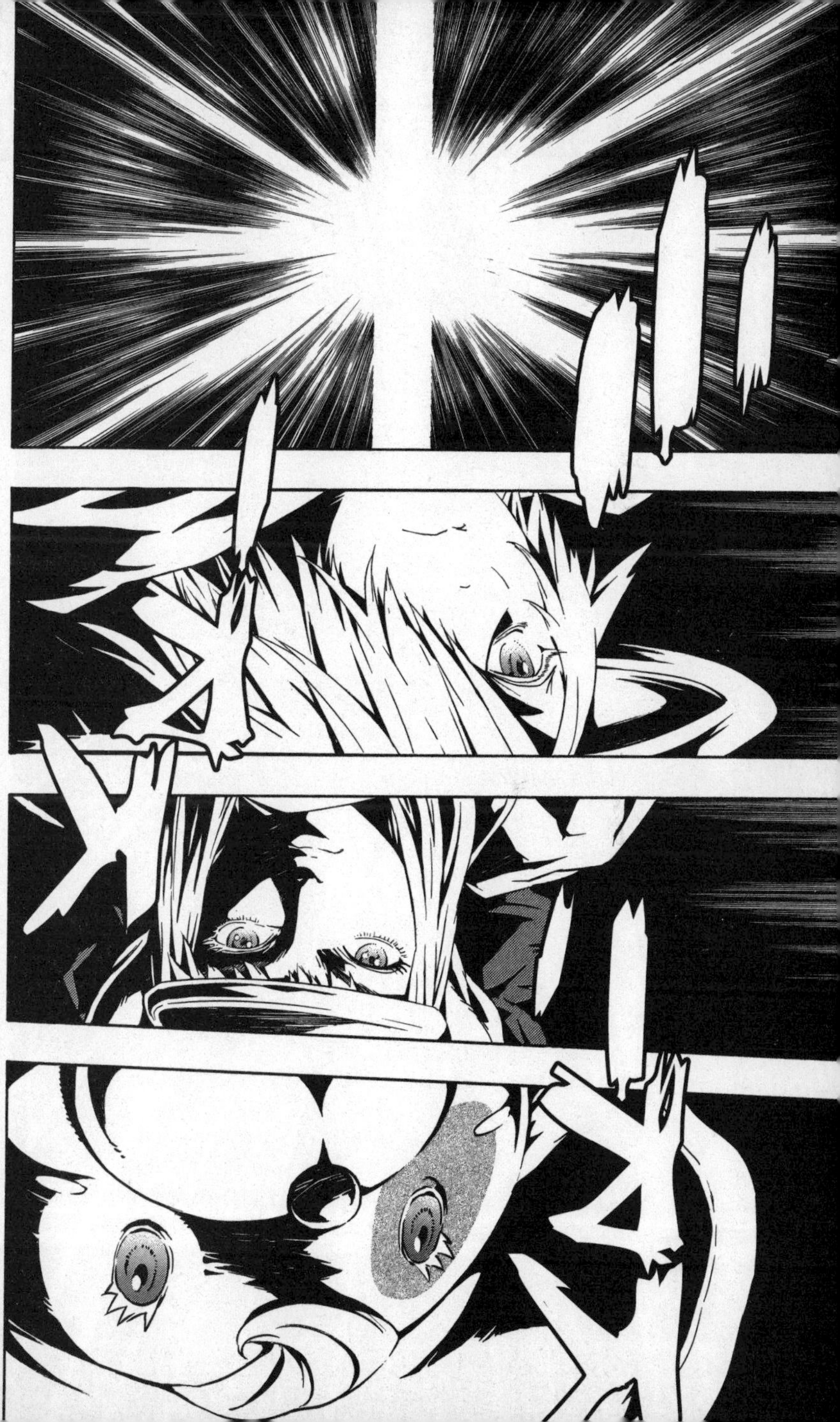

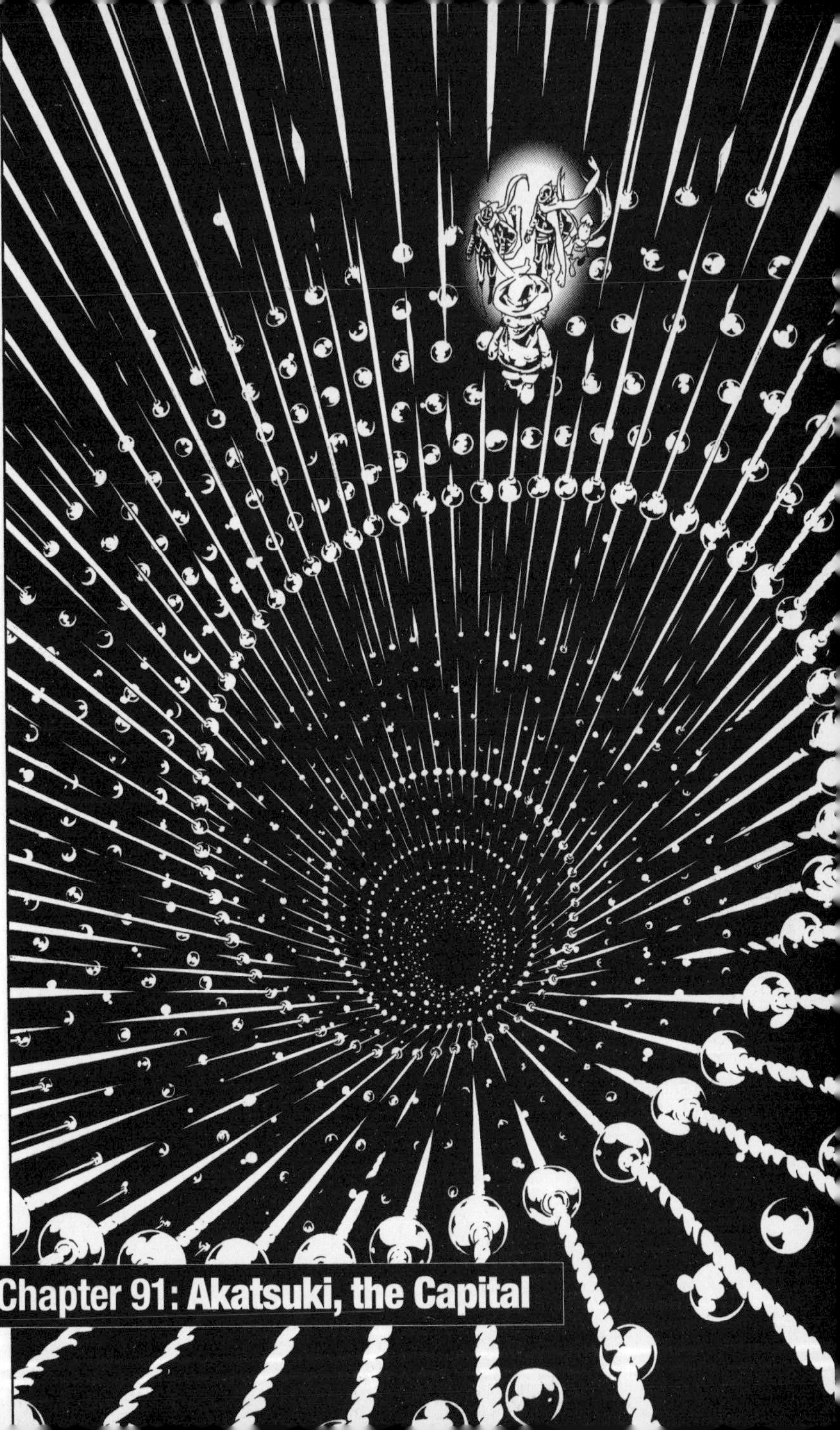

Chapter 91: Akatsuki, the Capital

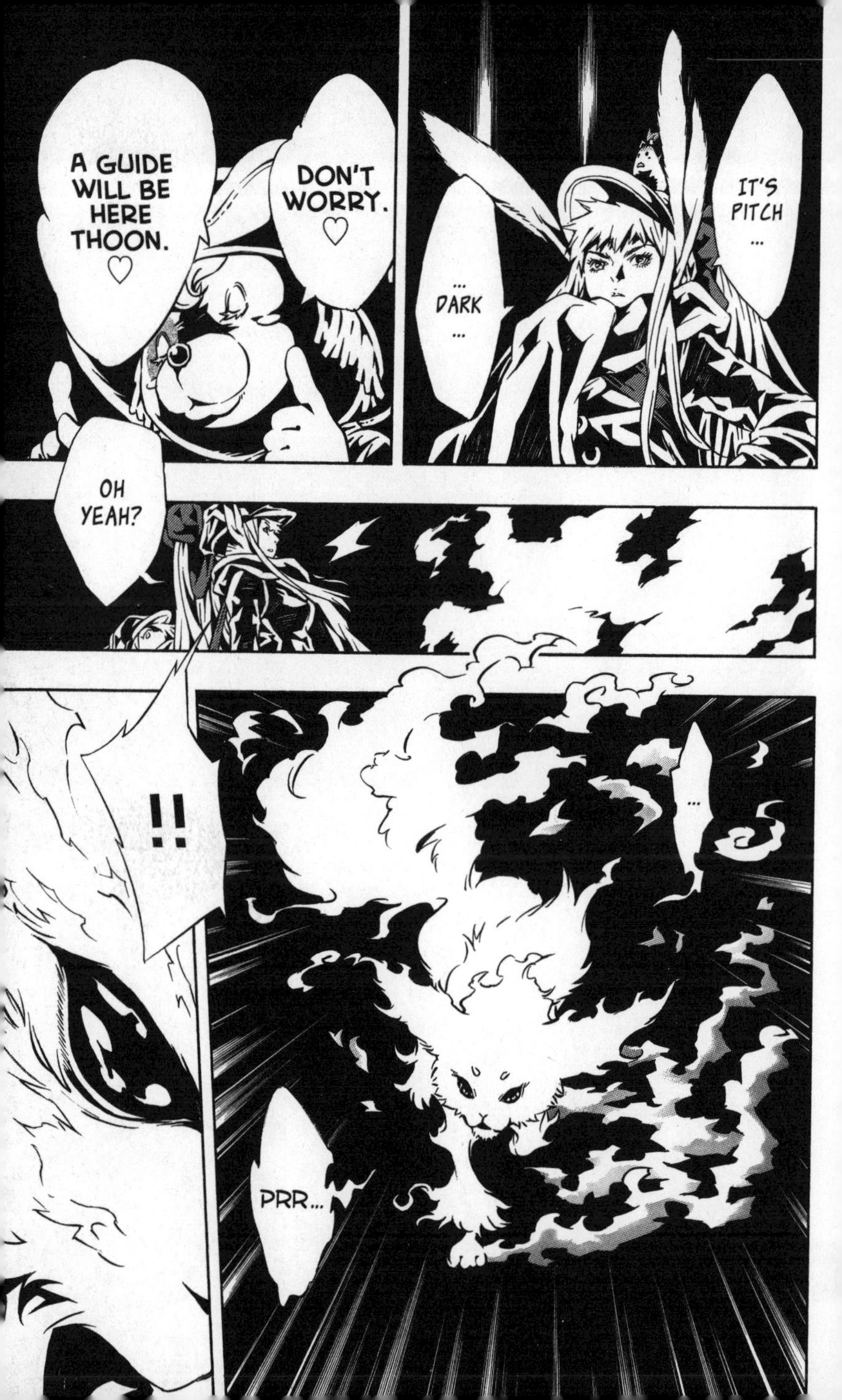
IT'S PITCH ...
... DARK ...
DON'T WORRY. ♡
A GUIDE WILL BE HERE THOON. ♡
OH YEAH?
...
PRR...
!!

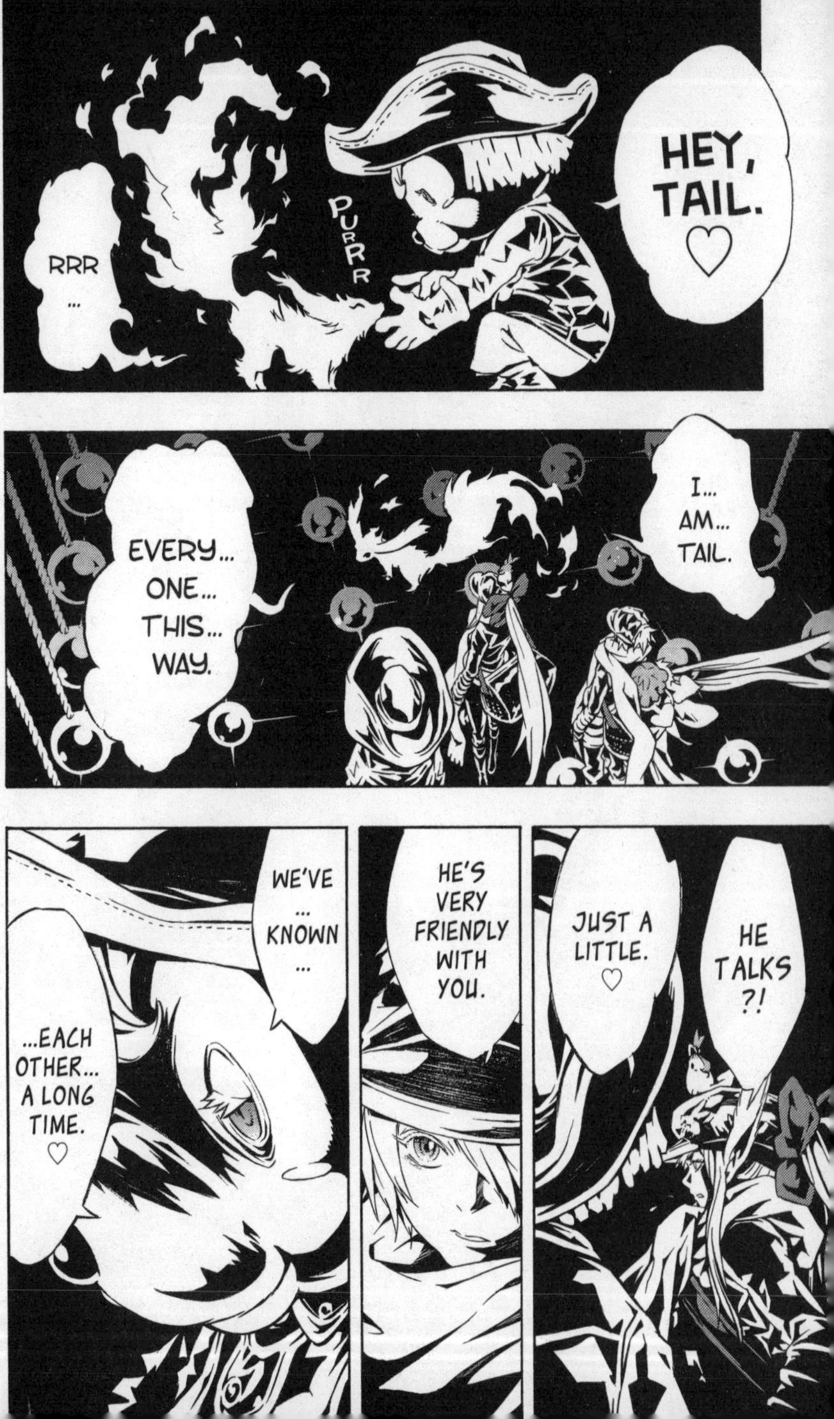
HEY, TAIL. ♡
PURRR
RRR ...
I... AM... TAIL.
EVERY... ONE... THIS... WAY.
HE TALKS ?!
JUST A LITTLE. ♡
HE'S VERY FRIENDLY WITH YOU.
WE'VE ... KNOWN ...
...EACH OTHER... A LONG TIME. ♡

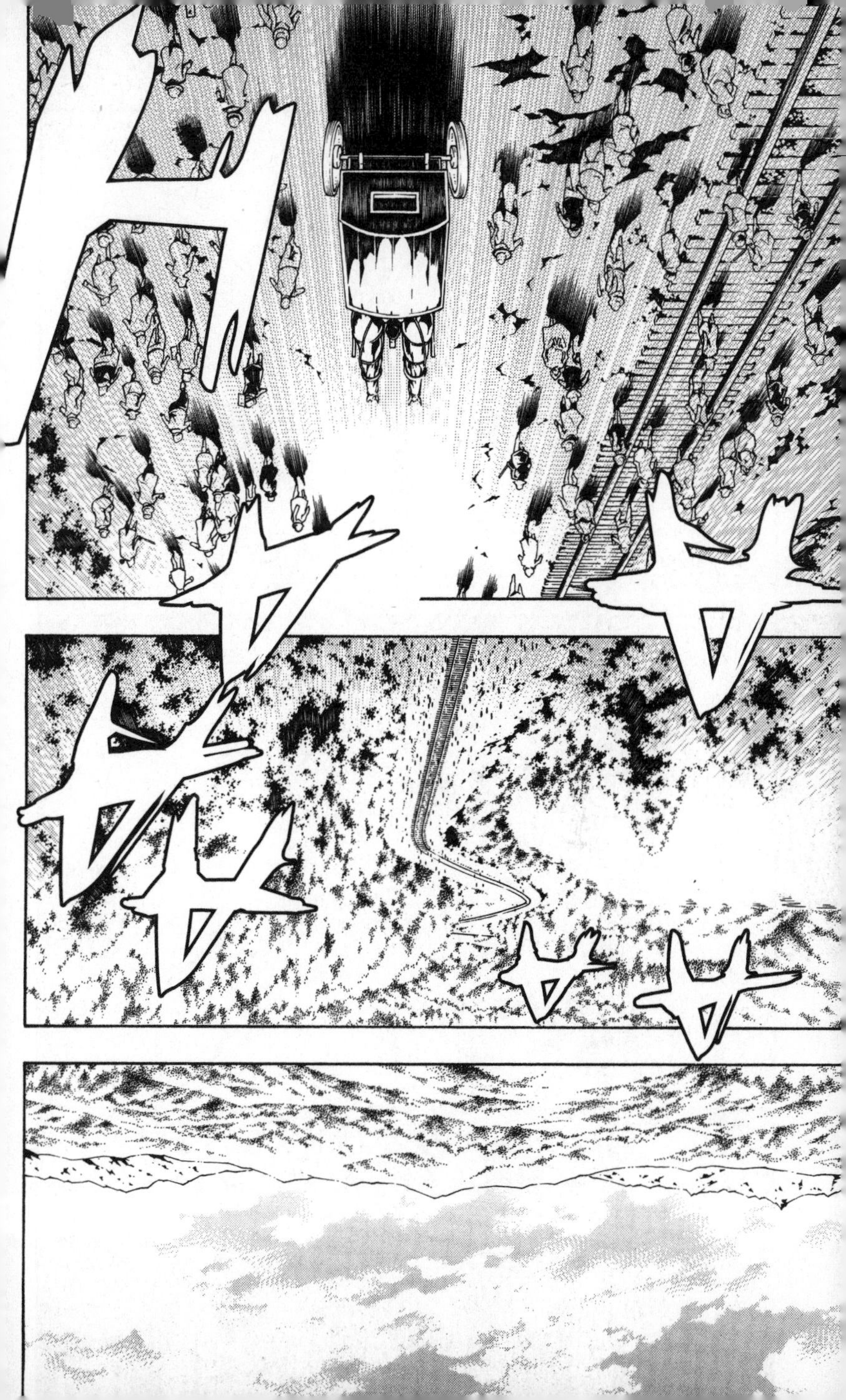

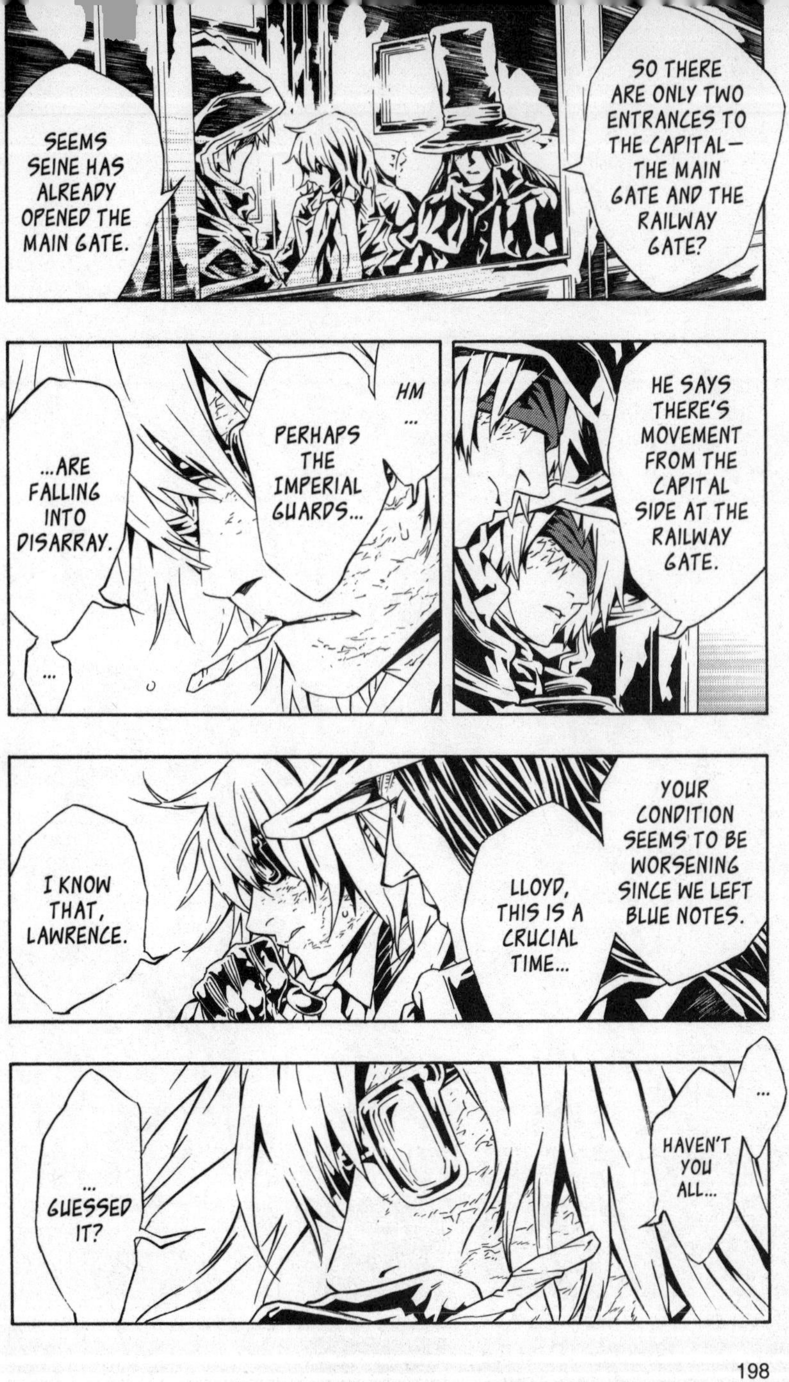
SO THERE ARE ONLY TWO ENTRANCES TO THE CAPITAL— THE MAIN GATE AND THE RAILWAY GATE?
SEEMS SEINE HAS ALREADY OPENED THE MAIN GATE.
HE SAYS THERE'S MOVEMENT FROM THE CAPITAL SIDE AT THE RAILWAY GATE.
HM ...
PERHAPS THE IMPERIAL GUARDS...
...ARE FALLING INTO DISARRAY.
...
YOUR CONDITION SEEMS TO BE WORSENING SINCE WE LEFT BLUE NOTES.
LLOYD, THIS IS A CRUCIAL TIME...
I KNOW THAT, LAWRENCE.
...
HAVEN'T YOU ALL...
... GUESSED IT?

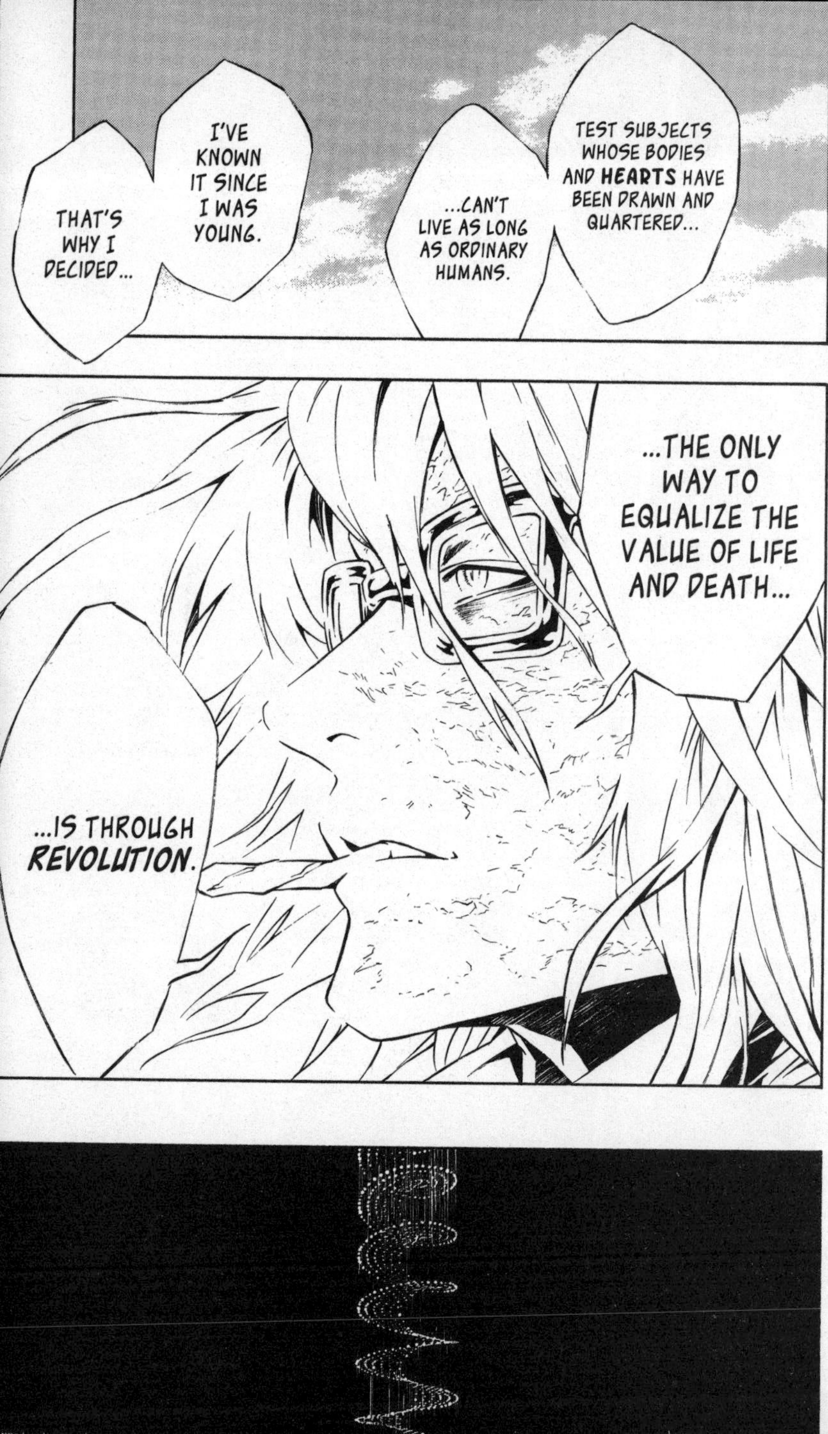
TEST SUBJECTS WHOSE BODIES AND **HEARTS** HAVE BEEN DRAWN AND QUARTERED...
...CAN'T LIVE AS LONG AS ORDINARY HUMANS.
I'VE KNOWN IT SINCE I WAS YOUNG.
THAT'S WHY I DECIDED...
...THE ONLY WAY TO EQUALIZE THE VALUE OF LIFE AND DEATH...
...IS THROUGH ***REVOLUTION***.

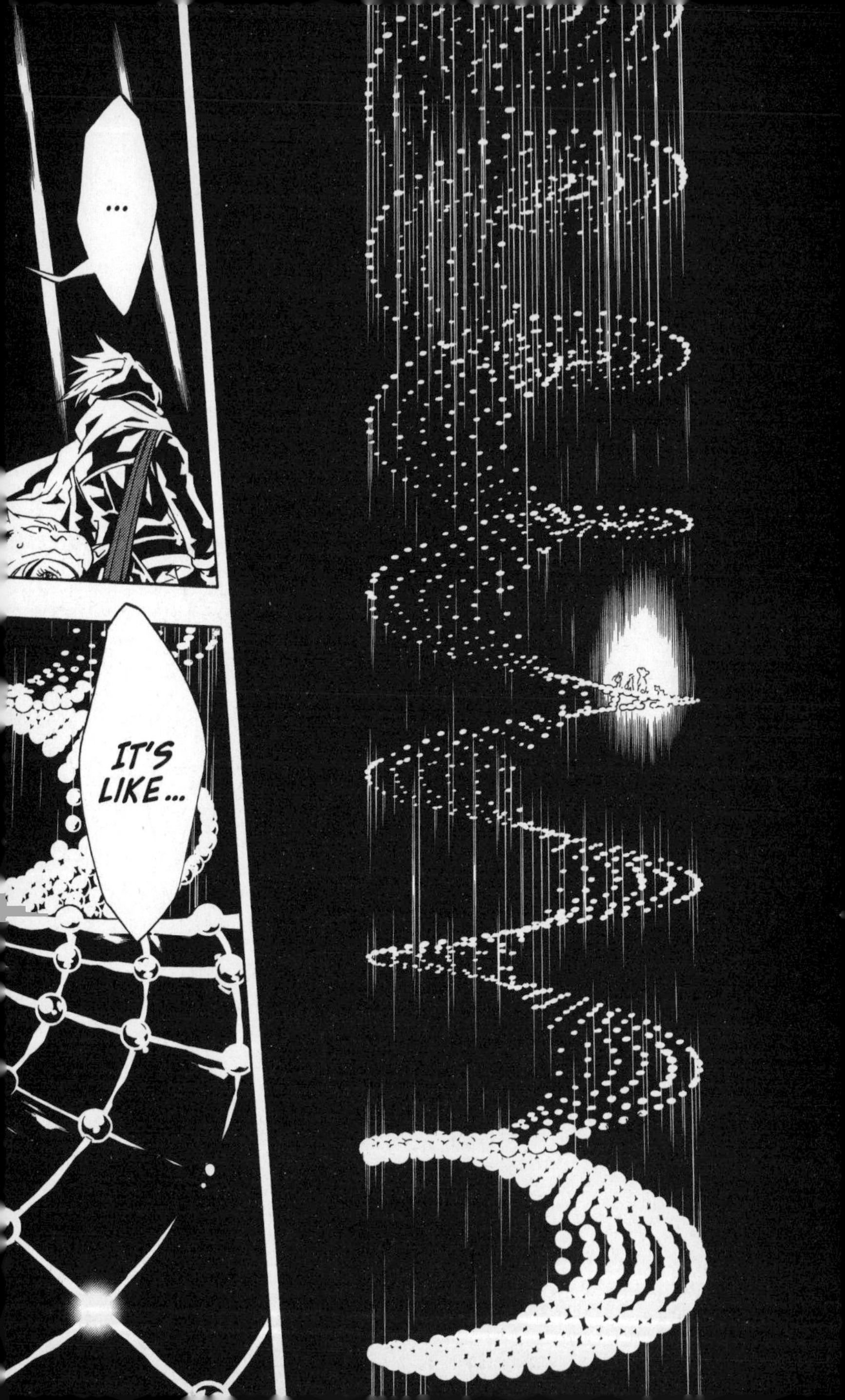
...
IT'S LIKE...

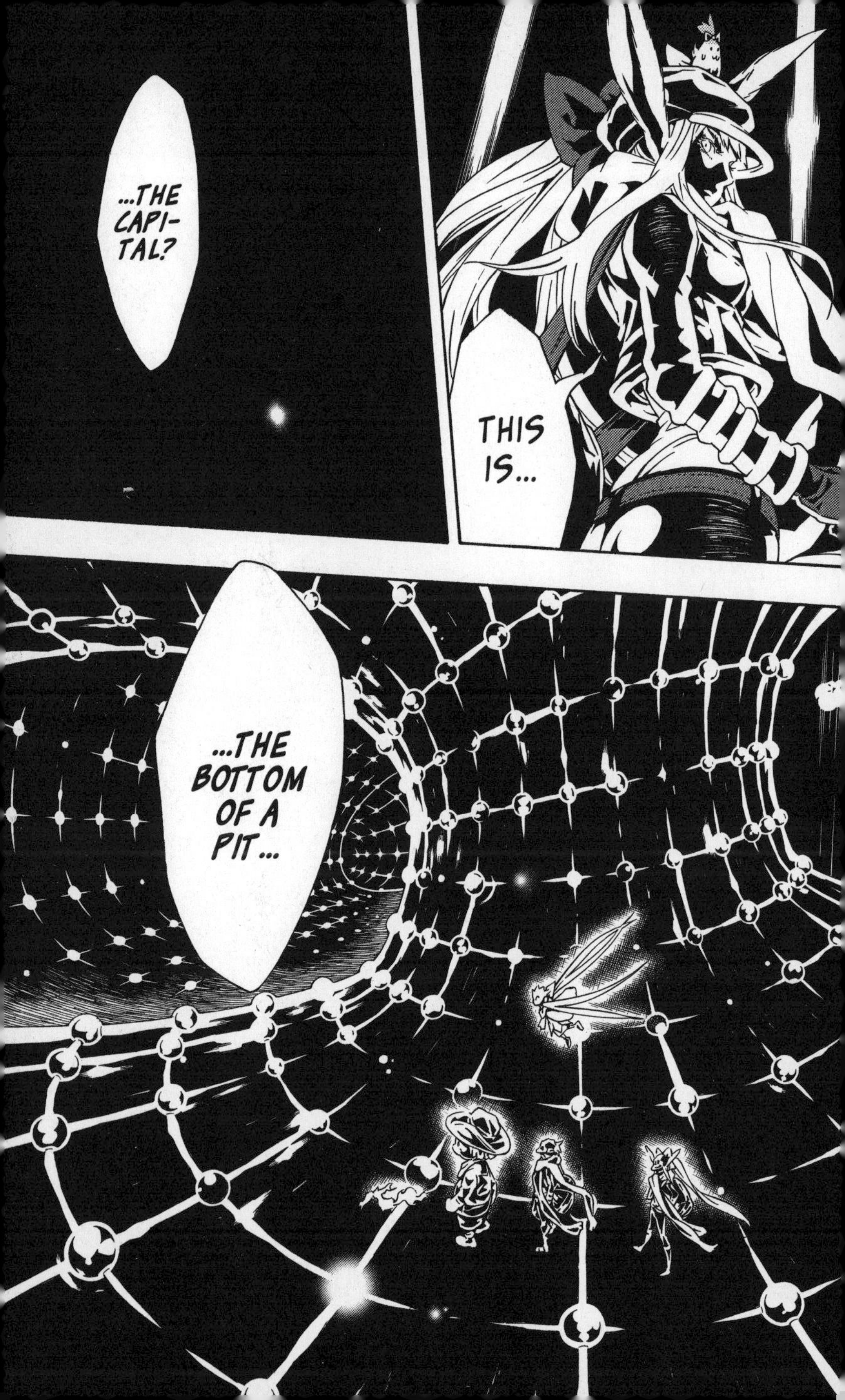
THIS IS...
...THE CAPITAL?
...THE BOTTOM OF A PIT...

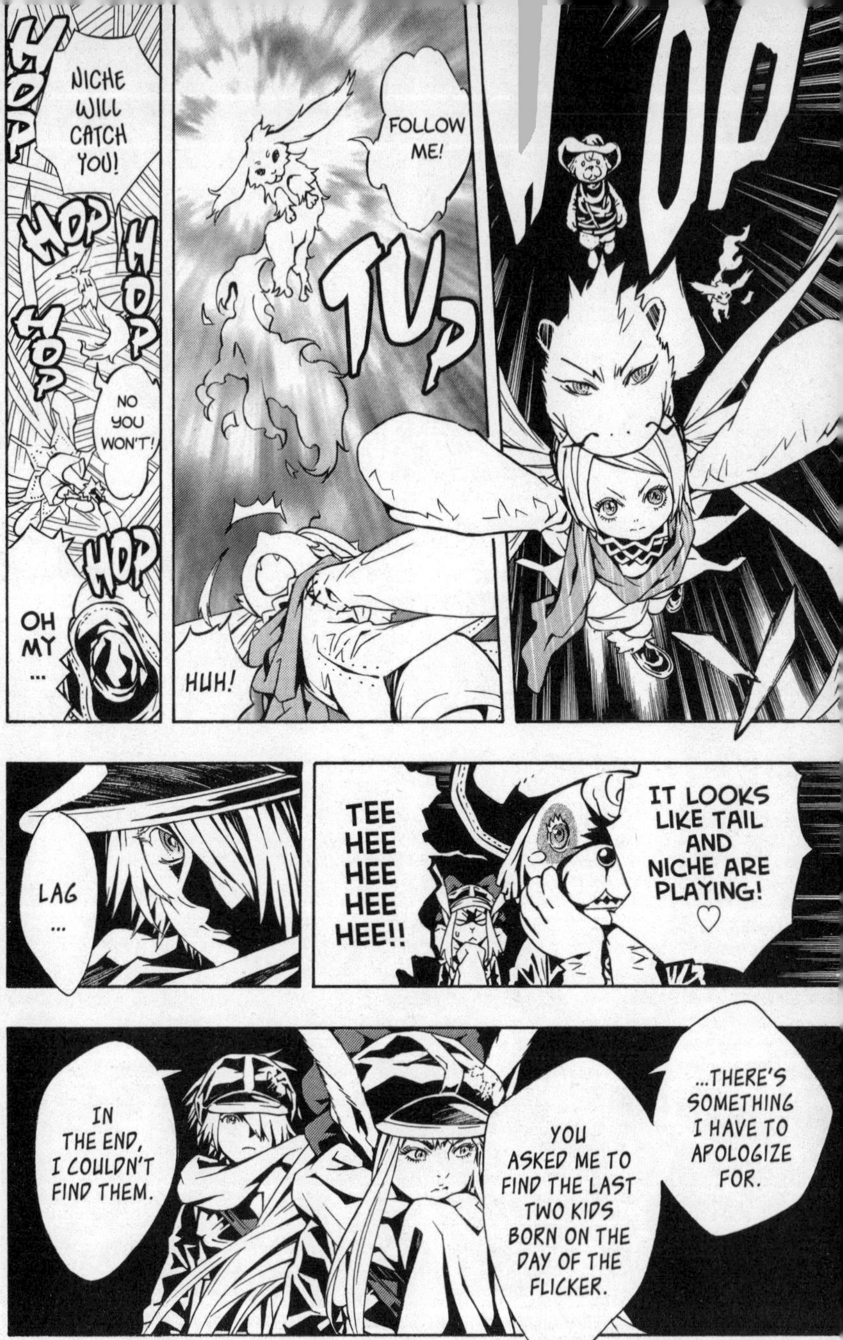
TUP
FOLLOW ME!
HUH!
NICHE WILL CATCH YOU!
HOP
HOP
HOP
HOP
NO YOU WON'T!
HOP
OH MY ...
IT LOOKS LIKE TAIL AND NICHE ARE PLAYING! ♡
TEE HEE HEE HEE HEE!!
LAG ...
...THERE'S SOMETHING I HAVE TO APOLOGIZE FOR.
YOU ASKED ME TO FIND THE LAST TWO KIDS BORN ON THE DAY OF THE FLICKER.
IN THE END, I COULDN'T FIND THEM.

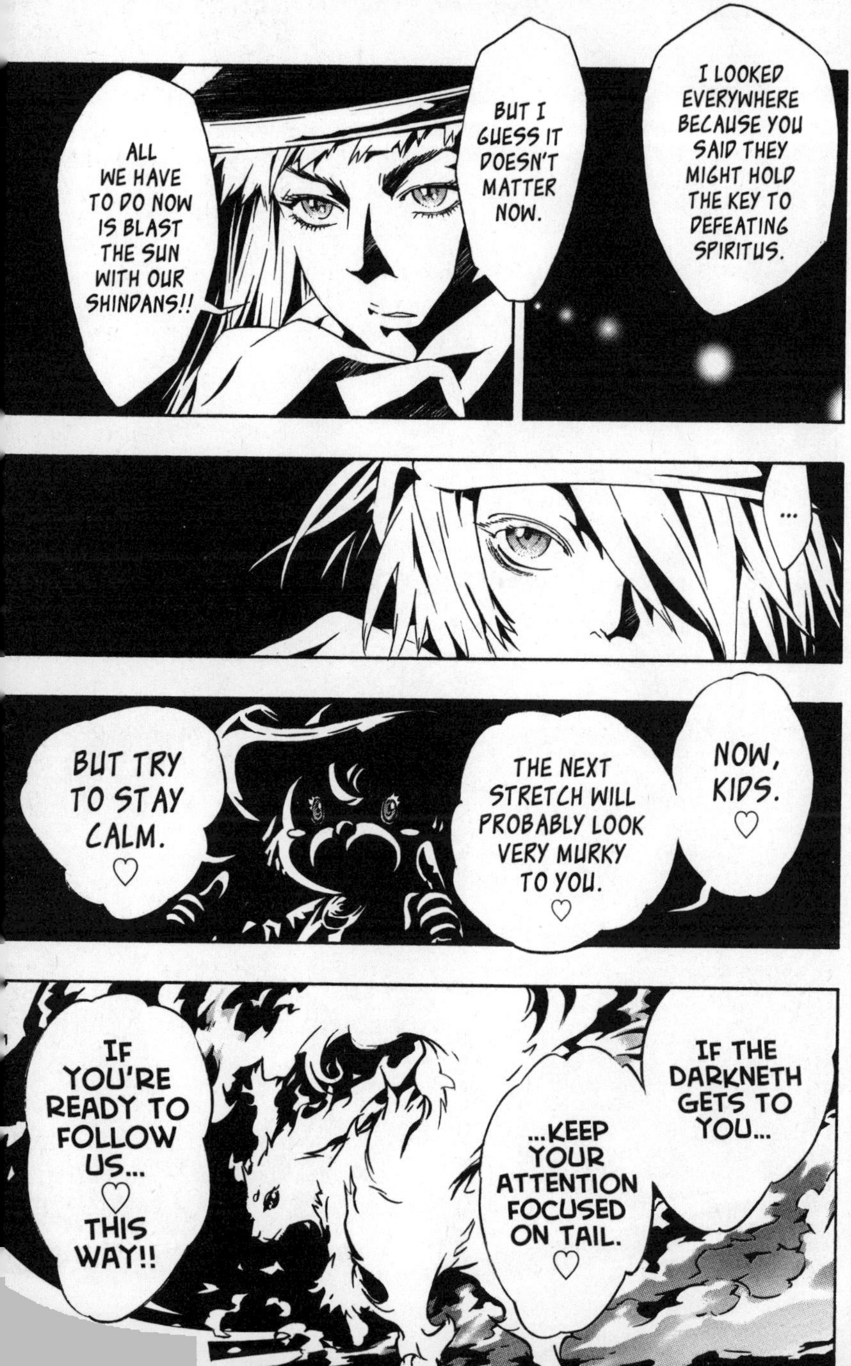
I LOOKED EVERYWHERE BECAUSE YOU SAID THEY MIGHT HOLD THE KEY TO DEFEATING SPIRITUS.
BUT I GUESS IT DOESN'T MATTER NOW.
ALL WE HAVE TO DO NOW IS BLAST THE SUN WITH OUR SHINDANS!!
...
NOW, KIDS. ♡
THE NEXT STRETCH WILL PROBABLY LOOK VERY MURKY TO YOU. ♡
BUT TRY TO STAY CALM. ♡
IF THE DARKNETH GETS TO YOU...
...KEEP YOUR ATTENTION FOCUSED ON TAIL. ♡
IF YOU'RE READY TO FOLLOW US... ♡ THIS WAY!!

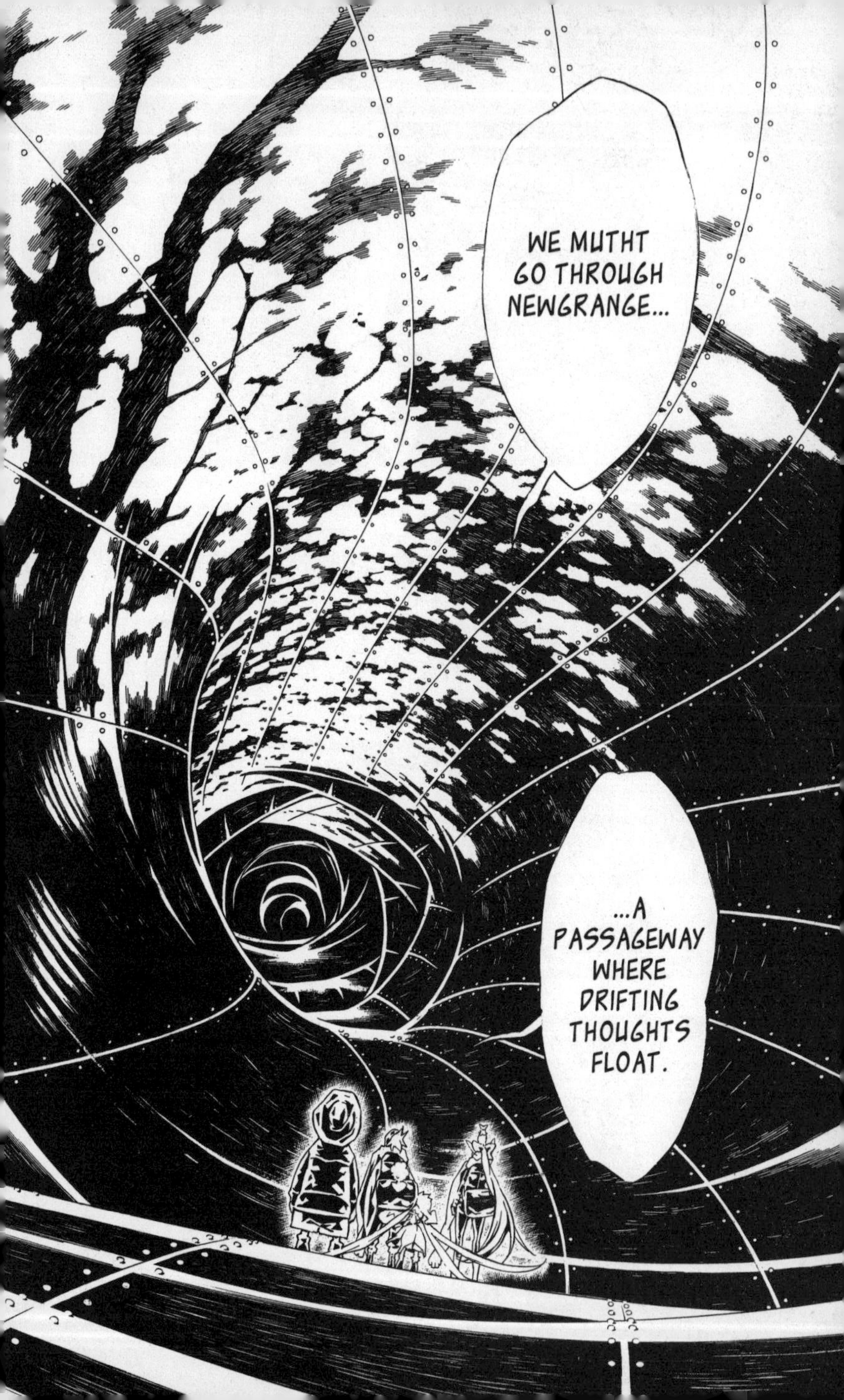
WE MUTHT GO THROUGH NEWGRANGE...
...A PASSAGEWAY WHERE DRIFTING THOUGHTS FLOAT.

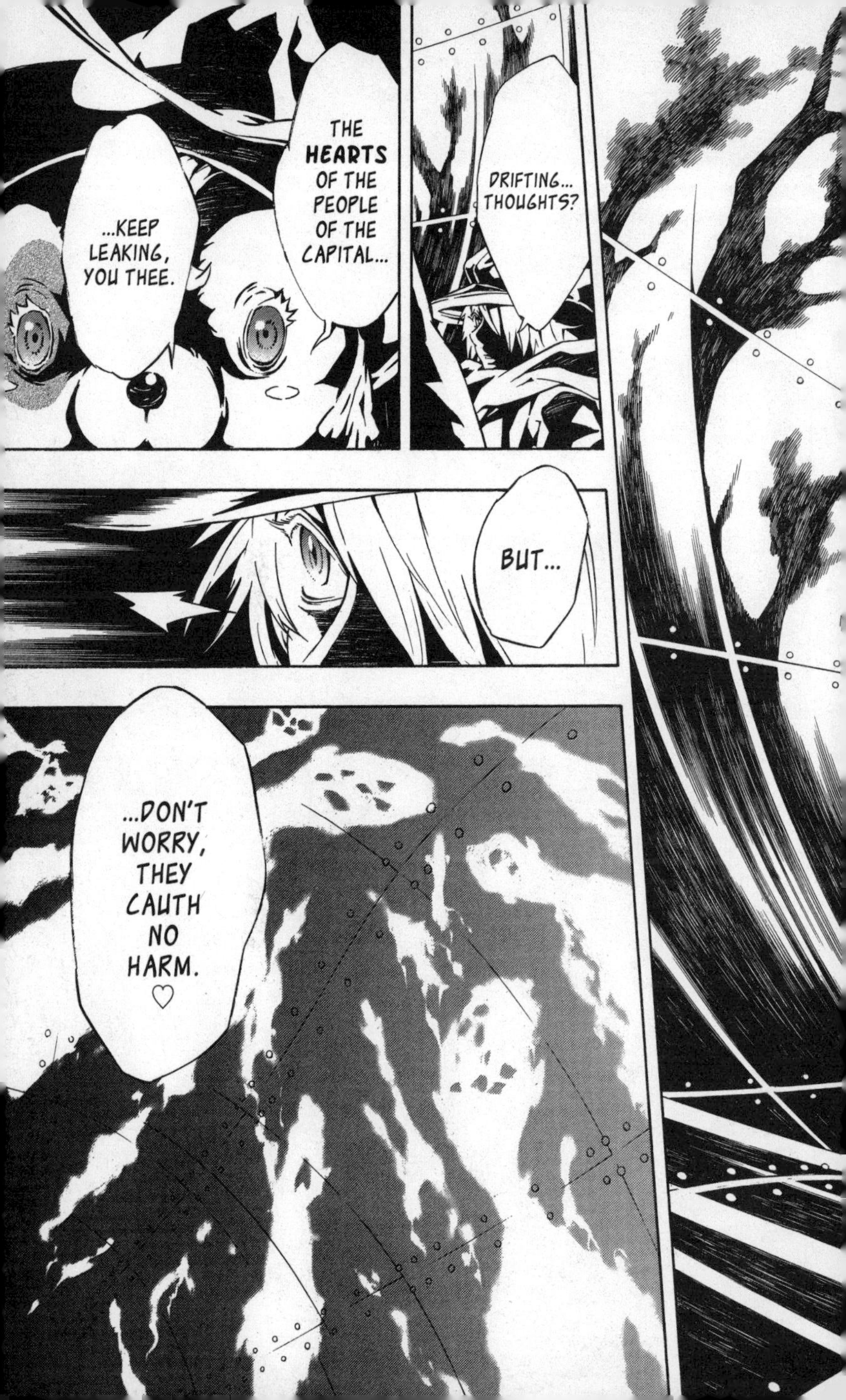
DRIFTING... THOUGHTS?
THE **HEARTS** OF THE PEOPLE OF THE CAPITAL...
...KEEP LEAKING, YOU THEE.
BUT...
...DON'T WORRY, THEY CAUTH NO HARM. ♡

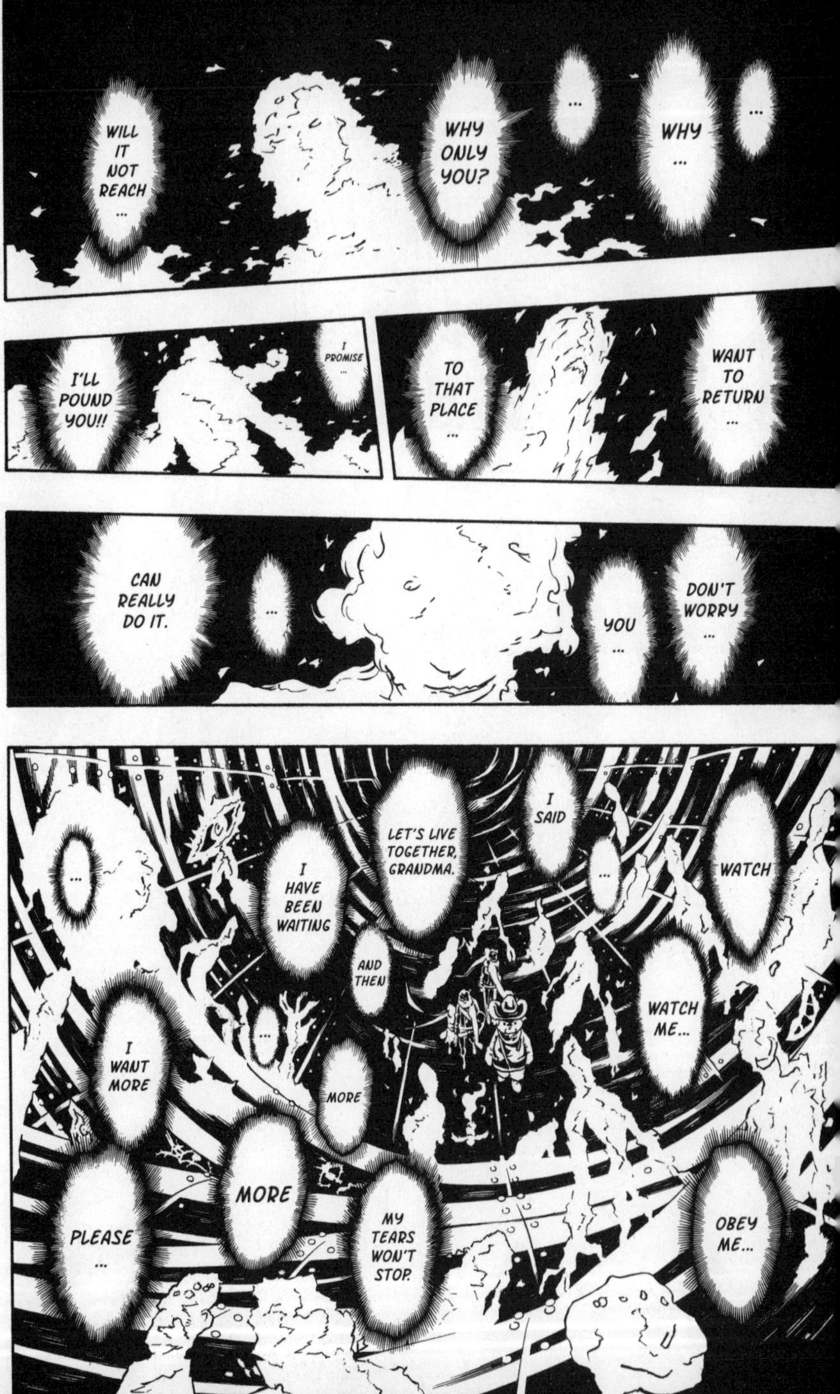
...
WHY ...
...
WHY ONLY YOU?
WILL IT NOT REACH ...
WANT TO RETURN ...
TO THAT PLACE ...
I PROMISE ...
I'LL POUND YOU!!
DON'T WORRY ...
YOU ...
...
CAN REALLY DO IT.
WATCH
...
I SAID
LET'S LIVE TOGETHER, GRANDMA.
I HAVE BEEN WAITING
...
WATCH ME...
AND THEN
...
I WANT MORE
MORE
OBEY ME...
MY TEARS WON'T STOP.
MORE
PLEASE ...

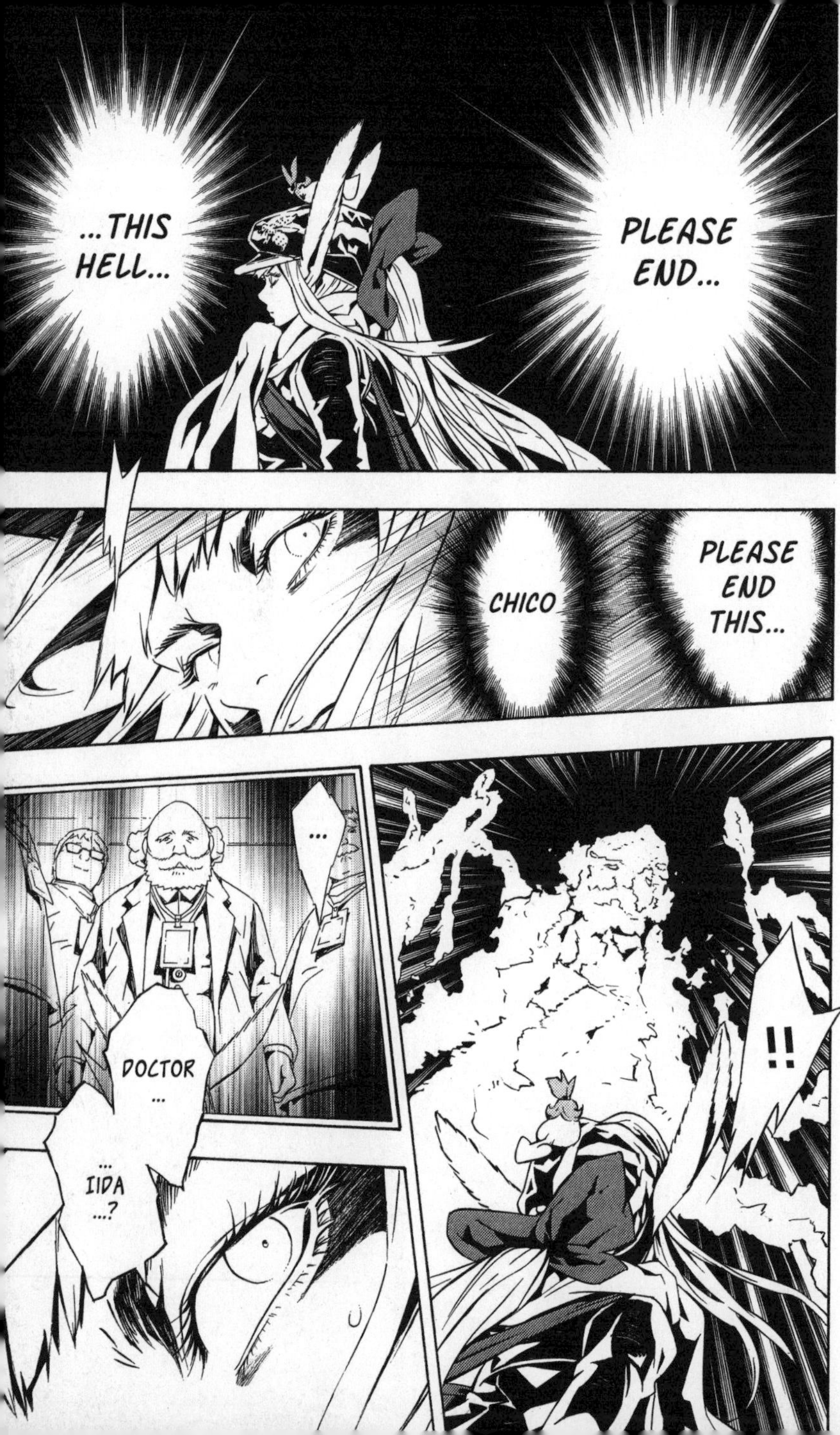
PLEASE END...
...THIS HELL...
PLEASE END THIS...
CHICO
!!
...
DOCTOR ...
... IIDA ...?

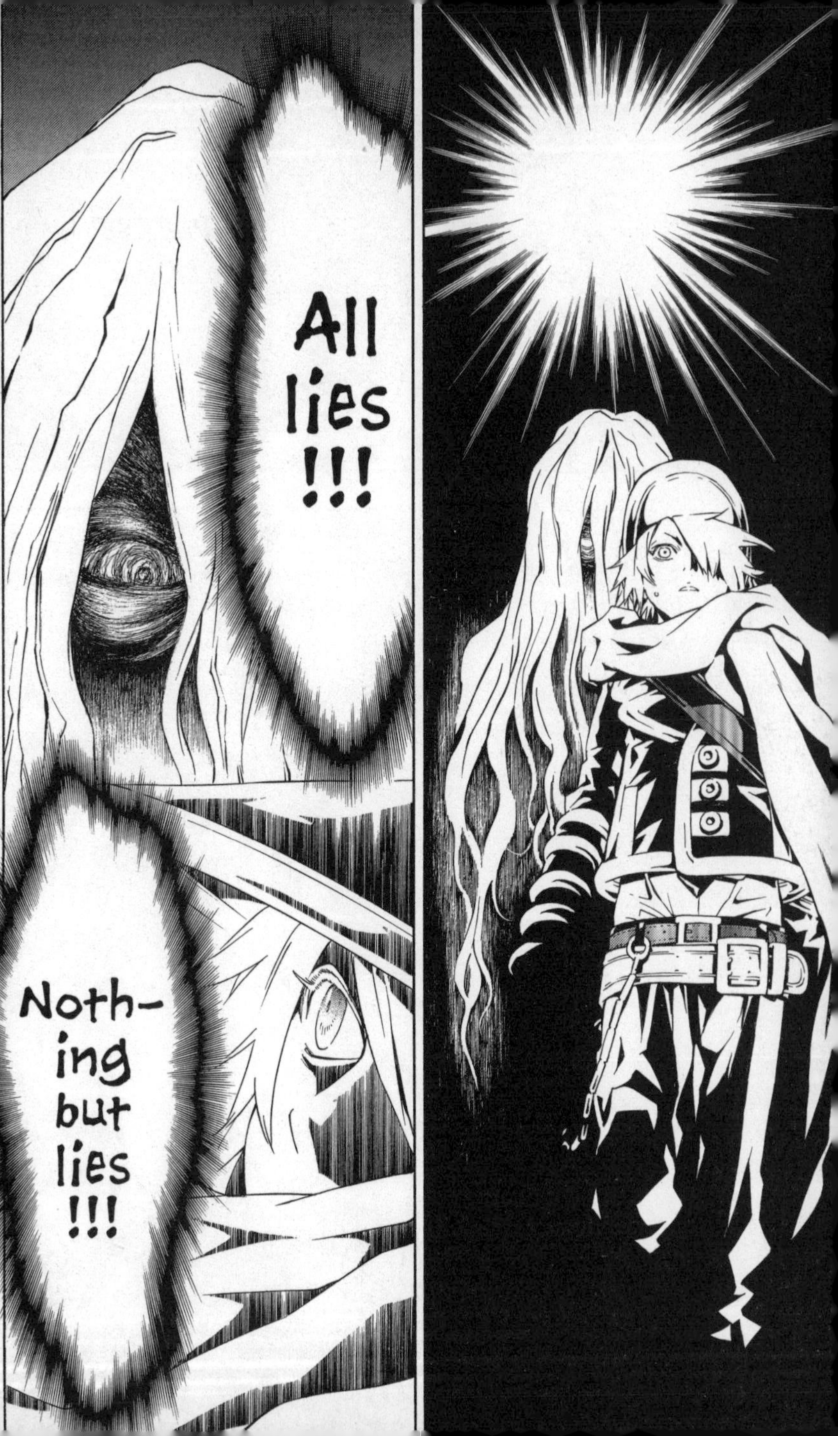
All lies!!!
Nothing but lies!!!

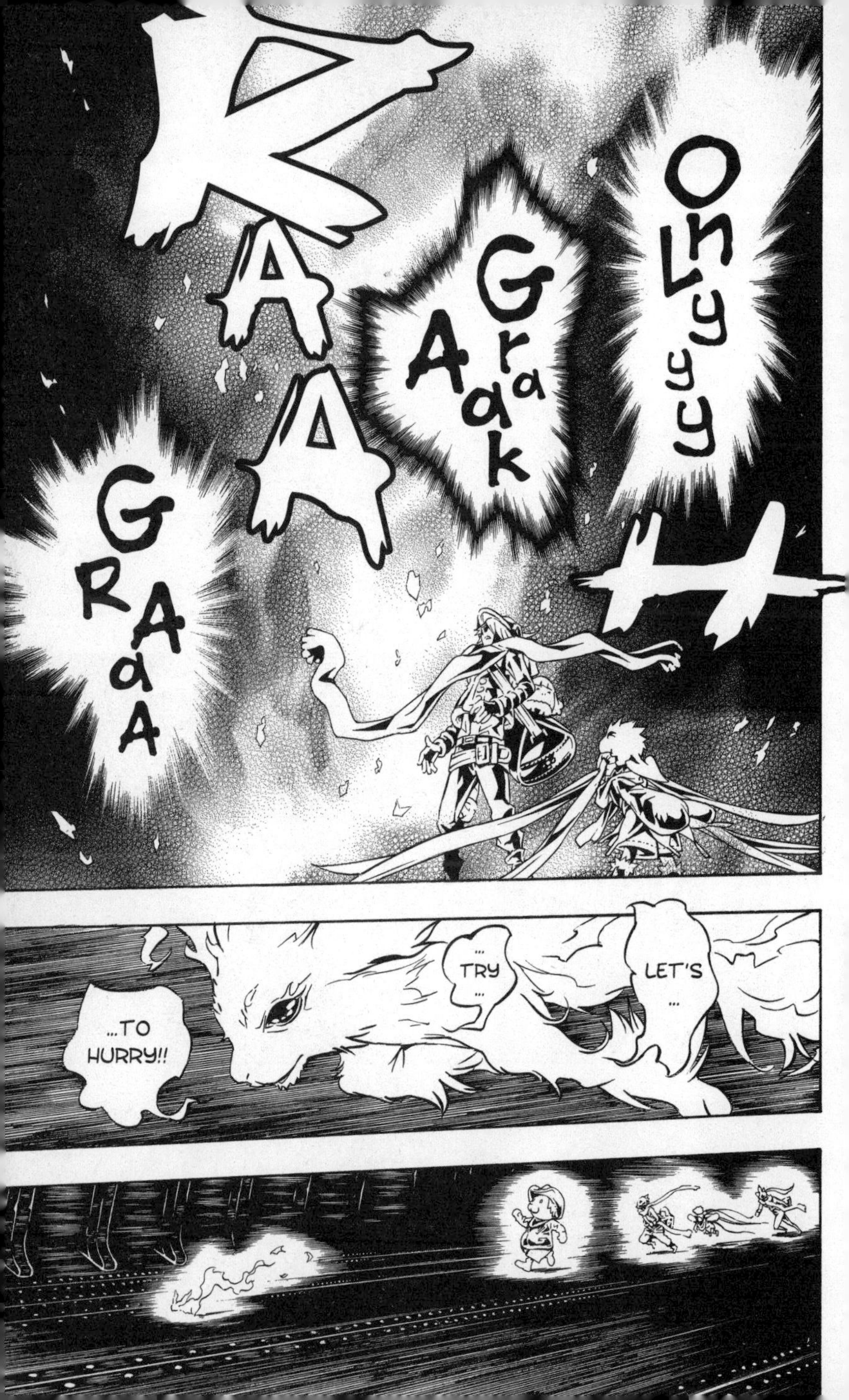
Onlyyy
KAA
GrAaak
GRAaA
LET'S ...
... TRY ...
...TO HURRY!!

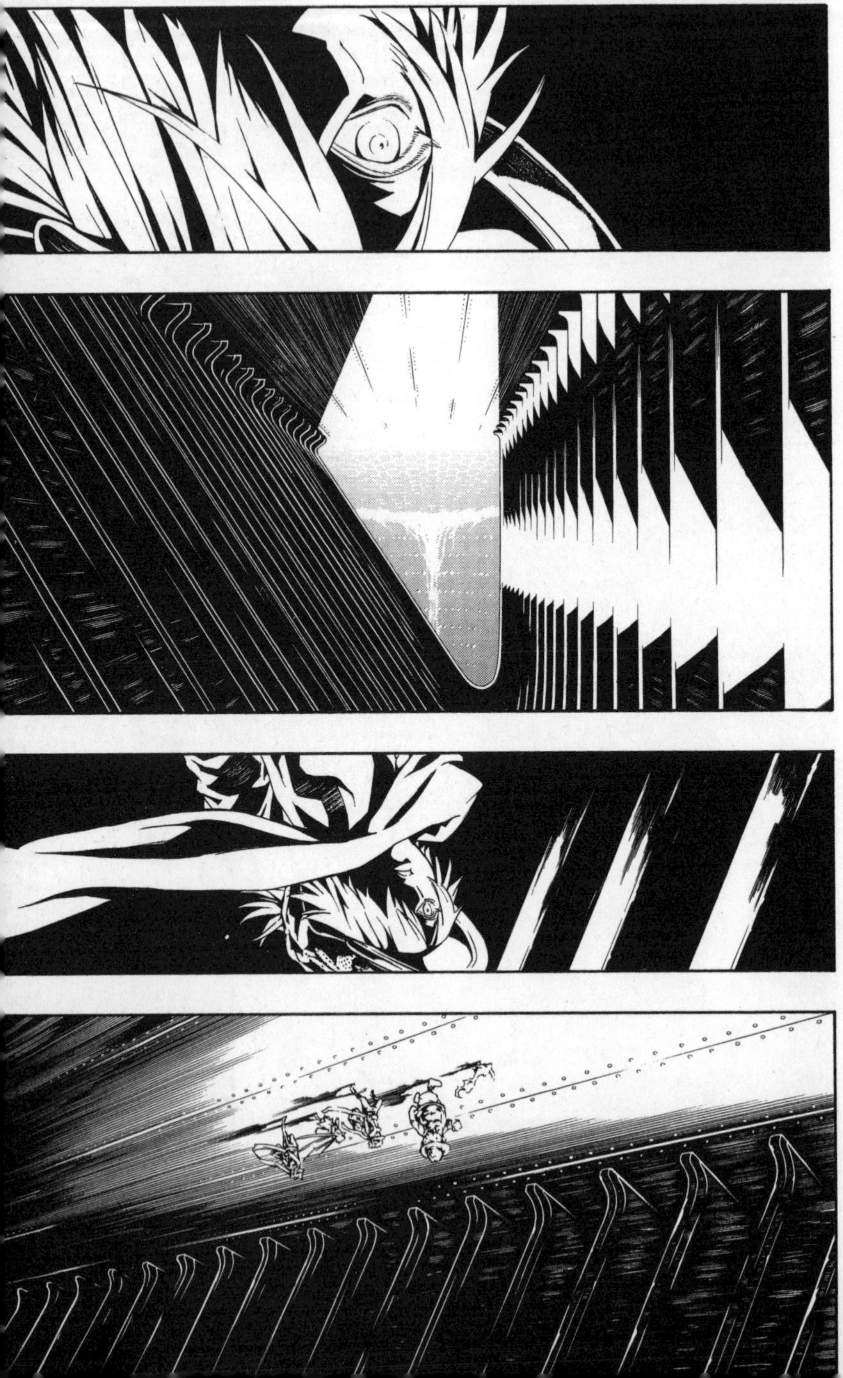

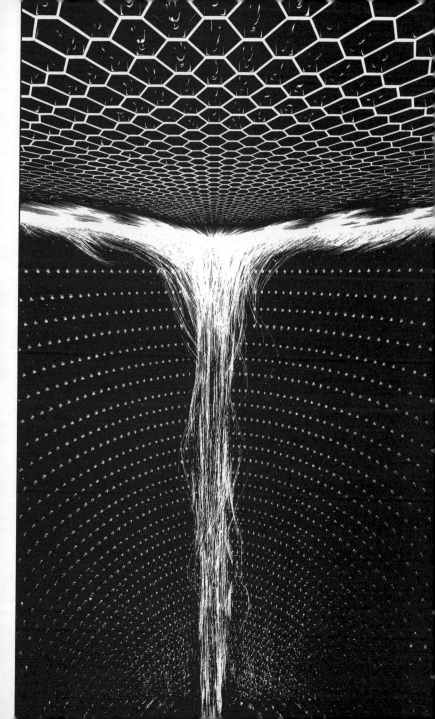

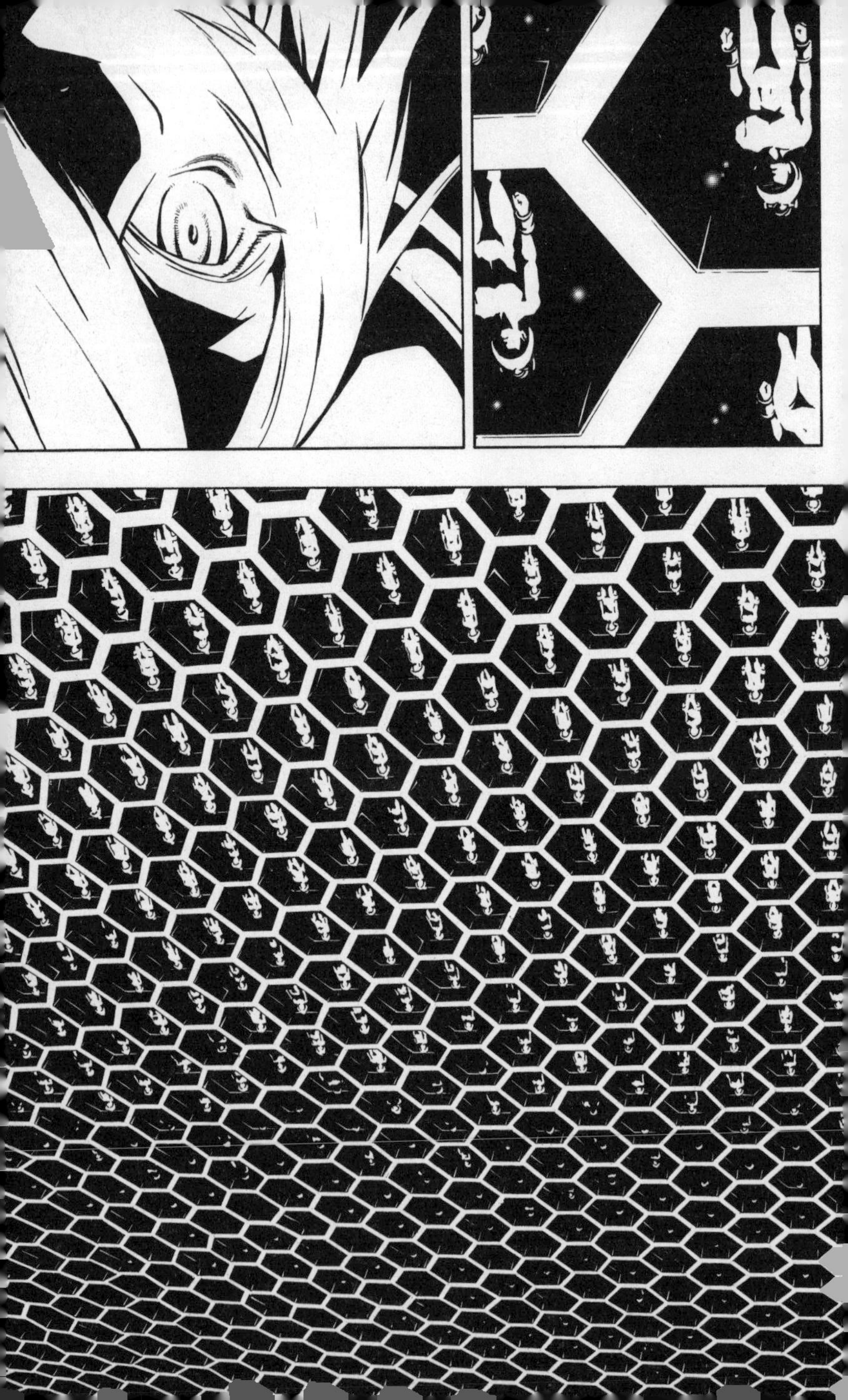

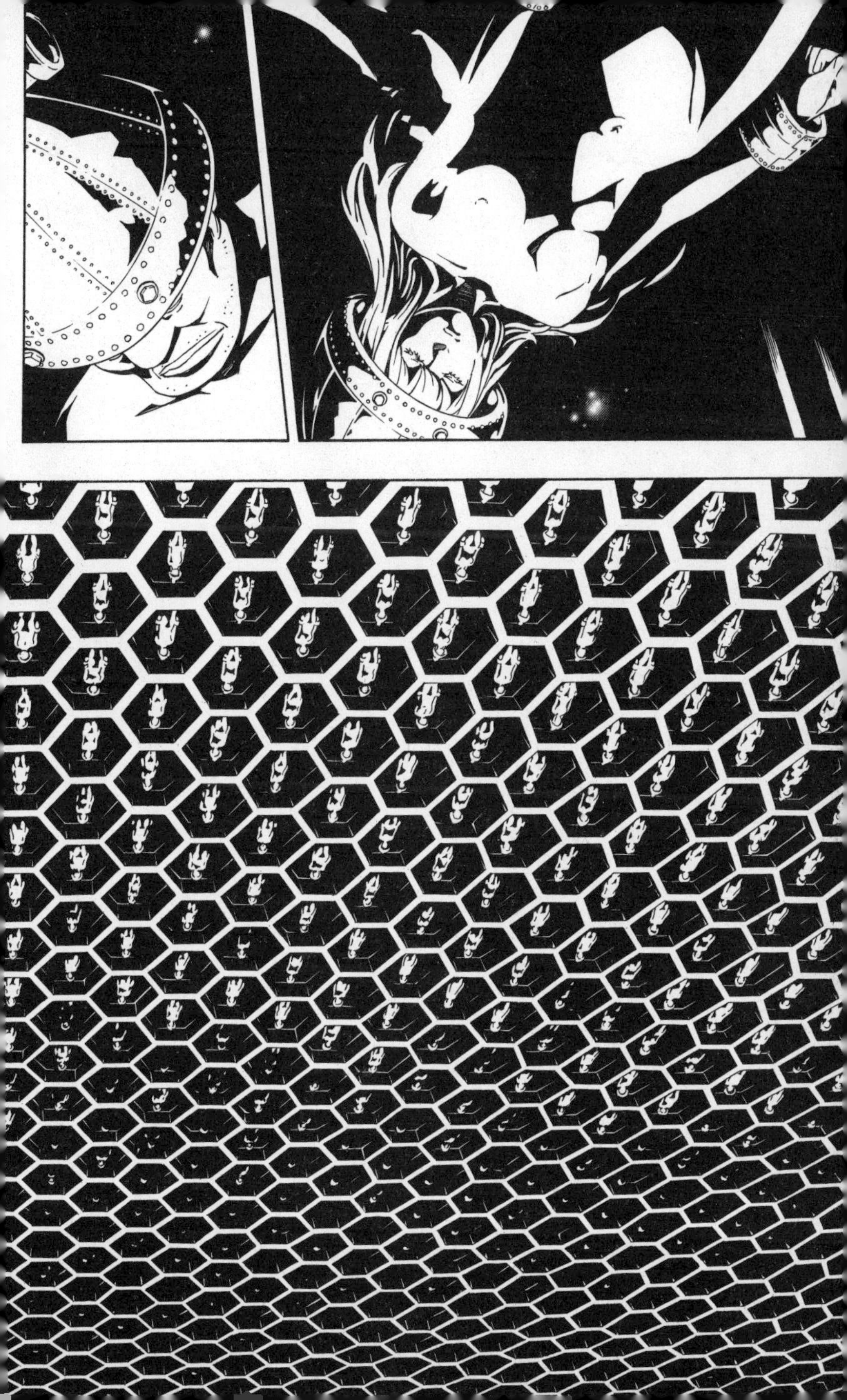

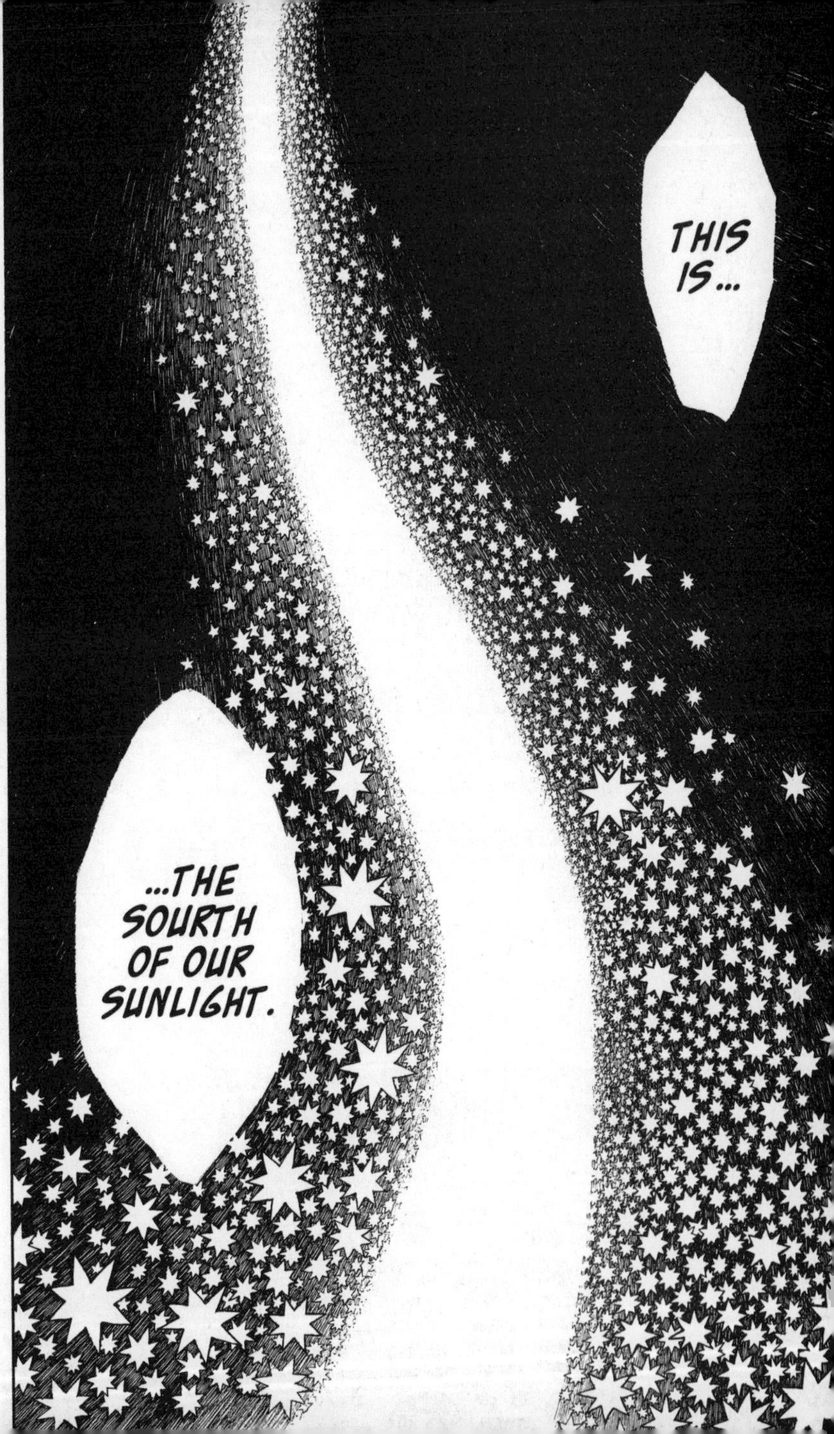
THIS IS...
...THE SOURTH OF OUR SUNLIGHT.

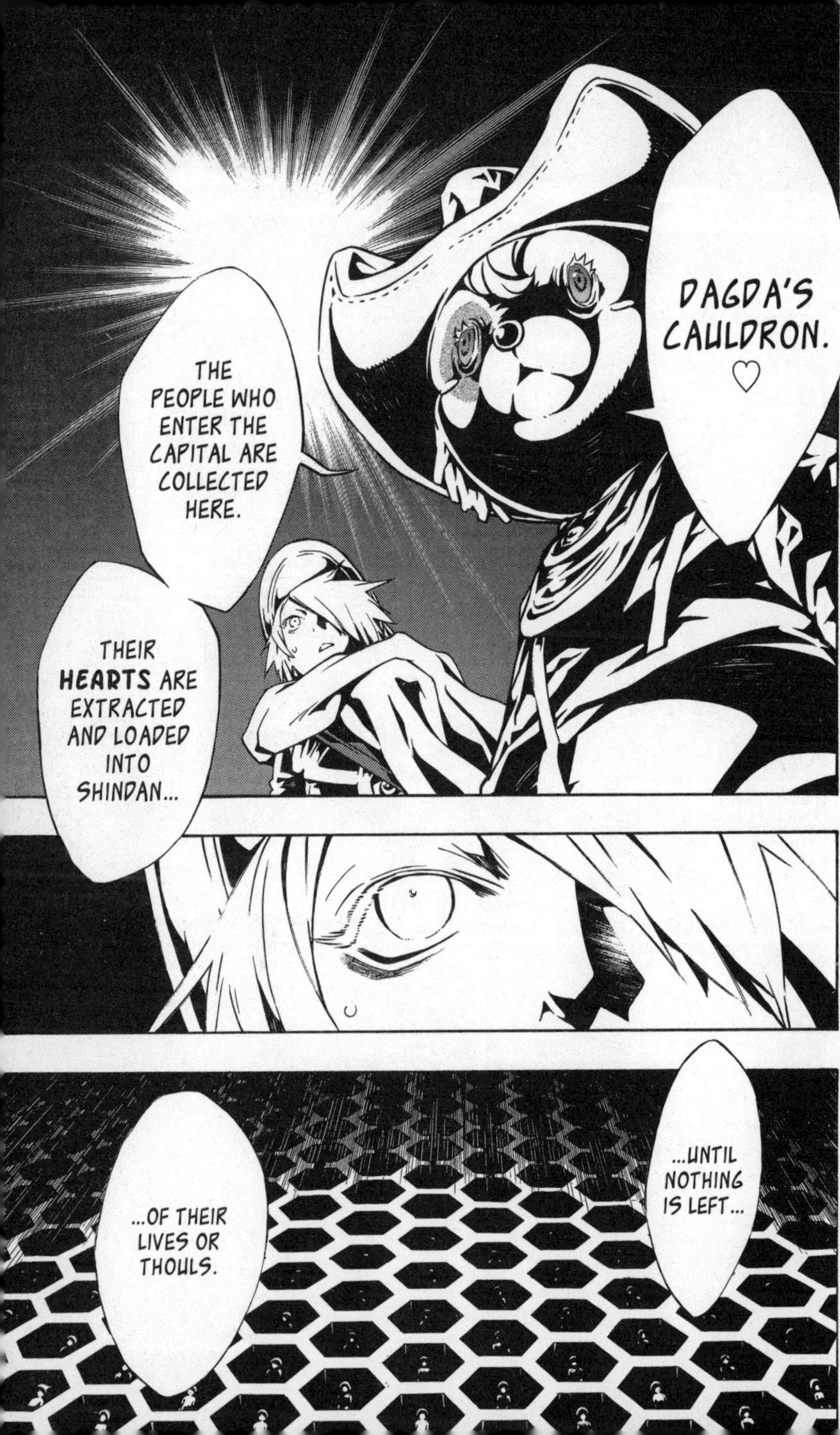
DAGDA'S CAULDRON. ♡
THE PEOPLE WHO ENTER THE CAPITAL ARE COLLECTED HERE.
THEIR **HEARTS** ARE EXTRACTED AND LOADED INTO SHINDAN...
...UNTIL NOTHING IS LEFT...
...OF THEIR LIVES OR THOULS.

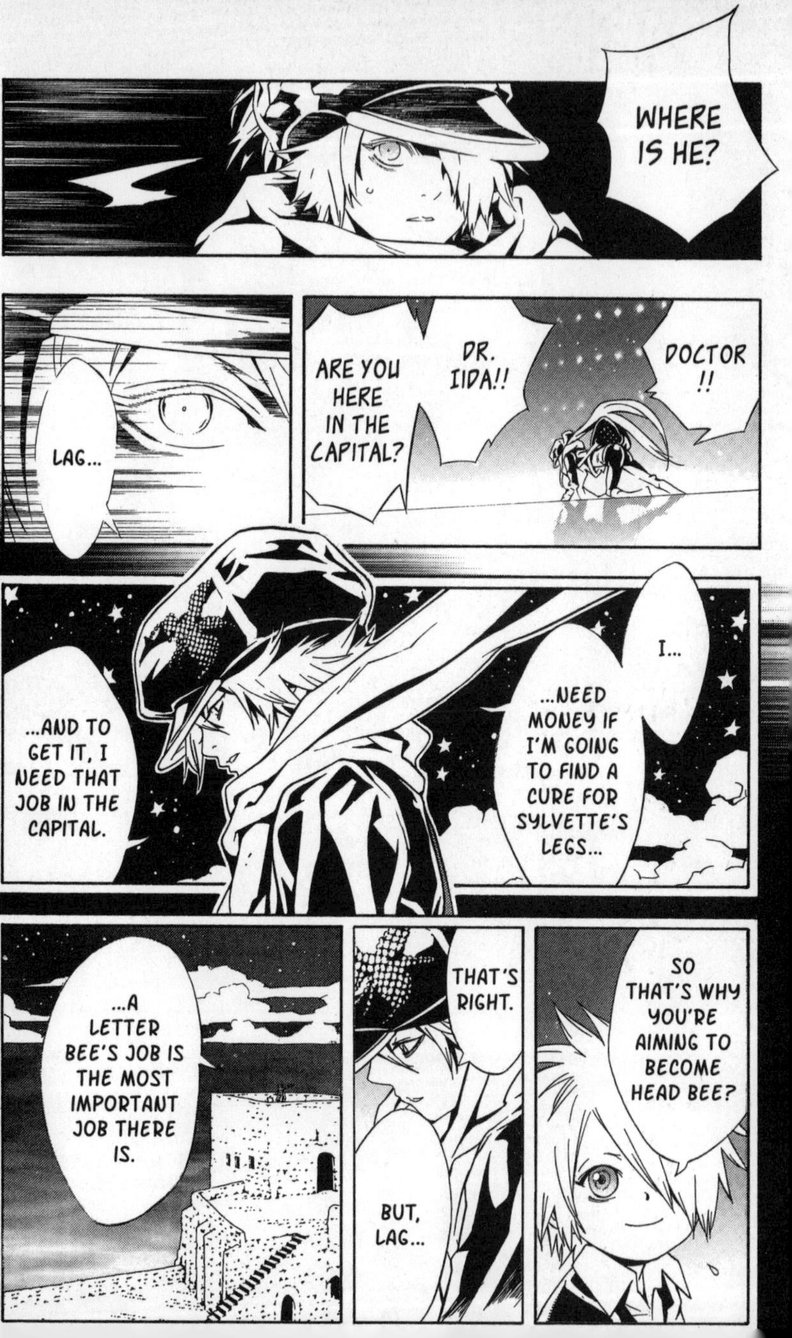
WHERE IS HE?
DOCTOR !!
DR. IIDA!!
ARE YOU HERE IN THE CAPITAL?
LAG...
I...
...NEED MONEY IF I'M GOING TO FIND A CURE FOR SYLVETTE'S LEGS...
...AND TO GET IT, I NEED THAT JOB IN THE CAPITAL.
SO THAT'S WHY YOU'RE AIMING TO BECOME HEAD BEE?
THAT'S RIGHT.
BUT, LAG...
...A LETTER BEE'S JOB IS THE MOST IMPORTANT JOB THERE IS.

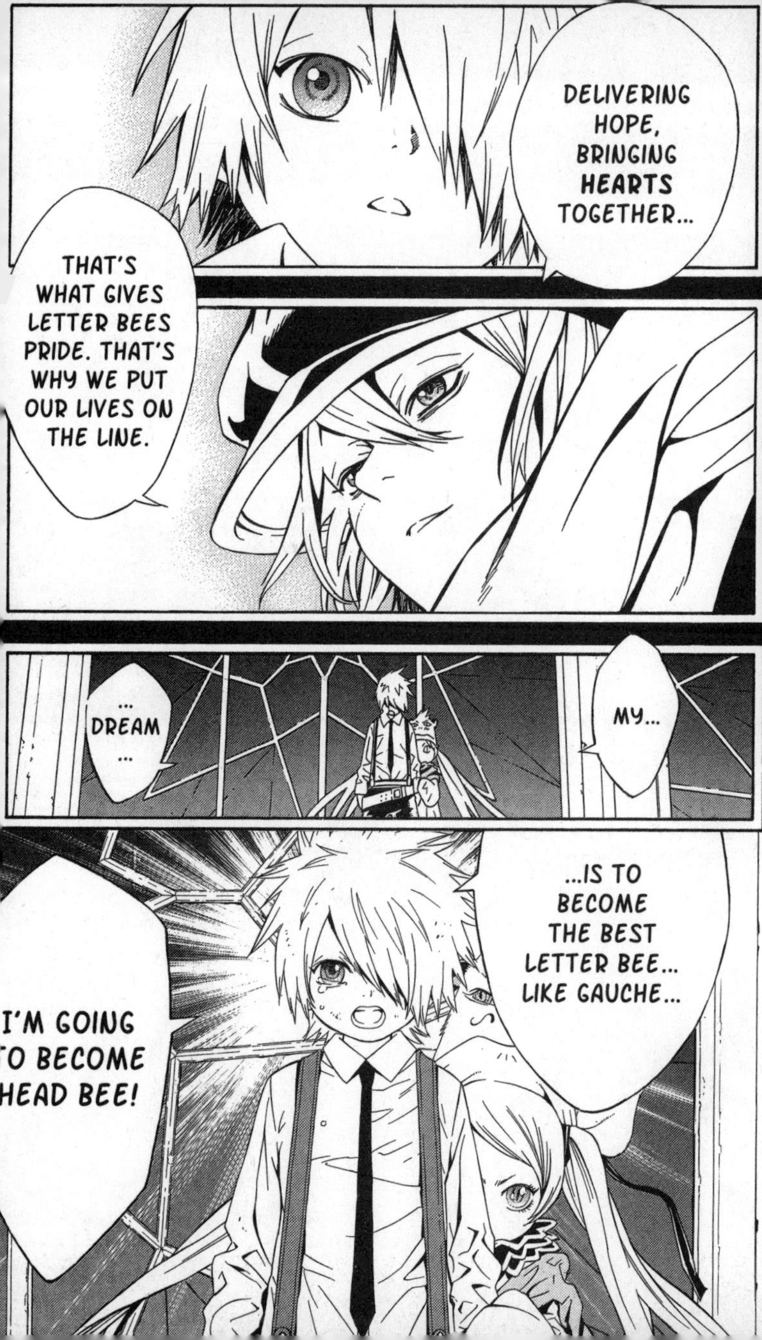
DELIVERING HOPE, BRINGING HEARTS TOGETHER...
THAT'S WHAT GIVES LETTER BEES PRIDE. THAT'S WHY WE PUT OUR LIVES ON THE LINE.
MY...
... DREAM ...
...IS TO BECOME THE BEST LETTER BEE... LIKE GAUCHE...
I'M GOING
O BECOME
HEAD BEE!

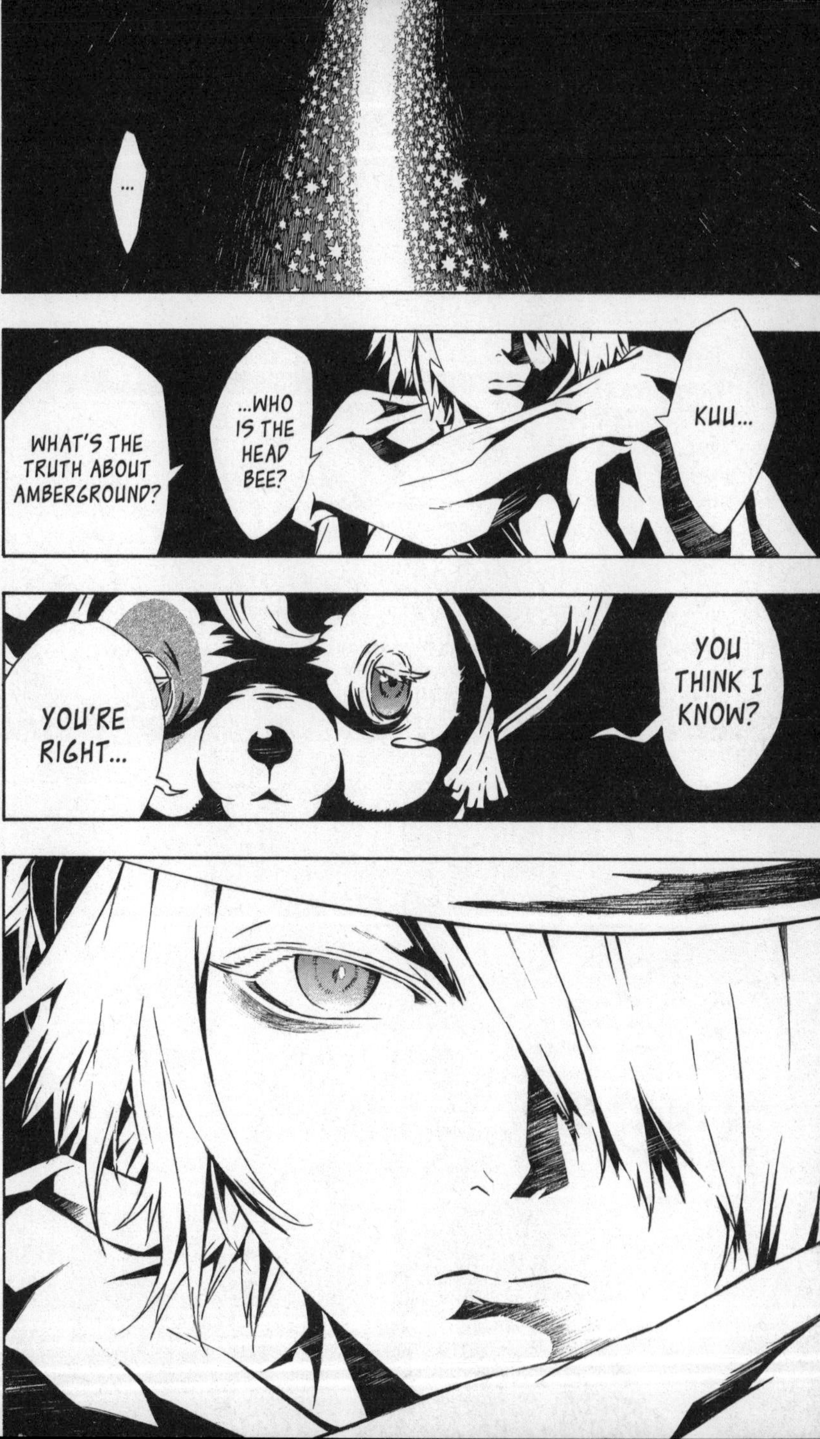
...
KUU...
...WHO IS THE HEAD BEE?
WHAT'S THE TRUTH ABOUT AMBERGROUND?
YOU THINK I KNOW?
YOU'RE RIGHT...

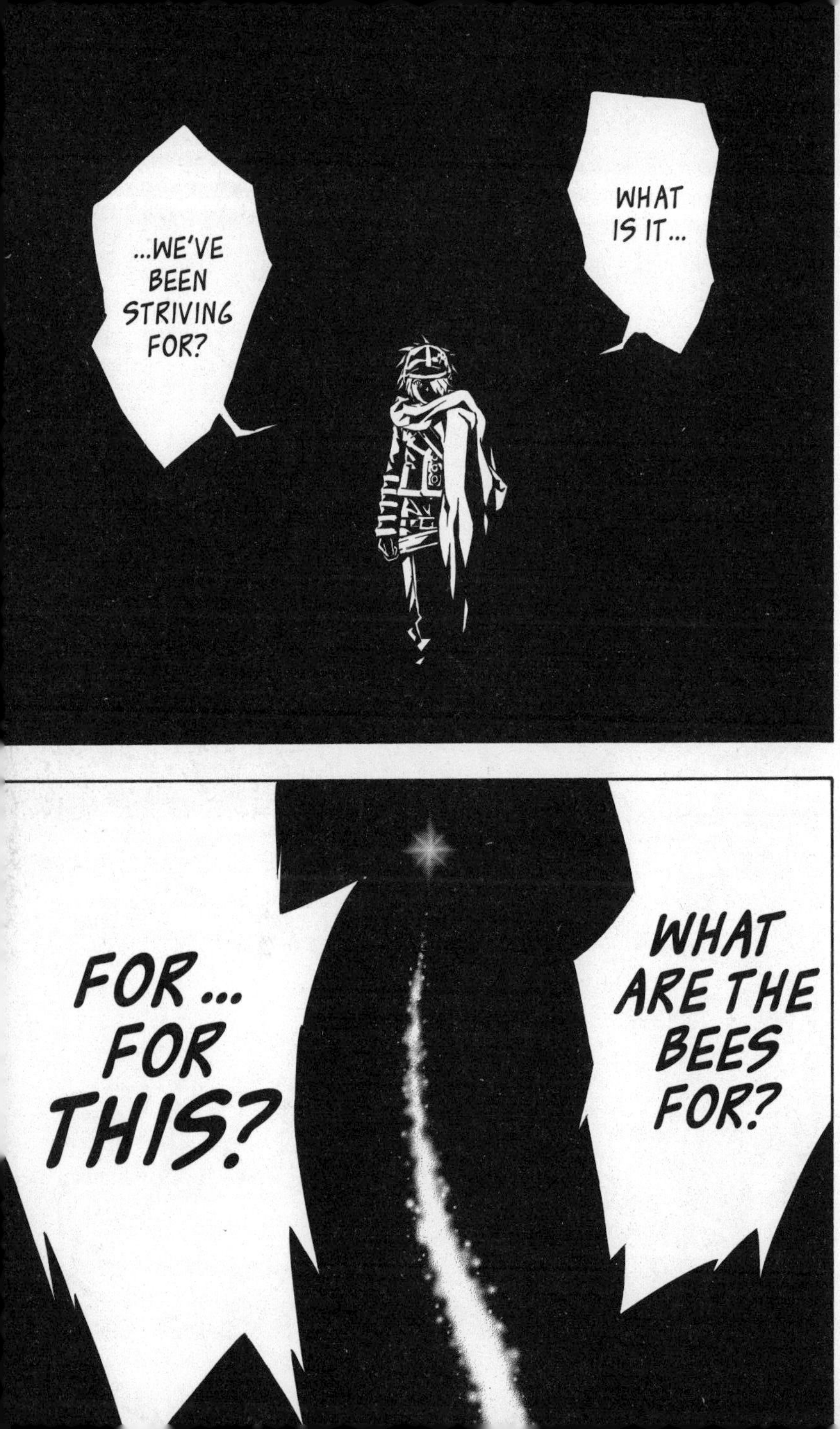
WHAT IS IT...
...WE'VE BEEN STRIVING FOR?
WHAT ARE THE BEES FOR?
FOR... FOR THIS?

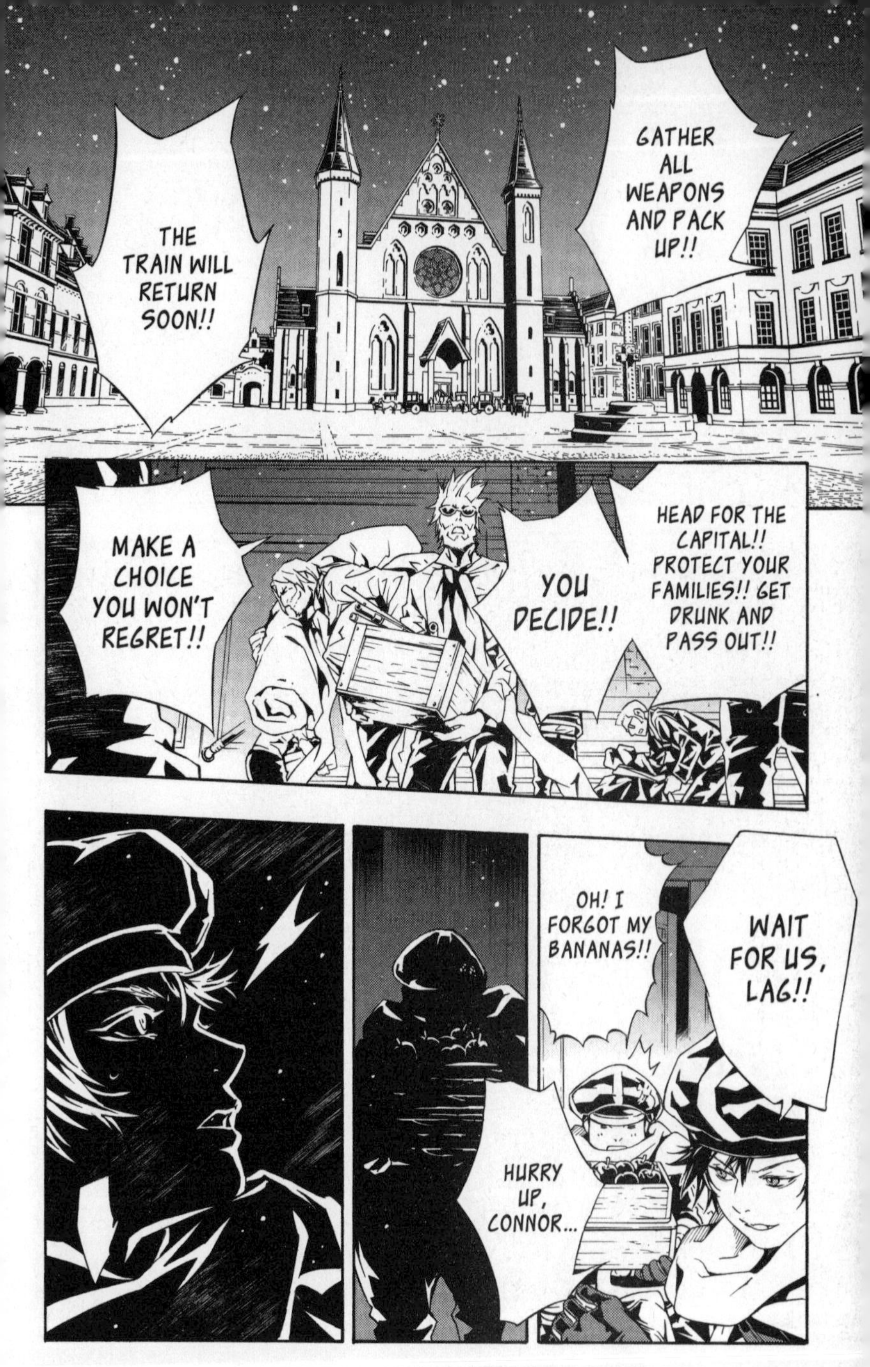
GATHER ALL WEAPONS AND PACK UP!!
THE TRAIN WILL RETURN SOON!!
HEAD FOR THE CAPITAL!! PROTECT YOUR FAMILIES!! GET DRUNK AND PASS OUT!!
YOU DECIDE!!
MAKE A CHOICE YOU WON'T REGRET!!
WAIT FOR US, LAG!!
OH! I FORGOT MY BANANAS!!
HURRY UP, CONNOR...

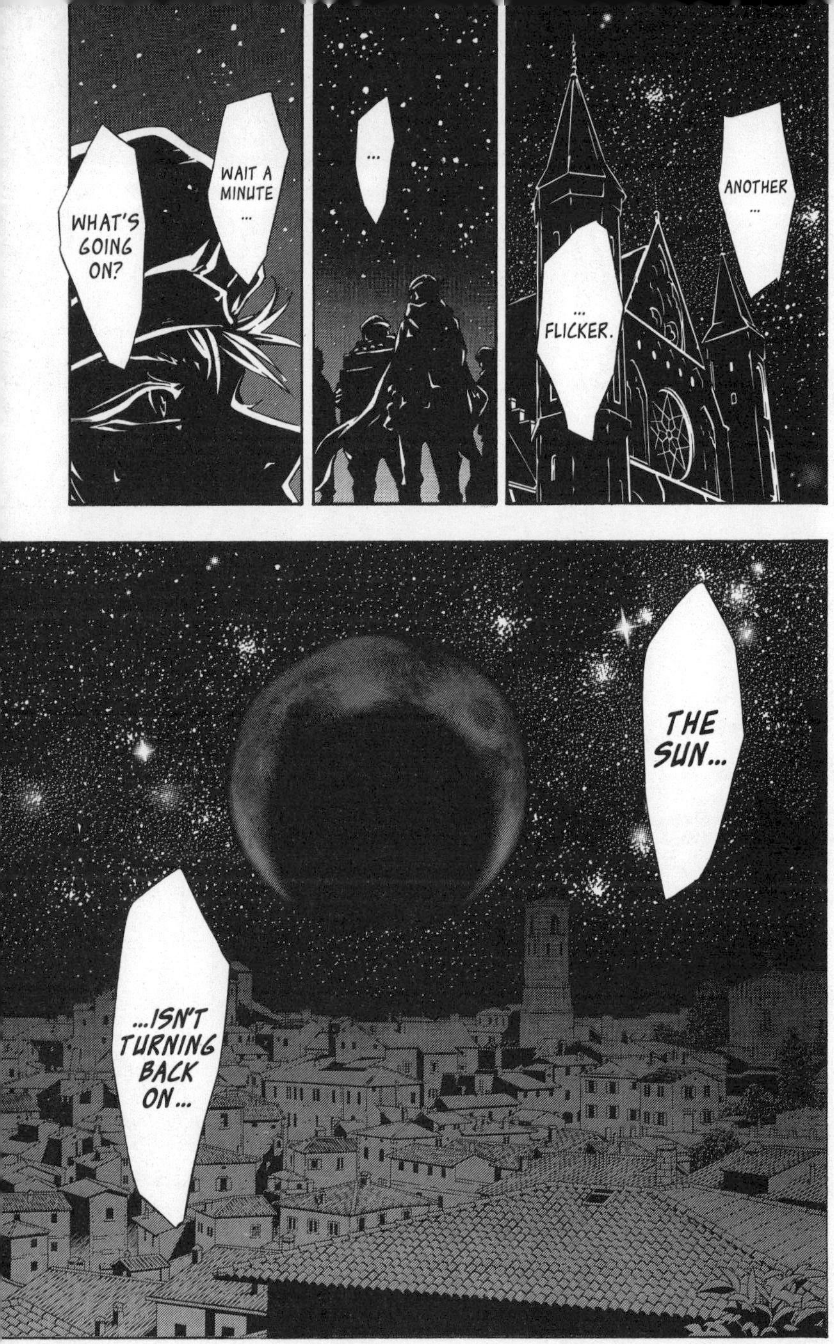
ANOTHER ...
... FLICKER.
...
WAIT A MINUTE ...
WHAT'S GOING ON?
THE SUN...
...ISN'T TURNING BACK ON...

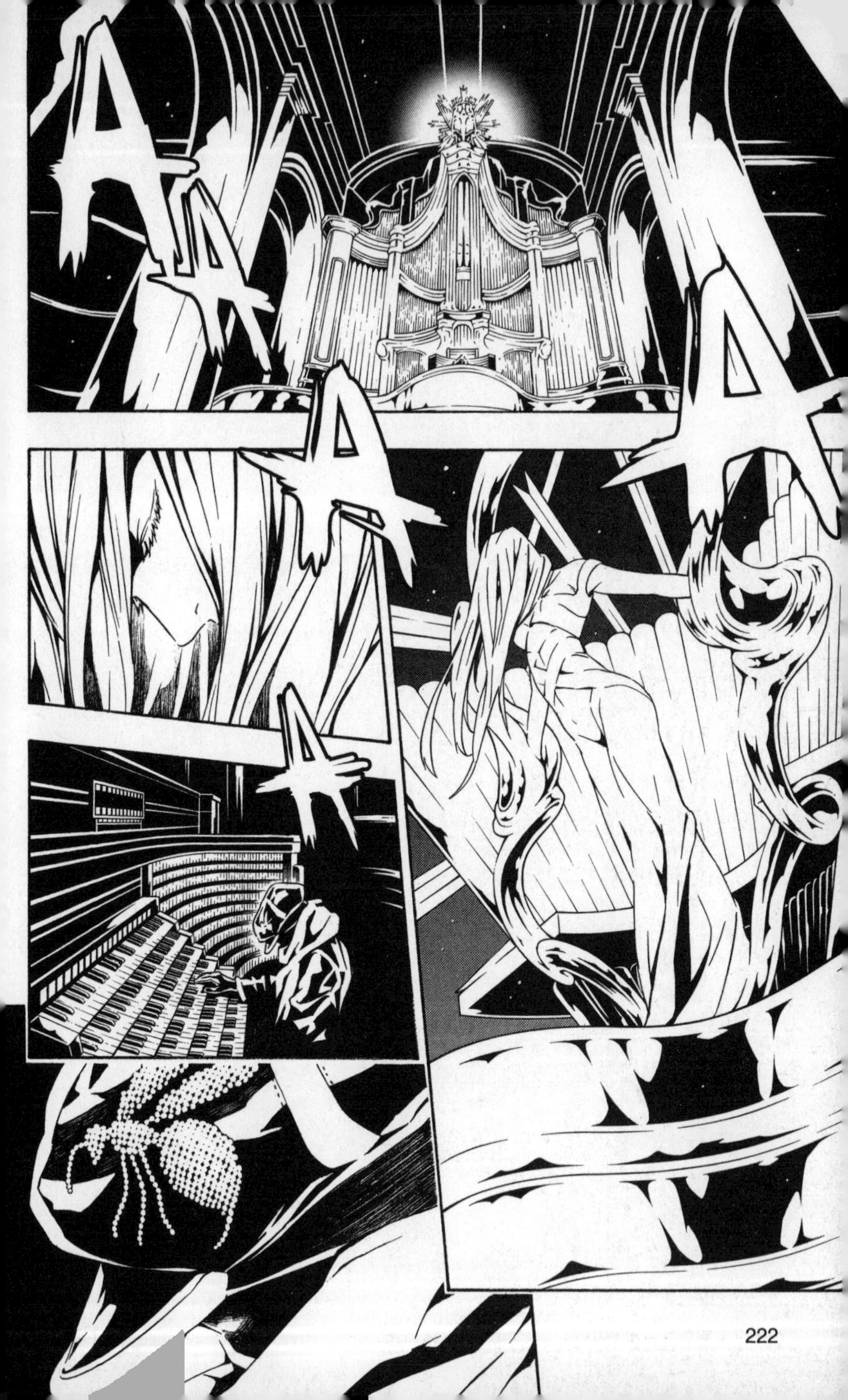

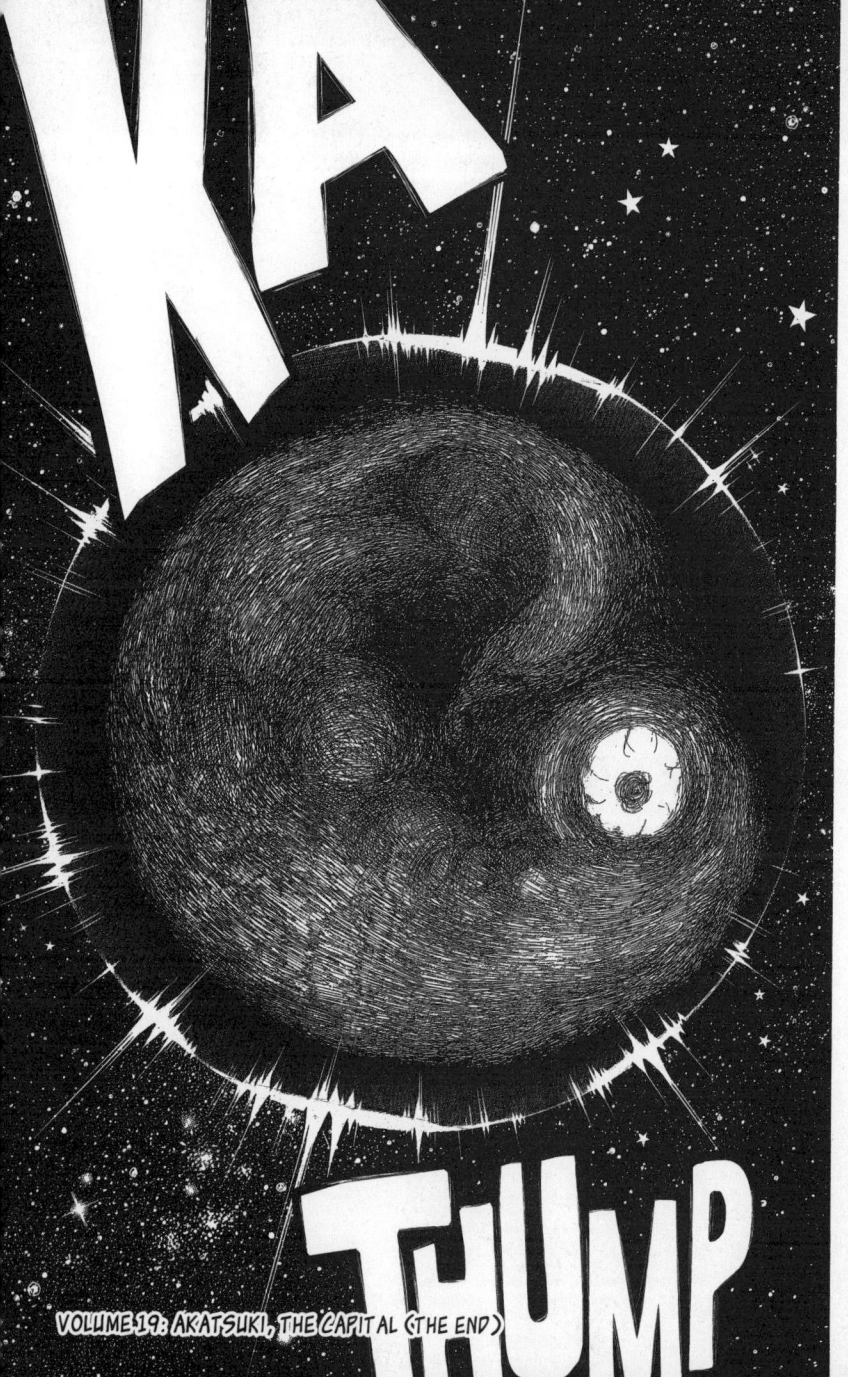

VOLUME 19: AKATSUKI, THE CAPITAL (THE END)

■ AKATSUKI, THE CAPITAL

We were always taught that Akatsuki was a city awash in the glow of the artificial sun, a place where everyone lived in wealth and comfort. The truth is the opposite—it's a dark pit. What the heck? Is this the utopia we all dreamed of? Oh my Empress! Speaking of which, where's the Empress? What about the Head Bee? Are they the last of their kind? They are, right? Oh man... Somebody tell me what's going on!

n.b.: Newgrange / An Irish passage tomb within the neolithic Brú na Bóinne complex. In Irish mythology it's a fairy mound. It's also connected to the legendary Tuatha De Danann race.

n.b.: The Dagda / A god of Irish mythology. He's a high king whose name means "the good god." He possesses a bottomless cauldron of food that leaves no man unsatisfied. He can also cook dead men in it to bring them back to life.

■ SPIRITUS

The light didn't just flicker, it went out completely! H-h-hang on a minute! *Ka-thump!* Is this the end? Is this it?

I can't just sit here! I'm going with them! I really will jump this time! I don't care what happens! I'll put my life on the line and leap to the next page!! Dr. Thunderland Jr., your daddy's coming! *Voom*!

...A PASSAGEWAY WHERE DRIFTING THOUGHTS FLOAT...

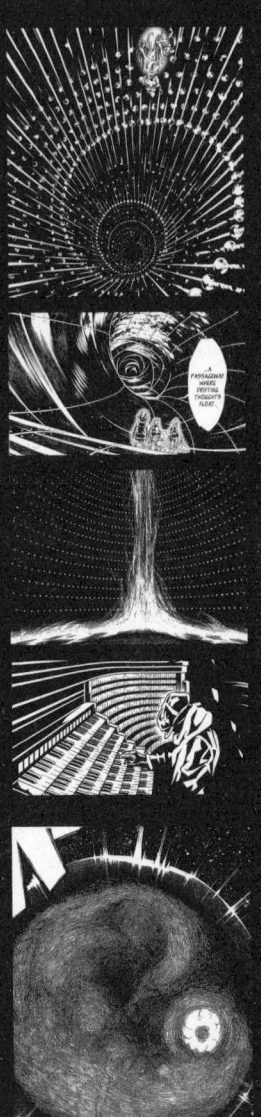

Route Map

Hff...hff...hff...

I did it! I finally did it! I've finally made it into the main story!!

...Huh?!

A: Akatsuki B: Yuusari C: Yodaka

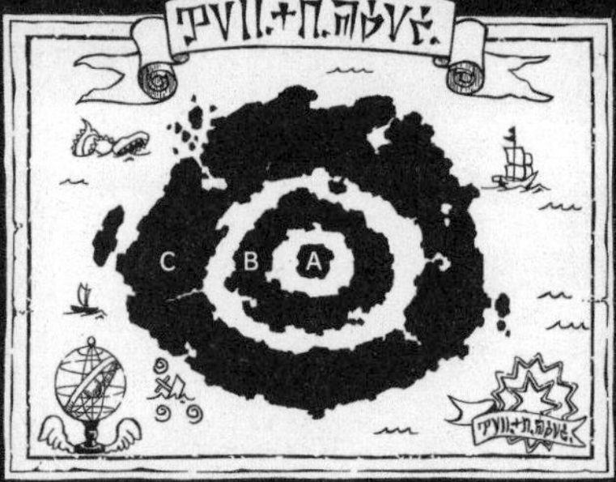

C
B
A

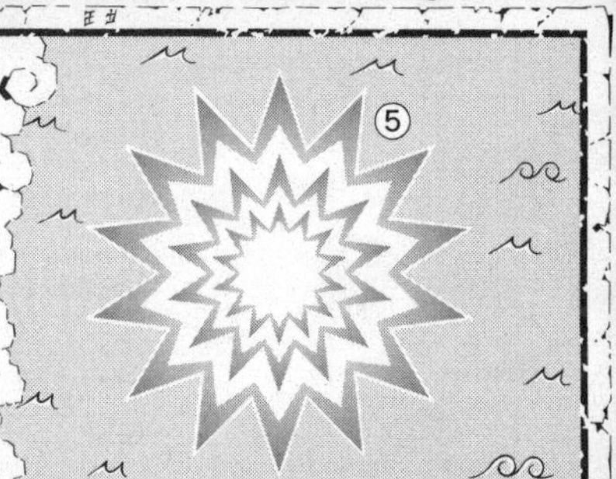

1
2
3
4
5

① Yuusari Central / Beehive
Cassiopeia Lamp (where Lag lives)
Auvers Sanatorium
Yuusari Central Station

② Waltz for Debby Inlet
(Final review point before entry to the capital)

③ Cobalt Glass River

④ Kagerou / Akatsuki
Newgrange Passage Tomb
The Dagda's Cauldron

⑤ Sun (the Gaichuu Spiritus)

I'm in the map... It's the end of volume 19...

What? The next volume is the last? Don't tell me that!!

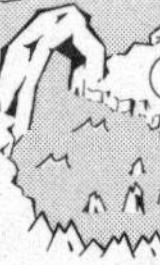

THE *BEST SELLING MANGA* SERIES IN THE WORLD!

ONE PIECE

Story & Art by **EIICHIRO ODA**

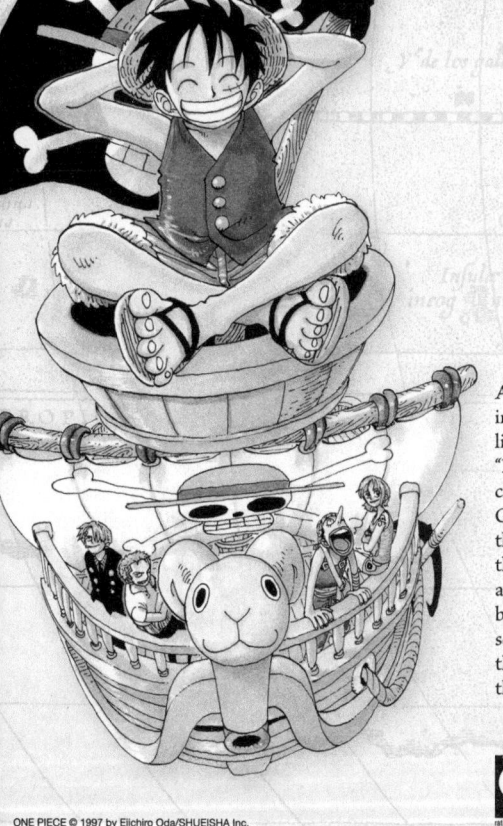

As a child, **Monkey D. Luffy** was inspired to become a pirate by listening to the tales of the buccaneer "Red-Haired" Shanks. But Luffy's life changed when he accidentally ate the Gum-Gum Devil Fruit and gained the power to stretch like rubber...at the cost of never being able to swim again! Years later, still vowing to become the king of the pirates, Luffy sets out on his adventure in search of the legendary "One Piece," said to be the greatest treasure in the world...

RATED T FOR TEEN
ratings.viz.com

SHONEN JUMP
www.shonenjump.com

VIZ media
www.viz.com

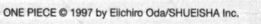

A PREMIUM BOX SET OF THE FIRST TWO STORY ARCS OF ONE PIECE!

A PIRATE'S TREASURE FOR ANY MANGA FAN!

STORY AND ART BY EIICHIRO ODA

Comes with EXCLUSIVE POSTER and the ROMANCE DAWN mini-comic!

As a child, Monkey D. Luffy dreamed of becoming King of the Pirates. But his life changed when he accidentally gained the power to stretch like rubber...at the cost of never being able to swim again! Years later, Luffy sets off in search of the "One Piece," said to be the greatest treasure in the world...

This box set includes VOLUMES 1-23, which comprise the EAST BLUE and BAROQUE WORKS story arcs.

EXCLUSIVE PREMIUMS and GREAT SAVINGS
over buying the individual volumes!

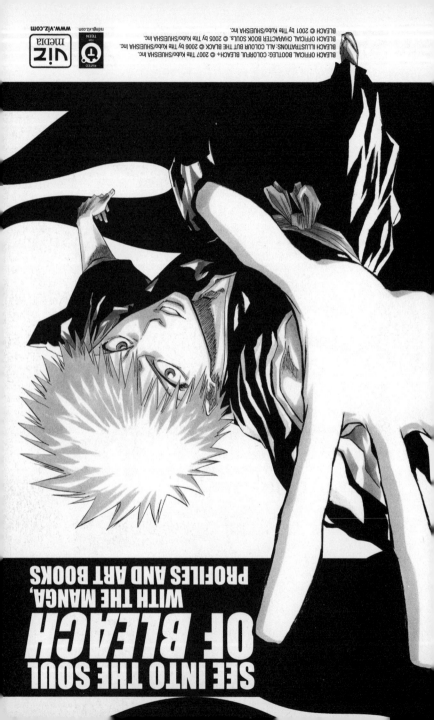

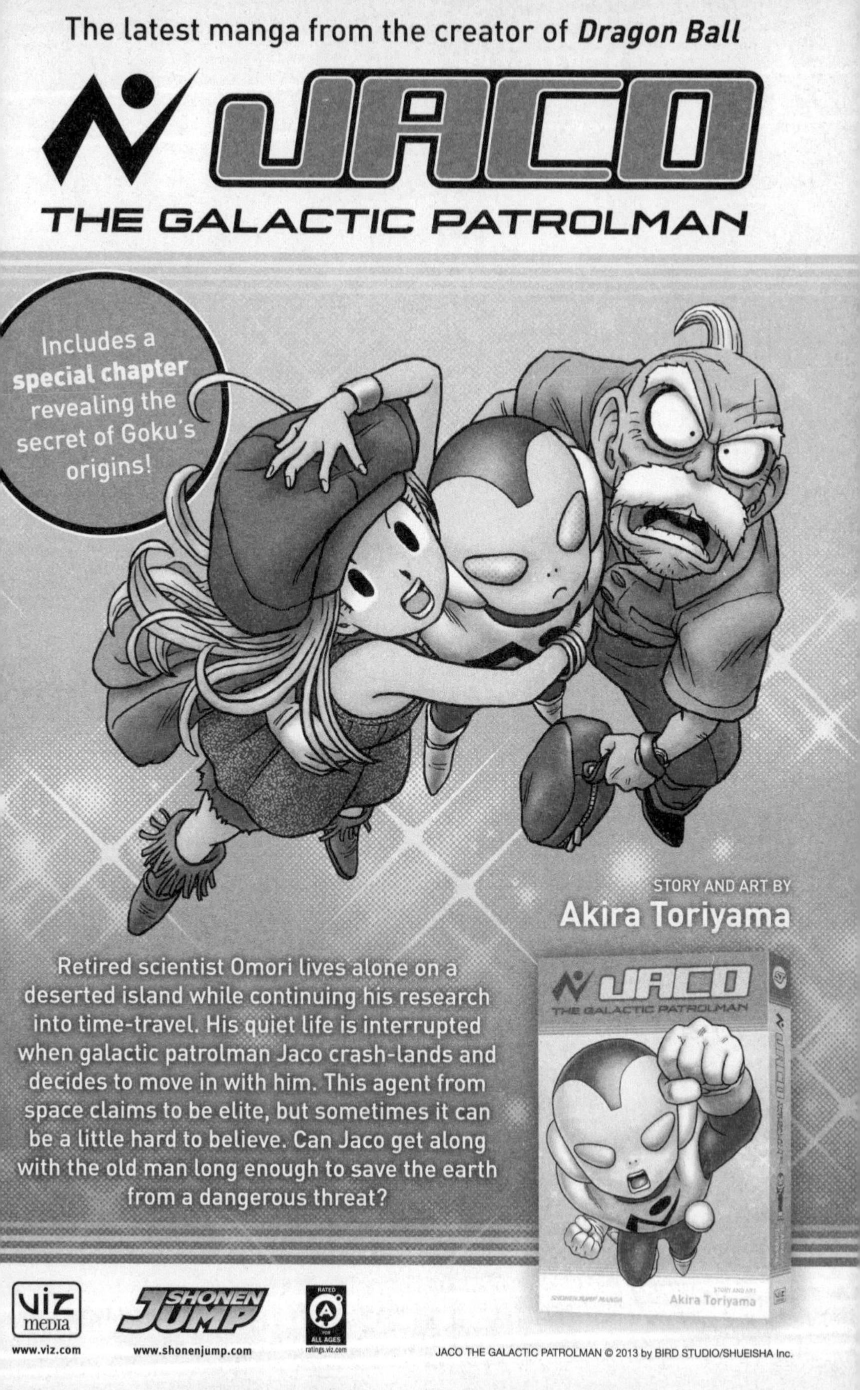

The latest manga from the creator of Dragon Ball
JACO
THE GALACTIC PATROLMAN
Includes a special chapter revealing the secret of Goku's origins!
STORY AND ART BY
Akira Toriyama
Retired scientist Omori lives alone on a deserted island while continuing his research into time-travel. His quiet life is interrupted when galactic patrolman Jaco crash-lands and decides to move in with him. This agent from space claims to be elite, but sometimes it can be a little hard to believe. Can Jaco get along with the old man long enough to save the earth from a dangerous threat?
JACO THE GALACTIC PATROLMAN
SHONEN JUMP MANGA
STORY AND ART
Akira Toriyama
VIZ media
SHONEN JUMP
RATED A FOR ALL AGES
www.viz.com
www.shonenjump.com
ratings.viz.com
JACO THE GALACTIC PATROLMAN © 2013 by BIRD STUDIO/SHUEISHA Inc.